THE
·*Real Food*·
SHOP AND
RESTAURANT
GUIDE

THE
·Real Food·
SHOP AND
RESTAURANT
GUIDE

CLIVE JOHNSTONE

Food Consultant:
Maurice Hanssen

EBURY PRESS

Published by Ebury Press
National Magazine House
72 Broadwick Street
London W1V 2BP

First impression 1985

ISBN 0 85223 493 7

Filmset by Advanced Filmsetters
(Glasgow) Ltd

Printed in Great Britain at
The University Press, Cambridge

CONTENTS

The *Guide* Explained	9
Restaurants	17
Other Recommended Restaurants	103
Shops	113
Other Recommended Shops	185
Supermarket Survey	191
Growers	197
Other Recommended Growers	221
Mills	225
General Reading	229
Maps	230
Glossary	244
Indexes to main entries:	
Restaurants	245
Shops	248
Growers	251
Report Form	253

Acknowledgements

Special appreciation is due to Caroline Walker and Geoffrey Cannon for the *Food Scandal*, though of whose activities I was blissfully unaware when the idea for the *Guide* was first floated. As much so to Nathan Pritikin for *Live Longer Now*, first noted on an airport bookstall but not with premonition of impending disaster. Also his other title, *The Pritikin Program for Diet and Exercise* which I enviously note has now sold well in excess of half a million copies. To Gayelord Hauser for his several pioneering works; Michael Balfour's *Health Food Guide*; *The Sunday Times Book of Real Bread*; *The Good Food Guide*; *The Good Hotel Guide*; *The International Vegetarian Handbook*; Maurice Hanssen's *'E' for Additives*; *The Organic Food Guide* edited by Alan Gear; Vicki Petersen's *Natural Food Catalogue*; and particularly Annabel Whittet for *Where To Eat If You Don't Eat Meat*, which was then the closest thing to a guide to places offering natural foods. Thanks to Jean Pink of Animal Aid and the several hundred correspondents who generously gave of their time to report on individual establishments included in the *Guide*.

Food Consultant: Maurice Hanssen

Contributors: Jean Case
Eunice Stokes
Barbara Strongitharm
Gerald Watkins

Designed by: Gwyn Lewis
Front cover illustration by: Catherine Wood
Illustrations by: John Woodcock
Maps by: M J L Cartographics

THE GUIDE
EXPLAINED

In this first edition *The Real Food Shop and Restaurant Guide* lists over 1,000 places throughout the British Isles where food is grown, prepared and served in ways where there is more than usual concern for quality These rare places yield good food in the best sense of the word and include shops whose prime interests are wholefoods, restaurants where ethical considerations have a high priority and growers who produce foods with careful regard for organic principles. Organically grown food supplies—which must be the basis for any sensible eating regimen—are still lamentably short, even if the future for them begins to look promising. Supplies are likely to improve as more and more come to appreciate, and are encouraged by the benefits of growing crops and rearing animals this natural way. The next best thing, until better organically produced supplies materialise, are wholefoods, in the sense that nothing has been added and nothing removed in the course of handling.

Fresh is best

Many foods only begin a downhill path after leaving the farm. Many more foods started life at the bottom of the hill, for which no warranties can be offered, but with the aid of the *Guide* the worst pitfalls can be avoided. The best restaurant, shop or baker can do little to improve on fundamentally poor raw materials. Fresh natural ingredients, eaten in peak condition are vitally important for a healthy diet. Some readers will be fortunate enough to be close to some of the organic growers we list, a good wholefood shop or a branch of that marvellous supermarket chain, Waitrose.

Food chains are long: perfection will remain an elusive objective for most, for the time being at least. But, there is one way by which the processes of change can be hastened. Those who love real food must stand up to be counted and not be prepared to take second best. Given this encouragement, and a larger market, growers, shopkeepers and restaurateurs, too, are likely to adapt to market forces. The sometimes hefty premiums for the privilege of natural food should begin to disappear. It will do much also for the welfare of man and animal down on the farm—or, in the bays of the forcing sheds as is often the case. The farm-worker and his family are more at risk than most from the detrimental effects of noxious chemicals and accidents involving them. The prospects for animal welfare are deplorable, unless there is a speedy turnabout in attitudes.

Before NACNE

The name NACNE (National Advisory Committee on Nutritional Education) rings familiarly if not melodiously. Recollections as to what it was all exactly about will have dimmed, so it is worth briefly recapping. It concerns the *Guide*.

Fifty years ago the nutritionist Gayelord Hauser was putting out much the same message as NACNE recently did. Modern thinking departs a little from a few of Gayelord Hauser's detailed recommendations but broadly, his advice for means of warding off degenerative disease, premature aging and early extinction was to eat wisely. The advice still seems to hold good, and in more ways than one. With hindsight and the passage of all those years, some of Gayelord Hauser's guidelines might seem faddist or even mildly quaint. He was in his day, the arch proponent of diets rich in fresh natural foods (fruit and vegetables in all their forms), yoghurt, skimmed milk, high fibre foods and lean meats. Vitamins whenever possible were to be taken in food form, not as expensive supplements. NACNE, about fifty years later, has got around to saying about the same thing. So much for any Governmental guidance. It was a bit late to do our grand-parents much good.

In 1984 the NACNE report was, in general, strongly supported by the government's COMA (Committee in Medical Aspects of Food Policy) report on Diet and Cardiovascular Disease. This was less dogmatic than NACNE but nevertheless gave much encouragement to those restaurants, shops and manufacturers moving towards wholefood principles.

Of course, it is perhaps easier said than done to make commendable changes in our established eating habits when the supermarket shelves are loaded with all the stuff we should not be eating and most restaurants cheerfully deal in meals irrespective of the consequences. One restaurateur's story wears thin— that customers go out to celebrate and do not want to be worried with nutritional considerations. But few of us can afford to go on cholesterol binges. We look to the restaurateur to take the trouble and have the resources and skills to put together meals which are both appetising and nutritious.

The Real Food Guide offers the consumer a detailed insight into the world of unadulterated natural foods. All the shops, restaurants and takeaways, as well as hotels and guest houses, in the *Guide* have been independently assessed for this purpose. In this way the *Guide* reflects what is now orthodox advice—eat more fresh natural food; eat less salt, sugar and fat and beware of the many additives which are used in the course of modern food processing.

How to use the *Guide*

The *Guide* falls broadly into three main sections (the places in which they are to be found are listed alphabetically within each section): restaurants, shops and growers. There are descriptive entries for 500 of these (indexed in alphabetical order on pp 245–252) and using all the information at our disposal we have done our best to project to the reader exactly what they are able to offer in the way of wholefood stuffs and services and sometimes their idiosyncracies as well. In addition a further 500 places are listed in gazetteer sections (other recommended restaurants etc.). In these, for this edition, the information available at the time of going to press has been more limited than we would have needed for a full descriptive entry. Names and addresses are listed along with times of opening. They fill a particularly useful need in parts of the country where places offering wholefoods are otherwise thin on the ground. We look forward to getting readers' reports from some of these places in due course when we might do them more justice. Among them are many excellent establishments and it in no way signifies lack of merit that they do not appear fully described in this edition in the body of the *Guide*. Also listed (on pages 225–228) are the fifty or more corn mills, restored to working order (including a few which were never out of production) and able to stonegrind corn. Several are not productive at the time of writing, but it is the aim of the *Guide* to keep tabs on all of these places. If the present interest in healthy fresh food can be maintained, there is every chance that nearly all could be returned to practical use. Mills are the best source of freshly ground flour, occasionally even, places where it is ground while you wait.

Maps

Firmly believing in the efficacy of English as it is written, we have resisted any slight urge to use symbols except for the maps. Readers may agree; there is a reasonable case here for some system to distinguish between the 500 or so places with descriptive entries, some of which have a shop, grower and a restaurant. Beyond that it should be mentioned, as with all maps published in guidebooks of this kind, that their principal value is for general purposes of location. If travelling in unfamiliar country we recommend the use of a large scale Ordnance Survey map. This is particularly necessary when seeking out growers or even some country house restaurants. They may well function in some delectable countryside but at times can be alarmingly elusive. (No map of Ireland is included as there are too few entries to warrant one. We hope that there will be more for the next edition.)

⌘ restaurant (*main entry*)	⌘ restaurant (*gazetteer entry*)
🏠 shop (*main entry*)	🏠 shop (*gazetteer entry*)
✿ grower (*main entry*)	✿ grower (*gazetteer entry*)
⚙ mill	

Prices

In the restaurant section all prices shown are approximate and should be confirmed when making a booking. The prices shown represent the cost of a three course meal and coffee, if this is the style of the establishment, and reflect the price of the least expensive dishes. The cost for a bottle of house wine is shown separately.

In the gazetteer section there are simpler price guidelines which give some indication of the house style. Inexpensive suggests that it is possible to get three courses and coffee for under £5. Medium means that it is likely to cost between £5 and £10 to eat. Wherever the price of a meal is likely to exceed £10 it has been annotated as expensive.

General information

Care should be taken to check personally on opening times, especially if you are planning a special visit or making a detour. The best information supplied by shops, restaurants and growers has been included but details of this kind are often subject to change according to circumstances.

Restaurants

Go to the country when in search of the finest wholesome foods. City restaurants even at their best (and some try very hard) are no match for the new breed down on the farm. Town restaurants never quite match the integrity found in some out of the way places, especially a handful of distinguished country hotels. More surprisingly these are not a clutch of affluent home counties' enterprises. Look further afield. Knights Farm, Burghfield, an exception in this last respect, has surprised by even retaining the services of Dr. Ann Wall, lecturer in nutrition at Reading University, in a consultancy role. At Knights Farm the Trevor-Ropers are very nearly self-sufficient with their own home-grown organic standard vegetables and free range eggs, finding time to home bake the bread and brioches. Even in the more modestly styled Old Bakery at Woolpit in Suffolk, Eileen Clarke—who makes a speciality of fish, game and poultry, the last all free-range as well as the eggs—manages to produce or acquire all organically grown fruit and vegetables. Mrs. Clarke's commendable philosophy is fresh and authentic. At Balcraig House, New Scone, most of the food is from their own farm—Aberdeen Angus cattle fed a natural diet and hung for four weeks. Their own lamb, kid and goats' milk. Veal is from calves reared humanely; bacon and pork from their own pigs are an alternative to fresh fish from local lochs. A good many appreciate the style of Liz and Andrew Whitley's pure food establishment at Melmerby in Cumbria. They amaze all by what they manage to produce from the smallholding behind the café, in striking but inhospitable countryside. At Dunain Park, south west of Inverness towards the loch, the operation is similar to that at Balcraig House where they make a point of growing a vast variety of herbs as well. Land locked in Bedfordshire, Somerset Moore makes a speciality of really fresh fish, shell fish and crustaceans which he partners with garden vegetables and fruits. Down in the South West, Teignworthy Country House Hotel shrewdly tracks down the best in produce that others prepare or rear. Milk and cream is unpasteurised, a combination of Jersey and South Devon. They know their fishermen well and have good supplies from Brixham and more especially the smoked kinds from Loch Fyne. Cranks, of course, have done much to popularise wholefoods over the past twenty years but more recently on the scene are work-a-day places such as Edinburgh's Country Kitchen. A rare find in the inexpensive range where the brown rice is organic as well as the baked potatoes. Polyunsaturates are an option as a matter of course. They can tell all of the ingredients in each dish and do a calorie count. Restaurants where a particularly high quality meal can be had are marked with a star.

Shops

These have been selected for inclusion on the basis of their wholefood interest although in a few instances they also carry a conventional grocery stock. They vary considerably from the useful but fairly predictable lines carried by the Holland and Barrett chain to the idiosyncratic style of the most enterprising such as the Granary at Truro. This shop is a world apart with the most fabulous range of unadulterated foods. Real Foods in Edinburgh and Infinity in Brighton are nearly into the same class. Wholefoods of Baker Street have a style all their own, for not only is everything pure and wholesome but they have that rare thing, a butchery department nearby where all the meats, sausages, terrines and pies are also to an organic standard. Harrods Food Halls have also gained their laurels for wholefoods. They can probably offer the largest selection of fruit and vegetable juices, many of organic origin, to be found anywhere. The Infinity range of organic pulses and cereals is carried and the selection of decaffeinated coffees and herb teas is amongst the best. Takeaway savouries are offered in increasing variety, the fresh fish counter is a special attraction and Springhill are amongst their several bakery suppliers. Springhill bake a wholemeal loaf with an excellent texture and an exceptionally good muesli loaf. When matched by quality, food here is no more expensive than in any other shop. At the other end of the shopping scale is the reliable local wholefood store, as good a place as any to go for advice when making the first tentative steps into the world of wholefoods. Just as long as you do not choose the busiest time of the day, the staff in these shops are the most helpful and sympathetic anywhere. For what they might not carry in stock they usually make compensation by their willingness to buy in to meet customers' needs. The local wholefood shop is often the best source of speciality wholemeal bread and will probably be the only place, if any, selling organically grown fruits and vegetables.

Growers

If you live in South West Wales, Devon and Cornwall, or Norfolk and Suffolk there is reasonable chance you will be within shopping distance of an organic grower. You will then be fairly certain to be able to get free range chickens and eggs, organically grown fruit and vegetables seasonally, goats' milk and sometimes ewe, as well as untreated cows' milk. Outside these areas it is tough, except for central London. Organically reared meats are difficult to get hold of anywhere. This is very often not because there is a lack of producers but because there are no established market channels. A good deal of organically reared meat goes unmarked into the ordinary meat distribution system. Whatever the inconvenience, you may still find it worthwhile seeking out the growers simply for the privilege of meeting a committed band who do it as a way of life rather than for any other motive.

Supermarkets and chain stores

These are still not the best places to go for wholefoods despite their partial response to changing needs and competition from the wholefood shops. Several well promoted media campaigns may well represent a change of course for them but it does not exactly make them epicurean wholefood centres. On pages 191–196 we have done a comparison shopping survey to show what eleven of them can offer (including the Holland and Barrett health food chain), then compared them with the stock available in a good independent wholefood shop, with Harrods Food Halls and with Wholefoods of Baker Street who are committed to stocking nothing other than food organically grown or reared. Sainsbury's came out of the survey quite well. You could fill a basket with goat and quark cheese, safflower cooking oil, natural fruit juices, canned vegetables in plain water, fresh poultry, soya milk and a selection of low-sugar jams and marmalades. But Waitrose are well ahead with all of these things and many more. Their eggs are free range, cooking oil sometimes cold-pressed, muesli sugar-free (their own and proprietary brands) and all of their stores carry fresh fish. Bread, whenever possible, includes a local speciality loaf in addition to commercial wholemeal bakes. Waitrose fresh fruits and vegetables are also in exceptional variety, the quality especially good. Dried fruits include an innovatory semi-dried range of vacuum packed kinds without preservatives. Reduced sugar jams are in greater variety than any other store. Boots, where they have a full in-store food section, are good for specialities like gluten-free and diabetic foods. Otherwise they are not serious competition. New ground has been broken by British Home Stores with a sugar-free muesli, untreated dried fruits, sugar-free snacks, and pickles and chutneys without added colour or preservatives. Their breads are amongst the best with organic rye, bran and grain loaves in addition to a muesli loaf. But like Marks and Spencer and Littlewoods they are still essentially stores for a limited range of convenience foods. Wholefoods of Baker Street are expected to be good, this is their raison d'être. Harrods were outstanding, easily living up to their reputation for being able to produce anything on demand. They surprised too with their prices. Standbys like bread, judged by quality, were no more expensive, if not cheaper, than elsewhere.

Artificial additives are being given serious attention by the large groups, following the example of the health stores. In June 1985 Safeway announced a two-year plan to remove 51 additives including colours, preservatives and anti-oxidants from their own brands. Others, including Waitrose and Tesco are cutting back on certain additives including tartrazine (E102).

RESTAURANTS

Bradfield House, Bury St. Edmunds

ABERAERON Dyfed ☆

The Hive on the Quay, Cadwgan Place TEL Aberaeron (0545) 570445

'Cwch Gwenyn ar y cei' is what patriotically minded Celts might really like to see emblazoned above Sarah Holgate's harbourside restaurant. There is an exhibition of bees as honey is her speciality, used for sweetening a delectable selection of ice creams. Sarah, with innocent deviousness, 'aims to draw interested eaters, families and unaware tourists' for her reasonably priced, home-cooked food. She puts much emphasis on flavour and fresh, locally grown produce which is made up into traditional British dishes. Simple, inexpensive lunches could start with paté and homemade bread and butter, sometimes a laverbread paté. Alternatively soup, pickled mackerel or quiche, all prepared in the kitchen. At night there are likely to be stuffed crispy pancakes with a choice of fillings: bacon and onion in a cheese sauce, mushrooms in a wine sauce and sweet peppers and tomatoes seasoned with garlic and herbs. Mackerel makes a reappearance stuffed with cockles and wrapped in bacon. Lamb chops have a pastry case and come accompanied by braised onions.

Organically grown vegetables; unpasteurised local Cheddar and Jersey cream; polyunsaturated fats used in cooking; minimum of salt and sugar; decaffeinated coffee. Vegetarian. Seats 50. Meals £2–£7.50. House wine £3.80. 10% service charge, evenings.

Open: June, 10.30 to 5; July/Aug, 10 to 9; Sept, 10.30 to 5.

ACCRINGTON Lancashire

The Health Food Restaurant, 1b Peel Street TEL Accrington (0254) 390743

MAP 6

Nora Growden has introduced the wholefood way to Accrington, the first such place in the town, so some explanation is warranted and this is offered in a neat hand-out she has had printed. Her aim is to provide tasty meals and snacks which have been prepared from ingredients specially selected for their nutritional properties. This means that everything is unprocessed, without additives, preservatives and colourings. And, being vegetarian, there are no animal fats which, she records, in the opinion of medical experts, is one of the major contributions to the epidemic incidence of heart-related disease in Britain. All her prices are modest, especially so for her hot specials of the day. Regularly you may have rice, pasta, bean and vegetable dishes. Main course salads are nutty mushroom, or with various cheeses or with a bit of everything. The homemade soup is affordable even by those at subsistence levels. Bread is wholemeal and rye. Puddings are crumbles, apricot and yoghurt flan, fruity yoghurt whip or simply a plain yoghurt. Any time of day, wholemeal scones, carrot and banana cakes, bran fruit and nut loaf.

Organically grown vegetables whenever possible; wholemeal bread; polyunsaturates in cooking and at table; fresh fruits at table; minimal salt and sugar; skimmed milk available. Vegetarian wholefood, vegan. Seats 32. Meals from £4, dishes from £1.

Open: Tue to Sat, 9.30 to 4.30.

ALFRISTON   **East Sussex**   ☆   MAP 3
Moonrakers   TEL Alfriston (0323) 870472

Folk are drawn to the village for a variety of reasons, including the delightfully restored
Old Clergy House, the first building to be acquired by the National Trust. Barry and
Elaine Wilkinson's timbered restaurant is less architecturally regular than the Clergy
House but does have some special merit in a one-price menu based on foods in season and
fresh vegetables only. Sicilian prawns are heaped in pasta shells, fortified with avocado
slices and a garlic and vinaigrette dressing. Soup could be a rich, creamy affair made to an
Old English recipe using Stilton and onions garnished with wholemeal croutons.
Croutons reappear with a lean haunch of venison marinated in wine, partnered by pork,
herbs and berries, goujons of sole met up with breadcrumbs, Parmesan, toasted almonds
and fried banana strips, and diners seem to approve. Something to finish included familiar
stand-bys like trifle—which we enjoyed—but all homemade, and supported by fruit
sorbets, if you had not opted for more cheese or the ices. Barry Wilkinson emphasises
their flexible attitude towards 'what we can do and our willingness to meet special dietary
needs'.

*Wholemeal breads; polyunsaturated fats used in cooking; minimum salt and sugar; fresh fruits at
table; freshly squeezed fruit juices; skimmed milk; decaffeinated coffee. Vegetarian, vegan, gluten-
free and fat-free dishes prepared on request. Seats 36. Meals £12. House wine £4.60.*

Open: Tue to Fri, 7 to 9.15; Sat, 6.45 to 9.45; closed mid-Jan to mid-Feb.

ALTRINCHAM   **Cheshire**   MAP 6
Nutcracker, 43 Oxford Road   TEL Altrincham 928 4399

A local regular lunchtime patron commends the 'excellent choice of sustaining dishes at
prices reasonable for such good quality food. A generous bowl of soup and a roll is almost
a meal in itself.' The two or three hot main dishes are served generously—zyldyk
casserole, lasagne or perhaps a fricassee. The numerous salads rate as interesting. Potatoes
are likely to be baked but as the produce is more than likely organically grown the skins
are scarcely a hazard. Puddings range from chocolate cream pie, cheesecake, Bakewell slice
to a fresh fruit salad. Self-service from the counter is friendly and considerate with the
emphasis on everything freshly made and wholefood.

*Organically grown produce when available; free range eggs; wholemeal bread; polyunsaturated
fats used in cooking; minimum salt and sugar; fresh fruits at table; occasionally freshly squeezed
fruit juices. Vegetarian, vegan. Seats 60.*

Open: Mon to Sat, 10 to 4.45; Wed, 10 to 2.

AMBLESIDE   **Cumbria**   MAP 6
Harvest Vegetarian Restaurant, Compston Road   TEL Ambleside (0966) 33151

You might well have to wait for a table in this successful restaurant but you may expect
good service, pleasant young staff and a wide choice, if you are vegetarian. Vegans fair
slightly less well but, with the tremendous upsurge of interest, menu adjustments are
already on the way. Gillian Kelly stays the course alone (after starting out with a partner)
offering good wholesome food, made with the freshest ingredients, organically grown
whenever she can get them. Brazil nut and mushroom roasts are served with a savoury
sauce of peppers and mushrooms, apple sauce as well. The cheese, leek and potato bake is
popular, as well as vegetable cobbler and her well spiced bean dishes. Large salad platters
alternate between avocado pâté, marinated mushrooms with hard-boiled eggs, cream
cheese with peppers, hummus. Bread is made here, using organically grown wheat from
The Little Salkeld Watermill. Desserts may be prosaic hot fruit crumbles, or fruit salads,
surpassed by ravani—adapted from a Turkish honey cake recipe and a house speciality.
(This is made with a great many eggs, ground almonds and semolina, later soaked in an
orange syrup and served up with cream!) Raisin and walnut vegan cake has apples but no

eggs. Animal rennet-free cheeses and natural yoghurts.

Wholemeal bread; polyunsaturates in kitchen and at table; fresh fruits. Vegetarian, vegan, gluten-free and other diets catered for—but advance warning preferred. Seats 45. Meals from £4—lunch and dinner. Bring your own wine, no corkage charge.

Open: Sun to Sat, 10.30 to 12, 12 to 2.30, 5 to 8; Thur closed except in summer.

ANSTY   Dorset   MAP 2
The Fox, Ansty, Nr Dorchester   TEL Ansty (0258) 880328

Peter and Wendy Amey's brick and flint inn, originally a private dwelling, now has a dining-room extension equipped to seat rather more than would ever have gathered around the largest Victorian table. Meats from the cold carvery are offered in at least twelve variations—pheasant, duckling, ham-on-the-bone, roast beef, salami, pâté and probably several pies. Salads number at least thirty and if the first serving does not entirely satisfy, just make a return trip. There is no extra charge. Meringues, gâteaux and Loseley ice cream are bought in.

Wholemeal bread; non-battery eggs; skimmed milk. Vegetarian. Seats 60. Meals from £4. House wine £3.75. Access/Visa.

Open: 11 to 2.30, 6.30 to 11.

ARBROATH   Tayside ☆   MAP 7
The But'n'Ben, Auchmithie   TEL Arbroath (0241) 77223

The local G.P. who has a youngster with a food allergy, first drew the *Guide*'s attention to Mrs. Horne's delightfully off-the-beaten-track cottage restaurant. It is down by the shore, several miles out of town. 'We have decided it is the only place where our family can eat out regularly. Sensibly few changes have been made to the whitewashed quarry tiled interior. Mrs. Horne, who does all the cooking herself, produces tasty, wholesome, unadulterated foods without any additives.' The atmosphere is cosy and friendly in this little enterprise which grew from three tearoom tables to take over the entire cottage. Salads are beautifully prepared and the vegetables always done to perfection. Meat and fish is shopped for daily, the latter just up from the shore. But'n'Ben Fruits de Mer is a selection of all the fish caught by the Arbroath boats, a local style chowder of prawns in their various sizes, crab, lobster, and 'anything else which seems to fit,' says Mrs. Horne. Steaks are from local Angus beef, the venison is from farm-reared animals in Fife, roasted with juniper berries and black peppers, served up with homemade rowan jelly, for which she scours the countryside in the autumn. Salads are according to season. Puddings are Drambuie cream—and others of that ilk—made of cream, oatmeal, walnuts and, of course, the liqueur to complete the highly caloric dish. N.B. 'But' was the living area; 'Ben' the parlour.

Wholefood vegetarian; wholemeal bread or oatmeal bannocks; fresh fruits; freshly squeezed juices; all cakes homebaked. Seats 30. Meals from £8. House wine £2.65 a litre carafe.

Open: 9 to 9.30; closed Tue.

ARDELVE   Highland ☆   MAP 7
Loch Duich Hotel, Ardelve, by Kyle of Lochalsh   TEL Ardelve (059) 985 213

Rod and Geraldine Stenson cook everything fresh daily at their modest inn on the sheltered sea-loch, and that includes the bread. Starters here always include a vegetarian option; main dishes always a roast using local beef. The locally caught fish varies according to sporadic landings in the vicinity so it is sometimes supplemented with supplies from further afield, but, it frequently means salmon, fresh or unevenly smoked nearby. Poultry means their own free range hens and ducks. Moussakas, vegetable platters, or quiche—which have all been commended by meat eaters—are available for vegetarians. A butcher in Turriff supplies all the meat and other game and the 'occasionally used veal' is not of the forced variety. Herrings and kippers are brought to the backdoor, the latter via 'an old man in Buckie who does not use any artificial aids to make them palatable'. Hopefully, with the aid of an Highlands and Islands Development Board grant, a smoker will shortly be setting up locally, using traditional methods. For desserts they make use of their own eggs, and yoghurt (there are goats in the back) for mousses. Yoghurt and cream cheese is used as a less fattening filling for sponges and the like. Preferences for double cream are as readily met. Geraldine is cautious too about her pastry for although all flour is organic, a lighter than wholemeal short crust is still more popular.

Wholemeal bread and oatcakes homemade; polyunsaturated fats used in cooking; minimum salt and sugar; skimmed milk; goats' milk ice cream and yoghurt; free range hen and duck eggs; own preserves, herbs and soft fruit—vegetables could be on the way. Vegetarian, vegan, wholefoods, macrobiotic, gluten-free and diabetic menus given notice. Seats 34. Dinners only £8. House wine £4.50 litre carafe. Bar lunches. Rooms 18 (bed and breakfast £15).

Open: daily 7 to 9. Closed Nov—Mar.

ASHBURTON   Devon   MAP 2
The Old Saddlery, North Street   TEL Ashburton (0364) 53127

Flanked by larger buildings, Annette Thomas' and Judy Roach's 14th century saddlery seems dwarfed. The old world atmosphere is maintained inside by the wheelback chairs and the huge granite fireplace, seen at its best in the depth of winter when a huge fire will roar. Mostly their cooking is vegetarian—*cordon vert,* they like to think—but there is always at least one meat dish which, more often than not, is a roasted free range chicken served with vegetables, or a cold cut to go with their especially good salads. All the vegetables are organically grown so this makes the salads particularly popular. There is also a specially sympathetic ear for anyone on a special diet but, of course, they can do these causes much greater justice if warned the day before. After two years, an increasing number of visitors are finding their way to the restaurant by word of mouth. It goes without saying that nothing is ever used in the cooking which includes preservatives, colouring or additives. Lunchtime customers sometimes make a meal of one of their starters, perhaps vegetarian pâté with toast from a homemade wholemeal loaf and salad garnish; hummus is equally popular. More substantial dishes include trout with salads or vegetables. Others will just opt for a toasted sandwich or a jacket potato and cheese with a salad garnish. Desserts may be sorbets, or ice creams with a hazelnut wafer. Meringues are extravagant affairs to which ice cream, fruit and dairy cream have been added. Daily there are special savouries and puddings written on the blackboard which local customers come to scan early in the day.

Organically grown vegetables; free range chickens and eggs; fresh herbs and spices; organic fruit and vegetable juices, the freshly squeezed kind, if the kitchen is not frantically busy; homemade wholemeal bread is salt and animal fat free. Wholefood, vegetarian. Seats 20. Meals from £2.50. Wine: bring your own. Rooms 2 (bed and breakfast £8.50).

Open: daily 10 to 3; Tue, Fri, Sat, 7.30 to 9.30; closed Mon.

AYLESBURY   Buckinghamshire   MAP 3
Counterpoint, 38 Buckingham Street   TEL Aylesbury (0296) 85275

At Counterpoint, lunchtime is the day's highpoint with fresh salads at reasonable prices to nourish the workers, some of whom sample the French organic wines while others try the fresh pressed fruit juices, rarer (in these parts) than any imported vinous beverage. Homemade is a recurrent theme and the fresh pasta dishes are made under contract by several local housewives and customers are invited to view the kitchens where soup of the day, a special hot dish or omelettes are prepared along with cold meats and pâtés to go with the salads. The breads used are Springfield's and may include pumpernickel and sprouted grains' types. Pastries have a low-sugar content and there are non-grain puddings. More inexpensive wholefoods (homemade) are on sale to take back for supper or to go into the freezer. There are tentative plans for evening opening, but increasing emphasis is being placed on the retail shop side so in due course look forward to free range eggs, teas, coffees and perhaps grains, flours and pulses, and vegetables from Springhill Farm and Organic Farm Foods.

Wholemeal bread; some organic fruit and vegetables; minimal salt and sugar; polyunsaturates in cooking and available at table. Wholefood, vegetarian, vegan. Seats 40. Meals £3.00. House wine 70p glass.

Open: Mon to Fri, 9 to 3; Sat, 10 to 3.

BAKEWELL   Derbyshire   ☆   Map 6
Green Apple, Diamond Court, Walter Street   TEL Bakewell (062 981) 4404

In addition to having been 'Cook of the Realm' in '77, Roger Green has been an active member in the past of the Soil Association. Just now with partners Jean Youatt and Revis Cruttenden, the kitchen is making too many demands on his time for him to indulge in the gentle art of gardening. When he discussed his menu he had just finished a carrot and coriander soup for a February dinner the night before Shrove Tuesday. It was to be followed by steak and kidney pie, or veal in a cream sauce. 'People come here to enjoy good food at a reasonable price, in a nice quiet atmosphere.' The very short menu is changed each week. Good wine is offered at prices with a fixed mark up. Vegetable lasagne and a choice from four salads was the meatless option—parsnip and brazil nut, peppers and courgettes, green leaves and a curried rice. 'Mango and almond tart is consistently popular, we just begin to worry lest we become too closely identified with it.' 'We do other things: chocolate meringues, chocolate cakes and a coconut cream tart,' Roger Green emphasised. Before coming to the restaurant, he had already established a reputation through his outside catering and cookery courses—these are still run, as ten week, one day a week courses. The restaurant comprises several linked cottages where they have tried to retain the domestic feel with old fireplaces—now flower filled—and interesting views through to each. Cooking is at times French, Chinese, Italian and vegetarian, inclined towards the wholefood. Dishes are always low on salt and thickening agents.

Wholemeal bread; minimal salt; skimmed milk; freshly squeezed fruit and vegetable juices; thick local yoghurts. Partly wholefood, vegetarian. Seats 65. Meals £6, lunchtime cheaper and self-service. House wine £3.70. Access/Visa.

Open: 10 to 5, 7 to 10.30; closed Tue; Sun, closed till Easter.

BANFF   Grampian   Map 7
The County, 32 High Street   TEL Banff (026 12) 5353

Mr. Moir has been installed in his high street hotel for a year, promoting local fresh food, and striving to improve on the sententious 'Taste of Scotland'. His strengths lie in the abundance of fresh meat, vegetables and fish. The last is literally from across the road, from the sea not a shop! Steak Glendeveron is sirloin rolled in oatmeal and, taking advantage of the locally produced malt liquor, served in a whisky flavoured sauce. Smoked fish is a breakfast speciality, likely to appear at lunchtime in a seafood pie.

Wholemeal bread; fresh fruits; minimal salt and sugar. Vegetarian, vegan, diabetic and gluten-free on request. Seats 36. Meals £3.50 to £12. Lunchtime only, main course and coffee £2.50. House wine £3.50.

Open: all day.

BANGOR   Gwynedd

Map 6

Grape Expectations, 322 High Street   TEL Bangor (0248) 355015

Timothy Pearce's high street bistro offers sensible home cooking in what he likes to describe as a Dickensian atmosphere. There are interesting dishes on his frequently changed menu, which always includes two vegetarian meals. Mrs. Pearce is an imaginative cook; soups have been harrira (Moroccan beans and lentils), Hungarian vegetable and paprika, sometimes the parsnip and apple popularised by Cranks. Avocados have been filled with an apple and walnut salad; mushrooms sautéed in a creamy sage sauce; mackerel marinated in white wine and herbs and given a soured cream dressing; and fresh pears have had a Roquefort cream stuffing. Rabbit and game are regular features. The former casseroled with bacon, dry cider and some juicy prunes. A Welsh game pie has pigeon, venison and pheasant, orange rind and port for flavouring, and chicken—alas, not free range—is casseroled Italian style. Fish dishes can be hake poached with ginger and wine, or American fish casserole (fresh white fish, prawns, peppers and tomatoes), and monkfish poached with mussels and prawns becomes Mariners' fish pie. Food for a meat-free regime includes spiced almond risotto, lasagne interleaved with fresh salad vegetables, or artichokes stuffed Italian style. Their bistro style delivers them from any formality and one would be just as welcome for a seafood smokie snack (smoked fish and prawns on hot buttered toast), delicious fresh herrings baked with thinly sliced potatoes and onions. 'Our puddings,' they stress, 'are not of the Black Forest gâteau school.' Instead they offer the sometimes scorned Eve's, a bread and butter pudding, apricot amber, and fresh raspberry and cinnamon whip. All, like the coconut slice, which was so good, homemade.

Wholemeal bread; organically grown vegetables when available. Wholefood, vegetarian, sometimes vegan. Seats 40. Meals from £4.20. House wine £4.10.

Open: Mon, 12.30 to 2; Tue to Sat, 12 to 2.30 and 7 to 10.

BARNSTAPLE   North Devon

Map 2

Heavens Above, 4 Bear Street   TEL Barnstaple (0271) 77960

For Nicole Rudd, vegetarian wholefood 'is just the accepted way to eat' and she prepares the food in the restaurant above a shop known as Sunfoods, run by friends. They are not ultra purist but they are, to quote, 'dirt cheap and seem to draw the office workers, the middle class, the lunatic fringe country dwellers and the judiciary, when in Session'. The style is freshly prepared vegetarian wholefood 'free from chemical nasties'. Customers commend the cleanliness, the wide choice of food, friendly service but, apparently above all, the willingness to discuss what is in each meal. Most lunch menu items are well under £1—cashew nut rissoles, lentil burgers, mixed salads, vegetable pasties, baked potato with cheese. Naturally they make everything themselves including soups, cookies, halva and fruit cake, even the lemonade. Cider is Hancocks, lager Pils, the stout Guinness. Organic wine is by the glass or carafe.

Organically grown vegetables; non-battery eggs; untreated milk; real ice cream; organic wines; wholemeal bread; minimal salt and sugar; polyunsaturates at table; fresh fruit. Vegetarian, vegan. Seats 50. Meals from around £1.50. Organic house wine, 2-glass carafe £1.25.

Open: daily, 10 to 3; Wed, 10 to 2; closed 2 weeks Oct and Mar.

BARROW-IN-FURNESS   Cumbria

Map 6

Pastures New, 64 Scott Street   TEL Barrow-in-Furness (0229) 33043

Only here a year, Richard Holmes' restaurant is principally a lunchtime operation but there are enough home-baked scones and cakes on the trolley to make it an attractive coffee and teatime venue. A former residential child care officer, Mr. Holmes has some very clear ideas about what will hold appeal for little fingers, without rotting their teeth prematurely. And he has some flexibility in his system, normally being able to provide a meal for most special diets, without prior notice. The dish of the day is likely to be nut roast, vegetable lasagne or vegetable curry. Hummus and salads—with cheddar or cottage cheese—are regular dishes, as are his inexpensive baked potatoes, with cheese and a mixed salad. Generous sandwiches have tahini and avocado, peanut butter and banana fillings, as well as the conventional cheese and salad. A vegan flan is filled with sweetcorn, peppers, tomatoes, onion and any other vegetables going, then given a milk-free sauce. There is cashew or regular cream, ice cream and yoghurt to go with the fresh fruit salads, fruit pies and muesli trifles.

Organically grown fruit and vegetables, very hard to get but used whenever possible; non-battery eggs; sugar-free cakes; wholemeal bread; polyunsaturates in kitchen and at table; fresh fruits at table; minimal salt and sugar; skimmed milk. Wholefood, vegetarian. Seats 24. Meals £3.25.

Open: Mon to Sat, 9 to 5.

BATH   Avon   Map 2
Evelyn & Owen's, 1 St. Andrew's Terrace   TEL Bath (0225) 333233

Brash but comfortable, in a former departmental store handy for the Assembly Rooms, the style is Trans-Atlantic. Encouragingly though everything is made on the premises including desserts, only fresh fruit and vegetables are used. The ebullience can be judged from the 'build your own pizza' approach. This means starting with a basic cheese pizza—the regular size sufficient for two—and adding mushrooms, green peppers, onions, sausages, anchovies, olives or more cheese. Taste, appetite and the pocket are the only limitations. There are of course side salads to accompany, and/or a baked potato with or without butter, or sour cream according to preference. Chicken burgers, barbecued baby back ribs are available for those who like something meaty. Some get by with the soup alone, supported by a chunk of their homemade garlic bread. Honey is used to sweeten the cream topping on the cheesecakes, cake is the carrot kind 'for people who don't even like carrots'. Wines, cocktails and beers, all at half price during the happy hour stretched between 5.30 and 7.

Wholemeal bread; fresh fruit and vegetables in cooking and fresh fruit at table; polyunsaturates used in cooking; minimal salt and sugar. Vegetarian. Seats 170. Meals from £1.95 (lunchtime special). House wine £4.50; the Californian variety £5.

Open: Sun to Sat, 12 to 2.30, 5.30 to 11.

BATH   Avon ☆   Map 2
The Hole in the Wall, 16 George Street   TEL Bath (0225) 25242

The name arose from the former need to dive beneath the raised footpath to get direct access to the near subterranean beamed and flagstoned restaurant. Beyond this there is nothing irregular about this thirty-year-old eating place or about its kitchen. The short, frequently changed menu is predominantly French provincial cooking. Expectations seem to be satisfied with terrines in variety, fish soups or a fish salad with a mango and basil sauce as starters. Carnivores find satisfaction in venison fruit pie, pheasant braised with celery, port and cream, or more cautiously the fish of the day. Vegetables and salads seem to rate well for outstanding freshness and presentation and a good enough selection of vegetarian dishes on demand, vegan with advance warning. There are always choice fresh fruits for those who have not succumbed to St. Emilion au chocolat, or brown sugar meringue with praline ice cream brulée.

Wholemeal breads; choice fresh fruits at table; freshly squeezed fruit juices; minimal salt and sugar. Vegetarian, vegan (warning preferred). Meals £14.50 to £17.50. House wine £6.30. American Express/Access/Diners/Visa.

Open: 12 to 2, 7 to 10; closed Sun.

BATH   Avon   ☆   MAP 2
Huckleberry's, 34 Broad Street   TEL Bath (0225) 64876

Shrewdly Robert Craven got in first and has, for the time being, cornered the lion's share of Bath's *cordon vert* market. The crowded, or maybe just cramped, bistro style premises are cheerful and informal. 'His menu is fairly imaginative and he tends to run out of food quickly which must be a good sign.' Or is he just a hopeless pessimist in assessing the attraction of mushroom moussaka, a tasty vegetable goulash, or Huck's salad pilaff special, the most expensive menu item at £2.25. Every day there is a tofu flan. Seasoning is with tamari, tahini, herbs and spices. Green bean, wheatberry, coleslaw and spinach salads are offered with a vegetable mayonnaise dressing. Other starters range from hummus to a cream of artichoke soup; to finish, more unrestaurant stand-bys of the flapjack, brownie, coffee cake school. Fruit juices are from cartons. Elderflower wine has appeal on several counts, not least that it is only £2.85. For more conventional imbibers, the house wine is by the litre carafe.

Wholemeal breads; polyunsaturates used in cooking and at table; minimum salt and sugar. Vegetarian, vegan, other diets by prior arrangement. Seats 35. Meals £3 to £5. House wine £2.85.

Open: 9 to 9.15; closed Sun.

BIRMINGHAM   West Midlands   MAP 3
Wild Oats, 5 Raddlebarn Road, Selly Oak   TEL Birmingham 021-471 2459

Jane Hulley's modest restaurant catering for a wide range of clientèle, is now in its sixth year. Just like the offspring at Bearwood (Wild Thyme—see entry) there are firm exclusion clauses regarding all packeted, tinned or preserved foods. Tinned tomatoes, tomato paste and sweetcorn are the only admitted exceptions. Lunches or dinners follow a pattern of five or six main courses, a battery of a dozen or so salads offered as support features. Main dishes, with your choice of any two salads or a baked potato, include spinach and cheese flan, mushroom timbale, Greek stuffed cabbage leaves and a substantial courgette and tomato savoury served with herby dumplings. Avocado with a Wild Oats blue cheese dressing or one of several soups or their own particularly sharp flavoured version of hummus are on offer for a first course. Brown bread ice cream they make themselves, the apricot pie has a wholewheat pastry, the fruit fool is natural yoghurt, honey and chopped fresh fruit. Tea and herb teas, coffee, homemade milk shakes. Cold takeaways attract a 15 % discount. Customers order in advance for the freezer food service, offering 100 variations on casseroles, hotpots, bakes and flans, and soups in thirty-plus different recipes.

Wholefoods; no tinned or packeted food except for tomatoes, purée and sweetcorn; everything prepared from natural ingredients, fresh vegetables and wholemeal flour. Vegetarian, vegan. Seats 30. Meals from £4.50.

Open: 12 to 2, 6 to 9; closed Sun and Mon.

BIRMINGHAM   West Midlands   MAP 3
Wild Thyme, 422 Bearwood Road, Bearwood   TEL Birmingham 021-420 2528

After being established five years, Wild Oats fathered Wild Thyme, credulous botanists are assured. Jane Hulley colonised this district, closer to Smethwick than Birmingham, just a year ago. Wild Thyme is up-market, immediately apparent from the gentle upward push given to prices, though still well within the grasp of most. Jane justifies the extra expense by more varied, more imaginative food and a short wine list. Salads still appear in the same twelve guises, including lentil—whole green lentils, radish, celery, apple, onion, basil and cottage cheese. Red cabbage is chopped with fresh oranges, sesame seeds, walnuts and dressed with orange juice. Brown rice is combined with celery, apple, grated carrot, radishes, raisins and herbs. Starters might be hummus served with pitta bread, soup, or a cashew nut pâté. Anything up to eight main dishes might include Brazil nut roast and tomato sauce, stuffed peppers and a sesame sauce or French mushroom tart. Follow-ups are strictly of the healthy life kind, maybe banana and apple crunch, a Middle Eastern fruit salad, with gentle deviations into homemade apricot ice cream and crème citron.

Wholefoods; no tinned or packeted food except for tomatoes, purée and sweetcorn; everything prepared from natural ingredients, fresh vegetables and wholemeal flour. Vegetarian, vegan. Seats 40. Meals from £5. House wine £3.75 a carafe.

Open: 10 to 2, 6 to 10; closed Sun and Mon.

BISHOPS LYDEARD   Somerset   MAP 2
Rose Cottage Inn, Bishops Lydeard, Nr Taunton
TEL Bishops Lydeard (0823) 432394

Homemade, wholesome, fresh and filling is the Dale-Thomas's philosophy at their inn in the busy village just short of the Quantocks. Meals are served in the restaurant and as it is freshly prepared to order, some lingering in the comfortable bar is usually inevitable. Light meals or starters include a smoked salmon mousse, gratin of prawns, mushrooms Provençale in a wine, herb and onion sauce, all offered with the option of wholemeal or French bread. Something more substantial might be a meatless pasta, cooked with an onion, mushroom and herb sauce and served with salad which was particularly appetising. Tortellini is the meat version. Large homemade vol au vents have a savoury lamb and tomato filling, with a carrot, potato and salad garnish and can be recommended too. Rose Cottage vegetarian moussaka can be adapted to meet vegan needs. Soups normally meet both vegetarian and vegan requirements. A brace of quails, stuffed with apricots and braised in cider, rack of lamb, roasted to order or a fillet steak are evening only menu extensions. Homemade ice creams.

Wholemeal bread; fresh fruits; polyunsaturates at table, if requested; minimal salt and sugar; organic wholemeal flour in some pastry crusts. Wholefood, vegetarian, vegan. Seats 45. Meals from £4.50. House wine £3.50.

Open: 12 to 2.30, 7 to 11; closed Sun and Mon and 1st week Nov, 2 weeks Christmas/ New Year.

BISHOP'S WALTHAM   Hampshire   MAP 3
Casey's, The Old Granary, Bank Street   TEL Bishop's Waltham (04893) 6352

There is reassuring atmosphere about this old granary in this small market town. Stephen and Janine Casey are new to the granary with fresh ideas about cooking standards. It is the kind of place which brings local business people for lunch, local families for coffee, lunch or tea and those bent on more leisurely relaxation for their all inclusive, evening menu. All their breads, biscuits and cakes are baked on the premises. Dinner dishes may be Pheasant Forestière, beef and Guinness pie, the fish, perhaps the sampled scampi Provençale with rice, from a choice of six dishes. Potted cheese, mushrooms Kiev or the homemade soup which provides an opportunity to put the house bread to good use, may begin the meal and cheese or dessert (on this occasion a sharp blackcurrant mousse), the coffee and homemade chocolates are included in price.

Homemade wholemeal or granary bread; fresh fruit and vegetable juices, organically grown fruit and vegetables; fresh fruits. Vegetarian always, vegan usually, gluten-free and diabetic on request. Seats 40. Meals, dinner from £9, 2-course specials £6, lunch specials from £1.75. House wine £3.75.

Open: Mon to Sat, 10 to 5; Tue to Sat, 6.30 to 10.30.

BLACKBURN South Yorkshire   MAP 6
Lovin' Spoonful, 76 King William Street   TEL Blackburn (0254) 675505

You reach the restaurant via an elegant stairway from the shop of the same name below. Decorated in cool greens and with Impressionists' prints, Jean Noble and John Banks make a special effort to make it as pleasing as possible, with fresh flowers always on the table. This is their third move in what seems an unlikely town for a fully-fledged vegetarian restaurant. At their first launch they could not even raise a £1,000 from the bank, but now their bank manager is an enthusiastic supporter and a regular diner. Booths and candlelight make a cosier atmosphere for evening in this large room. Unfortunately meat eaters still outnumber the herbivores so dining out has not taken off here just yet. Encouragingly though, the Christmas arrangements were booked up months in advance. Everything is cooked fresh daily. Imaginative main courses run to Mediterranean vegetable lasagne, courgettes Provençal, standbys such as moussaka or leek and mushroom flan, with more enterprise going into quiches of mushroom, celery and cream cheese. Another popular dish, cauliflower, broccoli and leek au gratin with a savoury rice. Naturally the soups, the pizzas, the fruit crumble and fruit pies are all freshly made on the premises. That goes too for the cheesecakes, apple gâteaux and particularly scrumptious fresh fruit ice creams. Small selection of French and German wines. Commended coffee, and bread from a local baker made to their recipe.

Wholemeal breads; soya bean oil or vegetable margarine in cooking; vegan margarines at table; fresh fruit; minimal salt and sugar; eggs free range—when used; organic vegetables sometimes. Vegetarian, vegan, diets with notice. Seats 50. Meals from £3, one course and coffee. House wine £2.50 a carafe.

Open: *Sun to Sat, 9 to 4.15; closed Mon.*

BOLTON Greater Manchester   MAP 6
Inpulse, 102 Newport Street   TEL Bolton (0204) 391672

The simple small café behind a shop is homely and cottagey, even if quite basic. The Robertsons re-opened here after managing a similar establishment in Amsterdam. They serve homemade soups, special lunches, coffees and teas to shoppers, students and business people. Better for hot dishes than salads, try them for kidney bean chilli, basmati, millet and buckwheat savouries and vegetable compotes, all offered with suitable sauces. Still all their own work are apple crisps, the speciality banana cream pie and fruit crumbles. Fruit salad, naturally, is fresh.

Wholemeal bread; freshly squeezed fruit juices; sugar only by customer request; non-battery eggs. Vegetarian, vegan. Seats 20. Meals from under £1, if you are happy with a baked potato.

Open: 10 to 4; closed Sun.

BOURNEMOUTH Dorset   MAP 3
Henry's Wholefood Restaurant, Landsdowne Road
TEL Bournemouth (0202) 297887

Recommended for their well cooked fresh and reasonably priced dishes, Nick Bishop manages the front of house affairs while former wholefood cookery teacher Karina Domeney masterminds the kitchen operation. Visual interest relies on the eight black-board menus hung around the room, their circular clothed tables, and intriguing glimpses into the kitchen beyond. Most of the people who come seem to do so because they like the cooking not because they don't eat meat. A crunchy nut roast is served with a cherry sauce; a vegetable curry is 'commended' but there seems to be more enthusiasm for the perennial lasagne. Moussakas, sweet and sour vegetables or Shepherd's Beany Pie or a butter bean casserole complete the menu, with ten or more individually dressed salads. Mangoes are a popular dessert as is the banana cake with a cream cheese and banana filling. Otherwise hot steamed fruit pudding, orange and coconut sponge and cheesecake are on offer. Bread can be an onion and herb speciality, made here like the other loaves. Main course dishes, including salad and baked potato or rice, never more than £1.75.

Homemade wholemeal bread; no added preservatives or colourings; wholewheat flour; freshly squeezed grape juice in season. Vegetarian, vegan. Seats 40. Evening meals average £4. House wine £2.50.

Open: daily, except Sun evenings and Mon lunch, winter, 11 to 3, 5 to 11; summer, 11 to 11.

BOURNEMOUTH   Dorset   Map 3
The Salad Centre, Post Office Road   TEL Bournemouth (0202) 21720

The Sloans' gentle reserve must mask some gritty determination to make life run smoothly at their restaurant, always identified as being opposite the post office which looms so large in this street. 'Salad Centre' is a misnomer for there are as many cooked dishes as the assembled raw vegetable kind. Strictly the Sloans abide by the rule of no artificial additives, salt and sugar heavily restricted, no refined flour. To make food tempting, natural herbs and spices are used extensively. There is always a homemade soup, something different each day. Salads—choose what you like from a selection of raw fresh fruit and vegetables, pasta, rice and beans—come in two bowl sizes. Mrs. Sloan makes her own mayonnaise to go with them, or with an inexpensive main dish, egg mayonnaise. Jacket potatoes might have a cottage cheese, celery and walnut filling. Every day there will be a choice of hot dishes from among broccoli and red bean casserole, West Country vegetable bake, ratatouille and brown rice, perhaps leek, tomato and potato bake with a cheesey nut-crunch topping. Always pizzas, flans and quiche and probably the nut roast of nuts, lentils, tomatoes and herbs with a savoury sauce. Light pancakes have a delicious savoury mix filling. Yoghurts they make themselves, also the cheesecake, Dorset apple cake and dairy cream whips. Anytime there are brownies or date and walnut loaf.

Wholemeal bread; free range eggs; freshly squeezed orange and carrot juices; fresh fruits; polyunsaturates in cooking and, on request at table; minimal salt and sugar; skimmed milk. Seats 50. Vegetarian, vegan. Meals from £4.

Open: Mon to Fri, 10 to 5; Sat, 10 to 2.30.

BOWNESS-ON-WINDERMERE   Cumbria   Map 6
Hedgerow Vegetarian Restaurant, Lake Road
TEL Bowness-on-Windermere (096 62) 5002

'Cosy, comfortable and very professional,' is the verdict for the small upper floor restaurant, 'with a good variety of food prepared in the visible kitchen.' Fresh fruit starters, with or without yoghurt are a minor innovation but there is always the soup, Brazil nut pâté, hummus and avocado cottage cheese pâté. Hot dishes are limited to two or three of the following prepared each day and always offered with a salad: mushroom and tomato risotto which is served with brown rice and tamari; ratatouille; variations on a cheese bake; bean casseroles; or a lasagne cheese bake with vegetables served with a tomato and garlic sauce. Salads of various kinds with any of the pâtés listed as starters, or with melon and cream cheese, or with cheddar, fruit and nuts are on offer. Fruit crumbles are always made using wholemeal flour, oats and sunflower seeds, cream and yoghurt according to preference. Otherwise fruit salads, fruit in season with coconut cream, cream or yoghurt, Hedges fruit cake, wholewheat cakes and banana slice. More extravagantly sherry trifles and banana honey and fruit split.

Wholemeal bread; polyunsaturates used in cooking; fresh fruit at table; minimal salt and sugar; non-battery eggs; organic fruit and vegetables when available. Vegetarian. Vegan only with notice. Seats 45. Meals from £3.50. Visa/Access/Diners.

Open: 11 to 9; closed Tue and Wed in winter.

BRIDGWATER   Avon   MAP 2
Bridge Restaurant, Binford Place   TEL Bridgwater (0278) 451277

Tony and Gail Shaw have been established fourteen years in their surprising, spacious café
with a loyal following. Every weekday there is a large variety of fresh salads and several
hot dishes from cauliflower cheese to lasagne. There are always jacket potatoes, usually
cottage pies and, not restricted to vegetarian items, cooked meats. Stand-bys are quiches,
while pizza with a full salad is a substantial offering. Sweets are tempting, including
seasonal specialities such as whortleberry (which some know as bilberry) pie, fairly
regularly apple pie and the more exotic pavlova, cheesecakes and trifles too. All day teas,
coffee and cake. The Shaws do not freeze or microwave any of their food which is bought
fresh daily.

*Largely home-grown fruit and vegetables; minimal salt and sugar; freshly squeezed orange
juice; wholemeal bread, with butter or nothing. Wholefood, vegetarian, vegan. Seats 60. Meals
from £3.*

Open: Mon to Sat, 9.30 to 5.30. No lunches Sat.

BRIGHTLINGSEA   Essex   MAP 3
Jacobe's Hall, High Street   TEL Brightlingsea (020 630) 2113

'Jacobe's is the only individually remarkable house in a not specially attractive town,'
records Nikolaus Pevsner. A fine fifteenth century half-timbered building, in this yachting
centre on the Colne, the town is also well known for its oyster fisheries. The aim is to use
the best fresh foods available at all times of the year which in practicable terms means
making the best of the sea's harvest. Fish figures importantly in the menu, from whole
Caribbean crawfish, split, smothered in garlic purée and butter at £16 down to an
economical seafood and French bread chowder in the wine bar at 95p. In between, the
prudent might consider the more sparingly dressed local sea bass at £5.95 or a local
grilled whole Dover sole, boned and filled with sliced scallops and smoked bacon for
£9.25. Back in Jacob le Clerk's wine bar, with fish still in mind, a pint of North Atlantic
shell-on prawns with French bread is a moderate £2.65. Or, for around the same outlay,
chicken and bacon casserole, carbonnade of beef, venison sausage and onion casserole and
a simple Lancashire hot-pot, all served with jacket potatoes, coleslaw and hot French
bread. Sweets tend to be ice cream with fresh fruits added in season or, instead, Stilton
cheese. The Turners make all their own breads and their menu changes seasonally.

*Homemade wholemeal bread; freshly squeezed fruit juices; non-battery eggs; polyunsaturates used
in cooking; minimal salt and sugar; skimmed milk. Wholefood, vegetarian, others on request when
booking. Seats 30. Meals from £4 in the Beriff Wine Bar, from £11 in Jacobe's Restaurant.
House wine from £4.20. Access/Visa/Diners/American Express.*

Open: 10 to 2, 7 onwards; closed Tue and Sun; closed 2 weeks Oct and Jan/Feb.

BRIGHTON   East Sussex   MAP 3
Clouds, 56 Ship Street   TEL Brighton (0273) 203701

A regular menu is built around charcoal-grilled rump steaks with deep fried clams,
similarly grilled leg of lamb with a redcurrant jelly or straight steak and a choice of sauces
which includes a 'vegetarian' special! French fries are offered with the barbecued chicken,
deep fried clams and the scampi. However there are always salads and jacket potatoes,
which will also go with the vegetarian quiche or cutlets. But beware the Clouds
Vegetarian Sauce hamburger, for it is beef beneath. Salads can be chicken, prawn or one
with cheeses, nuts and fruit. Spaghetti Bolognaise, mushroom and herb or vegetarian—
goes with garlic bread and salad. Wholemeal flour is used for the apple pie, There is
always fresh fruit salad. Tea and coffee all day. If your bill tops £15, a 12½% service charge
is added.

Wholemeal bread. Wholefood. Vegetarian. Seats 100. Meals from £3.25. House wine £4.25. Access.

Open: Sun to Sat, 11 to 11.

BRIGHTON   East Sussex   MAP 3
Food for Friends, 17A–18 Prince Albert Street   TEL Brighton (0273) 202310

Lunchtime crowds squeeze round farmhouse size tables but the pressure is often less at breakfast and dinner times. Friend and owner Simon Hope finds his recipe for success is increasingly acceptable to the lunchtime business trade, with his policy of low prices and healthy turnover. The rising light of morning brings the aroma of butter bean and Brussels sprouts, red bean and leek boulangère, stir fried vegetables and rice or, a herby onion quiche with a mixed salad which is more expensive, but worth it. The choice of salad dressings is imaginative: melon and ginger dressing; avocado; 1000 islands; or mayonnaise. Cauliflower and flageolet pie could have been a starter if preferred to a creamy little cheese soup. Orthodox Friend cuisine will supply chocolate and nectarine trifle, blackcurrant and apple crumble and fresh fruit salad. Bread is homemade, so are the hedgerow gâteaux, pineapple and banana eclairs, flapjack and sweet carrot cake. As a change from their apple and orange juices, consider a banana smoothy. Savouries are changed each afternoon to ensure variety for regulars. The breakfast menu offers wholemeal pancakes and fruit juice. Finish with dinner by candlelight. Unlimited coffee is 50p but be sure someone will be waiting to grab your seat as you get up from it.

Vegetarian, vegan. Seats 65, at a squeeze. Meals from £3.20. House wine £3.85 carafe.

Open: Mon to Sat, 9 to 10; Sun, 11.30 to 10.

BRIGHTON   East Sussex   MAP 3
Nature's Way, 89 Western Road   TEL Brighton (0273) 26181

The orange and brown treatment is a slight departure from the norm in wholefood restaurant décor. This decent basement restaurant, with stick back chairs and cane lightshades, offers a good range of vegetarian cooked dishes and bakers' goods in a fresh, clean setting. Coffee and cakes, all day, both to a good standard.

Vegetarian, vegan. Seats 30. Meals for £2.50.

Open: Mon to Sat, 9.30 to 5.

BRIGHTON   East Sussex   MAP 3
Slims Health Food Restaurant, 92 Churchill Square   TEL Brighton (0273) 24582

This modern piazza, bridging the gap between Marks & Spencer and The Lanes has, tucked in a corner beneath the hanging greenery, a popular cafeteria. Nut roasts are moist and tasty and come with mushrooms and pepper sauce. Other dishes look equally attractive and there are some decadent creamy things and egg dishes. Vegan and gluten-free curries. Homemade soups. Good value.

Wholemeal bread; polyunsaturates at table and in cooking; minimal salt and sugar. Vegetarian, some vegan and gluten-free daily. Seats 70. Meals from £2.50.

Open: Mon to Fri, 9.30 to 5.30; Sat, 9.30 to 6.

BRIGHTON   East Sussex   Map 3
Xavia's, Muttons Little Eating House Building, The Aquarium, Madeira Drive
TEL Brighton (0273) 695430

First considerations with Xavia and Glenn Mackay are those of health. Secondly comes satisfaction through taste, then presentation and finally cost. 'We try hard to keep the last as low as possible.' Then they have applied their minds to the question of comfort, so there is the luxury of generous upholstery, background music, flowers and soft lights, all some remove from the wholefood stereotype. The up-to-date kitchen with all stainless steel equipment and utensils forms part of the open plan arrangement with the dining area. As macrobiotic and vegan customers find it so difficult to eat out satisfactorily, special efforts are made with this kind of dish. Quenelles are offered with a variety of savoury fillings and they vary the recipe for the nut roast, and the accompanying sauces too. Starters include nourishing pea and lentil soups, all homemade like everything else. Alternatively, hummus dips, crudités and almond paté with brown rice snaps. Avocado pears as you care to have them. After conscience searching, fish steaks—turbot, halibut, tuna, salmon, swordfish and shark—make appearances on the menu. A mint and watercress sauce has appealed to some. Puddings include spiced hot fruit salad, their own cheesecake, date crumble, fresh fruit salad and Loseley ice cream. The olive oil used is first pressing; cider vinegar, Aspall's; the grains organic, including the rice. Demeter vegetable juices. French organic wines and possibly real ale soon.

Organically grown vegetables; free range eggs; wholemeal bread; polyunsaturates in cooking and at table; fresh fruits at table; minimal salt and sugar; freshly squeezed fruit juices. Vegetarian, vegan, macrobiotic. Some fish dishes. Seats 38. Meals from £7.00. House wine £4.25.

Open: Mon to Sat. 11–11; Sun to midnight.

BRISTOL   Avon   Map 2
The Guild, 68–70 Park Street   TEL Bristol (0272) 291874

It's a trek to find this pleasingly informal restaurant at the back of a Habitat-style store, but worth the effort. Euphemistically described as the Terrace, it's a series of several rooms overlooking one of the few areas of ivy, bramble and sycamore surviving in central Bristol. Appetising bakers' goods include their own home baked wholemeal rolls, scones, and pastries of the chocolate cake, flapjack type. The restaurant is clean and has a friendly waitress service. All food freshly prepared on the premises, free of preservatives, colourings and the like, and there is some lingering doubt in their minds as to what a microwave looks like. (Lunches bring cashew nut pâté or smoked mackerel, all presented with wholemeal rolls and side salads. Kitchen staff will usually prepare undressed salads on request. But don't expect to substitute the butter for your favourite margarine. They don't have any, or 'it is not of the polyunsaturated kind,' confided one member of staff. Chicken in tarragon sauce has approvers but there are no assurances about the bird's origins, though eggs we were reassured, were deep litter. The watercress and potato soups will normally meet vegetarian and vegan needs but if in doubt ask. Staff are well drilled in helping make a suitable choice. Puddings may be a chocolate brandy mousse, a sherry trifle or a safer apple and date crumble. Wholemeal flour is normally used in the cakes and pastries available through the day, with tea and coffee.

Wholemeal bread; erratic supplies of organic fruit and vegetables; deep litter eggs; wholemeal flour in cakes and pastries. Wholefood, vegetarian, vegan, other diets tackled. Seats 60. Meals from £4.20. House wine £4.20.

Open: Mon to Fri, 9.30 to 5; Sat, 9.30 to 4.30.

BRISTOL   Avon   MAP 2
McCreadies, 26 Broad Street   TEL Bristol (0272) 25580

'A nice little restaurant and takeaway with a good selection of wholefoods which are always labelled "vegan", milk-free and the like,' goes one report. 'Tasty and good sized portions at acceptable prices,' says another, contradicted by a third which claims, 'expensive but value for money as the food is of such a good standard.' So, judge for yourself! Soup of the day is 60p; paradise pie (smoked tofu) is £1.45 add to which 50p for a plain baked potato, 52p for the sweet and sour red cabbage, alternatively a side salad at 40p. A moussaka of red beans and mushrooms is priced the same as paradise pie. Desserts—cake, apple pie (vegan standard) and cheesecake—all homemade with praise for the cream and walnut cake. In the evenings there are more vegetarian dishes based on international menus from many countries. Three evenings a week there are more elaborate propositions: rough pastry rolls, Spenata kopita, are filled with spinach and cheese and served with some tasty salad. The lighter buckwheat crêpes may have a Russian style cabbage, caraway and cheese filling. Fettucini gusto, a recipe of noodles in a sauce of wine, cream, garlic and mushrooms, is delicious and very filling. Enchiladas are a lighter attraction. Puddings come as trifles, sorbets and mousse, or a selection of Loseley ice creams. Helen McCreadie's place has always been a café and it retains the old mahogany fixtures and fittings now softened with the green plants she so much admires. Food is cooked to appeal to popular taste, using all fresh ingredients and cooked on the premises. Coffee, tea and refreshments through the day.

Organic vegetables, when available; non-battery eggs; fresh and smoked soya bean curd as protein; wholemeal bread. Vegetarian, vegan. Seats 46. Meals from £3.50. House wine £3.95.

Open: Mon to Wed, 10 to 5; Thur to Sat, 10 to 10.

BRISTOL   Avon   MAP 2
Wild Oats II, 85 Whiteladies Road, Clifton   TEL Bristol (0272) 734482

In this provincial equivalent of Langan's, Mike Abrahams' aim is to produce 'nourishing alternatives to fatty and sugary foods, teas and coffees' although the latter are available, if you wish. His admirers feel that the food always looks good and tastes marvellous. Pâté maison is a combination of whole grains, vegetables, mushrooms, hazelnuts, red wine, herbs and spices. For a pickled vegetable starter the dressing is whey, natural lactic acid, rice vinegar and sea salt. Melon cocktail is served with a ginger syrup; a creamy watercress soup is vegan. Main dishes might be simply stir fried vegetables, bolstered with brown rice, Provençal potatoes or just garlic bread. More lavishly the tofu cassoulet is sautéed bean curd, chick peas, onions, peppers and tomatoes, prepared as an adaptation of the traditional recipe. Mushroom and cashew nut timbale is baked with millet and cashew nuts, the sauce a blend of sweetcorn, red peppers and white wine. An apricot and apple flan, Loseley ice cream, an apple and cider sponge with egg custard, sometimes cheesecakes, always fruit sorbets round off the meal. Wines, limited to ten, plucked from around Europe, and saké from Japan, are served in addition to natural organic wines from Bordeaux and Aix-en-Provence, matured without artificial aids. Real ale, real cider and lighter fare between meals.

Free range eggs, always; organic vegetables whenever possible; animal rennet free cheeses; wholemeal bread; minimal salt and sugar; polyunsaturated fats in kitchen and at table. Vegetarian, vegan, macrobiotic, diabetic, cancer diets. Seats 75. Meals, daily specials about £5.50, dinner from £7. House wine £4.50. 10% service charge for groups of ten or more and 15% discount for students and OAPs.

Open: Mon, Tue, 10.30 to 6; Wed, Thur, 10.30 to 10; Fri, Sat, 10.30 to 10.30; Sun, 11 to 5.

BROADWAY   Hereford and Worcester   MAP 3
The Lygon Arms, High Street   TEL Broadway (0386) 852255

It has been an inn since 1532 but the present character emerged this century, supported by American patronage and some skilful antique dealing. A timbered, massive stone fireplace in the dining-room is a certain attraction while waiting for salads of globe artichoke with palm hearts and mange tout, ogen melon with a raspberry sorbet and almond tulips, possibly better for you than avocado mayonnaise with Mediterranean prawns. Game and fish are usually table d'hôte features and appear prominently à la carte. Noisette of venison has a game sauce and a red cabbage garnish; baked guinea fowl cooked with juniper berries; angler fish has a bed of spinach or, more expensively, plain grilled Dover sole. Pan-fried cutlets of winter vegetables and nuts set on a tomato coulis is a vegetarian possibility. All dishes include fresh vegetables or mixed salads. The elaborate sweet trolley sports a better than average fresh fruit salad, and some choice cheeses.

Non-battery eggs; skimmed milk; wholemeal bread; freshly squeezed fruit and vegetable juices;
fresh fruits at table; polyunsaturates in kitchen and at table; homemade patisserie goods.
Vegetarian, other diets at short notice. Seats 120. Meals, lunch from £8.25, dinner from £15.50.
House wine £5.75.

Open: daily.

BURGHFIELD   Berkshire   MAP 3
Knights Farm, Burghfield, Nr Reading   TEL Burghfield (0734) 52366

This distinguished Queen Anne house has been opening its doors to epicureans for twenty years but keeps up-to-date with a 'modern' approach to cooking. The set price, four-course lunch and dinner menus change frequently. Impeccable suppliers of food are Garlands Farm and the Marigold Wholefood shop in Upper Basildon. With the brief respite between their twice daily ministrations, the Trevor Ropers manage to bake their own breads and brioches. In each course there is always a meatless dish. Fennel and cheese soup is made with a vegetable stock and lavishly finished with cheese and cream. A refreshing salad of William and avocado pears, if one is easy on the grapefruit mayonnaise, might be nutritionally more conforming, as might the chicken and walnut pâté. A commended salmon and white fish terrine — served warm and dealt with leeks and cream — sometimes appears as a second course in the evening, but at lunchtimes could have been a starter. Beef is scarce, but there is pan-fried calves' liver and spinach, seasoned with toasted pine kernels and nutmeg. The fish course will be Hobson's steamed fillets of turbot, sole and salmon, making partial amends for any earlier indiscretions. A mushroom filled artichoke topped with a walnut and orange sauce and served with a layer of vegetable mousse is the vegetarian option. To conclude there is Sicilian chocolate cake and a frangipane flan or a champagne sorbet with cassis sauce.

Organically grown vegetables; free range eggs; wholemeal home baked bread and brioches;
polyunsaturates or clarified butter in cooking; polyunsaturates at table, if requested; skimmed
milk; freshly squeezed fruit juices. Vegetarian, other diets, preferably with notice (advised
by Dr. Ann Walker, lecturer in nutrition, Reading University). Seats 45. 4-course meals,
lunch £13.50, dinner £17.25. House wine £5.75. Diners/Access/Barclaycard.

Open: Lunch, Tue to Fri; dinner, Tue to Sat.

BURY ST. EDMUNDS   Suffolk ☆   MAP 3
Bradfield House, Bradfield Combust   TEL Bury St. Edmunds (028) 486301

Arthur Young (the agricultural theorist) lived a wretched life here around 1820, but more recent reports suggest visitors could go further and fare worse. They speak of the 'pleasant tastefully furnished timbered restaurant, personal service, the felicity of the traditional cooking'. Likely as not the vegetables will be compost grown in Victoria and

Michael Stephenson's own large, yew fringed garden, the mushrooms possibly fresh picked from surrounding fields. Certainly the bread will be freshly baked in the kitchen. Soups include a delicate sorrel or wild mushroom; paté, trout en croute with a delicious horseradish sauce are all highly rated. Victoria Stephenson braises her recently popular ox tongue, with orange peel, dried wild fungi, grapes and red wine. Her diners commend the jugged hare, superb steaks and the loin of veal, sautéed in vermouth, mustard and cream. Strict vegetarians might be offered a yeast pastry case filled with a mixture of savoury rice, courgettes and seasoning. Inclusive Sunday lunches are felt to be particularly good value, offering, perhaps, an avocado and grapefruit salad with raspberry vinaigrette dressing, grilled lamb cutlets with gooseberry and mint jelly, finishing possibly with a fresh homemade strawberry ice cream (with Cointreau and orange juice in it), a raspberry sorbet, deliciously unhealthy rum babas and choux pastry cases mounded with cream.

Homemade wholemeal bread; free range eggs; largely organically grown fruit and vegetables; freshly squeezed fruit and vegetable juices on request and fresh fruit at table; no polyunsaturated fats at table—unsalted butter or nothing; vegetables cooked without salt. Vegetarian, vegan, gluten-free. Seats 24. Meals from £11, Sunday lunch £7.25 plus wine, coffee and service. House wine £6.

Open: 7 to 10.30; Sun, 12.30 to 2.30; closed Mon.

BURY ST. EDMUNDS   Suffolk   Map 3
Chalice, 28—29 Cannon Street   TEL Bury St. Edmunds (0284) 4855

Ruth Bolton's wholefood vegetarian restaurant is in two Victorian houses (at one stage a family bakery) and is twice a week (evenings) enlivened by musicians. Log fires and candlelight bring cheer to winter diners in the pine furnished room and the old bakery used for private functions. Among inexpensive, no nonsense dishes are cream of parsnip soup, butter bean pâté, and, quite often corn-on-the-cob. Ratatouille is served with garlic bread, the three bean casserole with a wholemeal roll and butter. Mushroom quiche or the hot lentil and hazelnut burger, the last with a tomato relish, might go well with one of her mixed salads. Chilli bean casserole is served with rice and has appeal for vegans. There is a choice of four puddings.

Wholemeal bread; free range eggs; some organically grown produce; polyunsaturates in kitchen and at table; minimal sugar and salt; skimmed milk; freshly squeezed fruit juices. Vegetarian, vegan, diabetic and gluten-free on request. Seats 50. Meals from £4. House wine £4.60 a litre.

Open: Tue to Sat, 12.30 to 2.30; Wed to Sat, 7 to 10.30.

BUXTON   Derbyshire   Map 6
Nathaniels Restaurant, 35 High Street   TEL Buxton (0298) 78388

Sue and Mike Jordan are secretive about the recipe for their lavish hot seafood cocktail, served in a Breton bowl, which has many devotees. King prawns are another speciality along with mushrooms Nathaniel, which has vegetarian approval when not topped with the customary sliver of paté, and melon with Cointreau. The inexpensive bistro menu includes the simpler garlic mushrooms, whitebait or a brandy pâté. Fillet of beef with Stilton is a popular main course along with duck and pears. Crêpes have fillings according to preference, vegetables for the totally pure, otherwise combinations of fish and cheeses. Lunchtimes bring the traditional dishes like steak and kidney pies, rice puddings and plum pies. Always the conventional confections, trifle and gâteaux. Dishes are always cooked to order and they don't possess a bain-marie, a microwave or a deep-freeze.

Wholemeal bread; freshly squeezed fruit juices; fresh fruits. Seats 50. Meals from £10 à la carte. House wine £5 a litre. Tue to Fri 4 courses, bistro menu £6.

Open: Tue to Sun, 12 to 2.30, 7 to 10.30.

CAMBRIDGE   Cambridgeshire   MAP 3
Hobbs Pavilion, Park Terrace   TEL Cambridge (0223) 67480

In a thirties brick and pantiled roof pavilion facing across Parker's Piece in the shadow of the monumental University Arms Hotel, Stephen Hill specialises in crêpes, having previously served only wholefood pizzas, quiches, salads and the like. He still offers the salads and everything except for the wholemeal rolls; the batters and desserts, and the fillings, are prepared in the kitchen. Packaged foods he has not escaped entirely—sweet corn and tomatoes come in tins. Many of the pancake fillings are vegetarian, sometimes vegan. Other dietary requirements require notice but he is happy to try and cope.

Organically grown vegetables as erratic supplies permit; wholemeal bread; freshly squeezed fruit and vegetable juices. Wholefood, vegetarian. Seats 67. Meals from £6.

Open: Tue to Sat, 12 to 2.30, 7 to 10.30: closed 1 week Christmas, Easter weekend, last 3 weeks Aug.

CAMBRIDGE   Cambridgeshire   MAP 3
Nettles Vegetarian Food Bar, 6 St. Edward's Passage   TEL Cambridge (0223) 350983

'People in this City crave for home-cooked and wholesome food which we do our best to cater for,' claims Maryanne Marks. Unequivocal as the name suggests, this establishment will seat just sixteen—that is cheek to cheek along the narrow bench. It is in a lovely peaceful backwater overlooking the tiny churchyard in the square of St. Edward King and Martyr. All the food is cooked on the premises daily. The sensibly limited bill of fare is likely to include lightly curried vegetables, lasagnes, a nut roast, several salads and wholemeal scones and rolls served with fresh vegetables. From 9 am muesli with fresh fruit; from mid morning and during afternoons, scones with homemade jam and cream. Prices are very modest.

Organically grown vegetables in season; wholemeal bread; polyunsaturates in cooking and at table; minimal salt and sugar. Vegetarian, wholefood. Seats 16. Meals from £3.75.

Open: Mon to Sat, 9 to 3.

CAMBRIDGE   Cambridgeshire   MAP 3
Xanadu, 7A Jesus Lane   TEL Cambridge (0223) 311678

Christopher Ryan has created a relaxed, informal family restaurant, everything homemade using, mainly, fresh ingredients. Exoticism extends to Xanadu's hors d'oeuvres trolley though there is a more simple and economical aromatic vegetable soup. Younger customers have been known to favour the alcoholic game pâté with herbs, salmon and shrimp mousse and an avocado stuffed with smoked chicken, served with salad. The price of the châteaubriand could be off-putting but it is divisible by two. Game, particularly the casserole of wild Highland grouse, is popular with its rich mushroom, apple and vegetable sauce. Abstainers feel that vegetarian traditions are upheld with a baked cheese mousse—cheddar, parmesan, cream and fresh herbs. 'Cheeky pear' is pear halves in a sauce of sweet chestnut and brandy cream, supplemented by a vanilla ice. Casablanca is a homemade ice cream cake with brandy and roasted toffee almonds, but more simply there is a cantaloupe melon sorbet or the homey red plum compote.

Non-battery eggs; no garlic or pork meat in any cooking; wholemeal bread; freshly squeezed fruit juices; skimmed milk. Wholefood, vegetarian. Seats 80. Meals from £8.25. House wine £5.

Open: Mon to Sat, 7 to 10/11.

CANTERBURY   Kent   MAP 3
Sweeney Todds Pizza Parlour, 8 Butchery Lane   TEL Canterbury (0227) 453148

This cellar restaurant is a haven for those who enjoy infinitely variable pizza, fresh salads, tuffed baked potatoes and their own-make chocolate cake. There is oregano but no wholemeal in the dough, and the cottage cheese and spinach version attracts a 5p contribution to Greenpeace, for every one ordered. Salads are appreciated for being reliably fresh and in variety. Non-vegetarian customers feel it is a better place to come for the ribs and chicken.

Fresh salads; polyunsaturates used in cooking; minimal salt and sugar. Vegetarian. Seats 84. Meals from £4.50. House wine £4.95. Access/Barclaycard.

Open: Sun to Sat, 12 to 12.

CARDIFF   South Glamorgan   MAP 2
The Armless Dragon, 97 Wyeverne Road, Cathays   TEL Cardiff (0222) 382357

Mark Sharples and David Richards are into wholefoods in as much that they use all fresh vegetables, and a lot of fish. Local meat and 100% flour are used in the traditional steak and kidney pudding. Laverballs, however, are entirely the product of their own imagination; 'putting other things in it, the laverbread is fried,' then served as a starter. Really fresh crab has appeal for others less adventurous. Sea fish is important in their perception of good food. 'Monkfish orientale' has become a staple but they are deemed good also for a fresh interesting chowder. Game, hare, pheasant and venison are regularly on the menu, with, occasionally, partridge and grouse. For vegetables they favour what is fresh and readily available—cauliflower with leek sauce, purées of root vegetables and 'what is wrong with spring cabbage, finely shredded and al dente?' Vegetarian platters are mushroom croquette, a laverball, a nut cutlet and a stuffed tomato with mushroom sauce. Alternatively a cream cheese and vegetable timbale in a leek sauce. The gâteau is wholemeal, the pudding chocolate, the cream caramel made with honey, the chiffon pie is made with cream cheese and the apricots are Hunza—with nut cream, if preferred.

Wholemeal bread; polyunsaturates used in cooking; minimal sugar in cooking. Wholefood, vegetarian, vegan. Seats 55. Meals from £6. House wine £4.50. Access/Visa.

Open: Tue to Sat, 12.30 to 2.15, 7.30 to 10.30.

CARDIFF   South Glamorgan   MAP 2
Crumbs, 33 Morgan Arcade   TEL Cardiff (0222) 395007

Adi Ashley has been running this shopping centre salad restaurant for fourteen years, organised to meet the lunchtime needs of workers, students, weight watchers and shoppers. Her fresh salads are supplemented in winter by her homemade soups. For £1.25 diners make up their own salad from a choice of six bowls. Supplemented with extras such as cottage cheese, cheddar and egg mayonnaise, if inclined.

Sugar is never used; fresh orange juice squeezed daily. Vegetarian, vegan. Seats 60. Meals from £2.50.

Open: Mon to Sat, 11.15 to 3.

CASTLE CARY   Somerset   MAP 2
The Old Bakehouse, High Street   TEL Castle Cary (0963) 50067

During the warmer months meals can be eaten out of doors in the courtyard and, what you fancied in the restaurant can be bought in the shop to take away! Carol Sealey (her husband runs the shop) sometimes includes dishes with fish and meat but she works in the general belief that her customers like freshly prepared interesting foods and as the place is small she is able to cook everything without any resort to convenience foods. As if that were not sufficient responsibility, she also gives talks and demonstrations on the subject of wholefoods and healthy eating. Main dishes may be spinach and tomato lasagne, preceded by one of her soups or egg curry served with brown rice. Sweet puddings—the toffee date kind, wholemeal apricot and fresh cream gâteaux. All her cakes, biscuits an scones are made here using brown flour and sugar, and the ice cream is also homemade.

Organically grown fruit and vegetables when available; semi-skimmed milk offered; non-battery eggs; wholemeal bread; polyunsaturates in cooking and at table; fresh fruits at table; minimal sa and sugar. Vegetarian, wholefood, vegan sometimes. Seats 24. Meals from £3.50.

Open: Mon and Thur, 9.30 to 1.30; Tue, Wed, Fri, Sat, 9.30 to 5.30.

CHAGFORD   Devon   MAP
Teignworthy Country House, Frenchbeer   TEL Chagford (064 73) 3355

A delightful 1920s house in a magnificent position on Dartmoor. At Teignworthy the take the business of looking after health quite seriously, though not so much so as to ris spoiling the relaxed atmosphere of a fine country house hotel. Cosseting commences wit the leisurely breakfasts from 8.30 onwards, when the juices are certain to be fresh (no fresh out of the carton), the main dish kedgeree (made, if not the genuine Loch Fyr kippers, at least with ones smoked without the addition of gaudy dyes). John and Gillia Newell show their refreshing attitude to food in their readiness to disclose all the source of supply. Apart from the fish sent down from Scotland, there are fresh supplies from th Solo Fish Company in Brixham and Brian and Jacie Lynch at Moretonhampstead send th fruit and vegetables. Cheeses mostly come from the farms where they are made. Egg come from hens which run around the neighbouring farms, and milk is a mixture of Jerse and South Devon, unpasteurised and making marvellous yoghurt and junket. The herb and a fair proportion of the vegetables are now grown by themselves. Using thes wholesome foods they serve noisettes of lamb with a mushroom sauce; soups made in th kitchen and the stock from their own stock pot. Dublin Bay prawns are baked in olive o quails are braised with a liberal amount of ground roast coriander. Ice creams ar homemade, sometimes the brown bread version, sometimes rum added. Soft fruit sorbe in summertime. Pork and bacon products hormone and antibiotic free from Anne Petc also her range of sausages and venison cuts; Loch Fyne, undyed kippers and smoke salmon, mussels, eel and trout from the same source; dry goods from the Granary, Truro

Wholemeal bread; polyunsaturates in cooking and at table; fresh fruits at table; minimal salt an sugar; skimmed milk available; freshly squeezed fruit and vegetable juices. Wholefood, vegetaria other diets with notice. Seats 24. Meals from £17.50. House wine £4.30.

Open: daily, 12.30 to 2, 7.30 to 9. Must book.

CHELTENHAM   Gloucestershire   MAP
Chives, 226 Bath Road   TEL Cheltenham (0242) 516676

Pure food has been late coming to Cheltenham, arriving only last year in the shape of th light and airy restaurant handy for the College. Catherine Hancox and partners Carolir Hancox and Jonathan Smith are now moving quickly, with a second branch planned fc Grosvenor Square in the town. For daytime self-service, a variety of mixed salads, n rissoles and a special main dish, from pasta to nut roasts, and jacket potatoes with variety of fillings are on offer and at night there are hot vegetables to go with the savou specials. Starters include soups, egg mayonnaise, hummus dip or cheese pâté. Puddings the order of honey and apple flan, fruit fresh in salads and in crumbles. Fruit yoghurts a made by themselves as are the variety of cakes.

Wholemeal bread and rolls; polyunsaturates in kitchen and at tables; fresh fruits; minimal salt and sugar; soya sauce used as far as possible; organic fruit and vegetables; free range eggs, from Mr. Roberts, the greengrocer and wholefood shop next door. Vegetarian, vegan. Seats 30. Meals about £5. House wine £3.75. Disabled access good.

Open: daily, 10 to 4.30; Wed close 2; Sat, 10 to 4.30; evenings Fri and Sat 7.30 to last orders 10.

CHESTER   Cheshire   MAP 6
Abbey Green Restaurant, Abbey Green, off Northgate Street
TEL Chester (0244) 319413

In this prettily sophisticated establishment, there are three rooms. The first, on the left, is where you can have morning coffee and digest the daily newspapers in armchairs or at one of the tables. To the right is the main restaurant beyond which a room where private functions can be held. To tempt the palate there may be mushroom gougère, savoury choux pastry in a mushroom and wine sauce, served with potato mountains, French carrots and celery; ravioli stuffed with cheese served with side salad and French bread. Moroccan cous-cous comes with the vegetables of the day. Stuffed aubergines have a stir fry vegetable garnish. Avocado and tofu dip is a favoured starter, more so than cashew nut and cream cheese pâté or the homemade soup of the night. Julia Lochhead's staff have a knack with pastry which makes the apple strudel a favourite choice if distancing oneself from the chocolate and rum gâteau, and in need of something more exotic than the always fresh and crisp tasty fruit salad. A good local baker makes the acceptable wholemeal and garlic breads.

Freshly squeezed fruit juices; wholemeal bread; fresh fruit at the table; only polyunsaturates at table and in kitchen; minimal salt and sugar; free range eggs; fruit and vegetables mostly organically grown. Seats 45. Meals, lunches from £2.50, dinners from £6. House wine £3.70.

Open: Sun to Sat.

COLCHESTER   Essex   MAP 3
Honeypot, 3 St. John Street   TEL Colchester (0206) 561676

Imaginative cooking but considerable secrecy about the recipes at this homely restaurant where everything is homemade down to the mayonnaise. With more than usual imagination, Vera Woodley and Clare Berrendero do quite lavish recipes like casserole primavera. Roughly translated as parsnips and leeks au gratin with gruyère and parmesan cheese, then topped out with spinach, tomatoes, eggs, cheese and cream. Torta serrana is a cheesy green pepper pie, accompanied by rice and a salad. Lunchtime standbys, at budget prices: vegetarian burgers, tuna fish quiche, hummus and pitta, savoury crêpes and omelettes. Desserts include fruit and nut flan, bananas and cream, or the more lavish fresh pineapple in cherry brandy with nuts, and crêpes suzettes with a liqueur cream.

Free range eggs; wholemeal bread; polyunsaturates at table; minimal salt and sugar; skimmed milk available; freshly squeezed fruit juices. Vegetarian, wholefood, vegan. Seats 65. Meals from £8.50, dishes from £2.60. Visa/Access/Diners' Club.

Open: 12 to 2.30, 6 to 11; closed all day Sun and Mon pm.

CRICKHOWELL   Powys   MAP 2
The Cheese Press, 18 High Street   TEL Crickhowell (0873) 811122

Mrs. Morgan-Grenville's cheerful small town café has particular appeal for shoppers and family parties. 'We bake on the premises and we bake in people's homes, all our food prepared without any "pre-made ingredients" and without any chemical additives.' The main dish of the day is frequently a free range chicken curry with organically grown rice. Very economically there may be a vegetarian bake, a soup (homemade with roll), quiches with mushroom or sweetcorn filling; lasagne of the meaty kind and baked potatoes with fillings. Filter coffee and pots of tea and lighter food throughout opening hours.

Organically grown potatoes always; free range eggs; duck eggs in season; organically grown rice; wholemeal bread; polyunsaturates in kitchen and at table; minimal salt and sugar. Wholefood, vegetarian. Seats 28. Meals from £3.35. Access/American Express.

Open: Mon to Sat, 9.30 to 5; closed Wed, pm; Sun, 2 to 5.

CROYDON   Surrey   MAP
Hockney's, 98 High Stret   TEL Croydon 01-688 2899

Matisse and Picasso prints on the wall and flowers on the tables, lend style to th
aesthetically pleasing spacious waiter-service restaurant. Openly set up to 'raise capital fc
Education through Art, in alternative Croydon'. Their version of peacock pie is coriande
cashew nuts, coconut cream, blackeye beans in a cheese and tomato purée, with
cauliflower cheese topping. Vegetable curry and rice has been on the mild side but som
feel the quality of the lasagne and macaroni cheese are sufficient to uplift their cookin
above the pedestrian. Aubergine marinade vies closely in popularity with a pâté maiso
and a pâté campagne. Making for a rich ice cream, blends of cream, cream cheese an
strawberries, with brandy or raisin and rum. The first, disguised with some fruit sala
apricot nectar and yoghurt turns out to be a 'Kim Philby'. The tall glasses of rum and raisi
ice cream, peaches and brandy snaps, turn out to be a 'Mine of Serpents'. Baking elevate
the carrot and the fresh fruit cake to the point where it is sought after supper far
sometimes served with yoghurt or cream.

Wholemeal bread; fresh fruits; polyunsaturates at table; free range eggs. Vegetarian, sometimes
vegan. Seats 80. Meals, evening from £5, main dishes from £2.75. Bring your own wine,
corkage £1.35. Access/Visa/Diners Club.

Open: Tue to Sat, 12 to 10.30.

DARTINGTON   Devon   MAP
Cranks, Shinners Bridge   TEL Dartington (0803) 862388

There are those who yearn for the bad old days when the place (Dartington Hall Cent
and its associated activities) symbolised an engaging purity and rural revival. At tim
there is all the frantic activity that only mass marketed tourism is able to beget. The earth
Crank's outpost dispenses much the same fare as the Marshall Street parent thoug
management reins seem looser here. Either that or the soft west country air has a
anaesthetising effect, for the activity behind the counter can be dispirited, and disorganise
One fares better with the actual food. The same good old breads, cakes, scones and salac
and hot dishes like savoury carrot layer, lentil and buckwheat slice, sustaining wint
hot-pot and some of the dishes now with soya protein, like soya egg and vegetable p
and burgers in baps. For puddings there is sometimes brandied prune mousse or 'toffee
rhubarb fool. Fruit juices are freshly extracted.

Homemade wholemeal bread; freshly squeezed fruit and vegetable juices; fresh fruit at table; free
range eggs; organic fruit and vegetables; stoneground organic wholemeal flour; biosalt with
cooking; polyunsaturates at table. Wholefood, vegetarian, vegan. Seats 52. Meals from £6.50.
House wine £4.90, organic wine (Bouchardon) £5.75. All major credit cards accepted.

Open: Mon to Sat, 10 to 5.

DARTMOUTH   Devon   ☆   MAP
The Carved Angel, 2 South Embankment   TEL Dartmouth (080 43) 2465

From the room with a riverside view, specialising in local fish dishes 'according
shopping on the quay', or items doing justice to any game larder, Joyce Molyneux ca
also satisfy gourmandising vegetarians. Green peppercorn noodles have made approve
appearance on more than one occasion and a vegetable filled pastry case with a chee
soufflé topping is a popular choice. Somewhere in a four-course meal, buckwhe
pancakes could be a feature. Lemon has lent astringency to celery soups and the Provenç
fish soup gained from sauce rouillé and garlic croutons. Another fishy starter was scallo
mousseline, mussels in saffron and ceviche of bass. Another meatless option is a tart
leeks and mushrooms in a cheese soufflé sauce. Pheasant may be served in pastry wi
pâté and mushrooms; roast half grouse more plainly with redcurrant jelly. Cheese

sorbets or a green salad come before the likes of passion fruit mousse cake, quinces in kumquat custard, apples cooked in butter and flamed in Calvados. Emphasis is on good quality local ingredients, simply and freshly cooked. Special requirements are cheerfully met but it is appreciated if these are made known at the time of booking.

Wholemeal bread; freshly squeezed fruit juices; fresh fruits at table; minimal salt and sugar. Vegetarian, other diets given notice. Seats 35. Meals, three courses from £17.70. House wine £5.50.

Open: Tue to Sat, 12.30 to 1.45, 7.30 to 10; Sun, 12.30 to 1.45. Closed all Jan.

DOVER   Kent   MAP 3
Curry Garden Tandoori, 24 High Street   TEL Dover (0304) 206357

Tourists turn up here, from the Continent, and from America making the crossing to mainland Europe. 'But they are not very very rich, hence the careful arrangement of prices.' Chef Abul Ahmed Khan mixes his own spices and readily adjusts seasoning to customers' particular likes and dislikes. One traveller appreciated the dum aloo (potatoes stuffed with nuts) more than her companions did the chef's special chicken dish. It is worthwhile remembering their takeaway service, as an improvement on seagoing fare, packed in special containers capable of retaining heat a long time.

Freshly squeezed fruit and vegetable juices; minimal salt and sugar; wholemeal bread. Vegetarian, vegan, special diet dishes by prior arrangement. Seats 52. Meals from £7. House wine £3.75. Access/Visa/Diners Club/American Express and luncheon vouchers accepted.

Open: daily, 12 to 3, 6 to 12.

DUBLIN   Dublin   No MAP
Shrimps Wine Bar, 1 Anne's Lane   TEL Dublin 713143/716110

Sheila Tynan's bar specialises in salads and customers seem happy enough with the generous if hit and miss arrangements for the seafood version. It all seems to be a question of what the sea yielded on any particular day. Salade niçoise is more than just greenery, the crab and the olives were liberally portioned, the dressing tangy. Chicken Caribbean was less exotic than it sounded but tastier than some fowl dishes tried elsewhere, leaving the unconfirmed idea that it might have been free range. Fresh pineapple ambrosia was confirmation that they were trying to do the right thing despite the fact that sticky toffee pudding is a perennial favourite most days. Always at least six hot dishes and everything is made in their own kitchen. 'We do a vegetarian salad but as all salads are made to order anyway we can do almost anything on demand.'

Wholemeal and malt breads; fresh fruit desserts; freshly squeezed fruit juices; minimal salt and sugar. Wholefood, vegetarian. Seats 48. Meals from £7, dishes from £3.50. House wine £6.75. Visa/Access.

Open: Mon to Sat, 12 to 12.

DUNDEE   Tayside   MAP 7
The Square Peg, 10 Constitution Road   TEL Dundee (0382) 28265

Honest to goodness wholefood fare of a basic kind in a town where the message has not yet been clearly heard. Toasted vegetarian cheese sandwiches are made with their wholemeal bread and served with a fresh green salad. Pâté is vegetarian but the filled rolls may be tuna or the moist and popular cheese and carrot version with a yoghurt dressing. Egg and creamed salad are recommended, being grated carrot, cabbage, worked with yoghurt, cream and mayonnaise. Scones and shortbread are wholemeal and there is a very acceptable banana and cherry bread. Chocolate flapjack is made from oats, fruit and honey with a carob topping.

Free range eggs; animal rennet free cheeses; low-fat milk; organic soya milk; wholemeal bread; fresh fruits and polyunsaturates at table. Wholefood, vegetarian, vegan. Seats 40. Minimum charge, 12 to 2, £1.

Open: Mon to Fri, 11 to 7: Sat, 10 to 5.

EASTBOURNE   East Sussex   MAP 3
Nature's Way, 196 Terminus Road   TEL Eastbourne (0323) 643211

There is more than a small amount of confusion between the various establishments in this town which trade as Nature's Way. Supporters, however, particularly identify 196 Terminus Road as the place to go because the food is varied and tasty, the only drawback being the small premises which quickly get very crowded. Prices are modest indeed for homemade soup, dumpling stew, crêpes Florentine, hazel nut roast and broccoli quiche which all reach very high standards, served with a selection of salads. Jacket potatoes, of course! Hot sweets may be bilberry and apple macaroon, an apricot sponge and banoffi pie. Apple strudel flan has takers all day. Cakes, scones, cheese scones and wholemeal rolls for afternoon teas or morning breaks. Everything the Fossitt's sell is homemade in their small kitchen. All ingredients are free from artificial preservatives and colour but all the fruit and vegetables may not be fresh.

Vegetarian, vegan. Seats 36. Meals from £3.50.

Open: Tue to Sat, 9.30 to 5.

EDINBURGH   Lothian   MAP 7
Country Kitchen, 4—6 South Charlotte Street   TEL Edinburgh 031-226 6150

New management have stepped into the shoes of McVities Guest who for many years, from these same cheerful premises, held the admirable reputation of catering for the masses decently. Now Howard Denton wears the mantle. 'Following the trend away from refined, over-processed and fatty foods, we serve salads, savouries, fresh fish, chicken, turkey, lean meat and high-fibre dishes.' Recipes are all researched with a special emphasis on low-fat content, salt and sugar reduced versions. But it is by no means a place for ostentatious self-denial and for afternoon loungers, there is piano accompaniment. A choice of soups is available every day. Traditional fried fillet of haddock (noted as particularly fresh) are not readily abandoned but American fish pie is a more healthy alternative. Each dish is marked showing calorie content, and description of ingredients. For burger-lovers there are cheese and onion burgers or try something spicy like the Ceylon curry and rice. Nuttie tatties are cheap and nourishing. Sampled date, raisin, apple and two bean salad rated well, and there are a dozen alternatives, including a sharp orange coleslaw to go with smoked haddock flan, turkey breast, chicken and liver or tuna pâté. Puddings are strong on mousse, cheesecakes and apple in strudel, crumble and pie. Homemade bran bread, fresh fruit salad and Copella apple juice are served.

Organic brown rice; organic potatoes used for baking; wholemeal bread; free range eggs; polyunsaturates in cooking and at table; fresh fruit at table; minimum salt and sugar; wholemeal pastas, flour. Wholefood, vegetarian, vegan, diabetic. Seats 200. Meals from £3. House wine £2.60 carafe.

Open: Mon to Sat, 8.30 to 7.30.

EDINBURGH   Lothian   MAP 7
Helios Fountain, 7 Grassmarket   TEL Edinburgh 031-229 7884

Erring towards the Bohemian and off the most worn tourist trails, Rosie Collingwood manages the genial café cum bookshop cum giftshop. Steiner principles apply to the food which is beautifully prepared from organically grown vegetables and grains by people interested in nutrition and creative cooking. The kitchen is central to all the trading and eating activity so customers see the food prepared. However for one, the observed finger licking in the kitchen held no appeal. Salads are in unusual combinations, and the beetroot soup has an optional yoghurt and cream garnish. Chestnut casserole is served with Brussels sprouts and mushrooms at a bargain price. But there are some problems with portion sizes, and it can end up quite expensive for lunch some regulars feel. Banana, lemon, yoghurt, cream cardamom and grapes are combined for a delightful dessert. The hot dish of the day is normally supplemented by a choice of vegetable pâtés, pies and croquettes. Salads are basically one grain, one leaf and one mixed root vegetable. There are cakes for vegans, some sugar-free, and above all, there is the excellent quality of the fruit and vegetables.

Bio-dynamic fruit juices and grains (they grind their own); organic vegetables; free range eggs; buttermilk; low-fat yoghurt and cream cheese in quiches; wholemeal bread; polyunsaturates in kitchen; minimal salt and sugar; freshly squeezed fruit and vegetable juices; sugar-free cakes. Seats 45. Meals from £3.

Open: Mon to Sat, 10 to 7.

EDINBURGH Lothian   MAP 7
Hendersons, 94 Hanover Street   TEL Edinburgh 031-225 2131

The warren of basement rooms beneath a wholefood shop of the same name, still has a streak of individuality though the improvisation wears thin at times. Opened in 1964, there is the same old integrity in the choice of raw ingredients, but a little of the zest has gone. Entirely wholefood, there is a wide range of imaginative salads, hot dishes and sweets, all made daily and on the premises. Their bakery still turns out good bread but pasties vary between the heavenly and the downright stodgy. Gone are the days when raspberry slices were melt in the mouth affairs. Savouries fare better and some marvellous vegetables go into the cauliflower bakes, the frittered aubergines, mushroom savouries and lasagne. Fruit salads, trifles, yoghurt creams still hold appeal.

Organic vegetables; free range eggs; wholemeal bread and baking; polyunsaturates in kitchen and at table; fresh fruits at table; minimal salt and sugar; freshly squeezed fruit juices. Wholefood, vegetarian, vegan. Seats 200. Meals from £6. House wine £4.90. Visa accepted.

Open: daily, 8 to 10.45; closed Sun, Oct to May.

EDINBURGH Lothian   MAP 7
Kalpna, 2–3 St. Patrick Square   TEL Edinburgh 031-667 9890

In this pleasing little restaurant they thrive with no small amount of support from the University. 'Vegetarian cooking may be a new cult in the west,' says Liz Mehta, 'but it has been a part of the cultural tradition of millions in India for centuries.' It is no accident that where the creative arts have flourished there has been a long tradition of imaginative cooking and a respect for wholesome foods. Indian food is what Liz regards as the original high-fibre diet. Dishes are mainly Gujerati but with some South Indian items too, that the proprietors were brought up on, but could never get in restaurants in the U.K. It is worth trying the Wednesday specials of deep fried vegetables and nuts, dhal and rice, and the Gujerati thali (stuffed vegetables) finishing with a sweet of sponge milk balls and rosewater. Starters worth considering are the vegetable cutlets and the stuffed lentil and vegetable pastry. Mughal kufta is a curry of peas, cheese curd, onions and nuts in a hot spicy sauce. Gajar halva is a carrot based sweet with almonds and cardamons. Also mango based Indian ice cream and fresh fruit sorbets. Fruit drinks—mango, and guava.

Wholemeal bread; minimal salt and sugar; polyunsaturates in kitchen and at table. Vegetarian, wholefood, vegan. Seats 66. Meals from £9, chef's special from £3.25. House wine £4.60. Access/Visa.

Open: Mon to Sat, 12 to 2, 5.30 to 11.

EDINBURGH   Lothian   MAP 7
Verandah Tandoori, 17 Dalry Road   TEL Edinburgh 031-337 5828

Much comment is made about the likability of the owners Wali (Tasar Uddin) and
Tommy (Ajman Miah) who came north together for the birth in '81 of the crisp modern
restaurant. Good value Bangladeshi specialities are the fairly hot and sour chicken
dhansak, the Jhali Bhuna curry and the milder Malayan prepared with pineapple, fruit
juices, coconut and cream, using chicken or king prawn, and the recommended biryanis.
Standard vegetarian dishes are thali, a selection of savouries including vegetable
massallam, tarka dhal, mushroom bhajee, unleavened wholewheat bread and pulao rice.
Madras sambar is a fairly hot vegetable and lentil curry, milder, is vegetable karai cooked
with fresh herbs and spices. Almond ice creams are homemade.

*Unleavened wholemeal bread; fresh fruit; minimal salt and sugar. Vegetarian. Seats 44. Meals
from £6.50. House wine £6.*

Open: Sun to Sat, 12 to 2.30, 5 to 11.45.

ELY   Cambridgeshire   MAP 3
Horizon Café, 29 Forehill   TEL Ely (0353) 61600

A number of reports confirm that the food is all quite nice in the pleasantly decorated
upstairs eating place above a wholefood shop (see entry). Prints on the wall and the
hanging greenery save the simplicity of the pine-furnished room from becoming austerity
and one of the partners, Sheila Dovey (an ex-S.R.N.), has an unusually sharp eye for
cleanliness. Soups are always homemade, alternating between the golden (lentils, carrots,
tomatoes, herbs), leek and potato, and green pea and mint. Main dishes can be vegetarian
moussakas, lasagne and a tempting nut roast from a recipe evolved in their kitchen. There
are always supporting quiches and a variety of salads each day—rice, three bean,
coleslaws, carrot and orange. Everything cooked for the café is available downstairs
as takeaway.

Open: Mon to Sat, 9 to 5.30; Tue, 9 to 2.

ELY   Cambridgeshire   MAP 3
The Old Fire Engine House, 23 St. Mary's Street   TEL Ely (0353) 2582

Feeling that 'food can after all be more than simply a means to prolong life,' Ann Ford and
Michael Jarman indulge customers by incorporating into the diet some meals which may
be thought over-rich or overseasoned according to the current dietary guidelines.
Nevertheless they insist that food is fresh, and unadulterated by the additives of the food
processing industry. Expect to be offered, in season, their roast pheasant, casserole of wild
duck, jugged hare, perhaps mackerel or pike baked in wine. Plaice is cooked with herbs but
never on Mondays, because it is fresh and there are no deliveries. Also seasonal and
rivalling Evesham is Wicken asparagus; the eel is from the Welney, smoked, and a more
regular offering. Pastry is a speciality used to make pies of pork and rabbit, steak and
kidney, pigeon and turkey. Roast of English lamb, beef and Yorkshire pudding and duck
with orange are, by their standards, more expensive standbys. One can finish the meal
with syllabub, gâteaux, sherry trifle, and meringues and cream. To bring balance to the
menu there is yoghurt with honey and almonds and fresh fruit salad. Coffee and tea
morning and afternoon.

*Home-grown vegetables; free range eggs; wholemeal bread; fresh fruits at table. Wholefood,
vegetarian with advance notice. Seats 35. Meals from £9. House wine £4.75.*

Open: daily, 10.30 to 2, 3.30 to 5.30, 7.30 to 9; closed Sun pm, 2 weeks at Christmas
and all Bank Holidays.

EXETER   Devon   MAP 2
Cooling's Wine Bar, 11 Gandy Street   TEL Exeter (0392) 34183

A convivial cavernous interior and cellar—down this narrow alleyway of street—offers
rumbustious food at bargain basement prices. David and Kay Belford probably have a fair
claim to be the town's most popular eating spot. It is worth facing up to quiche when it
comes with their fine array of inexpensive salads. Hot dishes (there are always three and
vegetarian) are no more expensive. Appetising aubergine Provençal and cottage pie with
red cabbage are frequently among the options. Meat and poultry are served cold. Chicken
Waldorf, spiced ham and egg or, moving up in price, sugar-baked ham or half a cold
chicken with salads. Lentil soup makes a cheap, nourishing starter. Puddings include
fragile, tempting frangipane tarts, Belgian fudge cake, hot chocolate pudding and black
cherry chiffon and cream. Regular standbys, cheesecakes, lemon meringue and syrup tart.
They cannot promise to please vegans and chip lovers are certain to be disappointed. No
food is fried and to avoid heavy seasoning they make all their own dressings from natural
ingredients.

*Wholemeal bread; fats high in polyunsaturates; minimal salt and sugar. Wholefood, vegetarian,
vegan sometimes. Seats 170. Meals from £3. House wine £4.10.*

Open: daily, 11 to 2.30, 5.30 to 10.30; closed Sun.

EXMOUTH   Devon   MAP 2
Round the Bend, 53 The Strand   TEL Exmouth (0395) 264398

'Nice decor, friendly atmosphere, a limited choice but what there is, is always freshly
cooked and imaginative, cutting above the usual nut roasts and pizzas,' commented one
reporter. Susan Glanville always manages a homemade soup, hummus and a vegetarian
pâté. To follow: lentil bakes, Japanese stuffed pancakes, nut burgers, scrumptious salads,
beanburgers which have achieved a certain popularity and simple baked potatoes with
cheese. She makes the savoury pasties in her own kitchen, the wholemeal bread is, as for
her shop, from Country Bumpkins, down the road. Sue Glanville emphasises, hers is a
wholefood restaurant. For seasoning she uses fresh vegetable stocks, sea salt and ground
pepper. There is animal rennet free cheese and live goats' yoghurt, and goats' cheese.
Prices are unbelievably cheap considering the quality and amount of food provided.

*Wholemeal bread; skimmed milk; organically grown vegetables; free range eggs. Wholefood,
vegetarian, vegan. Seats 35. Meals from £3. House wine £3.50.*

Open: Tue to Sat, 10 to 2; Fri, Sat, 7 to 10; in summer, Thur pm; spring and summer
Bank Holidays.

FALMOUTH   Cornwall   MAP 2
Kate's, 23A High Street   TEL Falmouth (0326) 311266

When Catherine Crombie recently took over, the menu was entirely vegan and
vegetarian but she has expanded the range to include a few meat dishes—though still
using entirely fresh ingredients and 100% wholemeal flour. 'Kates' takeaway—offering
large savings over restaurant prices—is a large part of the trade here offering a dozen
different salads, the ingredients varying with the seasons. Fish and meat pâtés have been
made a feature along with quiches, vegetarian pasties and the special hot dish of the day.
Except for the wholemeal, granary and pitta breads everything is freshly cooked on the
premises, the ingredients organic wherever possible. No artificial seasonings or colourings
are used, seasoning being mainly herbs and some mild curry flavouring. It is another one
of those places to come and live cheaply, healthily and well. A range of cheeses will be
coming shortly so increasing the variety of fare available for the tasty and generously
filled wholemeal baps which are so popular.

Organically grown fruit and vegetables whenever available; organic rice and flour; wholemeal bread; polyunsaturates in kitchen; fresh fruits at table; minimal sugar; sugar-free cakes. Vegetarian, wholefood, vegan. Seats 40. Meals from £4.

Open: daily, 9 to 9.30; winter, 10 to 3; closed Sun.

FAWLEY   Oxfordshire   Map 3
The Walnut Tree, Fawley, Henley-On-Thames   TEL Fawley (049 163) 360

Frank Harding has a busy country pub and his food is available wherever you can find space to eat it, and no surcharge for sitting in the restaurant. And he doesn't make much distinction between the vegetarian and other dishes, they like to cook to please people. Down in Henley, he gets a variety of customers from local farm workers and gamekeepers to celebrities, with and without local country homes. He buys in food which excites, and likes to do traditional dishes like steak and kidney pie. Also, expect to be offered vegan curried vegetable soup; nut and cheese stuffed mushrooms with a garlic mayonnaise; cheese leek and wine pancakes; or deep fried Camembert with a gooseberry dip. Smoked trout pâté comes with oatcakes, smoked fillet of beef has a horseradish dip. Wholemeal French bread is usually available.

Wholemeal French bread; fresh fruits at table; minimal sugar. Wholefood, vegetarian, vegan occasionally, other diets a welcome challenge. Seats 100. Meals from £5.50. Visa/Access.

Open: Sun to Sat, 11 to 2.30, 6 to 11.

FLITWICK   Bedfordshire   Map 3
Flitwick Manor, Flitwick   TEL Flitwick (0525) 712242

Trained at Pruniers (though that was some years ago), Mr. Moore actively promotes healthy food here and at the White Hart Inn in Flitton. He ploughs what he feels is 'a lengthy furrow' promoting interest in fresh fish, shellfish and crustaceans together with fresh vegetables and salads. Diners drawn to the gourmand menu of Sevruga caviar, Helford oysters and lobster at £45 will have laboured a little too or drawn on reserves, though in fairness it includes the bottle of Jacquesson Blanc de Blancs champagne. Setting aside his menu talking point, fish suppers of smooth scallop pâté with green peppercorns, a plate of shellfish including two varieties of prawn, crab, langoustines and a Helford oyster, are on offer for something nearer £12. That would include also the chocolate roulade and coffee. Choosing irregularly from his menu with few concessions to meat eaters, one can deliberate over the relative values of thick creamy finnan haddock soup or thinly sliced home-cured dill salmon. Sea bass is simply steamed on edible seaweed and served with hollandaise sauce. Large scallops are fried with bacon and Noilly Prat. Roast pheasant is served with bacon, bread sauce, game chips and red currant jelly. Potatoes are cooked in chicken stock and herbs, and winter vegetables include celeriac purée, fresh French beans and salsify. Vegetarians get an economical Greek feta cheese salad, followed maybe by a bowl of tagliatelle with a leaf salad, brown bread and butter, crème brulée with strawberries and coffee. But there are attractions in passion fruit and ginger ice creams, homemade at the Manor.

Vegetables, organically grown in kitchen garden; non-battery eggs; wholemeal bread; freshly squeezed fruit and vegetable juices; fresh fruit at table; minimal salt and sugar; polyunsaturates in kitchen and at table. Wholefood, vegetarian, vegan, calorie controlled diets devised. Seats 80. Meals from £7.50, vegetarian menu; from £12, regular menu. House wine £6.80. Access/ American Express/Visa/Diners' Club.

Open: daily, 12 to 2, 7 to 9.30; closed Sun, pm.

FOREST ROW   East Sussex   Map 3
Seasons Kitchen, Ashorne House, Lewes Road   TEL Forest Row (034 282) 3530

Elizabeth Boisseau is extremely particular about food, and if it falls below par, it is thrown away. Soups and salads in all their forms are generously acclaimed by her customers. So are cauliflower, Stilton and walnut tartlettes. Occasionally there is avocado mayonnaise; mushrooms and tempura sauce. Main courses include harder to find Mexican tostadas; light cheese and spinach crêpes with a rich mushroom or mornay sauce. There is a firm belief here that vegetarians have a sweet tooth, so sugar is used generously if not wisely in feathery Queen's pudding and cheesecake, so bear in mind the fruit salad and Loseley ice cream. Everything is cooked on the premises including the bread rolls. No additives, colourings or flavourings.

Only organically grown vegetables; wholemeal bread and rolls baked on the premises; polyunsaturates in kitchen and at table; free range eggs; fresh fruit at table. Wholefood, vegetarian, vegan. Seats 28. Meals from £7.50. House wine £3.75.

Open: daily, 6.30 to 9.30; closed Mon, Tue in winter; Sun, 12.30 to 2.

GLASGOW   Strathclyde   MAP 7
Poachers Restaurant, Ruthven Lane   TEL Glasgow 041-339 0932

Mrs. Scott and Mr. Bergious take pride in their menu written in plain English, with nothing too elaborate. Emphasis is on Scottish food, especially game, fish and shellfish, and they are happy to cater for most diets—preferably with a little warning—even macrobiotic. Mushrooms filled with pâté, wrapped in bacon and served with a white wine sauce are a speciality as well as a seafood tartlet of mussels, shrimps, saffron and cream. Vegetarians are usually asked what they would like, not helpful for anyone needing to be tempted. In practice one finishes up with aubergines stuffed with a savoury rice, peppers and mushrooms all given a creamy yoghurt topping. Turkey breast which followed—there being a dearth of game and fish that night—was appreciated for the chestnut and apricot stuffing and the sauce of port and cranberries. Jabron potatoes, sliced and baked with cheese, garlic and cream were nearly a meal in itself. To finish a meal there are meringues with winter fruit salad and cream; apricot brandy and chocolate trifle; and cranberry and orange sorbet and hazelnut torte.

Fresh fruits; wholemeal bread; polyunsaturates; non-battery eggs; only fresh vegetables but not necessarily organically grown. Wholefood, vegetarian, vegan, macrobiotic, gluten-free. Seats 45. Meals from £14. House wine £5.50. Access/Visa/Diners' Club/American Express.

Open: Mon to Sat, 12 to 2.30, 6.30 to 11.

GLASGOW   Strathclyde   MAP 7
Ubiquitous Chip, 12 Ashton Lane   TEL Glasgow 041-334 5007

Robert Clydesdale has everything cooked on the premises and there are no imported dyes in the cheese, or additives or colourings, with similar prohibitions on the tinned and the frozen. There is an affection for the harvest of the west coast seen in the Loch Fyne herring Lorraine; oak-smoked Loch Tay eel; Loch Torridon mussels marinière though we are left guessing where the creel was when it caught the langoustines! Monk fish and brill to which have been respectively added lightly curried sauterne sauce and Chambery butter sauce are another choice. Ham and lentil broth is a regionally sustaining dish and leeks with egg vinaigrette is something for the vegetarians, who might later be offered wholewheat, cheese and carrot flan or a chilli crumble. Otherwise the emphasis is on Scotch lamb, beef and game, with better than average treatment of vegetables like creamed parsnips with almonds, red cabbage with caraway seed. Puddings of the apple crumble, bread pudding kind, also fresh figs, without the lavish serving of cream, if necessary. Coffee in unlimited quantity.

Wholemeal bread; polyunsaturates in kitchen. Wholefood, vegetarian. Seats 120. Meals from £10 dinner, £7 lunch. House wine £4.25. American Express/Access/Visa/Diners' Club.

Open: Mon to Sat, 12 to 2.30, 5.30 to 11.

GRASMERE   Cumbria   MAP 6
The Rowan Tree, Grasmere   TEL Grasmere (096 65) 528

A small but delightful little place for a cup of coffee or a full meal, the menu is limited but very reasonably priced. There is appreciation for the real country atmosphere devoid of pseudo additions, and Robert and Jane Whittington manage to top several lists for tasty and imaginative food in an attractive setting. Hot dishes of the day—there are never more than two—vary between roasts, casseroles, curries and savoury pies in particularly fine pastry. The nut roasts are also served cold with a selection of salads or there is an animal free rennet cheddar or Blue Stilton to go with salads. Home-baked breads come with the soups, avocado and hummus served with salad garnish. Luscious lemon meringue seems to have the edge on the apple pie, while date and orange flan in honey syrup seems to exceed most expectations. Trifle is made using mead, fresh fruit, egg custard and cream, and they make their own ice creams and sorbets. Merrydown fruit wines and vintage cider. They also take guests in the house.

Wholemeal, homemade bread from organically grown wheat; polyunsaturates in cooking; free range eggs; some organic vegetables and dried goods; soya milk; fresh fruit at table; minimal salt and sugar. Vegetarian, wholefood, vegan, diabetic, gluten-free. Seats 40. Meals from £5. House wine £3.75.

Open: daily, 10 to 9 (Apr to Nov), 10 to 5 (Nov to Mar).

GREAT DUNMOW   Essex   MAP 3
Starr, Market Place   TEL Great Dunmow (0371) 4321

Locally there is a preoccupation with bacon. This is the town where a side of a pig is awarded to the married couple who can swear to have lived in complete harmony for a year and a day. There is a deep interest in other food and wines too and Brian Jones 'thanks God that there are people who can afford them' for his prices are not cheap. He takes a sensibly modern attitude to food however and each dish is carefully described. If there is a dish a customer does not like or should not have, then it is omitted. Menu changes are made daily and he uses only fresh produce, the only item bought frozen is the peeled prawns. Fish is well represented be it soft herring roe, seafood and mango salad or Mediterranean fish soup, to start. Similarly vegetables, with asparagus mousse and wholemeal toast; fruit curry and wild rice and celery and asparagus soup and Galia melon which is normally served with thinly-sliced beef. Wholemeal pastry is used for the steak, kidney and oyster pie. Fish reappears as a minty escalope of sea bass, baked red mullet with orange and fennel and paupiettes of lemon sole with crab and lemon hollandaise. Otherwise there is partridge, pheasant and duck in its tame and wild forms. The chef will consider any dish providing they have the raw ingredients.

Organically grown herbs and soft fruit; non-battery eggs; wholemeal bread; fresh fruits at table; minimal salt and sugar. Wholefood, vegetarian, vegan, diabetic. Seats 60. Meals from £14. House wine £6.60. Major credit cards accepted.

Open: Tue to Sat, 7 to 10; Sun, 12 to 2. Closed first three weeks in Aug.

HASTINGS   East Sussex   MAP 3
Brants Health Food Restaurant, 45 High Street   TEL Hastings (0424) 431896

John Gibbon's and Donald Brant's modest non-meat-eating establishment can offer only simple basic salads and savouries but all cooking is done on the premises. Expect tasty nut savouries, cheese flans and egg or cheese savouries. Salads are made up as meals in their own right. Soup is homemade and comes with a wholemeal roll. Apple pie is quite special and there is much to be said for fruit and nut flan cake, their fruit flans and fruit salads using dried and fresh fruits. Open through the day for coffee and teas. Only brown flour used in baking.

Organically grown vegetables; free range eggs; wholemeal bread; polyunsaturates at table; minimal salt and sugar. Vegetarian. Seats 32. Meals (light lunches) from £2.50. Wine by the glass 80p.

Open: Mon to Sat, 10 to 5; Wed, 10 to 2.

HEREFORD   Hereford and Worcester   MAP 2
Effy's, 96 East Street   TEL Hereford (0432) 59754

Helen Priday and Elspeth Parker struggle on in the centre of a farming community so changes have to be introduced gradually. Rather cleverly, they've persuaded a local organic grower to take over their own vegetable garden, and they make their own pasta, ice cream and their own highly regarded chocolates. There is an unusual selection of salads, pâtés, herby cream cheese and more. Spicy sausages are popular, seasoned with fresh herbs and infinitely better for being offered with Effy's special mustard, which they also pack in pots, if you want to relive the treat. A cheesey delicacy is deep fried and served with apple purée. Scallops are cooked in unsalted butter, mushrooms and white wine, served with the vegetables they take particular pride in. Diners seem to agree that chicken breasts are their speciality, cooked in a buttery wine sauce flavoured with tomatoes. Otherwise it might be the lamb steak cooked and served with a purée of shallots and fresh ginger, or pork kebabs marinated in local cider and spices. Profiteroles have a hot, plain chocolate sauce; the pavlova a coating of thick Jersey cream and blackcurrants. Effy's ice creams may be gooseberry and elderflower served with elderflower wine, the blackcurrant with port and the damson with cognac. Less calorific are their own fresh fruit flavoured sorbets. The in-house chocolates that come with the coffee are also available in takeaway packs. Wines, semi-organic, from the Broadfield Court Vineyard and Dunkerton's organic cider, in addition to a regular wine list.

Organic vegetables; fresh fruit at table; fresh fruit juices sometimes in the bar; polyunsaturates in kitchen and at table; non-battery eggs. Wholefood, vegetarian. Seats 50. Meals from £8. House wines £5.25. Access/Diners' Club/American Express.

Open: daily, 12 to 3, 6 to 12; closed Sun.

HEREFORD   Hereford and Worcester   MAP 2
Fodder, 27 Church Street   TEL Hereford (0432) 58171

All trace of the new Franciscan Friars has gone but Mr. Seddon-Harvey's bistro seems to be sufficiently well-entrenched to entertain evening opening, even if only on Fridays and Saturdays at present. His cheerful red and green room takes on a mellower tone by evening candlelight or there is space in the cool of the evening, for meals at courtyard tables. Tall Victorian iron gates are the only division between galley and saloon. Inexpensive, simple fare, it is food made to accompany the wine. Always freshly cooked, the dish of the night might be almond rissole, or a tofu vegetable casserole, perhaps moussaka or lasagne, nothing to break new ground but not the bank either. Marinated mushroom avocado has its devotees. Simpler stopgaps, available midday too, are the baked potato variations or the vegetable 'fodderburger' with a wholemeal bap. Crêpes with a tasty filling are popular and there are always salads. Strumble is a bean and vegetable dish with a crumble topping. Healthy puds may be farmhouse cheesecake or gâteaux. Anything on the menu can be done as takeaway. Conventional German and French wines plus the de-alcoholised kind. With wine, expect to spend £5 to £10 a head.

Open: Mon to Sat, 10 to 4.30; Fri, Sat, 7.30 to 11.30.

HEREFORD   Hereford and Worcester   MAP 2
The Marches, 24–30 Union Street   TEL Hereford (0432) 53712

The encouraging signs are that, after ten years, standards are going up not down. 'Everyone hopes it can last.' With exceptional energy Mrs. Vale runs both the restaurant ('the only serious alternative eating in Hereford during the day') and the adjacent wholefood shop. There are meat dishes too but most notice is taken of very substantial wholemeal quiches, nut roasts and about ten salads, the best of which are tomato and onion and the green leaf. Commendations for the soup and the breads, and hot savouries like cauliflower cheese and the lasagne. In the morning freshly made wholemeal fruit scones make a good breakfast. Helpings are generous, prices reasonable.

Wholemeal bread; wholemeal flour in baking; goats' milk yoghurt. Wholefood, vegetarian, vegan. Seats 190. Meals from £2.70. House wine 70p glass.

Open: Mon to Sat, 8.30 to 5.30.

HITCHIN   Hertfordshire   MAP 3
Flappers, 24 Sun Street   TEL Hitchin (0462) 50044

Decoration in a sharp '20s style has not surprised anyone. The reputation is for well seasoned alcohol-laden cookery, attracting not only vegetarians but others trying wholefood cooking, for whom there is the odd meaty dish. Country pâté is liver, chicken and garlic; fish is served as a seafood cocktail and smoked salmon. Otherwise starters are more likely to be vine leaves stuffed with buckwheat, pine kernel, sultanas and dill, a yoghurt dressing and pitta bread. Alternative pâté is made using cottage cheese, vegetarian cheddar, walnuts and wholegrain mustard. The cashew and almond nut loaf is served with a tomato and mushroom sauce, or try the vegetable curry, Flapper's pilau or the sometimes preferred galettes filled, mysteriously, with the speciality of the day, along with hot vegetables. A good value festive menu was breaded mushrooms, walnut and courgette pie and rum log with brandy cream. Vegetables are always fresh. Wednesday and Friday there is live jazz and folk music.

Wholefood, vegetarian, vegan. Seats 42. Meals from £3.50. House wine £4.40. Access/ American Express/Visa/Diners' Club.

Open: Tue to Sat, 12 to 2.30, 7 to 11.

HORTON CROSS   Somerset   MAP 2
The Lamb Inn, Horton Cross, Ilminster   TEL Horton Cross (046 05) 2524

This main road village inn, just west of Ilminster and convenient for Barrington Court (National Trust) reliably offers vegetarian and vegan cooking at reasonable prices. A good choice of main courses and salads especially during the summer season and always friendly service.

Wholemeal bread; sugar free desserts; salt free margarine. Vegetarian, vegan. Meals from £3. Wine by the glass.

Open: usual pub hours.

HOVE   East Sussex   MAP 3
Nature's Way Coffee Shop, 122 Church Road   TEL Hove (0903) 209931

Barry and Anne Lewis' three-year-old café has become an established venue for shoppers, local working people and students who care about what they eat. The cheerful staff, attractive pine furniture and green plants seem to account partly for its popularity. Interesting, varied, well-cooked food at reasonable prices is another reason. Daily specials may be hazelnut loaf or chilli con carne, with sometimes a wholemeal cheese and vegetable flan. Four kinds of salad in a standard bowl, nine kinds in the large bowl, are nearly meals in themselves. Soup of the day should also meet vegan needs. Puddings are fruit compotes, quite often a chocolate mousse and sherry trifle. Cakes—homemade—vary from time-to-time but one can usually expect honey sponge, carrot and chocolate fudge cake and flapjack, sometimes Australian chewie and Dorset apple cakes.

Wholemeal bread; polyunsaturates in cooking. Vegetarian, vegan. Seats 36. Meals from £3.50.

Open: daily, 9.15 to 5; closed Sun and Bank Holidays.

INVERNESS Highland ☆ MAP 7
Dunain Park, Inverness TEL Inverness (0463) 230512

In unspoilt countryside two and a half miles south of Inverness where the Caledonian Canal links Loch Ness with the Moray Firth, Judith and Michael Bulger keep a discreet country house hotel. They have a special regard for pure food. There are six acres of garden and woodland surrounding the hotel, Mr. Bulger proudly disclosing, 'We have two acres of our own kitchen garden and keep hens, geese, sheep and pigs. We grow all our own herbs and spices.' And, as he points out, the dining-room seems to have attained a considerable reputation for exceptional cooking, catching the attention of a good many good food publications. There is an abundance of local game, venison, grouse, pheasant, pigeon, which is made good use of in the kitchen. Salmon, scallops and lobster are also readily available. Menus are simple, all a question of doing a little, well. At dinner there will never be more than a choice of two main dishes, perhaps scallops and bacon kebab or chicken Provençal, preceded by mushroom soup and an avocado mayonnaise. As a general rule one of the main course choices is with a sauce and the other plain. Special dietary dishes are never on the menu but they are frequently catered for. The Bulgers take these demands in their stride, though 'we would appreciate more notice than we usually get'. Few tables are available for non-residents so it is sensible to make a booking. Last but not least, considerable importance is attached to breakfast. Choose from as many items as you wish—not forgetting the eggs which may have only just been collected.

Home grown organic vegetables and some fruit; home laid free range eggs; home reared chickens, geese, pork and lamb; wholemeal bread; fresh fruits at table; freshly squeezed fruit and vegetable juices. Wholefood, vegetarian, vegan, gluten-free, diabetic. Seats 20. Meals, set dinner only £15. House wine £5.20.

Open: daily; closed Oct to mid-Mar.

ISLE OF LUING Strathclyde ☆ MAP 7
Longhouse Buttery and Gallery, Cullipool TEL Isle of Luing (085 24) 209

The business of 'trying hard' really has some meaning here. Food is never prepared in advance and able and willing kitchen staff take special orders without blinking—faces more likely to crease into smiles than scowls. Lavish sandwiches are lunchtime specialities, filled with whatever fare is available. This can be gammon, salmon, prawn, venison paté, or cheese with lashings of salad. Or the meal can be more formal with their soup of the day, the venison pâté as a starter, or one of their really fresh fruit juices. Main dishes might be fresh Luing squat lobster tails, the local salmon and a Cullipool mixed platter with a little of all that is going. Indulgences like triple meringue cream, frozen Cullipool choc pot and frozen orange cream make desirable puddings. Dinners are only offered during July and August, three nights weekly—braised venison, Thursdays; baked salmon, Fridays; scallops poached and cooked on the spit, Saturdays. Note however that the island car ferry doesn't run at night. Edna Whyte and Audrey Stone have been here eight years now and persist with their aim of employing only island people. 'We can only achieve what is possible in such a tiny community so we keep things simple.' The owners are forever thoughtful, dogs can be tied to the big garden seat or left in the porch, a bowl of water provided. If a yachtsman asks for sandwiches to take away, perhaps to catch an early tide, there is no problem about opening hours. Homemade lemonade.

Home grown vegetables, herbs and salads, including sugar-snap peas and potatoes; island-laid free range eggs; wholemeal bread, also island-made by Mr. Davidson; dried goods from the Millstone Wholefood shop in Oban; fresh fruits at table; minimal salt and sugar; freshly squeezed fruit juices. Wholefood, vegetarian, vegan, diabetic and gluten-free requests handled as best as circumstances permit. Seats 34. Meals from £4.50. House wine £4.25.

Open: daily, 11 to 5; closed Sun and early Oct to Mon before Easter.

KENDAL   Cumbria   MAP 6
The Moon Restaurant, 129 Highgate   TEL Kendal (0539) 29254

Val Macconnell is spokesperson for this popular, lively little restaurant run by young people. 'Food is wholefood, cooked freshly every day with enthusiasm, care and creativity,' is one claim. The menu is a balance of meat and vegetarian dishes, using herbs and spices in an interesting way. 'It has the atmosphere of a French bistro—much green and white paint and curtains—Lakeland style,' says Val. They are not quite a co-operative but they make joint decisions which seem to work quite well, probably because they've appointed one of their number as manager. Some vegetarian dishes are more popular than the meat. Spinach and cream cheese lasagne with salad, mushroom and walnut pancakes and their regular flans have keen followers. Spiced meat balls or haddock and sweetcorn crumble are offered with either salad or hot vegetables; beef in red wine and lamb and aubergine curry complete a day's menu. People keep coming back for the sticky toffee pudding, so much so that it makes appearances midday and evenings served with cream or their homemade ice cream and custard. Fig and walnut sponge has also been known to please. Soups like the other dishes are all homemade.

Wholemeal bread; fresh fruits at table; minimal salt and sugar. Wholefood, vegetarian. Seats 30. Meals from £5. Wine £4.95 litre carafe.

Open: lunch, Tue to Sat, 11.45 to 2; dinner, Mon to Thur, 6 to 10: Fri and Sat, 6 to 11; Sun, 7 to 10.

KINGSTON UPON THAMES   Surrey   MAP 3
Clouds, 6–8 Kingston Hill   TEL Kingston upon Thames 01-546 0559

This large, relaxed eating place is run on much the same lines as the branch in Brighton. Although they can still produce French fries, wholefood is a more accurate interpretation of their style. Encouragingly all the pies, scones, cakes and meringues are made in their own kitchens using wholemeal flour. Vegetables are always fresh, and the meat is delivered daily as they try not to use frozen. Fresh and interesting salads go with the deep fried clams and the speciality charcoal rump steaks. The vegetarian menu should improve but already includes quiches or cutlets, and a chilli. But, as the *Guide* warned at Brighton, watch out for the Clouds Vegetarian Sauce hamburger, for it is beef beneath. Lavish creamy concoctions for dessert but there is always plainer apple pie and a fresh fruit salad.

Wholemeal bread; non-battery eggs; source of free range chickens being sought. Wholefood, vegetarian. Seats 110. Meals from £3.25. House wine £4.25. Access.

Open: Sun to Sat, 11 to 11.

KINGTON   Hereford and Worcester   MAP 2
The Blue Frog, Church Street   TEL Kington (0544) 230355

Supporters of the informal, friendly café report on the limited but valuable service here, given the dearth of such places in this region. The small menu can be erratic but there is usually at least one hot dish daily, made fresh, usually vegetable lasagne or spicy lentil rissoles with tomato sauce (both 90p each). In fact prices seem to be standardised for on some days there is cauliflower crumble which costs no more. A baked potato only adds another 35p to the bill. Whenever possible they use organically grown vegetables and free range eggs. Desserts are all of the cake kind but they are made on the premises with complimentary murmurings about the chocolate, and the chocolate and walnut slices.

Wholemeal bread; fresh fruit is non-existent; gluten-free or other special diets willingly catered for if notice is given first thing in the morning for lunchtime. Generous mugs for hot drinks—if you ask for a cup of tea a large pot is freshly made. Seats 20.

Open: Mon to Sat, 9 to 5.

KINGUSSIE Highland   MAP 7
Wood 'n' Spoon, 3 High Street   TEL Kingussie (054 02) 488

The Russells' bright, self-service restaurant offers a wide variety of wholefood fare for most needs. Vegetarian dishes are regular items and vegan are sometimes attempted. All the soups, baking and many varieties of ice cream are freshly made in their kitchens. Quiches are never frozen. Specialities are meat loaves, pork pies, fisherman's pie and hearty casseroles. Scotch eggs are the vegetarian variety. Salads tempt and, as a rule, they are ahead of their rivals this far North. During the quiet season there is table service and every Friday night until 1 am Saturday there is dancing.

Wholemeal bread; polyunsaturates in cooking; minimal salt and sugar. Wholefood, vegetarian. Seats 60. Meals from £3.75. House wine £4.20. Barclaycard.

Open: daily, 11 to 9.30 in summer; 11 to 8 in winter.

KINSALE County Cork   NO MAP
Vintage, Kinsale   TEL Kinsale (021) 72502

New owners at this established restaurant, Michael and Marie Riese, have a policy of fresh wholefoods. They make a particular point of serving fresh sea food, wild rabbit and game in season and free range duckling at all times. Sauces can be lavish—cream, wine, butter and eggs generously used—but 'nothing with preservatives, colouring or additives is allowed to enter into our cooking'. Soup may have been made with fresh tomatoes and oranges. Salmon will be local and oak smoked. Among hot starters, whole mushrooms in batter served with a lime curry mayonnaise is popular. Lavish sauces go with the sole Véronique or the brace of quail. Fillet of pork benefits from a spinach and mushroom stuffing and rabbit is casseroled in wine, olives, tomatoes and garlic. Vegetables are fresh. Vegetarian dishes are not a menu feature and the options for non-meat eaters are limited. Stir-fried vegetables with mayonnaise are as far as they go; soups and starters will be some compensation, as might the crêpes Marie, filled with a hot fruit mousse and flamed in cognac, hot raspberry jubilee flamed in Kirsch. Ice cream is homemade and so are the biscuits served with the cheese.

Wholemeal bread; free range eggs; fresh fruits at table; minimal salt and sugar; organically grown fruit and vegetables; polyunsaturates in cooking. Wholefood, vegetarian by arrangement. Seats 60. Meals from £13.50. House wine £6.75. All major credit cards accepted.

Open: daily, 7 to 10.30; closed Sun, Mon in winter. Closed last two weeks Jan and first week Feb.

KIRBY FLEETHAM North Yorkshire   MAP 6
Kirby Fleetham Hall, Northallerton   TEL Kirby Fleetham (0609) 748226

David Grant, in the Hall by the banks of the Swale, has an acre of walled garden which supplies a fair amount of his vegetables and fresh herbs. 'Not everyone in the North East wants the sort of food served here but there are those who do and are prepared to travel a long way for it! By limiting the choice on the menu, we believe we can maintain a reasonably high standard,' is David Grant's modest claim. He offers, at most, a choice of four main dishes at dinner, the fish perhaps being fresh salmon baked in wine. Lamb steaks have been marinated with orange and ginger, while a veal chop has benefited from the garden chervil, mushrooms and a vermouth cream sauce. Vegetarian items are not regular menu features but from a four course menu a celery soup, followed by peach salad and savoury cream, or perhaps the deep fried mushrooms, will be foundations for what this conscientious kitchen can dream up after placing your order, while enjoying drinks in the Georgian drawing-room—there is no bar. Refreshingly, prices include a service charge.

Home grown vegetables and herbs; wholemeal bread; fresh fruits at table; freshly squeezed fruit and vegetable juices. Wholefood, vegetarian on request. Seats 40. Meals from £13. House wine £6.50.

Open: lunch, Sun only, 12.30 to 1.30; dinner daily 7 to 9

KNARESBOROUGH   North Yorkshire   MAP 6
Schwallers, 6–8 Bond End   TEL Knaresborough (0423) 863899

Caroline and Martin Schwaller are enthusiastically for the natural way, going as far as to offer wine, Côteaux des Baux de Provence, which fits the prescription. Conveniently it comes via Martin's sister who operates Bond End Wines. A pleasing little restaurant, both the à la carte and the fixed priced menu change daily to incorporate the fresh produce they have been able to buy. 'All food is made by ourselves, bread baked fresh for each session for example.' When they are not finding time for baking bread they are busy about their homemade ices and sorbets. The four-course prix fixe menu doesn't present problems for those bent on eating out the healthy way. Fish, chicken and a vegetarian surprise (mixed bean hot-pot topped with walnuts and cheese) are reliable entries. Starters usually run to melon, a Greek salad, with a choice of the favoured gazpacho or sorbet to follow, always with fresh vegetables and salad. Then there is the à la carte offering scope for sizzling citrus plate, smoked quail and, for parties only, they will do a traditional fondue. To follow there is Jambon Braise au Celeri or Entrecôte Café de Paris, for the committed steak and pint sort. One of the house ice creams to finish, or the speciality cheese board, an individual platter of fine English and Continental cheeses specially selected. A Sunday lunch special: roast beef and pudding.

Free range eggs; wholemeal bread; freshly squeezed fruit juices on request; polyunsaturates in cooking and at table; fresh fruits at table; minimal sugar; all dishes cooked to order and salt omitted if requested. Wholefood, vegetarian, salt free diets—will try and meet other requirements. Seats 35. Meals from £10.25 dinner, Sunday lunch £6.25. House wine £6.50. Access/Visa.

Open: Mon to Sat, 7 to 10; Sun, 12.30 to 2; closed Tue.

LAUGHARNE   Dyfed   MAP 2
Stable Door Wine Bar, Market Lane   TEL Laugharne (099 421) 355

Leaving aside the Dylan Thomas connection, Laugharne survives as a pretty little place at the mouth of the Taff, protected from commercialism by being slightly out of the way and without too obvious attractions like marvellous beaches or bathing. This is interesting because Nick Prestland has become well established, in an unlikely setting. Enterprisingly he admits to 'attempting to introduce new and different tastes and styles of cooking', though his enthusiasm for garlic has given alarm on occasions. Nevertheless most enjoy his soups 'in hot and chilled varieties', his avocado mousse with prawns, some the hummus. Bread is garlic, salads are help yourself. For something really substantial Mexican beef tacos, or, more lightly, lemon chicken, from a bird which once roamed a yard. Vegetarians take to his aubergine and tomato casserole and the curried nut roast is a more moist affair than many. Fresh fruit pavlova, mint chocolate mousse and cheesecake follow.

Organically grown fruit and vegetables; wholemeal bread; free range eggs. Wholefood,

vegetarian, vegan, other diets by request. Seats 70. Meals from £5. House wine from £4.85.
Access.

Open: Tue to Sun, 11 to 3, 7 to 11; in winter, Thur to Sat only.

LEAMINGTON SPA   Warwickshire   MAP 3
Rainbow Vegetarian Restaurant, 9 Regent Place
TEL Leamington Spa (0926) 311056

Shoppers, students, office workers, young professionals all regularly patronise this simply
appointed popular workers co-operative. Daily they vary the menu, which is two soups,
quiche, pizza, two or three main meals, three salads, suiting the style of a principally
lunchtime operation. Only Fridays and Saturdays are they open late. Then, enlivened to
suit the mood, there is spicy vegetarian Mexican food. Says worker spokesperson, anony-
mously, 'Our aim is to cook tasty and exciting wholesome food, though not over-rich or
elaborate.' Soups are variable but on balance good, and there is the confidence from
knowing that only good safe ingredients go into them. Stir fried vegetables and
mushrooms and cashew nut pie are popular. Salads are good and quiches come with
imaginative fillings. A reliable fruit salad, and yoghurts are always available together with
applecake, flapjack and hearty wholemeal scones.

Free range eggs; animal rennet free cheeses; organically grown vegetables when available; soya
milk and tofu; wholemeal bread; polyunsaturates in kitchen and at table; fresh fruits at table.
Wholefood, vegetarian, vegan, sugar free desserts, other diets on request. Seats 40 (plus
30 outdoors in summer). Meals from £3.50. House wine £4.25.

Open: daily at lunchtime; Fri and Sat pm.

LEDBURY   Hereford and Worcester   MAP 2
Applejack, 44 The Homend   TEL Ledbury (0531) 4181

Having learnt the ropes under an earlier regime, Cynthia Sheppard has eased into the
management hot seat without disrupting bar or restaurant calm. Her bistro-type food
finds favour with most groups in this delightful little town with the black and white
houses. Miss Sheppard is handily placed too for supplies from the growing band of
organic producers in the district. Flexibility is the keynote and snacks or starters can be
kipper to chicken pâté, or ham and celery gratinée, if taste does not run to the popular
Applejack burgers. Main courses are of the lemon sole, clam fries, grilled Portuguese
sardine, school, or a casserole of the day, for which the standard accompaniments are side
salad and sauté potatoes. Meatless dishes include curried cheese savoury, aubergine bake,
vegetarian nut paella and fried avocado with tofu. Evening menus produce the more
elaborate venison casserole, griddled lamb and baked shark steaks. Puddings do not
disappoint—homemade sorbets, hot blackberry pancakes and an old English type
syllabub, coffee and marshmallow cream. All food is freshly made, from soup to sweets.

Some organically grown vegetables; free range eggs; soya milk and tofu; wholemeal bread; fresh
fruits at table; minimal salt. Wholefood, vegetarian, vegan. Seats 52. Meals, lunch from £4.50,
dinner from £8, bar dishes from £1.40. House wine £5.25. Access/Diners' Club/Visa.

Open: daily, 12 to 2.30, 7 to 10 (Fri and Sat, 7 to 11); closed Sun pm.

LEEDS   West Yorkshire   MAP 6
Salvo's, 115 Otley Road, Headingley   TEL Leeds (0532) 755017

Mobile Salvo Dammone and his family frequently make trips, usually to the Far East, Asia
and the United States 'to expand our progressively minded family's horizons'. This is
sometimes reflected on the daily blackboard menu of highly seasoned dishes at this zesty
Italian restaurant. However, they know Italy well too and tried and approved Gamberi

allo champagne, prawns sautéed in a rich champagne and mushroom sauce. Alternatively Sogliola walewska, a fillet of sole filled with prawns and 'polished off' with a crab, white wine and cream sauce. Strictly fruit and vegetable: melanzane moda nostra, a spicy combination of onions, beans and tomatoes topped with aubergines and cheese; fresh melon filled with fruit and sherry; nova alla florentina, poached eggs on spinach and cheese sauce. Failing all else, there is vegetable minestrone. Main courses, breast of chicken on a spinach bed, cream sauced and grilled; steaks; lamb kidneys in a peppery and mustard sauce; fillets of sole cooked in wine, with tomatoes, capers and herbs. Pasta opens vegetarian possibilities as well as several pizzas including the hot one topped with chilli pepper, garlic and onions. The enterprising make up meals from side dishes such as garlic mushrooms, Italian bean salad, rice pilaff and a tomato and cucumber salad. Cheesecakes, gâteaux, fruit salad and elaborate ices to finish.

Wholemeal bread; fresh fruits at table; skimmed milk; freshly squeezed fruit juices. Vegetarian, other diets by prior arrangement. Seats 50. Meals from £10. House wine £5.35 litre.

Open: Mon to Sat, 12 to 2, 6 to 11.30.

LEEDS   West Yorkshire   MAP 6
Strawberry Fields Bistro, 159 Woodhouse Lane   TEL Leeds (0532) 431515

Kevin and Yvette Clarke steer a careful course between the dietary needs of meat eaters and vegetarians and the romantic requirements of couples, young and middle-aged. If expansion plans come off they will probably manage something for other age ranges. In any circumstance they really cater for customers interested in wholesome homemade food at reasonable prices. They manage more variety than some larger rivals of their style with ratatouille, rollmops, corn on the cob, hummus and homemade soups. Most dishes are better for the good herb and garlic breads, bearing in mind it is normally hot and oozing with butter unless ordered otherwise. Pancakes are stuffed with mushroom and nut, ham and cheese, chicken and sweetcorn (both available with cream sauces), mushroom and lentil and chilli con carne. Burgers in some outsizes; croustade, bean and a meat moussaka are still modestly priced. Roman beef in a simple wine sauce and chicken in several styles, steaks and conventional salads of prawns, chicken, cheese and pâté are available. Desserts include: 'A touch of class' with lemon syllabub, 'Your favourite drink' with tipsy ice and chocolate fudge brownie downed with cream.

Wholemeal flour and bread; polyunsaturates in kitchen and at table. Wholefood, vegetarian, vegan, diabetic and gluten-free with notice. Seats 40. Meals from £5. House wine £5.10 litre. Access/Visa.

Open: Mon to Fri, 11.45 to 2.30; Mon to Sat, 6.30 to 11.

LEEDS   West Yorkshire   MAP 6
The Restaurant at 'The Leeds Playhouse', Calverley Street
TEL Leeds (0532) 442141

Flippantly known as the 'As You Like It food bar' this University precinct restaurant offers one of the best views of the power station, from the expanse of glazed walling. Indoors Sally Craven tops up morale with her good cooking. 'Remarkable food at reasonable prices.' She's more popular with lecturers (for her food) and the better paid from the hospital than students. Cheese pies, courgette and tomato flan have a melt-in-the-mouth pastry. Pizzas have lavish toppings and vegetable pies—leeks and broccoli and the like— and savoury rice rolls have strong followings. Cooking perhaps really comes into its own with a rich and creamy vegetable filled cheesecake, served with one of a dozen salads all well dressed. The tuna loaf and the chicken (free range of course) and pâté pie are both popular. For vegans there is mushroom and nut roast and ratatouille. Soups and pâtés, meat and vegetable to start. A selection of puddings is available, from the popular treacle tart through ten or so different kinds to pavlova dripping in raspberries to crème brûlée.

Early and middle of the day, light fresh scones, chocolate brownies, gingerbread, applecake, coffee and various teas.

Free range farm eggs; wholemeal bread and flours; freshly squeezed fruit juices; polyunsaturates in kitchen and at table. Wholefood, vegetarian, vegan. Seats 100. Meals from £3.50. House wine £3.

Open: 10.30 to 12, coffee and cakes; 12 to 2.30, lunches; 2.30 to 5, teas; 5 to 7.30, supper; closed Sun.

LEICESTER   Leicestershire   Map 3
Bread and Roses, 70 High Street   TEL Leicester (0533) 532448

Admirers rate this an attractive small, town-centre self-service restaurant. It is debatable whether or not one can define the cooking left wing, as the Blackthorn bookshop beneath is. In a town which does not rate well for culinary prowess, it is something of a find. Special approval is for the quiches, deemed absolutely delicious, nice crumbly pastry generously filled with vegetables, spinach, mushrooms, leeks and sweetcorn. Crisp, fresh salads. Prices are reasonable and portions generous.

Wholefood, vegetarian. Meals from £3.

Open: Tue to Fri, 10 to 4.

LINCOLN   Lincolnshire   Map 6
Wig and Mitre, 29 Steep Hill   TEL Lincoln (0422) 35190

Food is in perpetual motion from 8 am breakfasts until last orders late in the evening, and the menu changes twice daily. In a bustling fine old pub with all the character anyone might call for, restoration in 1977 won a Government award. The general attitude is eat what you like when you like. In the formal menu there are the conventional steaks, pork, gammon and fish to be found anywhere, though the quality is not in question. Look to the blackboard for real enterprise, where a modest start could be made with a carrot and orange soup (hot or chilled) or melon and honey cocktail or taramasalata salad and toast, blue cheese pâté or cauliflower Portugaise with garlic toast. Build up an inexpensive meal, choosing other items at no more than the cost of starters. Avocado and mackerel bake, rice croquettes in tomato sauce, beef upsidedown pie, pork and lime casserole or the salmon dumplings which are served with a prawn sauce. Non-meat eaters can expect to find half the items will suit their needs. Fast turnover keeps the pudding menu going apace with chocolate roulade, ginger mousse, pavlova and milles feuilles. Teatime brings teacakes, gâteaux and sandwiches.

Freshly squeezed fruit and vegetable juices; fresh fruits at table; minimal salt and sugar. Wholefood, vegetarian, vegan. Seats 100. Meals from £7.50 restaurant, from £1.10 blackboard menu. House wine £5.60 litre.

Open: daily, 8 'til late.

LITTON   Derbyshire   Map 6
Red Lion Inn, Litton, via Buxton   TEL Litton (0298) 871458

Handy for Miller's Dale and some stimulating walking, the Hodgsons offer some substantial fare at reasonable prices. Overlooking one of the village greens, all three small ground floor rooms have been given over to the business of eating. Coal and log fires cheer on winter week nights when it is unlikely you will get in if not booked. Fresh, good, simple cooking and cheerful service is what the food 'regulars' like. The nightly changing menu might bring tomato soup, or prawn salad, rather than a cocktail. Roast beef and steak and kidney pie for traditionalists; haunch of venison for higher flyers; good quiches, vegetable rissoles, and savoury rice dishes for those so inclined. Finish with brown bread and butter pudding, jam roly-poly and, quite naturally, Bakewell tart. Cheese if you really feel you can take more. No wine seems to be more than £7.

Wholemeal bread; fresh fruit at table; non-battery eggs. Wholefood, vegetarian, vegan, gluten-free on request. Seats 45. Meals from £5.75. House wine £4.80 litre. Access.

Open: Tue to Fri, 7 to 11; Sat and Sun, lunchtime.

LIVERPOOL   Merseyside   MAP 6
Carrageen, Myrtle Parade

'The owner is a Buddhist chef, who observes a completely compassionate approach to all forms of life, including vegetables,' reports a Wirral-based healthy life enthusiast. 'The quality, flavour and variety—and the quantity—of all the dishes is stupendous, more than value for money.' A full plate of salad plus spinach roulade, £1.75. But they do not have a telephone and do not answer correspondence so until more reports are received this is the best information available. Meals from £3.50.

Open: Mon to Fri, 10 to 6; Sat, 10 to 3. Seats 50.

LIVERPOOL   Merseyside   MAP 6
Everyman Bistro, Hope Street   TEL Liverpool 051-708 9545

Enormous tables in the first room, seating 10 or 12 for gregarious gatherings, smaller in the second room where you are served from the impressive buffet. They are attached to the theatre, nearer to the Roman Catholic than Anglican cathedral, at night attracting family groups, theatre and concert goers. Daytime customers come from the University community. The menu is seasonal and changes daily, never using frozen foods and only the tomatoes and sweetcorn tinned. All the food is prepared on the premises and generally low-fat, more yoghurt than cream used. Leek and potato soup is 45p and a whole avocado only 50p. Hummus and bread and taramasalata, or pork country pâté are all under £1. Reports mention the spicy lamb, kedgeree, and sweet and sour pork. Vegetarian meals have been spaghetti with lentil and tomato sauce, and courgette and mushroom casserole. Expect the salads to shine because partners Paddy Byrne and David Scott have just had *Seasonal Salads* published (Ebury Press) and *Grains, Beans and Nuts* will follow soon. To round off the meal take the Dundee cake, French apple tart, almond slice or cheesecake; or sample the pear in eau de vie, apple amber, lemon syllabub, fruit in yoghurt, farmhouse Cheshire cheese plus several others. Fresh fruits, including dates are a feature.

Organic vegetables when available; animal rennet free cheese; wholemeal bread; polyunsaturates in kitchen; fresh fruits at table. Wholefood, vegetarian, sometimes vegan and gluten-free. Seats 200. Meals from £4. House wine £3.40.

Open: Mon to Sat, 12 to 11.30.

LIVERPOOL   Merseyside   MAP 6
Farmhouse Fare, West Derby Road   TEL Liverpool 051-260 3511

Actually it is a former West Derby shop but as John Jones' wife has some talent for interior design, transformations have been made. It isn't exactly low beams and flag floors but an enormous individual working fireplace and an amount of bric-a-brac give the stamp of 'home'. Value for money is sought and seems to be given. Food is all fresh produce, backed by Mr. Jones' butchery business, with nothing frozen, nothing tinned. Some think they make an evening out very special by their kindness, service and thoughtfulness. Quantities are staggering! Rack of lamb seems to mean as many as six chops, a T-bone steak could weigh in at 1½lb only matched by the size of the buckwheat pancakes filled with mushrooms and onion, joined by stuffed tomatoes, sauce, glazed and put into the oven to bake. Sustaining the farmhouse image, there is a return to popularity for braised beef and oxtail. Trout in a pink coat has a wrapping of smoked salmon, halibut has a ginger and lime sauce and the salmon a greeny mint dressing. It is only consistent that the sweet trolley is outsize, never less than a dozen choices, pineapple cheesecakes, coffee and pineapple charlottes, and trifle for which they can never match demand. But the chef nowadays seems happier with old fashioned bread and butter pudding, cherry pie, and fruit and spices in a puff pastry case which has not really been found a name. Cheese is strictly English. Don't drop by on chance: there is a three to four week waiting list which is why they never advertise!

Wholefood, vegetarian. Seats 40. Meals from £10.50. House wine £4.75.

Open: Tue to Sat, 6 to last orders 10.30.

LLANDRINDOD WELLS Powys
Good Food Café, High Street

MAP 2

Sue Early and Heather Williams run a simple, homely good value café in this former Victorian shop. Soaring ceilings and white painted matchboard walls are softened by the abundance of greenery, cherished as much as the food. 'We do soups, rolls, salads, meat and vegetarian casseroles every day.' Sweet and sour pork and a steak and kidney make occasional appearances. Desserts are creamy pies, cheesecake and the apple pie kind, again all homemade, as are the daily soups, all with vegetable ingredients so it suits vegans. No wine except that which goes into sauces along with lots of herbs, spices and garlic. Coffee, tea and cakes throughout the day. 'We steer clear of processed natural foods,' say Sue and Heather.

Free range chickens and eggs; organic vegetables; wholemeal bread; homemade wholemeal rolls daily; soya oil used in kitchen. Wholefood, vegetarian, vegan. Seats 45. Meals from £3.25.

Open: Mon to Fri, 10.30 to 2.30.

LLANDUDNO Gwynedd
Carrington's, Gloddaeth Avenue   TEL Llandudno (0492) 70359   MAP 6

It's a steepish climb to the Victorian style open-plan room above a shop but regulars feel it is worth the effort. One half is the pre-dinner drinks area from where you can study the battery of framed 19th century political prints, ex-Punch, laments for lost liberal causes. Fresh salmon comes handily from the Conway. Vegetarians have been adequately satisfied by mushroom stroganoff, and nut roast which strangely appears here by popular vote. Vegetable pancakes are tried and tested. Breast of chicken is stuffed with smoked ham and cheese, but peppered sirloin steaks are regularly ordered! Chilled melons are filled with Mr. Carrington's raspberry sorbet and for grilled mushrooms there is the option of an almond or a liver pâté stuffing. Crab bisque soup is another example of local produce put to good use. Syllabub is the coffee and whisky kind. Honey and brandy ice cream is a homemade achievement, like the sorbets. Grilled bananas have a butterscotch sauce. Fresh juices—especially raspberry are kept frozen and blended with freshly pressed apple juice—one of the most popular items.

Freshly squeezed fruit juices; polyunsaturates in kitchen and at table; fresh fruit at table; free range eggs; goats' milk, cheese and yoghurt. Wholefood, vegetarian, vegan, other diets as circumstances permit. Seats 24. Meals from lunch £3.50, dinner £11. House wine £4.60.

Open: Mon to Sat, 11.30 to 2.30, 6.30 to 9.30 (last orders).

LONDON
Almeida Wine Bar, 1 Almeida Street, Islington, N1   TEL London 01-226 0931   MAP 4

A lively theatre wine bar with a friendly atmosphere. Frances Aston aims to provide good wholesome food as cheaply as possible though she does try to make a profit. 'We are a charity and all our surplus goes towards the building fund.' Seasonal salads are always interesting, the vegetables are fresh and you can always expect a vegetarian dish. Soups usually offer a choice between something like turkey and ham and carrot and tomato. Main dishes might be turkey pie, courgette in cheese with salad. Cold things include guacamole, hummus, taramasalata, broccoli and cheese flan and salad. Salads are often free of dressing or yoghurt has replaced mayonnaise. All will be served with a choice of wholemeal, rye or French bread, or biscuits. Interesting puddings—yoghurt often again substituted for cream—like the seasonal raspberry mousse, an excellent banana cake, a generously made fruit salad—are available.

Homemade yoghurt; wholemeal bread; polyunsaturates in cooking; fresh fruit at table; minimal salt and sugar. Wholefood, vegetarian, vegan. Seats 50. Meals £4.75. House wine £4.15.

Open: Mon to Sat, 11 to 3, 5.30 to 11.

LONDON ☆   Map 4
Angela and Peter, 300 Battersea Park Road, SW11   TEL London 01-288 6133

The pretty greenhouse-type extension has been a boon to Jonathan Blakeley's Victorian style, pine-panelled restaurant/wine bar. Now there is more room for diners and imbibers to co-exist harmoniously, and for the former to take advantage of reliable fresh produce served fast food style. Deliberately, menus avoid being obviously ethnic. There is always at least one vegetarian first course, a second course negotiable according to circumstances, but it will not be dull whatever the outcome, and then there is a daily fish dish. Freshly prepared choices could be a tomato and mozzarella salad, chicken liver and brandy pâté, and deep fried mushrooms with garlic mayonnaise. Chicken supreme cooked in tarragon and white wine, breasts of duck, or ham risotto might follow, with fresh vegetables as required. Chocolate and banana mousse, or lemon syllabub, complete the menu. Sampling ran to avocado and prawn salad, satisfactorily followed by the grilled lamb chops in garlic butter, together with broccoli and leeks which had both been sensitively treated. To finish, apricot crumble and the lemon syllabub which with coffee and wine came to a little over £26 for two.

Wholemeal bread; fresh fruits at table; freshly squeezed fruit and vegetable juices; minimal salt and sugar; polyunsaturates in cooking. Wholefood, vegetarian, other diets preferably with prior notice but not essential. Seats 65. Meals from £6.50 lunch, £8 dinner. House wine £4.10. Access/Visa.

Open: daily, 12 to 3, 6.30 to 12.

LONDON   Map 5
Avery's Salad Bar, 149 Fleet Street, EC4

No. 149 could be confused with Mick's place: it isn't. Try the alleyway to the right-hand side. This basement salad room is only open 11.30–3, Monday–Friday, but it does a take-away service and there are usually three or four meat dishes as well as chilli con carne, chicken curry, maybe a roast and vegetable and shepherd's pie. However, these are always supported by a matching number of meatless dishes such as lasagne, macaroni cheese, cauliflower cheese, leek mornay, mixed vegetable crumble, jacket potatoes and lovely salads. Interesting puddings, with syllabub and fruit fools for the warmer weather; crumbles and pies for the cold. General style is cheap and cheerful.

Wholefood, vegetarian. Seats 25. Meals from £3.

Open: Mon to Fri, 11.30 to 3.

LONDON   Map 5
Bubbles Wine Bar, North Audley Street, W1

'If only this wine bar's stools were more sympathetically contoured to posteriors . . .' comments one observer. Well, you are less likely to be dislodged from chairs and tables, and at the mezzanine level it even runs to comfortable, upholstered banquettes. Sensible no-nonsense layout and popular with imbibers from 5.30 onwards, it has related branches—the Cork and Bottle, Methuselah's and Shampers—all specialising in decent food and wine. Seafood dishes, with good fresh salads in variety, duck, and pastas in appetising sauces, make regular menu appearances. The freshness of all the food is self-evident. Dessert dishes are the kind to attract return visits. A variety of wines by the glass, clearly displayed for selection behind the bar.

Wholefood, vegetarian. Seats 42. Meals from £2.50. House wine £5.10.

Open: daily, 5.30 to 11.

LONDON   Map 5
Carlo's Place, 855 Fulham Road, SW6   TEL London 01-736 4507

A little of rural France in the Fulham Road is translated into cheerful gingham-clothed tables and a rustic heating stove. However when it comes to food Mme. Nimier is a fervent believer in fresh local produce and does not care to see her dishes drenched in sauces. Apart from fishy starters and delicious soups of the day, there is likely to be a light savoury salad of apples, nuts and chicory with a sweet wine vinaigrette, or a warm salad with sautéed chicken breasts. Her other bistro-type food includes several choices of fish and game in season, the fresh vegetables of the day always being a feature.

Wholemeal bread; fresh fruits at table; minimal salt and sugar; freshly squeezed fruit juices; on request meals with no animal fat, no salt; vegetables sautéed in their own juices. Wholefood, vegetarian on request. Seats 65. Meals from £8. House wines £5.40. All credit cards accepted.

Open: Mon to Sat, 12 to 3, 7 to 11.30; closed Christmas week and last 2 weeks Aug.

LONDON   Map 4
Chalk and Cheese, 14 Chalk Farm Road, NW1   TEL London 01-267 9820

A pleasing informal establishment, not vegetarian as the name might at first suggest. It is a place for reliably fresh food from a small selective menu supplemented daily by blackboard specials. Several of the starters are suitable for vegetarians and vegans, though for the latter more difficulty is encountered when the main course is reached. Avocado, grapefruit and orange salad, pancakes with cream cheese and garlic, spinach and cheese tartlet, grilled mushrooms in garlic suggest the scope. Main courses offered very acceptable lambs' liver, rack of lamb in good pastry, and grilled salmon with watercress sauce. The vegetarian dish of the day is likely to be lasagne, or mixed bean casserole, while the blackboard surprises might be a leek and cheese turnover or an almond pancake. Supporting vegetables and salads are up to standard and good value. Ice cream quite good, otherwise there is a fairly heavy emphasis on trifles, pavlovas and gâteaux.

*Fresh fruit at table; freshly squeezed fruit juices; wholemeal bread. Wholefood, vegetarian.
Seats 25. Meals from £6.50. House wine £4.30. Barclaycard/Access/American Express/Diners'
Club.*

Open: Tue to Sat, 6.30 to 11; Sun, 12 to 3.

LONDON   Map 4
The Cherry Orchard, 241–245 Globe Road, Bethnel Green, E2
TEL London 01-980 6678

A cheap cheerful place with a nice atmosphere and a nice garden too, to sit out in during the summer. Food is carefully prepared and with thought for the cholesterol content. Run by the Pure Land Co-operative, peaceable Buddhists, they are popular with those living and working in the area, doctors, social workers, teachers and families and there is enough interest to bring visitors from further afield. 'In accordance with an ethic of non-violence, we work as a vegetarian restaurant and sell our food as economically as costs permit.' Notwithstanding this, admirers appreciate the fresh flowers on the tables, the pleasant staff and nice atmosphere. Each day one of the two main dishes will be vegan. Also there is always fresh fruit salad and vegan or sugarless cakes. Ingredients (except in some cakes) are always fresh and unprocessed and 'we hope we are doing our bit to raise the nutritional standards of one of the poorer London Boroughs.' Black bean curries, Hunza pie, hummus, quiches and savoury rices are all popular and regular menu dishes. Salads are good and the selection of cakes are made daily.

Soya milk; animal rennet free cheeses; wholemeal bread; free range eggs; polyunsaturates in kitchen and at table; minimal salt and sugar. Vegetarian, vegan, macrobiotic. Seats 56 inside, 20 in the garden. Meals from £4.

Open: Tue to Sat, 10 to 8.30; Thur, 10 to 2.30; closed 1 week Aug and Christmas/New Year.

LONDON   Map 5
City Wholefoods, 73 Queen Victoria Street, EC4

It is a worthy place to drop by anytime from 8.30 am onwards. They close just after the lunch rush as they are really geared to City workers and the few visitors who get into this neck of the woods. Baking, except for bread from Goswells, is all done on the premises, using Doves Farm organically grown flour. Good hot scones but butter is obligatory, 'people expect it' they seem to think, but Sunflower goes onto the lavishly filled sandwiches which are not notably expensive. More organised than most places of the kind, the near spartan furnishings are relieved by modern prints decorating the walls. Big, big bonus, they back on to delightful small gardens maintained by the Metropolitan Gardens Association. A safe, civilised retreat with vine covered pergolas and sheltered sitting spots, if the weather is fine, a better bet than eating in.

Wholemeal bread and rolls; fresh fruit; polyunsaturates. Wholefood, vegetarian. Seats 14. Meals from £3.

Open: daily, 8.30 to 2.

LONDON   Map 5
Country Life Vegetarian Buffet, 123 Regent Street, W1
TEL London 01-434 2922

Not to be confused with other restaurants of the same name, this gets enthusiastic references from medical sources. Run by a Seventh Day Adventist laymen's organisation, the only recorded criticism is that the opening hours are all too short, Saturdays and Tuesdays not at all. The highlight of Mr. Loland Moutray's pure food operation is the 'all you care to eat specials'. There are warm words of praise for the imaginative and well presented buffet, which starts at £2.50 for soup and salad, progressing to £3.20 with the addition of hot entrée and vegetables. £3.90 brings a fruit salad as well for which one may return for more. It is a 100 % no smoking zone and, for those interested in more than immediate sustenance it holds health courses and has a large natural food shop. There are firm beliefs here in the natural laws of health, sun, water, air and exercise, and abstemiousness. Wine is not available. Note for globetrotters, there are branches in New York, Los Angeles, Osaka and, nearer home, Paris.

Organically grown fruit and vegetables at their own Godalming Farm; wholemeal bread; polyunsaturates in kitchen and at table; fresh fruit at table; minimal sugar and salt free dishes. Vegan, vegetarian, diabetic, gluten-free and others. Seats 100. Meals from £2.30, all you care to eat specials.

Open: Mon to Fri, 11.30 to 2.30; shop, 10.30 to 6; Fri, 10.30 to 3.

LONDON   Map 5
Cranks, Covent Garden, WC2   TEL London 01-379 6508

Cramps might well be more appropriate: tables and benches don't come narrower anywhere and, in this tiny branch customers sit facing each other across the narrow central corridor under a vaulted ceiling. It doesn't detract from the quality of the fare but like several of their other outposts, choice is more limited than in Marshall Street (see entry). The upstairs take-away is a big bonus and as good as one will find anywhere with a marvellous array of their own filled bakers' goods and wholesome cakes.

Open: Mon to Sat, 10 to 8.

LONDON   Map 5
Cranks, 8 Marshall Street, W1   TEL London 01-437 9431

Simple pine furniture, woven cane lampshades and handthrown pottery are the hallmarks of this wholefood restaurant, an image born here. A well designed place, though it has less of the airy wholesomeness than their branch in the old Heals furniture shop used to have. Credit normally goes to the late David Canter, his wife and Daphne Swann for changing the face of the British salad. Cranks brought a totally new view to the world of vegetables when the restaurant opened in 1961 with crisp fresh vegetables teamed with equally fresh wholemeal rolls, soups and savouries. There have been changes during the intervening years but the pottery, solid oak tables, quarry tiled floor and white painted walls survive as reminders of their near revolutionary notion. They specialise in salads, soups and savouries, their own wholemeal rolls, cheeses, yoghurts and fresh fruit salads. A juice bar offers vegetable and fruit juices and a good many health drinks, as well as fruit pies, cakes and biscuits. By day there is a continuous buffet service, by night a not quite so successful restaurant service. Hauser soup was inspired by Gayelord Hauser, the American nutritionist, influential to the Directors in setting up Cranks. Delicious but simple enough— carrots, onion, milk and seasoning. See the details in the Cranks Recipe book which describes most of the dishes available in their various restaurants. The Florida salad would be as good for breakfast as for dessert. Mushroom and potato pie is an equally delicious mixture. The blandness of cheese and millet croquettes is improved by a variety of herbs. A bean casserole of one kind or another is a regular dish; sometimes there is a hot-pot of vegetables, all again with special thought for the seasoning. They really come into their own with puddings, not wanting to go too far down the road to puritanism, preferring to subscribe to the view that 'a little bit of what you fancy does you good'. Banana yoghurt is one of several flan possibilities, the standby trifle a beguiling combination of orange and banana. Otherwise, junkets, spiced bread pudding and the plainer apple pie.

Homemade wholemeal bread; freshly squeezed fruit and vegetable juices; fresh fruit at table; free range eggs; organically grown fruit and vegetables; stone ground organic wholemeal flour; Biosalt in cooking; polyunsaturates in cooking and at table. Vegetarian, wholefood, vegan. Seats 170. Meals from £6.50. House wine £4.90. Organic wine (Bouchardon) £5.75. All major credit cards.

Open: Mon, 10 to 8.30; Tue to Sat, 10 to 11.

LONDON   Map 5
Cranks, Peter Robinson, Oxford Circus, W1   TEL London 01-580 6214

Reaching this Cranks outpost entails a first floor assault on the rag trade. The objective is only just perceptible (dim woven cane shaded lamps) beyond the brighter felt hats. An eat-in and get away quickly place. A more limited range of food than in Marshall Street but still quite strong on the bakery goods. Perhaps a sign of the times, some of the food here is served on paper plates.

Open: 10 to 5.30; Thur 'til 7.30.

LONDON   MAP 5
Cranks, Tottenham Street, W1   TEL London 01-631 3912

Recent restoration work has done much to restore some dignity to this Georgian building designed to fill the gap left by the closure of the branch in Heals across in Tottenham Court Road. Open from 8.00 in the morning, this is the first branch in the group to offer continental breakfasts. There is the full range of their well known dishes served in Marshall Street branch (see entry) and a take-away service.

Open: Mon to Sat, 8 to 8.

LONDON   MAP 5
Crumbs, 48 Holborn Viaduct, EC1   TEL London 01-236 8970

Convenient cafeteria style, the health conscious should not be deterred by their main feature which is bacon and egg breakfasts from 7.30. They also have other meat and fish dishes but they are well into salads, wholemeal bread and various tempting non-meat casseroles. Salads are the lunchtime speciality served with a wide choice of meats and cheeses, preceded by good homemade soups. Hot dishes may be cauliflower cheese, lasagnes (vegetarian and meat), curried vegetables, and macaroni cheese. Puddings range from simple crumbles to gâteaux and flans.

Wholemeal bread; fresh fruit at table. Wholefood, vegetarian. Seats 54. Meals from £3.

Open: Mon to Fri, 7.30 to 4.

LONDON   MAP 5
Dining Room, Winchester Walk, SE1   TEL London 01-407 0337

The coal gone, this cellar now has spartan pink walls and mosaic floor. Once part of the Borough Market, Sandra Cross and William English run an imaginative vegetarian restaurant here, using all organically grown materials. You can indulge in leek and potato soup, almond and tofu pâté or sweet and sour salad from a weekly changing menu. Main dishes include cauliflower cheese pudding, and fried aubergine slices served in basil mayonnaise and with couscous. They make something of a speciality of stuffed pepper in a mushroom sauce with a mixed sprout salad. Puddings have ranged from pumpkin tart to baked pear with melted cheese and walnuts, to Greek yoghurt and whey. Neal's Yard provides the organic cider from Dorset. Châteaux Chavrignach is an organic wine they import themselves. Otherwise there is Copella apple juice.

Always organic produce; free range eggs; wholemeal bread; polyunsaturates in cooking; minimal salt and sugar; organic wine and cider. Vegetarian, vegan. Seats 32. Meals from £5. House wine £4.50.

Open: Tue to Fri, 12 to 3, 7 to 10.

LONDON   MAP 4
Di's Larder, 62 Lavender Hill, SW11   TEL London 01-223 4618

'All the best ingredients in the world will not be of use in the hands of a bad chef' is, broadly, the philosophy of Bill and Di Kilpatrick here now for seven years. The small restaurant is linked with their health food shop where most of the regulars, sometimes theatre people, sometimes those working in the district, have been coming for a long time. They are vegetarian and wholefood and use only fresh, organic where possible, natural foods. Prices are amazingly modest, a main dish no more than £1.50 which would buy the vegetarian Shepherd's pie made using lentils, carrot and onion, topped with potato. Short cut macaroni is wholewheat and the sauce made of tomato and nuts, topped with cheese and baked. A Spanish omelette is about £1.25, quiche nut roasts and interesting salads less. Sweet and sour artichokes, with a mustard wine and honey sauce are other specialities. Finish with cheesecake, apple crumble or the pears poached in brandy.

Organic fruit and vegetable as they become increasingly available; free range eggs; wholemeal bread; polyunsaturates in cooking; minimal salt and sugar; homemade yoghurt. Wholefood, vegetarian specifically but there is usually something for vegans, gluten-free and diabetic. Seats 18. Meals from £3.25.

Open: Mon to Sat, 10 to 6.

LONDON   MAP 4
Earth Exchange Collective, 213 Archway Road, Highgate, N6
TEL London 01-340 6407

At the end of its first decade this co-operative excels for the purity of the food rather than the ambiance or even the elegance of wholesome inexpensive dishes. Log fires for cosy winter evenings, a garden to rest and play in summer. An exhibition of photographs lines the dining-room walls. Emphasis is on wholegrain and fresh salads, the last always vegan. Japanese foods are understood so tofu and seaweeds make appearances though they are by no means macrobiotic. Nori rolls are with miso sauce. Lasagne is made with spinach and cheese. Blackboard menus are likely to offer a lentil and lemon soup, hummus and pitta or a salad, followed by a three bean tablah. Bean sprouts will have been mixed with seeds. Then there is always the organic brown rice or salads, or a combination of each, to complete the dish. Quiches are the tofu kind and go down well, though like many of the dishes they are hearty rather than light-hearted. Finish with cake type sweetmeats, some vegan, coconut fresh fruit trifle or a fruit salad, the topping cream, yoghurt, plamil or egg custard. The licence is new and the wines incredibly good value.

Organic vegetables when available; organic brown rice; soya milk; free range eggs; wholemeal bread; fresh fruits at table; polyunsaturates in cooking and at table. Wholefood, vegetarian, vegan, usually gluten-free and diabetic. Seats 50. Meals from £4. House wine from £3.25.

Open: Fri to Mon, 12 to 3, 6 to 10.30.

LONDON   MAP 5
East-West, 188 Old Street, EC1   TEL London 01-608 0300

Dishes are elegant and thoughtfully presented but seasoning and sauces are scarcely distinctive features under this friendly aesthetic regime now ably directed by Wilma van Kempen. The restaurant is a simple, well maintained room within this former school, sheltering associate activities. At lunchtime the needs of committed City workers are met. Fully macrobiotic, all their food is painstakingly prepared on the premises, from fresh vegetables, fruit, wholegrains, beans and nuts, to seeds and soya base foods. There is total prohibition on canned and frozen foods. Sparingly, fish is served just once weekly, limiting any temptation to deviate, and Wednesday lunches are set aside for ethnic wholefood vegetarian fare—perhaps Indian, Italian or Jamaican. Main dishes might be tofu soufflé, rice and barley, hijiki-seaweed with spring onions and sesame seeds. Sautéed onion and white cabbage is served with lemon and tahini sauce. Carrots are pickled, and may be the main ingredient for a soup. Sourdough bread and filled pitta bread.

Wholemeal bread; sugar-free desserts; soya milk; organically grown cereals and grains; cold pressed oils; malt replaces sugar; sourdough replaces yeast. Vegetarian, vegan, macrobiotic. Seats 70. Meals from £4.50. House wine £4.

Open: Mon to Thur, 11 to 10; Fri, 11 to 9; Sat, 11 to 3.

LONDON   MAP 5
Elephants and Butterflies, 67 Charlotte Street, W1   TEL London 01-580 1732

Sharply differing from some of the wholefood vegetarian fraternity in that it actually looks like a restaurant, proprietress Florence Vincent believes in doing her own thing. Mrs. Vincent does farmhouse style cookery with a hint of the South Seas. Sylvia, in the kitchen, brings that influence. Avocado pâté is more popular than the cheddar (animal rennet free of course), cottage and cream cheeses. Reflecting the southern feel: chicken with peaches and brandy and spicy meat balls. For the Northern hemisphere, vegetable moussaka and a chickpea stroganoff made with soya milk, which is drawing in vegans. Imagination undimmed, desserts include carob roulade, wholewheat profiteroles, better than the white version, brown sugar meringues and white grape cream. The last is cream, yoghurt and sour cream, white grapes, cinnamon and brandy. 'Organic house white and red is a little dearer than the regular,' apologises Mrs. Vincent. Norfolk Punch and a growing bookshelf, for those inclined that way.

Organic meat; free range eggs; organic fruit and vegetables; wholemeal bread; polyunsaturates in kitchen and at table; minimal salt and sugar; skimmed milk. Many sugar-free desserts. Wholefood, vegetarian, vegan, gluten-free. Seats 36. Meals from £7.50 vegetarian, £9 meat dishes. House wine £4.50.

Open: Mon to Fri, 12 to 3, 6 to 9.

LONDON   MAP 5
Fenchurch Colony, 14 New London Street, EC3   TEL London 01-481 0355

'Generous helpings, good value in luxurious light, air-conditioned surroundings' seems to be the general consensus. This seems to pay off for, in the same style a new branch has opened, the Holborn Colony in Brooke Street EC1. Lunchtime crowds are here for the two tempting food displays of appetising salads, huge, overstuffed sandwiches and several hot dishes. Boeuf bourguignon, chicken Florentine or simple and cheap, a baked potato and cheese. Rare roast beef with horseradish seems to have a good many takers among the sandwich enthusiasts. Puddings come with cream, chocolate roulade, black-currant cheesecake, rich rum fruit and chocolate biscuit cakes. All the food is done on the premises except for the rough pâté and the ham. Vegetarian hot dish of the day varies between lasagne, a cottage pie, courgettes and cauliflower in a tomato sauce.

Wholefood, vegetarian. Seats 130. Dishes from £1.75. House wine £4.20. Access/Visa/ American Express.

Open: Mon to Fri, 11.30 to 3, 5 to 9.

LONDON   MAP 5
Food for Health, 15–17 Blackfriars Lane, EC4   TEL London 01-236 7001

The profligate might desert before reaching this corner (at the Ludgate Cellars, prominently featuring oysters) but a good many don't as around 650 meals a day are served. They get by on their value food but bakers' goods are not one of their strengths. Sandwich fillings are highly flexible but wholemeal Chelsea buns somehow ring a wrong note. Otherwise Mr. Highton fills a much felt need. Open from 8.00, breakfasts are among the cheapest anywhere. Mushrooms on toast 43p—egg on toast, if you prefer—muesli 38p. By lunchtime there is an appetising array of hot and cold fare, starting with another bargain in green pea soup. Chef's dish may be fresh mushroom, egg, leek and potato bake, under a creamy cheese topping. Escalope of fresh cauliflower in a red wine sauce is good, so is the moussaka à la Grecque. The salad selection is balanced with fresh fruits, vegetables and protein. Or melon suprême with cottage cheese, or egg and asparagus. Sample sweets as old fashioned as jam and coconut sponge with custard, as up to date as homemade yoghurt, or an indulgent pear and chocolate sponge with cream, scarcely ever spending more than 50p. Loseley ice creams or sorbets.

Seats 230. Meals from £3.

Open: Mon to Fri, 8 to 3.

LONDON — MAP 5
Food for Thought, 31 Neal Street, WC2 — TEL London 01-836 0239

In a mildly disordered avant garde entrepreneurial take-away at street level, Guy Garrett is also strong on some self-conscious improvisation—narrow, treacherous steps down to the eat-in part: 'You'll remember the "trip", if not the food.' Concessions—or oversight— to technology, green plastic flower boxes. Otherwise a colonial air. Deservedly popular but little space between tables and knees knock beneath, elbows above, the crush indicates the value. Mr. Garrett's aim is to serve delicious food inexpensively. In an unpretentious menu the emphasis is on wholesome fresh food, delicately flavoured without additives. Most dishes, starters or main courses can be had for around £1 or less. Soups are tasty and substantial, carrot and potato, country lentil, mixed vegetable type. There are always at least three hot savouries including lentil roast and apple sauce, stir fried vegetables and rice. For something cold, leek quiche, a salad ordinaire, or the mega version, the most expensive menu item. Finish simply with fresh fruit salad, a yoghurt, the cheesecake or fruit crumble of the day. Wholemeal bread from round the corner in Neal's Yard. Drinks— limited to apple juice, barley cup, herb teas and coffee.

Wholemeal bread; fresh fruits at table; minimal salt and sugar; freshly squeezed fruit juices; non-battery eggs; nothing tinned except tomatoes and sweetcorn. Vegetarian, vegan. Seats 52. Meals from £3.40.

Open: Mon to Fri, 12 to 8.

LONDON ☆ — MAP 4
Frederick's, Camden Passage, N1 — TEL London 01-359 8728

You can eat very cheaply in this smart, part greenhouse restaurant, now in its sixteenth year, particularly if you are not of meat-eating persuasion. So there are compensations even if the vegetarian options are limited but in advance of well-known smarter places. There might even be recognition of Government health advice, for first courses can be terrines of capsicums in a fresh tomato sauce, avocado mousse with or without its cream sauce, melon, orange and pink grapefruit. Strips of fresh pasta are in a tasty ratatouille sauce and soup of the day is made from fresh vegetables; deep fried mushrooms with a tartare sauce. Rabbit, pheasant and chicken put in an appearance but sensibly fish is better represented, a grilled sole being affordable and salmon trout cooked as you like, positively bargain-priced. Cuisine minceur low-calorie dishes have a showing in lean steak of grilled lamb and sirloin steak. Vegetarians get a three vegetable mousse with a creamy herb butter sauce and mixed salad, or simply grilled dried goats' cheese with salads and walnuts. Homemade ice creams are good, so is the patisserie.

Wholemeal bread; fresh fruits at table. Wholefood, vegetarian. Seats 150. Meals from £12. House wine £5.75. All credit cards accepted.

Open: Mon to Sat, 12 to 2.30, 7 to 11.30.

LONDON — MAP 4
The Garden, 616 Fulham Road, SW6 — TEL London 01-736 6056

Hungarian rather than health considerations govern menu planning and choice of ingredients, though Charles Brodie acknowledges making a special effort to seek out the natural and unrefined. His smart, intimate restaurant offers vegetarian food cooked and served to be acceptable to non-vegetarians along with game, fish and free range poultry. First courses include onion soups, cheese and spinach puff, deep fried croquettes of Brie, stuffed mushrooms, the Garden Quiche, smoked fish en croûte. Supporters hope he has got the balance right when it comes to main courses, predominantly on the theme of vegetable moussaka, crêpes stuffed with spinach and soured cream and chestnut loaf with West Riding sauce. Pasta of the day is popular as is chicken and artichoke pie and game, if it is available. Fish, solitarily, appears as goujons of sole. Occasional sorties into desserts with fruit pie, trifle and mousse. Wines from the list or house elderflower.

Wholemeal bread; polyunsaturates at table; fresh fruits at table; minimal salt and sugar; freshly squeezed fruit and vegetable juices; free range eggs and poultry. Wholefood, vegetarian. Seats 26 and 20 in the garden. Meals from £10. House wine £5.25. Visa/Access/American Express/ Diners' Club.

Open: Mon to Sat, 7.30 to 11.

LONDON   MAP 5
Gaylord (India), 79 Mortimer Street, W1   TEL London 01-580 3615

Included for vegetarian rather than wholefood interest, this large well appointed restaurant is of more fame here (and in India where it has branches) for its Tandoori dishes. Mr. Lambe is as at home serving his customers vegetable biryani; spiced green peas, cottage cheese and rice; the dhal special; aubergine and potato and as many as half a dozen more similar. Tandoori specialities of interest, king prawns cooked in a clay oven, as well as fish as available. There is a skewer roasted chicken, chicken tikka kebab. The prawn cocktail or grapefruit maraschino are safer to begin than soups. Traditional Indian sweets such as kulfi (ice cream) ras malai (cream cheese balls) and ragulla (curd balls).

Fresh fruits at table; freshly squeezed fruit and vegetable juices. Vegetarian. Seats 100. Meals from £4.50. House wine £4.30. American Express/Diners' Club/Barclaycard/Access.

Open: daily.

LONDON   ☆   MAP 5
Green and Pleasant Salad Restaurant, 117 Long Acre

At the back of the Covent Garden General Store (open until midnight) this in-house cafeteria with the American-style chrome and cane chairs and oilcloth covered tables, offers a wide range of salads not saturated in dressings. Homemade dressings and mayonnaise you add to taste. In all there are 32 salads to choose from and, if that is not enough, fortify them with the chicken pieces and patés or the wide selection of their own quiches. Alternatively, try the chilli and chicken curry and the chicken and ham pie. Start with homemade soups. Free coffee refills.

Wholemeal rolls; wholemeal pastry and pitta bread; fresh fruit at table. Wholefood, vegetarian. Seats 68. Meals from £3. House wine £4.25.

Open: 11 to 11.

LONDON   MAP 5
The Greenhouse, 16 Chenies Street, WC1   TEL London 01-637 8038

A bright, simple and exceptionally clean basement beneath the drill hall. It's also home to the G.C.A.E.A.F. Theatre Company, a Camden Borough and G.L.C. jointly funded enterprise. Sisters Julie and Angela Haslam are the new incumbents, a change for the better. They took over after Julie had done a feasibility study on the place for her dissertation. A useful blackboard menu offers several attractive hot savouries and it is even worth a try for an appetising quiche, in its courgette form light and delicately seasoned. Salads are good and inventive, and the plum crumble appealed with the pleasing sharpness of nectarine and was not disintegrating in a sea of syrup. Puddings have now taken off. Apple tart is Danish, and another tart is carob and nut, and the strudel rhubarb. Expect also carrot cake, scones and simpler stuff for in between meals. Service is friendly and informal, the atmosphere relaxed. Conveniently placed in a no-man's land between Russell Square and Tottenham Court Road, there is considerable evening interest with the longer opening hours.

Wholemeal bread; honey used instead of sugar; often natural juices; fruit at table; free range eggs. Wholefood, vegetarian, vegan. Seats 38. Meals from £3.75. Bring your own wine, no corkage charge.

Open: Tue to Fri, 10 to 10; Sat, 4 to 9; Mon, 10 to 6.

LONDON   MAP 5
Hare Krishna Curry House, 1 Hanway Street, W1   TEL London 01-636 5262

Any dignity Hanway Street might ever have had has vanished and external appearances here suggest a degree of improvisation which is not the case across the threshold. Somehow the large handwritten blackboard menu by the door doesn't come off in these circumstances where dustbins seem to be permanent street furniture. Enterprising vegetarians have not been deterred. They turn up regularly over the years for Harish Patez's appetising snacks. Samosas really are thin crispy pastry with nicely spiced mixed vegetables. Gram flour steamed sponge cake pieces are served with chutney. Puffed rice, onions and potatoes dressed with sweet and sour sauce can be hot or mild. More elaborately come the split black pea and whole rice pancakes. Main course, Gujarati style, might be their whole stuffed aubergine in curry, the bhindi special (okra) or chana (chick peas) and potatoes. Sweets include almond gulfee, shrikhand (yoghurt sweetened and spiced with cream cheese) and gulab jamun (sponge milk balls with rose water). A change from another fruit salad—mango slices, lychees. There is a wide range of fruit juices including mango and passion fruit, also yoghurt drink.

Vegetarian. Seats 52. Meals from £5. House wine £5.25.

Open: Mon to Sat, 12 to 10.30.

LONDON   MAP 5
Harrods Juice Bar, Brompton Road, SW1   TEL London 01-730 1234

'Nothing clever, just honest unadulterated juices without preservatives and the like,' says manager, Mr. Guyatt. A late breakfast here (they are not open until 9) is possibly a safer bet—healthwise—than Knightsbridge hotels. Days are launched with a not quite Bircher-Benner style muesli and natural yoghurt, milk if you must. Morning 'pick-me-ups' to follow are egg orange, banana milk and honey. Juices will, of course, have been freshly extracted from fruit and vegetables in the bar, a simple, almost rare experience in British restaurants and hotels. This, along with their marvellous choice of wholefoods in the various Food Halls, puts Harrods in the forefront as a source of natural food. Try the juices blended—the staff recommend combinations and some work better than others: grapefruit and watercress, carrot and beetroot. A blend of tropical fruits, or banana, apple and strawberry—the permutations and delights are limitless. Lunches have attractions for slimmers and vegetarians. Sweet and sour salads and perhaps a drink consisting of carrot, spinach, yoghurt and wheatgerm for the latter, and a low calorie cottage cheese salad and a grapefruit, yoghurt and honey drink for the former. For others, fruit salads with cream. Until 11 am decaffeinated coffee is served.

Seats 36. Meals from £4.50. Most credit cards accepted.

Open: Mon to Fri, 9 to 5; Wed, 9.30 to 7; Sat, 9 to 6.

LONDON   MAP 5
Institute of Contemporary Arts, 12 Carlton House Terrace, SW1
TEL London 01-930 7579

To get in you need to join as a member for the day which is 50p, less than the cover charge at some establishments, and it is worth it because not only is it a pleasantly casual, relaxed place to eat, but one can view at the same time the Sloanes, students, trendies and the more fashion conscious who mingle with office workers. There is the added virtue that each of the sensibly limited range of dishes is homemade. One of the three main dishes will be vegetarian and there is an interesting selection of puddings. Picnics in St. James' Park; there are foil containers and poly cups for take-aways.

Fresh fruit at table; polyunsaturates in cooking; sugarless puddings. Wholefood, vegetarian. Seats 80. Meals from £5. House wine £4.50.

Open: Tue to Sat, 12 to 8.

LONDON   Map 4
Julie's, 135 Portland Road, Holland Park, W11   TEL London 01-727 4585

High calorie, sensational dishes still sell best in this popular restaurant—with a wine bar too—held in high regard by the Sunday lunch fraternity. Mr. Ekperigin is, however, alert to the requirements of those interested in trying something different and offers a menu going some way towards meeting the needs of those seeking a healthy diet. He is always anxious to help, so expect a sympathetic ear to special requests. Recently, dishes like croissant and baked artichoke, red mullet on a bed of fennel and mixed smoked fish dishes have been gaining ground. Sole with real ginger and limes still lacks the popular appeal of its counterpart in a rich bearnaise sauce. Vegetable and hazelnut pie is baked in a half wholewheat pastry. Quiches come with wine bar salads at lunchtime. Among the puddings expect the likes of kiwi fruit in a wine sauce or plain bread and butter pudding.

Wholemeal bread; fresh fruits at table; minimal salt and sugar; skimmed milk; freshly squeezed fruit and vegetable juices. Seats 98. Meals from £12.
All credit cards accepted.

Open: daily, 12.30 to 3, 7.45 to 11.30.

LONDON   Map 4
Manna, 4 Erskine Road, NW3   TEL London 01-722 8028

Delicious food, very nice atmosphere and reasonable prices, feel supporters, the only difficulty being to get a seat at one of the long tables (ex-British Rail sleepers). Gas lamps complete the idea of the 'country' image in this former cobbler's shop. Rodney Kitchen's restaurant has been running twelve years, the second of its kind in London, some have said. Curried casseroles, sweet and sour, sometimes a country vegetable pie will have appeal for vegans too. Fruit starters are a speciality. Melons turn up in different guises including melon, ginger and curd cheese, along with grilled grapefruit and orange cups; mango and avocado salad. Pecan pie has greatest appeal amongst the puddings, but butterscotch and banana with yoghurt are good too. Loseley ice creams.

Wholemeal bread; fresh fruit at table; organic wine; polyunsaturates in cooking and at table; always one sugar-free pudding. Vegetarian, vegan. Seats 50. Meals from £6.50. House wine £3.10.

Open: dinners, daily, 6.30 to 11.30 (last orders).

LONDON   Map 5
Ménage à Trois, 15 Beauchamp Place, SW3   TEL London 01-589 4252

Stripped of the expense and sometimes pretentiousness of main dishes, it is possible to eat fairly economically (if not exactly soup kitchen style) down in this smart Knightsbridge basement. Only 'befores and afters' are served but there may be live musical accompaniment. Whilst Anthony Worrall-Thompson's philosophy is to give the customer what he or she wants and not what he wants them to have, the menu comes close to meeting the requirements of the new consciousness. Mr. Worrall-Thompson provides enough scope, he will say, for all appetites to conjure up menus of their choice, be it one or several dishes, yet still feel virtuous. Scallops, oyster and lobster, cooked with courgettes, asparagus and tomato is one of several dishes he offers as 'warm'. Several salads, too, fall within this scope, including the vegan—young stir fried vegetables with soy, garlic, ginger and coriander; and the quails' eggs, avocado and Roquefort. Specialities of the kitchen, a terrine of lobster, salmon and broccoli bound with a scallop mousse; Josephine's delight, a trio of creamed eggs, smoked salmon and more scallop mousse. Western Japanese-style, marinated sea bass is served with fresh coriander and warm scallops in a spicy sauce. More enthusiastically, puddings may be *hot* apple, blackcurrant and mint crumble; a pear en croute laden with chocolate mousse and two sauces—vanilla and chocolate. The fresh fruit sorbet has a raspberry coulis; a whole white peach is filled with pistachio ice cream. Cheeses are unpasteurised.

Wholemeal bread; fresh fruits at table; minimal salt and sugar; freshly squeezed fruit juices. Wholefood, vegetarian, vegan. Seats 75. Meals from £10. House wine £6.25. Visa/American Express/Access/Diners' Club.

Open: Mon to Fri, 11.30 to 3, 7 to 12.15.

LONDON
MAP 5
Neal Street, 26 Neal Street, WC2   TEL London 01-836 8368

Prices here are more expensive by comparison with the modest outlay for wholesome fare in some neighbouring establishments. Neal Street and the Yard are synonymous with earthier promotions. Nevertheless, for those prepared to bare their pockets, Anthonio Carluccio makes strenuous efforts to ensure the odds favour repeat visits. There is a powerful awareness of what might be good for you without making it obvious. Of fifteen main dishes ten are meat or game, sauces are minimal, and only fresh, natural ingredients are used. Game is used in a ravioli for starters, fish in five others including the scallop, squid and prawn salad or simply crab from Cornwall. Wild mushrooms are used in the soup; pâté de foie gras and the salmon tartare make expensive options. Main course game is partridge and pear; venison with more wild mushrooms. Breast of turkey comes with chestnuts and stuffing and the monkfish with a delicate lime sauce. Savoy cabbage is smoked; carrots and celeriac are puréed and the sprouts combined with chestnuts.

Wholemeal bread; fresh fruits at table; minimal salt and sugar; freshly squeezed fruit and vegetable juices. Wholefood, vegetarian. Seats 70. Meals from £20. House wine £9.15. All major credit cards accepted.

Open: Mon to Fri, 12.30 to 7.30.

LONDON
MAP 5
Nuthouse, 26 Kingly Street, W1   TEL London 01-437 9471

Seen from the seedy exterior, it has none of the attractions of nearby Marshall Street (see Cranks) but it has distinct merit not least because, as proprietor Mr. Abraham will say, 'we are the cheapest you can buy in W1'. Inside food is dispensed in simple, clean surroundings with friendly service. 'We use only fresh food, everything is made on the premises, and little or nothing of what is not good for you.' Seasoning and sauces are minimal as the customers help themselves. It is one of a handful of places where the nut roasts are a matter of pride. Three bean pasta, with a herby sauce and flaked almond topping is tasty but best at lunchtimes when freshly made. And that goes for the lentil and mushroom hot-pot with a cheese topping. Generally better for hot dishes than salads. Decent banana bread, date and walnut slice, carrot cake and gingerbread or fruit salad.

Free range eggs; wholemeal bread; fresh fruits at table; minimal salt and sugar; skimmed milk available; freshly squeezed fruit and vegetable juices; soya milk. Wholemeal flour in baking. Wholefood, vegetarian. Seats 100. Meals from £3.25.

Open: Mon to Fri, 10.30 to 7; Sat, 10.30 to 5.

LONDON   Map 5
Pappagalli's Pizza Inc., 7–9 Swallow Street, W1   TEL London 01-734 5182

The claims are bold: 'We are the originators of the wholemeal deep pizza (as well as the white) and the largest and most varied salad bar in Central London.' Pasta comes in 24 varieties. Meals include popular items like hot baked mushrooms, a build-yourself salad starter and smoky garlic barbecued chicken wings. The Sicilian-style pizzas are more economic if, by remote chance, four can be persuaded to make the same choice. Two, the Original and the Mighty Mushroom have mozzarella cheese, the remainder anchovies, Italian sausage, ham and the like, but there is considerable flexibility which will meet many needs. Of course, the salad bar may be a main course choice, adding the protein of your preference—cottage cheese and walnuts, or egg mayonnaise. The half dozen pasta dishes include two with meat sauces, one with fish. Apart from chocolate fudge brownies, puddings are ice cream variations, making a food watch next to impossible, but halve any harm by sharing—just ask for an extra spoon!

Wholemeal bread; fresh fruits at table; minimal salt and sugar; bean sprout selection at salad bar organically grown. Wholefood, vegetarian. Seats 100. Meals from £7. House wine £4.95. Visa/Access.

Open: Mon to Sat, 12 to 3, 5.15 to 12.

LONDON   Map 5
Peppermint Park, Upper St. Martin's Lane, WC2   TEL London 01-836 5234

Alan Lubin's and Roger Myers' American-style soda bar is big, bright and brash—and increasingly popular. The music is loud, with cabaret in the evenings at weekends and the nights are long. Dancing is from midnight Saturdays and Sundays. Hamburgers, frankfurters and steaks are features but there are moves all the time towards wholefoods and meatless dishes which get very fair representation. There are now aduki burgers as well. Among starters there is hot pepper soup, tagliatelle (with a tomato or cheese sauce), corn on the cob and a dish of scallops, mussels and prawns. Gumbo soup in real life is really a chowder—crab claws, prawns and mussels amongst other produce of the sea goes into the making. Chicken Kiev, peppered pork and Scotch beef are frequent features. There is a big demand for their rather special Californian fresh fruit salad as a main dish: mango, pineapple, grapes, oranges, lychees and kiwi fruit go into the making in addition to a few temperate fruits, cottage cheese, alfalfa and bean sprouts. Blueberry and apple pie—made by themselves—is a predictable feature. Ice creams (not theirs) are in thirty varieties and become blackouts when drenched with the liqueur of your choice.

Lots of fresh, sometimes exotic fruits; wholemeal bread; freshly squeezed fruit and vegetable juices; minimal salt and sugar; probably coming shortly—free range eggs and chickens. Wholefood, vegetarian, vegan. Seats 160. Meals from £8.50. House wine £5.20.

Open: Mon to Fri, 12 to 12; Sat and Sun, 12 to 2 am.

LONDON   Map 5
Pizza Express, 29 Wardour Street, W1   TEL London 01-437 7215

In this chain of nearly thirty restaurants around London and the south east, there are customarily sixteen pizza choices of which seven usually meet vegetarian needs. The remainder include meat or fish of some kind. Customers for the Venetian version—it is a vegetarian standard—can glow with the satisfaction that for every one they eat 10p is donated to the 'Venice in Peril' fund. Over £50,000 has been donated so far which doesn't take too much market research to calculate its popularity since the chain's inception in '65. Substantial affairs and a decent light pastry base, the nutritional balance might be improved if sizes were halved and a side salad or baked potato thrown in for the same price. Decent coffee, Italian lager and wines. Colourful surroundings, wholesome for the kids and music thrown in, all means that this is far from being a bad deal even if it is not the style for a special night out.

Free range eggs; olive oil used in cooking; fresh fruit at table; minimal salt and sugar. Wholefood, vegetarian. Seats 70. Meals from £4.50. House wine £4.60.

Open: daily, 11.30 to midnight.

LONDON
Plummers, 33 King Street, WC2   TEL London 01-240 2534

MAP 5

Leaving aside the hamburgers and steaks, this pretty restaurant, popular with Covent Garden patrons and tourists, offers a number of menu items that are interesting to thoughtful diners. Starters include several fish dishes, a fish chowder and crudités. Salads come with meats and fish or there is the substantial all-in-together version generously fortified with fruit, peanuts and raisins. Fish dishes are usually grilled and the trout and salmon are done without too much reliance on rich sauces. Vegetarians fare well for choice, with a casserole of vegetables, a better bet than the nut crumble with the spinach and cheese topping and the vegetable cottage pie. Sorbets are probably a good choice for desserts; the mature cheddar is offered with celery or apple and the bread rolls are good.

Wholemeal bread; fresh fruits at table. Wholefood, vegetarian. Seats 70. Meals from £13. House wine £5.35. All major credit cards accepted.

Open: Mon to Sat, 12.30 to 2.30, 6 to 11.30.

LONDON
Ravenscourt Park Teahouse, Ravenscourt Park, W6

MAP 4

There are occasions when the closing times at Tom Alley's teahouse are governed by those arranged for the park, which will be dusk in winter. The Paddenswick Road gate may be the most convenient point of access. He is worth seeking out for his inexpensive wholefood, all of which is prepared and cooked on the premises, including the bread. The former stable block is an agreeable venue for a leisurely lunch, or lighter refreshments from 10 in the morning onwards. Several main dishes may be red bean, leek and rice pie; a spinach and potato curry, perhaps a mushroom slice. Burgers are the vegetarian form, and there is pizza on a wholemeal base, naturally. Warming starters may be pea and mushroom soup or the substantial teahouse broth. Some days there are tofu balls with sweet and sour sauce, sweet pumpkin pie, lasagne and red bean casserole. Salads solo or with other dishes—butterbean, coleslaw, green, tabouleh. Cake to finish, ginger, honey, fruit, chocolate brownies and apple and apricot shortcake.

Organically grown vegetables; homemade wholemeal bread; polyunsaturates at table and in cooking; fresh fruits at table; minimal salt and sugar. Wholefood, vegetarian, vegan. Seats 40 (plus 40 outdoors in summer). Meals from £4.25.

Open: daily, 10 to 6 (earlier in winter).

LONDON
Ravi Shankar, 133–135 Drummond Street, NW1   TEL London 01-388 6458

MAP 5

There is an appealing, wholesome appearance about this bright, clean place with the plain pine tables—a well-scrubbed look. The unassuming Mr. Iqbal only opened his doors recently but already has an enthusiastic following. A deliberately limited menu is also an attraction and there is more than usual confidence that the food is fresh and everything prepared on the premises. Try him for inexpensive snacks or starters like potato poori (potatoes, pooris, onions with sauces), chick peas and potatoes cooked with yoghurt, sauces and spices. The freshly squeezed fruit juices include passion fruit, grapefruit and pineapple. Set meals, South Indian style, may be Mysore Thali (dhal, mixed vegetables together with raita, papad and pooris or chapattis) perhaps followed by kulfi. Lentil pizza, Indian style, has some of the conventional topping ingredients to which coconut and spices are added. Pancakes are served with three separate vegetable fillings, sambhar and coconut chutney. Indian desserts or an ice cream.

Wholemeal bread; fresh fruits at table; minimal salt and sugar; skimmed milk available; freshly squeezed fruit and vegetable juices. Vegetarian, wholefood. Seats 70. Meals from £4.25. Diners' Club/Access/Visa/American Express.

Open: daily, 12 to 11.

LONDON   MAP 5
Raw Deal, York Street, W1

On the corner of York Street with Wyndham Place, by the side of Sir Robert Smirke's Parish Church of St. Mary's, Bryanston Square (1824), there is daily a steady stream of regulars to this simple little café. Seating, at simple wooden benches, can be cramped and there is a fair amount of togetherness. Dishes of the day are modestly priced, around £2 for lentil roast or a risotto, possibly better value than the fresh though more expensive salads. Interesting puddings of the fruit crumble, mousse, fruit salad kind, with cream or yoghurt. Animal rennet free cheeses.

Wholemeal bread; fresh fruits at table; minimal salt and sugar; freshly squeezed fruit juices; polyunsaturates in cooking and at table. Vegetarian. Seats 24. Meals from £4. Bring your own wine, no corkage charge.

Open: Mon to Sat, 10 to 10.

LONDON   MAP 5
Slenders, 41 Cathedral Place, EC4   TEL London 01-236 5974

Concessions to creature comforts include modestly upholstered bench seats, spaced along the window frontage with views into the precinct. Salads and good wholemeal bread for take-away are a speciality. Bread rolls are baked in the kitchen. Cooked dishes include asparagus and courgette soup, vegetarian shepherd's pie, nut rissoles, quiches and good tasty soups. Lasagne is with spinach and mushrooms. There is normally a vegetable casserole, and always baked potatoes. Puddings will be fruit salad or crumbles, carrot and banana cakes and flapjack. Mousse, trifle and cheesecakes. White flour and sugar are not used in any of the dishes.

Free range eggs; wholemeal bread; polyunsaturates in kitchen and at table; minimal salt and sugar. Vegetarian, wholefood, vegan. Seats 50. Meals from £4.

Open: Mon to Fri, 7.30 am to 6.15 pm.

LONDON   MAP 5
Spud U Like, 79 Camden High Street, NW1   TEL London 01-387 0960

The most frequent complaint by customers at this chain of fast food outlets is that the healthy life advantages stop short of getting polyunsaturated margarine in lieu of butter. Otherwise there is much to commend them. In pleasant, clean surroundings some simple, nutritious food is produced for less than the usual price of fish and chips. Healthy fillings: mushroom and rice, spring salad, cottage cheese with several different additions like chives or onions, tuna or cheddar, apple and celery. Hot fillings might be chicken curry, hot sweetcorn, chilli con carne or baked beans. Quite a number meet the needs of vegans.

No fat used in cooking. Vegetarian and gluten-free items, vegan. Seats on average 30 in each unit. Meals £2.50. Around 50 units in London and country.

Open: Mon to Sat, 11 to 11; Sun, 12 to 11.

LONDON   MAP 4
Sree Krishna, 192–194 Tooting High Street, SW17   TEL London 01-672 4250

Mr. Ramamarayanan enjoys some popularity for his South Indian specialities in addition to a choice of other dishes. Expect masala dosai, avial and sambar and, Fridays and Sundays only, iddly, a steamed rice cake of rice and black gram. Biryanis include the vegetarian mushroom version, otherwise there is egg, chicken and a prawn. Chicken comes in a number of other ways—bhuna, Madras, Vindaloo, Bombay—some diners taking to it fried with chips and peas. A fair range of vegetables including the green banana bhaji. Sweets mean mango or lychees, fruit salad, ice creams or combinations of these. Almond cake and kulfi mango.

Some vegetarian dishes. Seats 70. Meals from £5.50. House wine £5.20.

Open: Sun to Sat, 12 to 3, 6 to 11.

LONDON   MAP 4
Village Taverna, 28 Ridgeway, Wimbledon Village, SW19
TEL London 01-946 4840

The policy here is that 'we make it ourselves or we do not have it' but that does not apply to the pastries and ice cream. These are bought in (some rich fare), except for their own homemade yoghurt and orange blossom honey. Only olive oil is used for cooking and all of Mr. Manoras's meats are charcoal grilled. Additives, there are none. Starters are yoghurt and hummus dips, dolmades, whitebait, melon in season, a casserole of mixed vegetables flavoured with herbs and top of the price range, meaty charcoal grilled king prawns. The tasty vegetable casserole appears again, in a larger portion, as a main dish, beyond that there are no other dishes without meat or fish. Souvla is a generous chunk of English lamb on the bone, marinated and spit cooked. Afelia is pork casseroled with coriander seeds. Mezze, the only meal not served with salad, a selection from three of the starters and a choice from seven main dishes with feta cheese. Figs are the preserved kind.

Wholemeal pitta bread; polyunsaturates in cooking; minimal salt. Wholefood, vegetarian, diabetic. Seats 56. Meals from £4.50. House wine £5.80 a litre. Visa/Access.

Open: Mon to Sat, 12 to 2.30, 6 to 11.

LONDON   MAP 5
White House, Albany Street, Regent's Park, NW1   TEL London 01-387 1200

Rank Hotels bastion in NW1 does not quite manage park views but is close enough for pleasurable training runs and gently working off any heavier fare to which you may succumb. Plushly appointed, the dining-room caters adequately for plainer eating needs with main interest in fish dishes. Except for chicken, poultry and game are scarce. To commence, the yield from the sea might be a light fish mousse; quenelles of pike, sole and carp; herrings with soured cream; whitebait and the fish soup. Artichokes are served with an unspecified, suitable sauce, and they make a point of serving asparagus whenever obtainable but be alert to the quantities of melted butter! Trout are stuffed with a mousse of sole, red wine and mushrooms. Fresh and smoked salmon is in a puff pastry case. Meat-free meals might have started with a selection of vegetable hors d'oeuvres, followed by the noodles cooked with tomato, field mushrooms and cheese. A pastry case has a filling of spinach, mushrooms and mozzarella cheese. Other possibilities—nut and vegetable cutlet and a vegetable casserole. Desserts include water ices, lavish crêpes with peaches, bananas and cherries, fresh fruits from the trolley.

Wholemeal bread; fresh fruits at table; minimal salt and sugar; skimmed milk available; freshly squeezed fruit and vegetable juices. Wholefood, vegetarian, vegan. Seats 120. Meals from £12.50. House wine £5.60. All major credit cards accepted.

Open: Mon to Fri, 12.30 to 2.30, 6.30 to 11; Sat, 6.30 to 11.

LONDON   Map 5
Wilkins Natural Foods, 61 Marsham Street, SW1   tel London 01-222 4038

It is difficult to imagine life for the Rossiters without the D.O.E. commuters from Coulsdon, Caterham and Croydon rolling up from 8 am onwards, seeking healthy life breakfasts in a smokeless zone. Their reputation is based on tasty soups, absolutely delicious vegetable pies (vegan standard), and excellent pizzas. Most of the food is prepared on the premises and is also sold in the shop (see entry). A hummus filled pitta bread is popular, and a fruit pudding is warmly approved. Date slices and carob chip cookies are made without sugar. Generously filled sandwiches are made with their homemade bread. Cooking is done with free range eggs (when used) and sometimes organically grown vegetables. Loseley ice creams. There are dishes suited to those on gluten-free diets and diabetics.

Homemade wholemeal bread; polyunsaturates in cooking; fresh fruits at table; minimal salt and sugar; freshly squeezed fruit and vegetable juices. Meals from £3.50.

Open: Mon to Fri, 8 to 5.30.

LONDON   Map 4
Whole Meal, 1 Shrubbery Road, Streatham, SW16   tel London 01-769 0137

Customers to David Martin's café are a mixture of trendy Guardian readers, social workers and, very occasionally, the Metropolitan Police from the station across the road. Smarter than the name might first suggest, food is served in an open plan kitchen/dining-room furnished with fashionable caned seating, low lights and a string ceiling! Lightly seasoned, inexpensive food includes a soup of the day, several quiches and salads. There is usually special approval for the hot main dishes which might be spinach and mushroom crumble and an Indian chick pea casserole. Yoghurts or cream to go with the apple and cinnamon crumble, fresh fruit and honey, or the chocolate and hazelnut pudding. Hot food offered throughout opening hours or more simply, herbal teas, coffee and juices.

Non-battery eggs; wholemeal bread; polyunsaturates in cooking; fresh fruits at table. Vegetarian, vegan. Seats 36. Meals from £5, dishes from 85p. House wine £4.50.

Open: daily, 12 to 10.30.

LONDON   Map 4
Windmill Restaurant, 486 Fulham Road, SW6   tel London 01-385 1570

Particularly note the apostrophe between the 'Mc' and the 'Donald' for there is a comfortable touch of Ireland in Mr. Mc'Donald's restaurant with lots of green winter plants, cheery open fire (wintertimes) and flickering candlelight. The interesting complex has a corridor running alongside the restaurant to the little warehouse shop, hidden away at the end (see entry). The menu offers sunflower seed and millet burgers—it comes with a salad, one of about ten, the cabbage and bulgar bake looks as good. Begin the meal with carrot and orange soup or the creamier cheese and parsnip. There is a different lunch menu. Desserts run to banana cream (cream, yoghurt, bananas and honey), apple crumble, but the trifle goes fastest. They had run out before getting to us. Plainer tastes might have gone for the carrot cake, made by themselves as is everything else. Along with a wholewheat sponge and a chocolate cake, everything is available as a take-away. No frozen foods are used. People sometimes come for birthday parties and such but they really bustle here, not the place for a quiet evening out. Bring in your own wine, corkage only 40p. Eat well from £4, even £3.

Wholemeal bread; polyunsaturates in cooking; minimal salt and sugar; only free range eggs. Meals from £3.

Open: Mon to Sat, 12 to 11; Sun, 7 to 11.

LONDON Map 5
Woodlands, 77 Marylebone Road, NW1   TEL London 01-486 3862

Coming here is more like visiting a carefully designed, conscientiously maintained modern home, with nothing spurious. It holds appeal, too, appreciative correspondents feel, for the amazing variety of the delicious South Indian dishes. Enterprising, welcome recipes like tomato omelette, using creamed wheat without any eggs; lentil pizzas topped up with coconut, (briefly and inventively, conututhappam). A mixed utham is a lentil pizza with tomatoes, onion and coconut. There are vegetable cutlets with salad and bisi bele hulianna, a spicy rice and lentil preparation. Cream of wheat pancakes have a potato, onion and nut filling. Chappatis are wholewheat. For sweets, badam latlawi (ground almonds with milk sponge and saffron); sherra (a wholewheat semolina pudding).

Wholemeal chappatis; no eggs used. Vegetarian, wholefood, vegan. Seats 28. Meals from £8. House wine £5.50.

Open: daily, 12 to 3, 6 to 11.

LUDLOW   Salop Map 2
The Feathers, Bull Ring   TEL Ludlow (0584) 5261

This notable picturesque inn, first licensed in 1521 still meets the traveller's needs. Meals are prepared with much regard for simplicity, sufficiently forward thinking to be able to offer a decent separate vegetarian menu. Osmond Edwards' paramount concern is with the freshness of his ingredients and the care with which they are prepared—lightly cooked to order. Dinner menus include herb pâté using fresh herbs studded with ham, tongue and chicken livers, oriental salads are a trio of cucumber, prawns with beansprouts and lobster, each in individual dressings. Pigeon breasts are served with wild rice and mushrooms. Dover sole fillets—for main dishes—are tossed with nuts, white wine and lime vinegar. A light bacon sauce is served with the poached turbot, the lobster and prawns with wild mushrooms and a julienne of leek. An apple sauce laced with calvados is an accompaniment for venison. Traditional fare includes roast beef and Yorkshire pudding, roast pork and apple sauce with vegetables cooked as you like them. Mushroom pie has a cheese sauce, sweetcorn and a puff pastry case. Nut and macaroni curry has a cucumber and tomato side dish, otherwise there is vegetable and savoury bake, several salads, quiches and omelettes. Always two fish dishes at breakfast as well as fruits, yoghurts and muesli.

Wholemeal bread; fresh fruits at table; minimal salt and sugar; polyunsaturates in cooking. Additional vegetarian menu. Seats 80. Meals from £15 dinner, from £3.75 vegetarian dishes, £10 special lunch. House wine £5.60. All credit cards accepted.

Open: daily, 8 to 10, 12 to 3, 7 to 9.30.

LYMINGTON   Hampshire Map 3
The Old Bank House, 68 High Street   TEL Lymington (0590) 78888

Newly reopened—after being leased and run into the ground—the omens are better for Mr. Halliwell's refurbished establishment in this popular yachting centre. There is the customary run of steaks and burgers, so his bistro appeals to all tastes, but the place is worth considering as well for tasty homemade soups, savoury crêpes which may be filled with seafoods, Mexican chilli, mushrooms, ratatouille and the Hawaiian mushrooms, ham and pineapple. Fondues are served with seafood, cheese or steak, all with jacket potatoes and salad. Pasta is fresh. Puddings are pancakes too. Light classical music.

Wholemeal bread; freshly squeezed fruit and vegetable juices; fresh fruits at table; minimal salt and sugar. Vegetarian, vegan. Seats 60 café wine bar, 40 cellar bistro. Food, wine bar from 75p, bistro meals from £5.50. House wine £3.65.

Open: Tue to Sun, 12 to 12.

MACHYNLLETH Powys   MAP 6
The Quarry Shop, Maengwyn Street   TEL Machynlleth (0654) 2624

Admirers, mainly holidaymakers doing a round Wales trip, cannot speak too highly of this
quite simple little place behind the wholefood grocery shop of the same name (see entry).
The menu is a simple as the décor but prices will not break the bank and the ingredients
are more likely than some to leave the body unscathed. It is a coffee to teatime operation,
lunches in between. Annie Lowmass and Barry Wise offer savoury sweetcorn flans, pizzas
and leek and mushroom bakes, all priced within a few pence of 90p. Customers are known
to have been well satisfied by a substantial bean and vegetable soup, so much so as to
make further eating difficult. You could try something lighter: such as the rice and nut
salads, the pasta version, or a green one to accompany one of the hot dishes. It is
rewarding to do a test run on the lemon spice cake, an apricot slice, carob pie or, more
degenerately, trifle and a dollop of raw cream. Only teas, coffees and fruit juices available
to accompany the food. They use wholefoods, organic when available, raw milk, vegan
margarine, other ingredients are vegetarian—and, they like to think, less sugar and salt.
More garlic and herbs are used than in most cafés.

Vegetarian, wholefood, vegan. Seats 30. Meals from £3.

Open: daily, 9 to 5; closed Sun except Jul and Aug, Thur pm.

MALDON Essex   MAP 3
Acorn Natural Food Café, Oakwood Arts Centre, Market Place
TEL Maldon (0621) 52317

Gill Fordham and Nigel Walker do all of the cooking on the premises and are virtuously
aiming to reduce fats and sugar in the food. Part of a privately run arts centre in this listed
building, the café, with bentwood chairs and Laura Ashley and Sanderson decoration, is
perhaps cosy rather than smart. Across the garden at the back is the old warehouse which
the same people have converted into craft workshops. Gill Fordham finds time, too, to run
vegetarian wholefood cookery classes. Specialities are nut roasts, lasagne, vegetable
curries, and always a quiche. Crusty home baked baps have tahini and tofu salad fillings, in
addition to more familiar cheese, egg mayonnaise, locally made herb cheese, peanut butter
and banana, all with a side salad if required. Baked potatoes have coleslaw dressings, low
fat cheese or garlic butter. From time to time fruit flans, fruit salads and crumbles, and the
exotic carob and date ice cream sundae. Cakes include, principally, spicy tea bun, ginger,
malt and honey, carrot and sunflower. Milk shakes are made with real bananas, other fruit
flavours in season, soya milk option, too. No artificial flavourings or preservatives.

*As much organic produce as possible; free range eggs; soya milk; wholemeal bread;
polyunsaturates in cooking; tahini and peanut butters available at table; fresh fruits at table;
minimal salt and sugar. Vegetarian, wholefood, vegan. Seats 30. Meals from £3.50. Bring your
own wine, small corkage charge.*

Open: Mon to Sat, 9.30 to 5; Sat, also 6.30 to 9.30.

MALDON Essex   MAP 3
Maldon Coffee Shop, 63 High Street   TEL Maldon (0621) 57146

There is a very pleasant atmosphere in these old cottage premises behind the bookshop,
with old oak beams, leaded window lights and an old range. For warmer days there is a
quiet garden courtyard to sit out in. It is the sort of place to find coffee drinkers, tea talkers
and those having light lunches. Generally there is an emphasis on the homemade right
down to the mayonnaise. Similarly with the quiches though likely as not these will have
been reheated from the freezer. Wholefood rather than vegetarian, expect vichyssoise,
smoked mackerel on toast and ratatouille. Pancakes might normally have a pork filling
unless something else is organised, like spinach and cream cheese. Baked potatoes come
with salad. Quiches are sometimes imaginative like walnut and cauliflower. The dish of

the day might be a vegetable lasagne. Desserts of the almond and apricot pudding kind and homemade ice creams are good. And that goes for the flapjacks, brownies, gâteaux and cheesecake often made with wholemeal flour.

Free range eggs; sometimes free range chickens; wholemeal bread; homemade ice creams; minimal salt. Wholefood, vegetarian, vegan salads. Seats 35 indoors, 20 outside in summer. Meals from £4.25, dishes from £1. House wine 50p glass.

Open: Mon to Sat, 10 to 5.

MANCHESTER   Greater Manchester   MAP 6
The Chaise Lounge Too, Lower Ground Floor, Royal Exchange
TEL Manchester 061-832 4842

In an open basement shopping precinct in the old cotton exchange, Mr. and Mrs. Eyre run a friendly vegetarian café, a good deal of the food being homemade. Tricky fire regulations mean that most of the greenery is plastic (which puzzles), but this scarcely detracts from the comfortable arrangements. In addition to lasagne, moussaka and nut roast there are burgers of the tofu kind. Salads rate as something of a speciality, build them up according to taste. Good on cakes of the carob, carrot and chocolate fudge sort, and fresh fruit and fruit salads too.

Wholemeal French bread and rolls; vegetarian margarine; soya and goats' milk; fresh fruits at table; minimal salt and sugar; freshly squeezed fruit juices on special request. Vegetarian, wholefood, vegan. Seats 60. Meals from £5.20. House wine £4.20.

Open: Mon to Sat, 9 to 5.

MANCHESTER   Greater Manchester   MAP 6
Farmhouse Kitchen, Fountain Street   TEL Manchester 061-236 5532

There are two branches in the city of these large self-service restaurants (the other in Blackfriars Street) with masses of horizontal light pine boarding reminiscent of a corral in a Western. Only natural ingredients, the management insist, are used. Herbs, nut oil, fresh fruit and vegetables, and butter too, which 'makes our food taste so much better'. An interesting range of salads—all inexpensive—will include pineapple and celery, Russian, spring, winter (anytime), coleslaw and beansprout. Fish and meat dishes of a conventional kind, the former sometimes in a baked dish, otherwise deep fried. For other tastes there are cheese topped pizzas, quiches in several kinds, mushroom and barley casserole, sweet and sour cheese, vegetable moussaka. Fruit salads and natural yoghurts. In-house baking produces wholemeal cheese, fruit and plain scones and cakes of the brownie, banana, carrot sort.

Wholemeal bread; wholemeal flour in baking; fresh fruit at table. Wholefood, vegetarian. Seats 200. Meals from £4. Wine 75p glass.

Open: Mon to Sat.

MANCHESTER   Greater Manchester   MAP 6
Gaylord India, Amethyst House, Spring Gardens   TEL Manchester 061-832 6037

Authentic North Indian cuisine, Mr. Chadha makes a more powerful impact with the number of his vegetarian listings. Fifteen items are offered varying from paneer makhani (homemade cottage cheese cooked with tomatoes and cream) to vegetable balls, peas and mushrooms, fresh ladies' fingers, lotus roots and lentils and ginger. The special vegetarian thali includes three varieties of vegetables, samosa, pulao, raita, purées and papad. The tandoori mix offers several chicken and lamb dishes, pulao rice, mixed vegetables, dhal special, papad and salad. Among soups and starters, European conventions—prawn cocktail, grapefruit, mulligatawny. Seasonally available sweets, mango and paw paw.

Wholemeal bread; polyunsaturates in cooking; minimal salt and sugar. Vegetarian, vegan. Seats 86. Meals from £6.40. House wine £5.60. American Express/Diners' Club/Visa/Access.

Open: daily, 12 to 3, 6 to 11.30.

MANCHESTER   Greater Manchester   Map 6
The Market Restaurant, 30 Edge Street   TEL Manchester 061-834 3743

Broadly the style here is 3 starters, 3 main dishes and 3 sweets, with special emphasis on the freshness of the ingredients. Like Mrs. Jones' front room might have been in the forties, the walls are primrose, decorated with plates from the flea markets, the tables white cloth covered with candles. Menus are changed by the week but you could find, to start, smoked salmon and taramasalata timbale, a beetroot and sour cream soup, and a pâté; and fruit fresh from the market which might meet vegan requirements. Nuts are popular for dressings. Circassian chicken will have a walnut and hazelnut sauce, with more walnuts in the cauliflower and Stilton flan. Fish is not used as often as they like because they insist on it being fresh, not frozen. Ice cream is homemade which with a mango or guava sorbet and something more substantial like a chocolate flan will make up an evening's choice. Cheese is a farmhouse Cheshire.

Non-battery eggs; wholemeal bread; polyunsaturates in cooking usually; minimal salt and sugar. Wholefood, vegetarian, vegan and gluten-free with notice. Seats 30. Meals from £7. House wine ½ litre carafe £2.70.

Open: Tue to Sat, 6.30 to 10.30; closed 1 week Christmas, 1 week spring, all Aug.

MANCHESTER   Greater Manchester   Map 6
Nut and Meg, Palantine Road, Northenden

Tricia Hulme's business is in a thirties shopping parade. The eating part here is nothing more than four chunky pine tables between the grocery goods on the shelf-lined walls. It has habituées: local shoppers and business people turn up regularly for their main meal of the day, chosen from several tempting hot dishes. Broccoli and walnut bake, zyldyk casserole (vegetables in a mildly curried sauce) and chilli made with bulgar wheat are among the most popular. Good apple pies and in summer when there is more demand, fruit salads. Everything is made on the premises including the high fibre fruit cake, date slices, wholewheat parkin, carrot and date and walnut cake. There is also a vegetarian mince slice. Goats' milk ice cream and natural yoghurts. Tofu dips.

Wholemeal bread; fresh fruits at table; minimal salt and sugar; free range eggs; organic vegetables. Vegetarian, wholefood, vegan. Seats 16. Meals from £3.50.

Open: Mon to Sat.

MANCHESTER   Greater Manchester   Map 6
On the Eighth Day, 111 Oxford Road, All Saints   TEL Manchester 061-273 4878

A basic sort of place is the general consensus but most people are impressed by the incredible value for money and consistently good quality food. Even other restaurateurs (among them Yorkist adversaries) commend this restaurant. They also know the best places from where to buy in for the confections not made themselves. Bread from the spiritedly independent Green Door Bakery, samosas from Chunis Chaat House and pies from Sunrise, all the way from distant Shropshire countryside. Theirs is a multi-ethnic style. 'We use non-battery eggs—when recipes call for eggs, which is not often. We generally avoid recipes with milk fat and always use organic rice and flours.' Fats high in polyunsaturates are always used in cooking and margarines of this kind are usually offered at the table as well. There is a daily baked dish, perhaps lentil and cauliflower (£1.80). Spinach and potato curry with rice is a mere £1.30. Both may have been preceded by a well flavoured minestrone (45p). Salads priced according to size come with mung bean pâté (60p and £1.10) or salad with savoury rice 50p and 90p). Cashew nut cream served with the date and walnut or cinnamon and sultana cake is scrumptious. All their dishes are vegetarian and most are vegan. Beverages—soya milk, barley cup, coffee and regular herb teas. Next door is the wholefood shop of the same name (see entry).

Wholemeal bread; polyunsaturates in cooking and at table; fresh fruits at table; minimal salt and sugar; free range eggs; organic flour and rice. Seats 45. Meals from £3.

Open: Mon to Sat, 11.30 to 3.30.

MELMERBY   Cumbria   MAP 6
Village Bakery, Melmerby   TEL Melmerby (0768) 81515

Lis and Andrew Whitley's mission is pure food. They are special in more ways than one with a distinctive converted 18th century barn alongside a rugged thirteen acre village green. Behind is eyecatching Melmerby Fell (2,331 feet), Cross Fell (2,930 feet) is nearby and a road out to Alston, touches a spectacular 2,000 feet. Much of the food served comes from their organic smallholding out at the back where pigs rummage and bullocks and sheep graze. It is a matter of regret but no surprise, that with all these diversions there is not time for evening opening. Days get under way with breakfasts of Loch Fyne oak-smoked kippers; free range eggs done as you like; starters, perhaps Granola topped with yoghurt and fresh fruit. Lunchtime soups come with the house cheesebread, the grapefruit with rum and stem ginger. Hearty follow-ups may be roast beef salad; curried vegetables; their special hamburger in a bap (the likes of which are not often found) or Village Bakery Brick oven pizza. Baked potatoes, and side salads are a matter of course. The winter menu offers mince pies from homemade vegetable mincemeat, rich in fruit, low in sugar. There are always lavish banana splits and Cumberland Rum Nicky. Lighter, even more inexpensive is shepherd's pie snack, 54p; Cumberland sausage roll, 29p; curried vegetable pastie, 40p. Coffee—as many cups as you like—is 45p. Real ale comes from Carlisle's independent Theakston's Brewery. There are just a few wines chosen with light lunchtime drinking in mind.

Organically-grown fruit and vegetables. Seats 40. Meals from £5.50. House wine £3.90.

Open: Sun, Tue, Thur, Fri, Sat, 8.30 to 5.

MELTON MOWBRAY   Leicestershire   MAP 3
Harboro Hotel, Burton Street   TEL Melton Mowbray (0664) 60121

This well-appointed Georgian hotel is part of the Anchor Hotel group, taking its name from one Robert Sherrard, a town benefactor who in 1770 became 4th Earl of Harborough. Today's owners specialise in various set meals which offer particularly good value. Poacher's Bag is a fixed-price buffet offering a selection of cold cooked joints. It operates on a self-help basis with numerous salads, jacket potatoes and wholemeal bread. If inclined, you may make a second visit to the salad table. Lesser delights are local Stilton (Huntsman's Choice) or Leicestershire cheese with wholemeal bread and salad—a variation on the ploughman's lunch. The restaurant offers a venison and beef pie in a flaky pastry; plaice, shallots and mushrooms in a pastry case. There are appetisers such as melon and cucumber salad, turkey mousse, avocado pear filled with celery, apple and walnuts in a horseradish mayonnaise. A special vegetarian menu provides fritters (tomatoes, peppers, mushrooms and garlic, moulded with cheese) served with a salad. Stuffed savoury pancakes come with baked potatoes. Also available are vegetable risotto and a mixed nut omelette.

Wholemeal bread; fresh fruits at table; minimal salt and sugar. Wholefood, vegetarian. Seats 60. Meals from £3.20 lunch, £8.60 dinner. House wine £4.65. Access/Visa/Anchor/American Express/Diners' Club.

Open: lunch, daily, 12 to 2; dinner, 7.30 to 10, Sun 7.30 to 9.15.

MEVAGISSEY   Cornwall   MAP 2
Mr. Bistro, East Quay, Mevagissey   TEL Mevagissey (0726) 842432

Chris and Romer Robins are descended from a fishing family which may partly account
for the special selection of fresh, locally landed catches available in their bistro. Few cod or
haddock are found hereabouts but there are Dover and lemon sole, plaice, squid,
monkfish, John Dory, red mullet and mackerel on the menu. Fresh salmon and salmon
trout come from the Fowey River, oysters come from the Helford. Scallops, crab and
lobster are plentiful too. Simple lunches may be the catch of the day or a seafood platter,
pâtés—smoked salmon or rough farmhouse—or perhaps a home-baked flan. Dinners
bring deep fried squid, hot devilled crab, hot grilled lobster and John Dory with prawn
sauce. Hungarian-style mushrooms, Mr. Bistro's vegetarian speciality, are cooked with
soured cream. All meat and poultry is fresh and often local. Convenience foods are not on
offer. 'If we run out of any dish you want, apologies—we cannot extract a frozen dinner
and blast it with a microwave because we don't have one,' say Chris and Romer Robins.

*Wholemeal bread; polyunsaturates at table; fresh fruits at table; minimal salt and sugar; freshly-squeezed fruit juices; a fair proportion of fruit, vegetables and herbs come from the garden.
Wholefood, vegetarian, gluten-free by arrangement. Seats 30. Meals from £9 dinner, lunch
dishes from £1.50. House wine £5.25 litre.*

Open: Sun to Sat, 12 to 2, 7 to 10; closed Nov to Feb.

MONTACUTE   Somerset   MAP 2
The Milk House, The Borough   TEL Montacute (0935) 823823

Mr. Stead's cottage restaurant may well predate the village's Elizabethan great house of
1580 (National Trust) which first really put the place on the map. The impressive lintel
above the porch may well be the largest single piece of worked stone ever to have come
out of Ham Hill Quarries. Mr. Stead is new to this old-established restaurant but, like his
predecessor, he insists on fresh produce, and as dishes are mostly prepared to special order
there is little difficulty in coping with special diets or requirements. He continues to offer
many of the dishes for which the restaurant had established a reputation. These include
Stilton, sage and potato puffs—light savoury choux balls deep fried and served with an
anchovy and gherkin mayonnaise. His mushrooms are served in a white sauce with a
crunchy nut topping; thin pancakes are filled with shellfish and topped with cheese.
Honey and melon liqueurs are served with the fresh melon, and smoked Scotch salmon
has a fennel sauce. Venison is marinated in port before being cooked in red wine, with
bacon, onions, mushrooms and cream. Dolmas are one of two vegan dishes—mushrooms,
onion, celery and peppers, wrapped in a cabbage leaf and baked in tomato and herb sauce.
The other is walnut and tomato casserole. The vegetarian lasagne is made with
mushrooms and aubergines. Puddings on offer may be cold coffee soufflé, a sorbet, or a
walnut and apricot roulade.

*Non-battery eggs; steamed fresh vegetables; wholemeal bread; freshly squeezed fruit juices;
diabetic wines. Wholefood, vegetarian, vegan, gluten-free. Seats 42. Meals from £14. House
wine £4.95. American Express/Diners' Club/Visa/Access.*

Open: 12 to 2, 7 to 10 except Sun, evening; closed Mon.

MORPETH   Northumberland   MAP 6
The Gourmet, 59 Bridge Street   TEL Morpeth (0670) 56200

There is something forbidding about the sheer size of the menu in Mr. Paesano's
restaurant, because it's nearly large enough to cover the table! A large section is devoted
to fish dishes and to hot and cold appetisers which would meet many special food needs.
Most are offered either fried or sautéed but there is a grilled Dover sole, and scampi is
served in a curry sauce with rice pilau. Special requests are cheerfully accommodated.

Pastas and noodles are prominent among the hot starters. Duck, venison and chicken make appearances among main dishes. Vegetarian specials include aubergine lasagne, crêpes bergère, champignons Provençale (mushrooms in béchamel sauce baked with rice) and vegetables in a mild curry. For dessert there are poached pears, crêpe Pierre (banana, soft meringue and orange juice), zabaglione Garibaldi or sorbets.

Wholemeal bread; fresh fruits at table; minimal salt and sugar; skimmed milk available; freshly-squeezed fruit juices on request. Wholefoods, vegetarian, vegan. Seats 25. Access/Visa/Diners' Club/American Express. Meals from £13. House wine £4.85.

Open: 11.30 to 2, 6.30 to 11; closed for Sun and Mon lunch, for 2 weeks in Feb.

MUCH WENLOCK   Shropshire   MAP 6
Scott's, 5 High Street   TEL Much Wenlock (0952) 727596

The olde worlde café and shop with the slightly plush bottle green interior gets the overflow trade from the Ironbridge Museum. It also rates a listing as a building of architectural interest with a rather unusual Georgian window. All of the limited menu in Mrs. Walsh's coffee shop is homemade and she now more and more offers vegetarian and wholefoods. At lunchtimes there is likely to be at least one sustaining soup, sometimes green pea and mint, sometimes hearty vegetable, always made with a vegetable stock. Main dishes are macaroni cheese, lasagne (both meat and vegetarian), Welsh rarebit, with a selection of salads and baked potatoes. Mrs. Walsh and her staff score with fig and banana slices, or Guinness cake and some generously-filled meringues which sustain the coffee and tea trade as well. Eighty-five per cent grade flour is used in all her baking, and there is an increasing range of wholefoods on offer in the shop.

Non-battery eggs; mostly skimmed milk; wholemeal bread; polyunsaturates at table; minimal sugar. Wholefood, vegetarian. Seats 25. Meals from £4.10, dishes from £1.50. House wine 80p glass.

Open: 10 to 5; closed Wed and Christmas to beginning of Feb.

NAIRN   Highland   MAP 7
Clifton Hotel, Nairn   TEL Nairn (0667) 53119

Gordon MacIntyre's plushly appointed hotel in this little royal burgh, watering place and golfing centre on the Moray Firth has rosettes from the motoring organisations for its food. Mr. MacIntyre does not believe in short cuts and adheres to some very traditional cooking methods. He is also flexible; as you like it, is the order of the day and he is insistent that customers should not feel obliged to pay for several courses if all they want is an omelette. It is no surprise, so far north, to see game figuring so importantly on the menu. No less important is the quality of the vegetables and herbs used—always fresh and a good many come from the hotel garden. Listed among the numerous vegetable dishes are spinach roulade, tabouleh and aubergine charlotte.

Free range eggs and chickens; free range ducks and duck eggs; some home-grown vegetables; homemade wholemeal bread; polyunsaturates at table; fresh fruits at table; minimal salt and sugar. Wholefood, vegetarian. Seats 40. Meals from £7.50. House wine £6.65. All major credit cards accepted.

Open: Apr to Oct, daily, 12.30 to 2.30, 7 to 9.30.

NEWARK   Nottinghamshire   MAP 6
Gannets, 35 Castlegate   TEL Newark (0636) 702066·

Customers commend the good quality, interesting home cooked food and wonderful pastry. Hilary Bower's restaurant is a hobby-turned-business so there is nothing cynical about her attitude to prices, mark-ups and profit margins. A lot of 20th century life has by-passed the town and hers is one of the many surviving listed Georgian buildings, saved in the nick of time when decay threatened to overwhelm them entirely. Inside, it is aesthetically pleasing with lots of pine and a cork tiled floor. Hilary Bower bridges the needs of most food interests. The homemade soups are both vegetable and meat based. There are pasta and beef bakes, lamb's liver casseroles and also vegetable casseroles, lasagne, mixed green salads as well as brown rice and coleslaw on offer. Indulgent puddings include strawberry pavlova, chocolate roulade, sherry trifle and a more unusual ginger, orange and caramel trifle. Fresh fruit crumble is made with wholemeal flour and there's a beautifully moist carrot cake.

Wholemeal bread; fresh fruits at table; minimal salt and sugar (raw); skimmed milk. Wholefood, vegetarian. Seats 38—more on the patio in summer. Meals from £4. House wine £4.25.

Open: Mon to Sat, 10 to 4.30.

NEWCASTLE-UPON-TYNE   Tyne and Wear   MAP 6
The Super Natural, 2 Princess Square   TEL Newcastle-upon-Tyne (0632) 612730

The airy, clean self-service restaurant and wine bar offer some reasonably-priced wholesome foods, with appeal for various dietary needs including vegan and orthodox Jewish needs. Stewart Read makes no claim to be a health food establishment—he sells fresh double cream, for example. However, like most vegetarian restaurants the menu holds attractions for slimmers and anyone averse to adulterated or chemically treated foods. A typical day's menu is likely to include lentil and sweetcorn soups, cauliflower Provençale, pan hagerty and aubergine in a cheese and tomato sauce. Pizzas have a wholemeal base and the pasta a savoury sauce. As many as twelve salads are usually on offer and there are simple things like boiled eggs—free range—for a late breakfast. For puddings, there's pumpkin and sultana pie, fruit salads, fools and gâteaux. Snacks are available throughout the day.

Free range eggs; wholemeal bread; polyunsaturates at table; minimal salt and sugar; animal rennet free cheeses; wholemeal flour in baking. Wholefood, vegetarian, vegan. Seats 100. Meals from £3.60. House wine £3.

Open: Mon to Sat, 9.30 to 10.30.

NEWENT   Gloucestershire   MAP 2
Soutters, 1 Culver Street   TEL Newent (0531) 820896

In spring a good many people come into the district to see the true wild daffodil growing in profusion. A few stay on to sample the cooking at Fred and Paula Soutter's comfortable old cottage, which is scarcely any younger than the notable 16th century market hall nearby. The style is French, the food all fresh and nearly all homemade. All the bread, ice cream, sorbets and sweets are the Soutters' own. Wherever possible the lamb is Scotch; beef and game is English and the vegetables fresh and delivered by local growers. Starters of interest are sautéed mushrooms with a spicy tomato sauce; vine leaves filled with courgettes, celery, peppers, herbs, almonds and olives. The mousse is sometimes made of smoked salmon. A speciality, walnut supreme, is a superior and tasty nut roast, grilled with a sauce topping. Venison steak is split and filled with chicken livers, then wrapped in lean bacon. The puff pastry savoury is basically mushrooms, onion and soya mince with herbs and wine. Poultry could well be duck; fish, Cornish crawfish. A second vegetarian dish, town house pie, includes mushrooms and wine, making it a cut above the average vegetable casserole. Homemade sorbets and honey sweetened ice creams available.

Non-battery eggs; wholewheat flour; honey and molasses in place of white sugar; wholemeal bread; polyunsaturates in cooking; fresh fruits at table. Wholefood, vegetarian, special diets by arrangement. Seats 18. Meals from £9. House wine £4.35. American Express/Diners' Club.

Open: Mon to Sat, 7.30 to 9.30.

NEWPORT Dyfed MAP 2
Cnapan, East Street TEL Newport (Dyfed) (0239) 820575

The demure Georgian village house on East Street takes overnight guests too. Eluned Lloyd is new to East Street but before coming to Cnapan she had already established an enviable reputation for herself in a wholefood cottage restaurant not far away. Devoted locals and holidaymakers still support her here. During the season there is a daily wholefood lunch, using organically-grown raw vegetables in imaginative salads. A student of John Seymour living near by has been persuaded to grow the vegetables. Free range eggs are supplied locally. Oats are a favourite base for courgette and nut bakes, the fluffy fisherman's pie, humble pie (sausage, apple, mince and sage) and spinach and cottage cheese. Smoked mackerel gets the now familiar gooseberry sauce. More elaborate dinner menus bring steaks, chicken breasts with a curry sauce, herby pancakes with broccoli, Greek herbs, cashews and a cheese sauce. Fresh salmon and crab have appropriate dressings. To follow there is squidgy chocolate roll and apricot and ginger cream.

Organically-grown vegetables; skimmed milk used in yoghurts; free range eggs; wholemeal bread; polyunsaturates in cooking and at table; fresh fruits at table; minimal salt and sugar; skimmed milk; freshly squeezed fruit juices. Wholefood, vegetarian, some vegan dishes. Seats 35. Meals from £8 dinner, £5 lunch. House wine £4.85. Access.

Open: Easter to end of Oct, daily, except Tue, 10.30 to 5, 7.30 to 9. Winter Fri evenings, all day Sat and Sun lunch.

NEW SCONE Perthshire MAP 7
Balcraig House, New Scone TEL New Scone (0738) 51123

Luxurious self-sufficiency is the order of the day at Michael and Kitty Pearl's well-appointed Victorian country house in some fine Perthshire countryside. Apart from their farm there are ten acres of surrounding gardens and, for the mildly active, gentle walks to the folly on the hill at the back. Even without the food there are creature comforts in the fine antique furniture, pictures, richly patterned oriental rugs, relaxation on the terrace or activity on the tennis court. But most remarkable of all is the astonishing amount of food which Mr. and Mrs. Pearl manage to produce themselves from their 130 acres. They don't stop at a few grazing bullocks; something like sixty different kinds of herbs alone are grown. The cooking does not slavishly follow any particular school. The priority is to make good use of their own, or wild, rather than bought-in produce. So expect seasonal variations—fungi in the autumn and fresh peas in the summer months. None of the vegetables are frozen. The kitchen is never idle: pâtés, ice cream, wholemeal bread, rolls, pastry and sweetmeats are all made there. A light style of cooking has evolved, easy on the salt and on cream. Grilling, roasting, steaming and stir frying are favoured, rather than frying with fat. A favourite dish is sliced breast of duck grilled for a few minutes at high temperature, then served on a bed of green salad. Baked stuffed field mushrooms are done with a farce of onions, herbs and breadcrumbs and baked in a white Galloway cheese sauce. Local hare is pot roasted; estate pheasant comes with kumquats and game gravy. Puddings may be junket and Southern Comfort; shortbread boxes filled with walnut, fig and amaretto cream; sweet rum and pineapple omelette. For breakfasts there are Arbroath smokies. Vegetarian dishes are not regular main course features, but it would scarcely mean improvisation to have the choux pastry starter, filled with mushrooms and pine kernels in a tomato and fennel sauce.

Largely home-grown fruit and vegetables; own honey; free range chickens and eggs; own Aberdeen Angus cattle fed a natural diet and hung four weeks; own lamb; own goats' milk and kid; veal calves reared humanely; own bacon and pork; homemade wholemeal bread; wild brown trout from local lochs; minimal salt and sugar; fresh fruits at table. Wholefood, vegetarian main dishes on request. Seats 36. Meals from £16. House wine £6.25. Access/Visa/American Express/Diners' Club.

Open: hotel, all day; dinner, 7 to 11, Sun, 7 to 10.

NORWICH   Norfolk MAP 3
Britons Arms, Elm Hill

The Civic Trust put Elm Hill on the national map a good many years ago when they did their first historic street restoration scheme. Distinctive pretty pastels, hallmarks of much of their work, have gone, but the spirit of taking care persists. The Britons Arms, a former pub, is a marvellous example of thoughtful restoration with old elm benches and tables. The regular menu includes sandwiches with fish and meat. Dishes of the day are usually entirely vegetarian; a pasta, leek and lentil casserole with crusty dumplings has had much appeal, as does the sweetcorn and cheese salad and baked potatoes with a cream cheese filling. Sweets include a lovely light orange flavoured sponge with orange icing and cream.

Wholemeal bread; minimal salt and sugar. Wholefood, vegetarian. Seats 28. Meals from £4.

Open: Mon to Sat, 10 to 5.

NORWICH   Norfolk MAP 3
Café at Premises, Reeves Yard, St. Benedict's Street   TEL Norwich (0603) 660352

The one-time church hall is now a lively co-operative meeting place, sometimes with banjo accompaniment. There's extra seating in the gallery above, beneath which is the kitchen. Locals come for their inexpensive midday meals which can vary in style and quality according to who is on duty. Main dishes might be a spicy parsnip and sweetcorn pie or spaghetti bake, preceded by tomato, lentil and leek soup. There are simple snacks like wholemeal cheese and salad rolls. Cakes and pastries include some sugar-free, a fruit flan and cider apple cake. Organic ingredients as available.

Organically grown vegetables when available; free range eggs; wholemeal bread; polyunsaturates in cooking and at table; minimal salt and sugar. Wholefood, vegetarian, vegan. Seats 50. Meals from £4, dishes from £1.40.

Open: Mon to Sat, 12 to 5.30; also Thur to Sat, 7 to 10.

NORWICH Norfolk MAP 3
Sasses, 2 Thorpe Road   TEL Norwich (0603) 622424

Any lingering doubts about the usefulness of the close relationship with British Rail Thorpe Station can be allayed: the chance to park on their car park across the road is not one to be missed. Willum Middlemiss and Duncan Wells have taken a pair of substantial '20s pseudo Tudor houses and decorated them '30's style, down to radios and gramophones. Music is Fats Waller. Easy, pleasant and unpretentious, they offer innovative, well-prepared food using good ingredients. They also attract attention for their vegetarian section, usually two main dishes any day. Ripe juicy melon is a good foundation for the melon, orange and port starter. Smoked fish and prawn mousse is (as one would hope) a delicate affair and baked mushrooms, in season, are the field kind. Steaks they will do with pleasure but the menu is interesting for roast guinea fowl, the chicken cooked with bacon and olives and finished with brandy. An escalope of turkey is wrapped in a pancake and topped with Gruyère cheese. Aubergine and pepper bake is quite sumptuous; the mushroom and garlic stuffed pancakes close contenders. Beware: vegetables and baked potatoes come swimming in butter unless discussed beforehand. Fresh wholemeal bread has a fine nutty flavour. Desserts err towards extravagance but there is fresh pineapple and kirsch, sorbets and a rum and chocolate torte. The chef will gladly cook dishes from former menus where possible.

Wholemeal bread; fresh fruits at table; freshly squeezed fruit juices. Wholefood, vegetarian, vegan dishes on request. Seats 70. Meals from £7. House wine £4.85. Access/Visa/American Express.

Open: Sun to Sat, 6.30 to 11.30.

NORWICH   Norfolk   MAP 3
The Waffle House, 39 St. Giles Street   TEL Norwich (0603) 612790

This is best located by seeking British Telecom's surprisingly elaborate rococo confection next door. In the simpler accommodation offered by this old Georgian house, waffles—wholemeal, if wished—and their accompaniments beguile just as much. Of particular interest are the fresh fruit sauces and the wholesome minor dishes.

Seats 42. Waffles from £1.35.

Open: Mon to Sat, 11 to 10.

NOTTINGHAM   Nottinghamshire   MAP 6
Ben Bowers, 128 Derby Road   TEL Nottingham (0602) 413388

Having weathered the recession, Tony Suthers and Tom Glancz are pushing ahead with plans to refurnish the restaurant, keeping the rustic olde worlde decoration. The place has taken a good deal of wear and tear with the large throughput of diners drawn by quality and modest prices. There is also the matter of the special effort only to use fresh foods cooked to order, except for soups and dishes which benefit from slow cooking. There is free adaptation of any European dish which includes two puff pastry bouchées filled with chicken livers in a Madeira sauce; smoked trout paté; hot garlic bread with prawns; barbecued chicken wings, and melon and paw paw cocktail, just some of the choices faced after gentle launches with the homemade soup and fruit juice options. In the brief calm before the main event, lemon sorbets, seafood shells and trout fillets are served. Ben's original steak and mushroom pie is done in a brown ale gravy. The Bavarian beef escalopes are served in a sauce of chopped bacon, mushrooms and Madeira sauce. The vegetarian platter is put together with a piece of quiche or a nutburger and a Provence sauce added. Then there are pears poached in ginger wine with lemon cream; apple and pear pie with cinnamon and brown sugar, and a cheeseboard with a selection of fruit and veg.

Wholemeal bread; polyunsaturates in cooking and at table; fresh fruits at table; freshly squeezed fruit and vegetable juices. Wholefood, vegetarian, vegan on request. Seats 50. Meals from £6.60. House wine £4.50. Access/Barclaycard/Diners' Club/Amexco.

Open: Mon to Fri, 12 to 2, 7 to 10.30; Sat, 7 to 11.

NUNEATON   Warwickshire   MAP 3
Drachenfels, 25 Attleborough Road   TEL Nuneaton (0203) 383030

Doreen Ryder can offer rooms as well at her largely vegetarian restaurant which is conveniently placed for the M6 and M69. A German nobleman, during a brief sojourn at the turn of the century, built the distinctive house with the turret. Mrs. Ryder provides steak, chops, gammon, fish and scampi for residents, then later in the evening wholefood vegetarian dishes for other diners, when no animal fat or produce is used. Most of her tasty interesting food is prepared even without dairy produce but responding to popular vegetarian demand, sweets tend to be rich, sticky creamy affairs. Wherever possible, sauces are served separately for those who prefer to go without. Mousses and dips are popular starters. Main dishes may be vegetable paella, cauliflower crisp, and pastas.

Wholemeal bread; polyunsaturates in kitchen and at table; fresh fruits at table; minimal salt and sugar; skimmed milk available; freshly squeezed fruit and vegetable juices; organic vegetable supplies being sought. Wholefood, vegetarian, vegan, other diets at short notice. Seats 24. Meals from £5. House wine £4.95 litre.

Open: Thur, Fri, Sat, 7 to 10.

OLDBURY   Hereford and Worcester   MAP 3
Jonathan's, 16 Wolverhampton Road   TEL Oldbury (021 429) 3757

This restaurant occupies a large chunk of a shopping parade, the interior revamped as
a warren of individually furnished rooms, some for eating, some just for drinks and
relaxation. Out at the back a spacious imaginatively laid out courtyard is dedicated to
Campari. Calorie counts are taken seriously, and Monday to Friday a three-course meal, as
good as a feast, is down to 1,200 calories. There are more takers for five-course Victorian
country house dinners (Saturday evenings only). Ham and turkey Cecils are sturdy
sausages of roughly minced turkey and ham blended with breadcrumbs (only a few they
claim), herbs, sage, and thyme, bound with egg and fried. Equally substantial, Dublin
casserole, solid beef steeped in Guinness and finished with prunes. Jane Grigson is given
credit for chicken cullis, jointed and boned and stuffed with ham mousse. Fish may be
poached salmon; starters include Russian salad, soup, fricassée of mushrooms and either a
chicken or mackerel pâté. For clients preferring not to eat meat, Winnett pie is in practice
a vegetable casserole. Pickles and preserves are in-house and available as take-away.

Homemade wholemeal herb bread; fresh fruits at table; minimal salt and sugar; freshly squeezed
fruit juices. Wholefood, vegetarian. Seats 100. Meals from £7.40 lunch, £14 dinner. House
wine £5.20. Barclaycard/Access/Diners' Club/American Express.

Open: Sun to Sat, 12 to 2, 7 to 10; closed Sat pm.

ONICH   Highland   MAP 7
Creagdhu, Onich, Nr Fort William   TEL Onich (085 53) 238

The splendid mountain view is of Garbh Bheinn, 2,903 feet. This elegant hotel dining-
room (there are twenty rooms for residents) overlooks Loch Linnhe and dispenses local
salmon, trout and venison. There are fresh herbs and some of the vegetables are grown in
the garden by Norman and Jessie Young. Each night they put on a vegetarian main course
dish which might be a substantial nut roast, a walnut and rice loaf or one of the several
casseroles in their repertoire. There is always a selection of salads, and there might well be
goulash with rice. Pastas come with particularly good sauces. There is heavy reliance on
cream in the puddings, so you may be driven to seeking the fruit salad and adding one of
their homemade yoghurts.

Organically grown vegetables; homemade wholemeal bread; polyunsaturates in cooking and at
table; fresh fruits at table; minimal salt and sugar; freshly squeezed fruit juices. Wholefood,
vegetarian, other dietary needs readily met. Seats 50. Meals from £5 lunches. House wine £5.20.
Visa/Access/American Express.

Open: daily, 8 to 9; closed Nov to Mar.

OSWESTRY   Salop   MAP 6
Good Companion, 10 Beatrice Street   TEL Oswestry (0691) 655768

Mr. and Mrs. Hickman do several interesting dishes in their popular wine bar cum
restaurant. The kofta kebabs are served in pitta bread with salad and yoghurt. Seafood
lasagne and crêpes with sweet praline and maple syrup and savoury fillings are frequently
demanded. Mr. and Mrs. Hickman make everything themselves, seasoning dishes
whenever possible with herbs, preparing light sauces using skimmed milk and polyunsaturated fats. Steaks, spare ribs and chilli con carne are all on offer. Then there is the
vegetable savoury, a quiche, or starters like homemade soups (usually two going at any
one time), hummus dips and the country pâté is served with French bread. Sweets include
fresh fruit pavlova, fudgy banana pie, ice cream, chocolate nut crunchy cake, or there's a
vegetable savoury.

Free range eggs; some organically grown vegetables; wholemeal bread; polyunsaturates in cooking
and at table; minimal salt and sugar; freshly squeezed fruit juices. Wholefood, vegetarian,

macrobiotic, gluten-free on request. Seats 35. Meals from £4.75, dishes from £1.40. House wine £3.50.

Open: Tue to Sat, 12 to 3, 7.30 to 11.30; closed first 2 weeks Jan.

OTLEY   Yorkshire   MAP 6
Pool Court, Pool-in-Wharfedale   TEL Pool-in-Wharfedale (0532) 842288

Michael Gill's restaurant in the Georgian country house, with rooms, offers abundant comfort. His four-course meals interestingly start off with a samosa, the filling minced meats and curry sauce. A salad is offered with roast hare; Morecambe mussels with garlic bread. Salmon is set in a clear jelly, with red and green peppers and herbs. Cream of fennel soup could be to follow, or grapefruit sorbet or consommé of beef. Dishes of the night could be fresh fish—from the coast daily—a charcoal tournedos, or the breast of chicken with two sauces—the wine in which it was poached and an onion one added. Medaillons of venison come with wild rice and field mushrooms. An alternative available to diners is pineapple gratin—the centre scooped, filled with a nut mixture, diced pineapple, peaches and figs, sprinkled with cheese and baked. Field beans and parsnips are casseroled in cider and stock, flavoured with tomato purée and seasoned. Desserts include amaretti soufflé (the soufflé topped with amaretti liqueur and crushed amaretti biscuits), pears in Chablis and Bavarian nut pudding (a steamed chocolate nut mixture). In season, fruits on the platter have included kiwi and pineapple.

Free range eggs; local duck; fresh fruits at table; freshly squeezed fruit juices; minimal salt and sugar. Wholefood, vegetarian, vegan, other diets by request. Seats 65. Meals from £18. Fixed price menu £11. House wine £6.45. Visa/Access/American Express/Diners' Club.

Open: Tue to Sat, 6.30 to 9.30; closed 2 weeks July/Aug and 2 weeks Christmas.

OXFORD   Oxfordshire   MAP 3
Brown's, 7 Woodstock Road   TEL Oxford (0865) 511995

Brown's is designed to be reminiscent of Charleston in the twenties, all good clean fun, bentwood chairs and board floors, so there is the best possible resonance for every noise. Veterans enthuse over Mrs. Brown's vegetarian salad—fantastic and marvellous value, as are all the dishes. Choice for first course is limited to small pasta dishes or soup. Then there are chargrilled steaks, roast ribs with barbecue sauce or a big salad—avocado, bacon and spinach, and bacon can be omitted on request. Brown's make a banana cream pie, apple and pear pies, and scones which are served mornings and afternoons, but not the dark chocolate cake. Disappointingly the bread is not wholemeal.

Fresh fruits at table; minimal salt and sugar. Wholefood, vegetarian. Seats 200. Meals from £6.50. House wine £4.25.

Open: Mon to Sat, 11 to 11.30; Sun, 12 to 11.30.

OXFORD   Oxfordshire   MAP 3
Holland and Barrett, King Edward Street

This is a one-off for the two hundred-strong chain of health food shops and particularly good value. The stairs in and out are narrow and there's little room for knees under tables but good honest fare, at modest prices is on offer. There are salads in great variety, bean casseroles, lasagne, stuffed courgettes and good soups. Cakes are bought in but are of high quality. There are tea, coffee and wholemeal scones available in the mornings and afternoons, and good bread, samosas and vegetable pasties to take away, in the shop.

Seats 40. Meals from £4, dishes from £1.40.

Open: Mon to Sat, 9.30 to 4.30.

OXFORD   Oxfordshire   MAP 3
St. Aldate's Church Coffee House, 94 St. Aldate's   TEL Oxford (0865) 245952

Tourists, students and shoppers find their way to this friendly atmosphere, handy for the
Westgate Shopping Centre. Sensible down-to-earth baking is of the banana bread, date
and walnut loaf, Guinness cake sort. By midday chicken curry, beef stroganoff and chilli
con carne are on the go. Quiches have a vegetable filling. Baked potatoes have sour
cream, cheese and pickles, or homemade tomato relish fillings. Start with corn chowder,
carrot and lemon, or tomato and rosemary soup. Then there are lentil and walnut loaf,
cheesy vegetable pie, and bean stews. To follow, choose between apple charlotte, fruit
crumble served with custard, fruit salad, trifle and yoghurt whip.

*Wholemeal bread; fresh fruits at table; minimal salt. Wholefood, vegetarian. Seats 50. Lunch
from £2.75.*

Open: Mon to Sat, 10 to 5.

PENRITH   Cumbria   MAP 6
Bluebell Bookshop, Three Crowns Yard   TEL Penrith (0768) 66660

At one time this comfortable little bookshop served lunches, but now to the regret of
many, only coffee, tea and cakes, the last using wholemeal flour and the best of other
ingredients. Coffee—particularly good—is from Mr. Higgins in Bond Street. With
advance notice, Pauline and Derek Robinson will prepare cakes and biscuits for special
diets, and all are acceptable to vegetarians. Grain coffee and coffee blends are sold in the
shop. Children's books are a speciality.

*Free range eggs in baking; home grown organic apples; Aspalls organic apple juice;
polyunsaturates in cooking; minimal salt and sugar. Wholefood. Seats 8. Another 8 outside in
summer. Coffee and teas only.*

Open: Mon to Sat, 9.30 to 4.30.

PENZANCE   Cornwall   MAP 2
Olive Branch, 3A The Terrace, Market Jew Street   TEL Penzance (0736) 2438

Patricia and Stanley Mellor use only wholefood ingredients for their varied and
inexpensive dishes. Their son does the cooking, Patricia Mellor the cakes. Meals begin
with homemade soup or egg mayonnaise. Regular hot meals are beefburgers with
barbecue sauce, parsnip and cashew nut patties, cauliflower cheese bake, and perhaps
celery egg and cheese casserole. There are salads, brown rice and potatoes as you like
them, including chips. There are daily specials for which locals and regulars keep watch,
and always omelettes, simple salads, sandwiches. For afters, the chocolate mould is
starch-free, otherwise there is spiced banana, banana split, fruit salad or cakes: oat slice,
farmhouse fruit, chocolate gâteaux, carrot and honey cake.

*Wholemeal bread; polyunsaturates in cooking and at table; minimal salt and sugar. Wholefood,
vegetarian, vegan. Seats 88. Meals from £3.75.*

Open: Mon to Sat, 10.30 to 2.30, 5 to 7.

PERTH   Tayside   MAP 7
Timothy's, 24 St. John Street   TEL Perth (0738) 26641

There's wholemeal flour in the pastry but wholemeal bread has yet to be fully accepted.
This apart, there is quite a jolly atmosphere in the family-owned and run restaurant. The
family are health food fanatics. Only fresh local produce is used: vegetables, raspberries
and apples from the garden—as well as the nettles for the soup. Snitters (Danish for
appetisers) might be sweet herring (with lemon and onion rings), the Vets Night snack

(Danish salami with potato salad and sweet pickle). Double M (mussels and mackerel), or homemade cheese and ham pâté. The more substantial smorgasbord runs to Norseman's Choice (the super prawn cocktail), roast beef, roaming Dane (home-cooked ham with the Laing's own curried banana concoction) and a dozen more of this style. There is uncertainty about what part beef Madras had to play in Viking life. Salads include a Bombay version—banana, nuts and curry. Also on offer: cold platters, Tay salmon and sea trout. A health food platter is based on rice, cheese, egg and tomato, and lots more. Mayonnaise is homemade; sultana tart is to a Swedish recipe.

Wholemeal baking; sometimes wholemeal bread; fresh fruits at table; minimal salt and sugar. Wholefood, vegetarian, other diets attempted. Seats 50. Meals from £4.50, dishes from £2.20. House wine £5.30. Access/Visa.

Open: Tue to Sat, 10 to 11.30, 12 to 2.30, 7 to 10.15; closed 3 weeks from mid-July.

POLPERRO Cornwall   MAP 2
Kitchen at Polperro, Fishnabridge   TEL Polperro (0503) 72780

Fresh food is important to husband and wife team, Judith and David Porter, in the small cottage dining-room where they prefer to do fixed price meals. Vegetarian food is always on offer, though vegan dishes pose more problems. Everything is made in the kitchen, the vegetables are always fresh and the bread home-baked. The short set menu might include lamb korna, a grilled sea trout and venison in red wine. The beef might be Provençale or a fillet steamed in a port cream and rosemary sauce. Down by the sea, there's less fish than one might expect, but there are crab fritters for starters or prawns in an avocado. Otherwise smoked pork sausages, or a soup—tomato and mint, and cream of Stilton. A regular vegetarian menu offers hazelnut and cashew savoury, cheese and millet croquettes, vegetable and hazelnut rissoles. The tourists' supper is good value and has some of the vegetarian options. Early in the evening something special for children is available.

Wholemeal bread; freshly squeezed fruit juices; polyunsaturates at table; fresh fruits at table; minimal salt. Wholefood, vegetarian, sometimes vegan. Seats 22. Meals from £7.50. House wine £4.90. Access/Diners' Club/Visa/American Express.

Open: summer from 6.30, otherwise from 7, except Fri and Sat, Christmas and New Year. Mid Mar to mid Nov, Tue to Sun, from 6.30. Winter, Fri, Sat and Christmas from 7.

RICHMOND Surrey   MAP 4
Mrs. Beeton's, 58 Hill Rise   TEL Richmond 01-940 9561

Mrs. Collie's friendly restaurant is unusual in that a group of housewives do the cooking on a rota. Much depends on the individual cook's inclination so consistent standards are not always maintained. Menus too vary from day to day but one can rely on the freshness of the ingredients. Starters could be mushroom and watercress pâté, well-flavoured soups and spinach tarts. To follow, lamb à la Grecque, beef Provençale and moussaka with fruit salads, orange mousse and fruit flans to finish.

Wholemeal bread; freshly squeezed fruit and vegetable juices; fresh fruits at table; polyunsaturates at table. Wholefood, vegetarian. Seats 30. Meals from £5. Bring your own wine. No corkage.

Open: Sun to Sat, 10 to 5, Tue to Sat, 8.30 to 10.30.

RICHMOND Surrey   MAP 4
The Refectory, 6 Church Walk   TEL Richmond 01-940 6264

Mary Kingsley delights in bringing to The Refectory her love of traditional British cookery. History is hazy about the origins of the place but buildings were shown on the site in a Prospect of Richmond dated 1726. Everything is cooked on the premises always

using fresh ingredients. Seafood flan, crab mousse and brandied chicken livers have
proved popular first courses. Cidered pork is served with apple and cheese sauce, veal is
cooked with lemon, the beef jugged and the chicken done with honey and orange.
Vegetables have included sweet and sour red cabbage, brown rice and nuts. There are
puddings like plum compote, Bakewell tart, ginger crumble cakes, cinnamon cheesecake,
Boodle's orange fool—or a prune version. Lunchtimes offer chicken and mushroom pie,
spiced lamb and apricot, Shropshire fidget pie, cheese-topped cottage pie. There are salads
according to season, and English-grown wines from Lamberhurst, Bruisyard and Pulham.

Wholemeal bread; polyunsaturates in cooking; minimal salt; freshly squeezed fruit juices;
polyunsaturates at table. Wholefood, vegetarian, other preferences if advised on booking. Seats 50.
Meals from £9, dishes from £2.50. House wine £5.15.

Open: Tue to Sun, 10 to 3; Thur to Sat, 7.30 to 8.45.

ROSS-ON-WYE   Hereford and Worcester   MAP 2
Meader's, 1 Copse Cross Street   TEL Ross-on-Wye (0989) 62803

Prices are amongst the most modest at Ann and David Reece's cottage in a side street.
During the day there's a simple self-service system and salads are a speciality. There are
always at least ten from which to choose and a main dish of the nut roast kind. In addition
there are quiches and pizzas. At the end of the day, set price three-course meals are based
on grills of gammon, steak and fried fish. Specialities are beef bourguignon, chicken
breasts stuffed with prawns and lobster, lemon sole in a prawn and mushroom sauce.
Simple starters include soup or prawn cocktail. Vegetable and nut roasts meet vegan
standards, and there's brandy fudge cake to follow. Throughout the day homemade
scones, coffee and tea are on offer.

Wholemeal bread; polyunsaturates in kitchen and at table; fresh fruits at table; minimal salt
and sugar; skimmed milk available; non-battery eggs. Wholefood, vegetarian, vegan, diabetic.
Seats 45. Meals from £6, vegetarian from £5. House wine £4.25 litre.

Open: Mon to Sat, 9 to 3, 7 to 10; winter, Mon to Wed, 9 to 3 only.

RUSHDEN   Northamptonshire   MAP 3
The Coffee Tavern, Coffee Tavern Lane   TEL Rushden (0933) 317644

Local enthusiasts commend John Walker for good, wholesome homemade fare. Meeting
popular demand means that prawn cocktail is on order for Friday and Saturday dinners,
but at other times there is reliance on the Cranks cookery book including walnut roast
with mushroom sauce. Other customers stand by his homemade soups, available also with
the simpler lunchtime menu. When not offering the Crécy pie (carrots, onions and herbs in
a pastry case) John Walker varies the mix of nuts and herbs for his nut cutlets. Puddings
are gâteaux, ice creams and pies, the last two homemade like the bread. Coffees, teas and
scones are on offer during mornings and afternoons.

Homemade wholemeal bread; freshly squeezed fruit juices. Wholefood, vegetarian. Seats 53.
Meals from £6.50. House wine £5.10 litre.

Open: Mon to Sat, 9 to 4.30; Sun, 12 to 2.

ST. ANDREWS   Fife ☆   MAP 7
Brambles, 5 College Street   TEL St. Andrews (0334) 75380

After teaching the merits of good diet for years in school, it is a joy for Jean Hamilton to
put theory into practice. 1983 was the real test, when she catered for the McCarrison
Society Conference. The budget-conscious start lunch with lentil, cinnamon and tomato
soup (or perhaps the carrot, apple and cashew version). Mustard rabbit is served with
brown rice; mushroom and leek croustade is probably accompanied by one of the salads

and a baked potato. And there is hummus and oatcake. Fresh herbs are homegrown. Frequently, vegetables are puréed for saucing Jerusalem chicken, using Jerusalem artichokes and mushrooms. Wholemeal rolls have egg and alfalfa, or cheese, peanut and apple fillings. Bramble and apple tart, fresh fruit salad, coffee and hazelnut gâteaux are good value, while banana cheesecake costs slightly more. Scottish organic wine is from Moniack Castle and it is difficult to get customers to drink anything else, though Silver Birch, Meadowsweet (collected on Skye) and elderflower wines enjoy popularity too. Regular customers with food allergies telephone beforehand to find what's on the menu.

Organically grown vegetables when available; free range eggs; wholemeal bread; polyunsaturates in cooking and at table; fresh fruits at table; minimal salt and sugar; freshly squeezed fruit juices. Wholefood, vegetarian, vegan, other diets with notice. Seats 38. Meals from £3. House wine 75p per glass.

Open: Tue to Sat, 10 to 4.30; closed for 2 weeks Sept and 2 weeks Jan.

SALISBURY   Wiltshire   MAP 3
Michael Snell, 8 St. Thomas's Square   TEL Salisbury (0722) 336037

There's emphasis on Swiss type pastries, homemade chocolates, and ice cream, tea and coffee. At lunchtimes there are salads with the choice of mushroom flan, pizzas, quiche of several kinds, and baked potato. Country lunches consist of English cheddar, pickles and an apple. Coffee is roasted on the premises.

Wholemeal bread; minimal salt and sugar; fresh local produce whenever available. Vegetarian. Seats 120. Meals from £4.50.

Open: Mon to Fri, 9 to 5.30, Sat, 8.30 to 5.30.

SCARBOROUGH   North Yorkshire   MAP 6
Sarah Brown's, 13 Victoria Road   TEL Scarborough (0723) 360054

An encounter with committee members of the Vegetarian Society was the start of Sarah Brown's road to fame, quickly discovered by the media after becoming the Society's cookery demonstrator. Somewhat surprisingly 90 % of the customers are non-vegetarian. But so far, fame has not had a slight influence on prices. A small pizza starts at 50p. Other lunchtime fare will be a savoury flan and Sarah's special spinach and cottage cheese lasagne. There are always several salads, baked potatoes, a hot pudding and fruit salad. The evening menu includes a delicate mint and cucumber soup; chestnut and wine pâté in celery boats; stuffed tomatoes with a filling of egg, mushroom and artichoke; and fresh melon boats. Main dishes include wholewheat pancakes with a herbed cheese filling and either a tomato or parsley sauce. Sarah Brown's almond croustade has a light cheese and nut base, is baked with a vegetable sauce and has more cheese for topping. The ice cream, like everything here, is homemade, and there's rum and raisin and chocolate mint chip flavourings. Hot puddings could be prune and ginger, banana and walnut with cream or a yoghurt and honey sauce. Carrot and cinnamon, apricot and coconut or tassajara cakes are just some from a selection of a dozen or so.

Organically grown fruit and vegetables; free range eggs; animal rennet free cheeses; sugar free cakes and preserves; wholemeal bread; polyunsaturates in cooking and at table; minimal salt and sugar; freshly squeezed fruit and vegetable juices; wholemeal pastry. Vegetarian wholefood, vegan, gluten-free with notice. Seats 32. Meals from £4.25. Wine 65p per glass.

Open: Mon to Sat, 10.30 to 4.30; closes Wed at 2, Thur to Sat from 7.30.

SHANAGARRY   County Cork   NO MAP
Ballymaloe House, Shanagarry   TEL Shanagarry (021) 652531

Homely country house style rather than smart meals, are served in two dining-rooms.

Locally caught fish, meat and poultry from the 400 acre farm are the foundations for dishes such as Mrs. Allen's popular French peasant soup, which regularly puts in appearances. The traditional salad is enhanced by the Shanagarry cream dressing, and there's grape, grapefruit and mint cocktail. Mrs. Allen provides oysters in champagne sauce, plaice stuffed with lobster and little pots of fish pâtés, baked bass served in a spinach butter sauce; salmon with hollandaise or, from the day's catch, hot buttered lobster. Ashore the farm produces roast pork, stuffed loin, steak au poivre. Chicken is served in a very traditional style with bacon, homemade sausages and bread sauce. Always available are soups using vegetable stock, Ballymaloe cheese fondue, spaghetti with herbs and garlic, cheese soufflé, or soft boiled eggs and a little hollandaise sauce. More notice will produce ratatouille, cheese turnovers, stuffed mushrooms, and nut rissoles. Desserts never disappoint and include mousses and trifles, with homegrown fruit.

Free range eggs and chickens; wholemeal bread; freshly squeezed fruit and vegetable juices. Wholefood, vegetarian, other diets on request. Seats 80. Meals from £16.50 dinner. House wine £8.50. Diners' Club/American Express/Access/Visa.

Open: daily, 1 to 2, 7 to 9.30.

SHEFFIELD   South Yorkshire   Map 6
Crucible Theatre Coffee Shop, Norfolk Street
TEL Sheffield (0742) 760621, Ext. 258

There is pride here in simple freshly prepared soups, salads and pastries using lots of fresh vegetables. Salads are mixed bean; cauliflower, peach and walnut; pineapple, cottage cheese and prawn; cream cheese and tuna. Soups include mushroom with red kidney bean, French onion and vegetable. Wholemeal garlic and herb bread, and quiches are served. Wholemeal mincemeat or date slices and chocolate mousse gâteaux provide the sweet.

Wholemeal bread; fresh fruits at table; polyunsaturates in cooking. Wholefood, vegetarian. Seats 70. Meals from £3.50.

Open: Mon to Sat, 10 to 6; closed 2 weeks Aug.

SHREWSBURY   Salop   Map 6
Delany's, St. Julian's Craft Centre, St. Alkmond's Square
TEL Shrewsbury (0743) 60602

Diners rate this well for the varied fare—the menu is changed daily. Others like the cosy relaxing atmosphere. Onion and toasted sunflower seed have been used for soup and there is a mulligatawny version too. Salads are regular features. Hot dishes of the day could be cauliflower paprikash bake or vegetable shepherd's pie. Vegan needs are recognised by a vegetable and macaroni casserole, and bean and tofu burgers. Sweets are limited to cakes; chocolate and orange, ginger and banana, apple and brazil nut, or almond shortbread. Sometimes there's Bakewell tart, and honey and yoghurt puddings.

Organically grown vegetables as available; free range eggs; wholemeal flour in baking; wholemeal bread; polyunsaturates in cooking and at table; fresh fruits at table; freshly squeezed fruit and vegetable juices. Wholefood, vegetarian, vegan. Seats 32. Meals from £4.

Open: Mon to Sat, 10.30 to 3.30, and every other Sat evening.

SILEBY   Leicestershire   Map 3
The Old School, 7 Barrow Road   TEL Sileby (050 981) 3941

The old village school has been pleasantly converted and as Jackie Fleet, the owner, would say none of their dishes will drive you into bankruptcy. Jackie does all the cooking herself. Menus change according to seasonal availability and naturally all the food is fresh. The ideas are simple; the approach enthusiastic. Homemade chicken and liver pâté, citrus fruit mixes, prawn and apple and a creamy vegetable soup make up the evening starters. There is poached salmon or a steak with a chasseur sauce to follow. Poultry may be supreme of chicken, game a casseroled pheasant. Puddings vary between lavishly rich chocolate gâteaux and lighter lemon mousse. For something quick and inexpensive, try the sister restaurant, Bunters, in the village, with pizzas and salad, coleslaw, or a baked potato, homemade soups and scones.

Wholemeal bread; fresh fruits at table; minimal salt and sugar; local vegetables; non-battery eggs; freshly squeezed fruit juices. Wholefood. Seats 65. Meals from £6.50 lunch, from £9 dinner. House wine £6.40 litre. Visa/American Express/Access.

Open: Tue to Fri, 12 to 2, 6.30 to 10; Sat, 6.30 to 10; Sun, 12 to 2.

SKIPTON   North Yorkshire   Map 6
Herbs, Healthlife Shops Ltd   TEL Skipton (0756) 60619

Soup is made in the kitchen, the rolls come from a pet baker. Main dishes are all salads, fortified with eggs, cottage cheese, cheese and onion pie, mushroom flan or, for vegans, the Herbs special green variety. Freshly-squeezed fruit juices are orange and grapefruit. More excitement comes with the desserts; Swedish apple cake, fresh fruit ice cream, ice cream gâteaux, sorbets, and fresh fruit salad.

Free range eggs; organically grown fruit and vegetables when available; wholemeal bread; polyunsaturates in cooking and at table; fresh fruits at table; minimal salt and sugar; skimmed milk available; freshly squeezed fruit juices. Wholefood, vegetarian, vegan, other diets on request. Seats 34. Lunch from £1.30.

Open: Mon, Wed, Thur, Fri, Sat, 9.30 to 5.

SOUTHAMPTON   Hampshire   Map 3
Bountiful Goodness, East Street Shopping Centre
TEL Southampton (0703) 30831

This bright modern town centre restaurant operates with more than customary brisk efficiency. Nut roasts turn up with tempting green salads, coleslaw and other salads of the day's selection. Moussaka is the traditional Greek kind using lamb, aubergines, herbs and cheese. Spaghetti Bolognese has a meat sauce and wholemeal pasta. Neapolitan spaghetti has a vegetable sauce. Salads have rice, fruit, and nuts in addition to tuna, prawns and egg. There is a choice of butter or Flora with the wholemeal rolls. Yoghurts come plain or with honey and there's homemade hot apricot slice, hot chocolate sponge or apple pie. Teatime treats include wholemeal tea cakes and own-recipe cakes. Orange, lemon and cinnamon, and just a hint of cloves, go into the hot spiced apple drink.

Wholemeal bread; polyunsaturates in kitchen and at table; minimal salt and sugar; freshly squeezed fruit juices; organic wholemeal flour for baking. Wholefood, vegetarian, vegan. Seats 130. Meals from £6, dishes from £1.10. House wine £3.30 carafe.

Open: Mon to Sat, 9.30 to 5.30.

SOUTHWOLD   Suffolk   Map 3
The Crown, High Street   TEL Southwold (0502) 724222

This brasserie and wine bar has only just reopened after refitting by Adnams Brewery. It serves well-cooked, fresh, locally grown or caught produce. The emphasis is on local fish and salads.

Organically grown vegetables; free range eggs; wholemeal bread; fresh fruits at table; minimal salt and sugar; freshly squeezed fruit juices. Wholefood. Seats 70. Access.

Open: Sun to Sat, breakfast to 9.30.

SPARK BRIDGE   Cumbria   MAP 6
Bridgefield House, Spark Bridge, Ulverston   TEL Spark Bridge (022 985) 239

David and Rosemary Glister manage to cherish diners and guests (there are six rooms) without obvious fuss. Pan-fried fillet steak and casserole of pigeon breast have been the only main courses, but special needs can be catered for given suitable warning. Scope for self-expression lies in the melon and cucumber salad with a yoghurt dressing, spiced pepper cream flan, smoked haddock pancakes, turkey and lemon croquettes, mushroom and pepper salad. Vegetable dishes are specialities. Celery is pan fried with walnuts, broccoli cooked with a hazelnut butter. Bridgefield bread and butter pudding is served with fresh dates and cream. There is stem ginger and cream in the meringues, whisky in the lemon syllabub.

Homegrown fruit and vegetables; own free range hen and duck eggs; own raw farm milk; freshly squeezed fruit juices. Wholefood. Seats 20. Meals from £12. House wine £4.50. Access/Diners' Club/American Express.

Open: daily, 7.30 for 8. Booking essential.

STOCKPORT   Greater Manchester   MAP 6
Coconut Willy's, 37 St. Petergate   TEL Stockport (061 480) 7013

Martin Rooney's knowledgeable interest (he is a chef by training and for seven years ran a health food shop) is appreciated in this restaurant with its modern red, blue and green décor. A minor drawback to some are less experienced junior staff. Seasoning is limited to fresh and dried herbs and spices, the minimal amount of sea salt, shoyu sauce, and miso. Delicious soups include cauliflower and cheese, tomato, pasta and red pepper. Other starters have included stuffed vine leaves, nut pâté and tofu dip. Among the eight main dishes at dinner (the same number of puddings and starters) might be mixed vegetable tagliatelle, butter bean and broccoli, lasagne or cheese and carrot slice. There may be chick pea and pine nut curry. Cheesecake, fruit salad, a strawberry sorbet and the soya and goats' milk ice cream could be among the pudding choices. During the day there's a self-service selection of salads, confectionery, wholemeal pizzas and quiches. Martin Rooney is himself macrobiotic and is always happy to discuss menus.

Organically grown fruit and vegetables whenever possible; organic rice; oats, cider vinegar; sea vegetables; organic stone ground flour; animal rennet free cheeses; wholemeal bread; polyunsaturates in cooking and at table; fresh fruits at table; minimal salt and sugar; skimmed milk available; freshly squeezed fruit juices. Wholefood, vegetarian, vegan, macrobiotic. Seats 55. Meals from £4, set 4-course dinner £6.95. House wine £5.25 litre.

Open: Tue to Sat, 9.30 to 11.30; closed 2 weeks early Jan.

TIVERTON   Devon   MAP 2
Angel Food, 1 Angel Terrace   TEL Tiverton (0884) 254778

The partners in this tiny enterprise supply only vegetarian food and some dishes are vegan and gluten-free. All is homemade using good quality oils, fresh herbs, organic cider vinegar and the like. Expect salads, pies, pasties and pizza, fruit juices, and homemade cakes.

Animal rennet free cheeses; soya milk; goats' and sheep's milk cheeses; wholemeal bread; polyunsaturates in cooking and at table; minimal salt and sugar; freshly squeezed fruit juices; free range eggs; organic vegetables when available. Wholefood, vegetarian, vegan, gluten-free. Seats 15. Meals from £3.50.

Open: Mon, Wed, Fri, 9.30 to 5.30; Thur, 9.30 to 2.30; Sat, 9.30 to 5.

TRURO   Cornwall   MAP 2
Pottles, Back Quay   TEL Truro (0872) 71384

Pottles aim is the serve only freshly prepared home cooked food, without shortcuts.
Nothing is prepacked, mass produced or microwaved. As soon as the shoppers are
about, coffee, croissants and Cornish yeast buns find buyers. Later there is demand for
homemade cakes and more extravagant gâteaux. By midday, meat platters—ham, pork,
beef and pâté—are in demand, all with generous green salads. Other customers make a
meal of the jacket potatoes or there is hot-pot of the day served with a simple salad.
Friday night is the weekly highlight when there is provincial French food, a classical
guitarist, sherry to start and coffee to finish, for an all-inclusive price. The four courses
offer a salmon mousse, courgettes gratinées or avocado dip and vegetable crudités. For
main courses choose from the Greek lamb, sautéed chicken with sweetcorn, peppers and
pine kernels, or a richly sauced casserole Provençale. The lighter puddings are port wine
jelly, Mexican mocha cream, chocolate mousse style. More substantially there's a treacle
tart and chocolate meringue gâteaux.

When available, vegetables organically grown by a local disabled group; wholemeal bread;
polyunsaturates in kitchen and at table; minimal salt; freshly squeezed fruit and vegetable juices.
Wholefood, vegetarian, vegan, diabetic, gluten-free, others with notice. Seats 60. Meals from
£8 dinner, dishes from £1.40. Bring your own wine.

Open: 9.30 to 5; Fri, 9.30 to 8; closed Sun and Mon pm.

TUNBRIDGE WELLS   Kent   MAP 3
The Pilgrims, 37 Mount Ephraim   TEL Tunbridge Wells (0892) 20121

It is more like a modest winter garden, the approach triumphal—beaux-arts style, from the
shop below. Sunny top-lighting, fresh greenery and management drive, make the simply
appointed restaurant a very popular meeting place. Extended hours dispel notions that
healthy life days are all over by five. Overawed by the computers she left behind, the
endearing Gabrielle Higgins views her achievements more modestly. The popular
Pilgrim's pizza is something out of the ordinary, 'the topping moist and succulent and
served in great big portions' which with the house speciality potatoes or a green salad
comes to about £2.50. Every day she offers three or four of her twelve main dish
repertoire which includes stir-fried vegetables, risotto and moussaka. There is always
something vegan, a nut roast or a pasta. Start with a homemade soup (a big bowl 75p) or
an egg mayonnaise. Salads come combined as you like them or with a cold 'roast'. Smoked
mackerel are a deviation from the vegetarian creed 'but some veggies like them!' For
puddings, fruit whip (yoghurt and fresh cream—80p), trifle, made with their own
sponges, fresh fruit and cream, or cheesecake made on the premises. Always a fresh fruit
salad; always a fruit tart. At teatime she serves a wholemeal sponge with a cream and jam
filling, homemade in her own kitchen.

Rombout's coffee; wine by the glass; produce is organically grown whenever possible; free range
eggs; extensions could be in the offing with table service offered.

Open: Mon to Sat, 10.30 to 8.

ULLAPOOL   Highland   MAP 7
The Ceilidh Place, 14 West Argyle Street   TEL Ullapool (0854) 2103

The vegetarian proprietors, Jean and Robert Urquhart, have been anchored here for all of
fifteen years serving little meat but plenty of fresh fish from the pier—lobster, prawns,
herring, haddock and salmon. The fish is cooked and served with lots of salads (hot and
cold), though so far north they do find it difficult to get organic supplies or grow their
own. Scones and vegan bread are homemade and there's a health bookshop. Staying the
night? Simple clubhouse beds through to rooms with bath.

Animal rennet free cheeses; free range eggs; wholemeal bread; polyunsaturates in cooking and at table; fresh fruits at table; minimal salt and sugar; freshly squeezed fruit juices. Wholefood, vegetarian, vegan, diabetic. Seats 70. Meals from £5.50. Diners' Club.

Open: daily, 8 to 11; closed Nov to Mar.

WALBERSWICK   Suffolk   MAP 3
The Potter's Wheel, Walberswick, Southwold   TEL Walberswick (0502) 724468

Whenever possible Lesley Scott uses locally produced raw ingredients and foods in season. Lunches are simple with the accent on fresh vegetables. Her dinner menus always include a game dish and a vegetarian meal. Sunday lunches are a time for roasts. Dinners, even after recent price increases, are still good value. Alternatives to the cauliflower soup could be smoked mackerel mousse or a Stilton and walnut pâté. Roast partridge or lamb cutlets are popular and other diners have gone for the hot avocado with a wine and nut stuffing. Meals can be accompanied by pure local apple juice, Perrier water or bring-your-own wine. The lunchtime blackboard might list soup with brown bread and butter, steak and kidney pie with fresh vegetables, mushroom or nut pancake with vegetables or salad, ratatouille, cheese baked potato. Puddings are an attraction—fruit and lemon cheesecake, frozen almond cream, a fresh fruit salad, lemon syllabub and apple pie.

Organically grown fruit and vegetables when available; free range eggs; wholemeal bread; fresh fruits at table, minimal salt and sugar. Wholefood, vegetarian, gluten-free. Seats 24. Meals from £4.50 lunch, £8.50 dinner. Bring your own wine, corkage charge 50p. Access.

Open: lunches, Wed to Mon, 10.30 to 5.30; dinners, Fri and Sat; closed Oct to Apr.

WALFORD   Hereford and Worcester   MAP 2
Walford House Hotel, Walford, Ross-on-Wye   TEL Walford (0989) 63829

Life is peaceable hereabouts and Raymond and Joyce Zarb descended on the district—after a more exotic lifestyle in London and Paris—because this is where all the fresh basic commodities are readily available. They have an acre of kitchen garden, and their own cow and goats. Butter and cheese are made in the traditional way. Mr. and Mrs. Zarb love to discuss guests' likes and dislikes, and produce their meals accordingly. There is no problem about producing a meal for any diet. People they know in nearby Newent produce their very good double and single Gloucester cheeses.

Seasonally self-sufficient in organically grown fruit and vegetables; free range eggs; fresh goats' and Jersey cows' milk; wholemeal bread; polyunsaturates at table; fresh fruits at table; minimal salt and sugar; freshly squeezed fruit and vegetable juices. Wholefood, vegetarian, vegan, other diets easily catered for. Seats 38. Meals from £7.50. House wine £7.40. American Express/ Diners' Club/Access/Visa.

Open: Sun to Sat, lunch from 12.30, dinner from 7.30.

WAREHAM   Dorset   MAP 2
Annie's, 14A North Street   TEL Wareham (092 95) 6242

Annie Barnham's place is in an old barn next to the post office with a garden which nearly doubles the seating capacity on warm summer days. The café is completely vegetarian, specialising in a variety of salads, and homemade soup with the now familiar garlic bread. Sustaining dishes are the moussaka, lentil bakes and pasta dishes. For a change there is sometimes a curry or a mushroom croustade. There are always baked potatoes and quiche which, like the cakes, are homemade. Bakewell tart and Annie Barnham's apple cake are particularly good.

Wholefood, vegetarian. Seats 30. Meals from £4.

Open: Mon to Sat, 10.30 to 5.30 winter, 10 to 10 summer.

WATERHOUSES   Staffordshire   MAP 6
Cindy's Kitchen, The Old School, Cauldron Lane   TEL Waterhouses (053 86) 431

Wholefood and food for the mind is provided at this former parish school now run as an independent arts and crafts centre by Lindy Hindle. Her policy in the kitchen is to use the most wholesome and natural ingredients. Lunchtimes bring a savoury cheesecake, vegetarian burgers, homity pies and curried fruit and vegetable pie. There are salads as side or main dishes and baked potatoes, and fruit pie with yoghurt or clotted cream to follow. There are cakes too, which also appear at teatime; apricot and sultana slice, orange muesli cake, lemon cake, carrot and chocolate crunch. Special set teas offer open sandwiches and cheese scones, and there are wholemeal scones with the cream teas.

Free range eggs; wholemeal bread; polyunsaturates in cooking and at table; fresh fruits at table; minimal salt and sugar; freshly squeezed fruit juices; animal rennet free cheese. Wholefood, vegetarian, vegan. Seats 45. Meals from £4, savoury teas £2. House wine £3.85. Visa/Access/ American Express.

Open: daily, 10.30 to 5.30, Apr to Oct; Nov to Mar, 10.30 to 5, Fri to Mon.

WATH-IN-NIDDERDALE   North Yorkshire   MAP 6
Sportsman's Arms, Wath-in-Nidderdale   TEL Wath-in-Nidderdale (0423) 711832

The long rambling stone-built inn faces the pretty green in this dales' village. Walkers in this moorland country turn up for the substantial breakfasts, more around midday for satisfying bar lunches. Ploughman's platters have mature Cheddar or red Leicester and crusty wholemeal French bread. Smoked trout is from the river Nidd which passes through the village. Some customers opt for an open wholemeal roll with garlic butter and prawns. Dinners produce Scotch salmon, local venison and pheasant, and lobsters fresh daily from Whitby. The asparagus season is extended with imports from South Africa. Mango is exotically combined with prawn mousse and a curried cream sauce. Puddings range between Norwegian apple cake, Italian pear macaroons and for a savoury there are bananas wrapped in bacon and served on toast. No frozen foods are used.

Free range eggs; locally grown vegetables; fresh fish from Whitby; wholemeal bread; polyunsaturates at table; fresh fruits at table; minimal salt and sugar; freshly squeezed fruits and vegetable juices available. Wholefood, vegetarian, all diets on request. Seats 50. Meals from £12.50, bar lunches £1.60. House wine £5.35. Access/Visa/Diners' Club/American Express.

Open: daily, bar, 12 to 2, 7 to 11.

WELLS   Somerset   MAP 2
The Good Earth, 4 Priory Road   TEL Wells (0749) 76800

Part of this house operates as a shop selling wholemeal, sunflower, muesli and granary loaves. Deliveries are daily and only stone ground flours are used. Cooking is done with fresh, unrefined ingredients. There are seasonally free range hen, duck and goose eggs, organically grown fruit and vegetables. Soups are all made with fresh vegetables. Hearty main-course dishes are made from a selection of nuts, seeds and pulses, cheese, eggs, grain and pasta. Expect mushroom and cashew nut pie, stuffed cabbage leaves, cheesy Scotch eggs, shepherd's pie. Salads are offered with homemade dressings of mayonnaise. Desserts are based on fresh fruit in a pie or flan; the ice cream is homemade—brown bread crumb, coffee and hazelnut, tutti-frutti. At teatime there is Somerset apple dappy and Brazil and cherry cake. The courtyard at the back is used on fine days.

Wholemeal bread; fresh fruits at table; minimal salt and sugar; skimmed milk available; freshly squeezed fruit juices. Wholefood, vegetarian, vegan. Seats 80. Meals from £3.75. House wine £4.60. Access/Visa.

Open: Mon to Sat, 10.30 to 4.30 ; Wed, 10.30 to 2; closed Christmas/New Year.

WHITBY   North Yorkshire   MAP 6
Magpie Café, 14 Pier Road   TEL Whitby (0947) 602058

Do not be deterred by the chip fryer. Sheila and Ian McKenzie do lots of interesting dishes
as well. But the built-in advantage is that in Whitby the fish comes straight from the pier.
Fillets of fish, chips, tea, bread and butter are the popular standby. When salads are not
being prepared with cottage cheese and fruit, marvellous fish is substituted. A de-luxe fish
platter includes crab, lobster, salmon and prawn and these ingredients also find their way
into starters. All the cakes and sweets are homemade. For sweets, there's frangipane,
hazelnut, rum and praline slice, fat-free sticky sultana loaf, wholefood banana slice and
always a special diabetic sweet is on offer. Cheese is Wensleydale.

Wholemeal bread; fresh fruits at table; minimal salt and sugar; skimmed milk available.
Wholefood, vegetarian, gluten-free, diabetic. Seats 95. Meals from £2.75.

Open: daily, 11.30 to 2.30, 3.30 to 6.30; closed Fri except July and Aug; closed first week
Oct to Apr.

WHITNEY-ON-WYE   Hereford and Worcester   MAP 2
Rhyspence Inn, Whitney-on-Wye   TEL Whitney-on-Wye (049 73) 262

A fine timbered drovers' inn this offers the combined facilities of a pub and a restaurant
and two well-appointed rooms with bath. Inexpensive bar food varies between the
landlord's favourites (which can be 'hammy', 'fishy' or 'mushroom'), to the substantial
stock pot soup and nine by two and a half—Swansea bread filled with thick slices of
home-baked ham and salad. Main meals—in either the Bottom Bar or Drovers' Kitchen—
are the homely steak and kidney pie, steak, fish and, usually a curry with side dishes and
brown rice. There are three vegetarian options, mushroom gratinée the most appealing. It
is worth monitoring the blackboard for daily specials.

Non-battery eggs; sometimes organically grown fruit and vegetables; wholemeal bread; fresh
fruits at table; minimal sugar; freshly squeezed fruit juices. Wholefood, vegetarian, other special
dishes for residents. Seats 40. Meals from £7. House wine £5.50.

Open: 12 to 2.30, 7 to 10.30 summer; closed Mon all year round, Mon and Tue
Nov to Mar.

WINDSOR   Berkshire   MAP 3
Country Kitchen, 3 King Edward Court   TEL Windsor (075 35) 68681

Salads are a strong feature, at least seven varieties and served according to requirements,
either as a main dish or to supplement hot dishes. Chicken pie, beef curry with rice, and
chilli con carne are popular meals. Lasagne comes in meat and vegetable versions. Paella
and a vegetable casserole are other vegetarian choices. Delicious sweets may be lemon
mousse, chocolate fudge, fresh fruit salad and passion cake. The last is more prosaic than it
sounds—carrots and walnuts. Wholemeal flour is used in much of the baking. Brown rice
with savoury recipes. In summer there's homemade lemonade.

Wholemeal bread; minimal salt and sugar; skimmed milk used in cooking. Wholefood,
vegetarian. Seats 200. Lunch from £5. House wine £3.25 ½ carafe.

Open: Mon to Sat, 10 to 5.

WITHERSLACK   Cumbria   MAP 6
The Old Vicarage, Witherslack, Nr Grange-over-Sands
TEL Witherslack (044 852) 381

Well away from main roads and as handy for the beach as the Lakes, the four partners in this country house hotel with a splendid garden make a point of catering for special diets. Seasonings in dishes are minimal and only sea salt is used. Ingredients are totally fresh. Cooking oils are likely to be sesame, soya or sunflower. The set five-course menu changes daily. There's no choice of main course, which could be fillet steak in the piece with a bearnaise sauce. Vegetable support is good and imaginative: carrot purée, cauliflower (Polish style), parsnips and bacon, broccoli. Puddings include wholewheat treacle sponge, bramble ice cream with a blackberry sauce, fresh fruit salad. For first courses, courgette soufflé and a hollandaise sauce, smoked goose breast, nourishing lentil soup. If you have an urge to stay, there are eight rooms all with bath.

Homemade wholemeal and white bread; low-fat dishes; vegetarian alternative on demand; polyunsaturates in cooking. Wholefood, other diets specially catered for. Seats 30. Meals from £14.50. House wine £5.25. All credit cards accepted.

Open: daily for dinner, 7.30 for 8; closed Christmas week.

WOODSTOCK   Oxfordshire   MAP 3
Brothertons, Market Square   TEL Woodstock (0993) 811114

Once an ironmongers (which locals still miss), now Brothertons' is a traditional gaslit brasserie serving continental breakfasts, coffees, lunches, afternoon cream teas and dinners. Good impressions are made with the cheery, civil service, and the quality of the food which appears to eschew all the convenience kinds. Russian blinis are enjoying a vogue; smoked Scotch salmon and sour cream sandwiched between two savoury Scotch pancakes are more Celtic than Slavonic. Still obeying the call of the north, Arbroath smokies, Brotherton style, are flaked and served in a cheese sauce. Supreme of chicken has a mustard seed sauce. Main course fish could be Portuguese sardines or seafood crêpes with a salmon and prawn stuffing. Deadly to the figure is chocolate rum truffle cake, while individual cheeseboards have Bath Olivers (with enough for two), or there are crêpes, again with cream and liqueur of your choice filling, topped with crushed macaroons.

Wholemeal bread; fresh fruits at table; freshly squeezed fruit juices at the bar; minimal salt. Wholefood, vegetarian. Seats 60. Dishes from £2.40. House wine £4.50.

Open: Daily, 10.30 to 10.30.

WOOLPIT   Suffolk   MAP 3
The Old Bakery, Woolpit, Nr Bury St. Edmunds   TEL Woolpit (0359) 40255

Eileen Clarke's cottage has medieval origins and a wealth of old beams. Conveniently just off the A45 to Harwich the clients can be amazingly cosmopolitan. Everything is homemade using fresh ingredients. Fresh herbs are used which Lesley Brumness supplies—she did the Pebble Mill Series on TV. Mrs. Clarke's philosophy is that foods should be seasonal, fresh and authentic. Special emphasis is placed on fruit and vegetables in summer, pies and dumplings in winter. She also has an acute awareness of modern nutrition and health. Pies and casseroles may be meat, fish, poultry and game, or all vegetable. Her poultry, including the turkeys, are all free range. Good fish comes fresh from Lowestoft. Soups are a speciality. If there is fresh fruit about, summer puddings put in an appearance, otherwise fruit is beautifully cut to display its virtues. Sometimes there is treacle tart, enriched with fruit and nuts, though not as rich as chestnut and chocolate pudding. Lunches are light, informal meals; soups, pâté or stuffed pancakes.

Wholemeal bread; polyunsaturates in cooking; minimal salt and sugar; organically grown fruit and vegetables; free range eggs; goats' milk. Wholefood, vegetarian, other diets by prior arrangement. Seats 30. Meals from £6 lunch, £9 dinner. House wine £9.

Open: Tue to Sat, 10.30 to 5; Fri and Sat from 7.30.

WORCESTER   Hereford and Worcester   MAP 2
Millwheel, 22 The Shambles   TEL Worcester (0905) 23353

Phillip Coward's crisp modern café in pine and light paint is at the back of a shop of the
same name, in this ancient city area, unapologetically in the Cranks idiom. The many
admirers feel it is none the worse for that in the place 'where they succeed in making
natural foods interesting'—just as long as you don't expect food after about 4.30 because
by 5.00 the shutters are firmly up. In this meatless establishment, fish occasionally puts in
an appearance. Otherwise it could be a lasagne using soya mince and a variety of herbs
which make it 'very appetising' and 'quite as good as the moussakas, with carefully varied
seasoning'. There is a selection of salads, and always potatoes, usually baked, to
accompany hot dishes. Dietary needs are sympathetically met, which may be gluten-free
or vegan, but you may not always find lunch dishes to meet your particular need. There is
always fresh fruit. Fats high in polyunsaturates are used in the cooking but you will be
disappointed if you seek an alternative to butter at the table. On the credit side, only
100 % organically grown wholemeal flour is used and the eggs are non-battery. Mr.
Coward persists with his search for sources of organically grown vegetables, so far
without success.

*Wholemeal bread; polyunsaturates in cooking and at table; minimal salt and sugar; skimmed
milk available. Wholefood, vegetarian, vegan, gluten-free. Meals from £4.*

Open: Mon to Sat, 9.30 to 5.

WORTHING   West Sussex   MAP 3
Nature's Way, 130 Montague Street   TEL Worthing (0903) 209931

This pine furnished restaurant above a coffee shop has a branch in Hove too. Barrie and
Jane Lewis launched the enterprise five years ago and their aim is to provide interesting
and varied vegetarian food which is acceptable to non-vegetarians as well. Everything is
homemade, they go easy on the salt and of the nine or so regular salads only half have
dressings. Flans have cheese and vegetable fillings and the daily special may be hazelnut
loaf or a chilli con carne with rice. Large bowls of salad include a portion of all nine
varieties. Puddings include sherry trifle, chocolate mousse, dried fruit compote and fruit
crumbles. Cakes—varying from time to time—are honey sponge, bran loaf, carrot cake,
brownies and Dorset apple. There are wholemeal cheese scones too.

*Wholemeal bread; polyunsaturates in cooking and at table; fresh fruits at table; minimal salt.
Wholefood, vegetarian. Seats 54. Meals from £3.50.*

Open: Mon to Sat, 9.15 to 5.

YARM   Cleveland   MAP 6
The Coffee Shop, 44 High Street   TEL Yarm (0642) 782101

Michael Richardson has been established here seven years serving good wholesome food,
using no preservatives, colourings or additives. Decoration is interesting bric-a-brac,
offsetting the plain wooden tables and chairs. Hot dishes are old favourites like steak and
kidney pie, cheesy prawns and usually something like leek and cheese flan for a meatless
alternative. Salads come in various sizes, the Richard III concoction has herbs, spices, figs,
dates and apple, and there are other salads—curried tuna, coleslaw, fennel, rice and green.
Mr. Richardson makes his own ice cream, Yorkshire curd pie, Bakewell tart, pavlova and
Dutch apple pie.

*Organically grown vegetables and non-battery eggs when available; wholemeal bread;
polyunsaturates in cooking; minimal salt and sugar. Wholefood, vegetarian. Seats 50.
Meals £4.75, dishes £2.50. House wine 75p glass.*

Open: Mon to Sat, 9 to 5; closed Sun except Dec.

YEOVIL   Somerset   MAP 2
Little Barwick House, Barwick   TEL Yeovil (0935) 23902

Christopher Colley grows a lot of his own vegetables, and in the cooking his wife, Veronica, uses a lot of West Country game, fish from Samways in Bridport and crabs and lobster from Weymouth. Regulars needing a special diet usually tell them when they are coming so vegetable pies, leek and tarragon tarts and stuffed mushrooms can be prepared. Puddings for diabetics are special pies and water ices, or fruit cocktail. For ordinary customers, baked smoked mackerel comes with mushroom sauce; mussels Provençale, baked pancakes and cream smokies form first courses. Plainer fare is the soup of the day or chilled melon. A brace of roast quail has a grape and walnut sauce; roast loin of lamb is served with mint and cucumber. Game depends on the season, and there is an individually baked pie of the week, perhaps ham and veal. Puddings include freshly poached peaches in a loganberry sauce; orange in caramel, brandy snaps with cream. The damson soufflé will have a chilled damson sauce, and there's blackcurrant water ice with cassis.

Own home-grown fruits and vegetables when available; free range eggs and chicken; wholemeal bread; polyunsaturates at table; fresh fruits at table. Wholefood, vegetarian, vegan, gluten-free, diabetic. Seats 30. Meals from £12. House wine £5.60. Access/American Express/Diners' Club/ Visa.

Open: Mon to Sat, 7 to 9.30.

OTHER RECOMMENDED
RESTAURANTS

Britons Arms, Norwich

Abersoch Porth Tocyn Hotel Gwynedd
TEL (075 881) 2966 *Lunch 12.30 to 2. Dinner 7.30 to 9.30. Wholefood · expensive · rooms.*

Aberystwyth Ceredigion Wholemake The Toll House 1 Llanbadarn Road Dyfed
TEL (0970) 611174 *Mon to Fri 10 to 6.30. Sat 10 to 9. Wholefood · inexpensive.*

Aberystwyth Connexion Restaurant 19 Bridge Street Dyfed
TEL (0970) 615350 *Mon to Sat 10 to 4.45, 6.30 to 10.30. Wholefood · inexpensive.*

Abingdon Harvest Café 37 Stert Street Oxfordshire
TEL (0235) 26660 *Mon to Sat 10 to 5. Wholefood · vegetarian · inexpensive.*

Aldeburgh Wateringfield Golf Lane Suffolk
TEL (072 885) 3104 *Dinners daily from 6.30. Inexpensive.*

Alfriston Drusillas East Sussex
TEL (0323) 870234 *Daily 10.30 to 5. Closed Nov to Mar. Inexpensive.*

Alresford O'Rorue's Restaurant Pound Hill Hampshire
TEL (096 273) 2293 *Dinners Mon to Sat 7 to 9.30. Expensive.*

Alston High Fell Hotel and Restaurant Cumbria
TEL (0498) 81597 *Daily 12 to 2, 7.30 to 9. Medium · rooms.*

Altrincham Ganders Wine Bar and Bistro 2 Goose Green Cheshire
TEL 061-941 3954 *Daily 10 to 3, 7 to 1. Medium.*

Ambleside Rothay Manor Hotel and Restaurant Cumbria
TEL (0966) 33605 *Daily. Morning Coffee 10.30. Lunch 12.30 to 2. Afternoon Tea 3. Dinner 8. Last 3 weeks Jan closed. Expensive · rooms.*

Ambleside Zeffirellis Compston Rd Cumbria
TEL (0966) 33845 *Daily 10 to 9.45. Inexpensive.*

Ashford Eastwell Manor Hotel and Restaurant Eastwell Park Kent
TEL (0233) 35751 *Breakfast 7.30 to 10.30. Lunch 12.30 to 2. Dinner 7.30 to 9.30. Expensive · rooms.*

Ashtead Snooty Fox Restaurant 21 The Street Surrey
TEL (037 22) 76606 *Mon to Fri Lunch and Dinner. Sat Dinner. Sun Lunch. Expensive.*

Bakewell Cavendish Hotel Baslow Derbyshire
TEL (024 688) 2311 *Daily. Expensive · rooms.*

Bath The Canary 3 Queen Street Avon
TEL (0225) 24846 *Daily 10 to 6. Inexpensive.*

Bath The Moon and Sixpence 6a Broad Street Avon
TEL (0225) 60962 *Daily 12 to 2, 6 to 10. Medium.*

Bath Sweeney Todds 15 Milsom Street Avon
TEL (0225) 62368 *Daily 12 to 12. Inexpensive.*

Beaminster Chedington Court Chedington Dorset
TEL (093 589) 265 *Daily 7 to 9. Closed 2 weeks Jan, Apr/May or Aug. Wholefood · expensive · rooms.*

Beattock The Old Brig Inn and Posting House Dumfriesshire
TEL (068 33) 401 *Daily 11 to 11. Inexpensive · rooms.*

Bexhill Corianders 66 Devonshire Road East Sussex
TEL (0424) 220329 *Mon to Sat 9.30 to 5.30. Vegetarian · wholefood · inexpensive.*

Bexhill-on-Sea Nature's Way Health Food Restaurant 10 Devonshire Road East Sussex
TEL (0424) 220052 *Daily 10 to 4. Vegetarian · inexpensive.*

Birmingham Whitakers 158 Broad Street Fiveways Shopping Centre West Midlands
TEL 021-632 5590 *Mon to Sat 11.30 to 10. Vegetarian · medium.*

Blackpool The River House Skippool Creek Thornton-le-Fylde Lancashire

TEL (0253) 883497 *Open Breakfast, Lunch, Dinner. Expensive · rooms.*

Blair Drummond Broughton's Restaurant Stirling
TEL (0786) 841897 *Open Tue to Sat 12.30 to 2, 7.30 to 10.30. Wholefood · medium.*

Botley Cobbetts Restaurant The Square Botley Southampton
TEL (048 92) 2068 *Sat, Sun, Mon 12 to 2. Sun 7.30 to 10. Inexpensive.*

Bournemouth Amadale House 21 St. Clements Road Boscombe Dorset
TEL (0202) 34848 *Open to residents only. Inexpensive.*

Bournemouth Flossie's and Bossie's 71 Seamoor Road Westbourne Dorset
TEL (0202) 764459 *Mon 9 to 5. Tue to Sat 9 to 10.30. Inexpensive · vegetarian.*

Bournemouth Chandelles Restaurant 747 Christchurch Road Dorset
TEL (0202) 36021 *5 evenings Oct to Mar open 7. 7 evenings Apr to Oct open 7. Inexpensive.*

Bovey Tracey Blenheim Hotel Brimley Road South Devon
TEL (0626) 832422 *Daily 9 to 10, 7.30 to 9. Wholefood · medium · rooms.*

Bovey Tracey Ullacombe House Haytor Road Newton Abbot South Devon
TEL (036 46) 242 *Open to guests' requirements. Evening Meal 7. Vegetarian · wholefood · medium · rooms.*

Breakish Langdale Guest House Waterloo Isle of Skye
TEL (047 12) 376 *Dinner daily 7 to 8.30. Wholefood · inexpensive · rooms.*

Brighton The French Connection Restaurant 11 Little East Street Sussex
TEL (0273) 24454 *Daily 12 to 2.30, 7 to 10.30. Expensive.*

Bristol Salad Kitchen 18 Park Row Avon
TEL (0272) 24539 *Mon to Fri 9 to 5. Vegetarian · wholefood · inexpensive.*

Bromley Carioca Tandoor 239 High Street Kent
TEL 01-460 7130 *Open daily 12 to 2.30, 6 to 11. Fri and Sat 6 to 12. Medium.*

Burnham-on-Crouch Contented Sole Restaurant 80 High Street Essex
TEL (0621) 782139 *Tue to Sat 12 to 2, 7 to 9.30. Inexpensive.*

Calver Bridge The Derbyshire Craft Centre Eating House Sheffield
TEL (0433) 31231 *Daily 10 to 5.30. Closed during week Jan and Feb. Inexpensive.*

Carbis Bay 'St. Judes' Guest House St. Ives Road St Ives Cornwall
TEL (0736) 795255 *Daily Easter to Oct. Breakfast 8.30 to 9. Evening meal 6.30. Vegetarian · wholefood · inexpensive.*

Chagford Thornworthy House Devon
TEL (064 73) 3297 *Daily 7.30 to 10. Wholefood · expensive · rooms.*

Charlton The Horse and Groom Inn Malmesbury Wiltshire
TEL (066 62) 3904 *Tue to Sun 12 to 2.30, 6.30 to 10.30. Medium.*

Cheltenham Fruit and Nut Place 4 Henrietta Street Gloucestershire
TEL (0242) 520577 *Mon to Fri 11 to 3. Sat 10 to 4. Fri evenings 7 to 10. Inexpensive.*

Cheltenham Wellingtons Restaurant 3 Portland Street Gloucestershire
TEL (0242) 30066 *Mon to Sat 7.30 to 10. Lunch Tue to Fri 12.30 to 2. Medium.*

Chichester Clinch's Salad House 14 Southgate West Sussex
TEL (0243) 788822 *Tue to Sat 8 to 5.30. Wholefood · vegetarian · inexpensive.*

Chinley The Bank Restaurant Green Lane via Stockport Cheshire
TEL (0663) 50151 *Sat 8 to 9.30. Tue to Fri 12 to 2, 7.30 to 9. Wholefood · medium.*

Chipping Campden Caminetto Restaurant High Street Gloucestershire
TEL (0386) 840934 *Mon to Sat 7 to 10.30. Medium.*

Coatham Mundeville Hall Garth Coventry House Hotel and Restaurant Darlington Co. Durham
TEL (0325) 313333 *Open daily. Closed 10 days Christmas. Stable Bar 11 to 3, 6.30 to 10.30. Medium.*

Coggeshall The White Hart Hotel Essex
TEL (0376) 61654 *Mon to Sat 12.30 to 2, 7.30 to 9. Inexpensive. Closed Aug and 1 week after Christmas.*

Colchester Bistro Nine 9 North Hill Essex
TEL (0206) 576466 *Tue to Sat 12 to 1.45, 7 to 10.45. Wholefood · medium.*

Cork Glassialleys 17 Drawbridge Street Eire
TEL Cork (or 010 353 21) 22305 *Mon to Sat 12.30 to 2.30, 7 to 10.45. Medium.*

Coventry Trinity House Hotel 28 Lower Holyhead Road West Midlands
TEL (0203) 555654 *Mon to Sat 6.30 to 9.30. Vegetarian · wholefood · inexpensive · rooms. Closed Christmas.*

Cranleigh Clouds High Street Surrey
TEL (0483) 271272 *Tue to Sun 11 to 11. Wholefood · inexpensive.*

Crickhowell Gliffaes Country House Hotel Powys
TEL (0874) 730371 *Closed Jan to mid-Mar. Daily 8.30 to 9.45, 1 to 2, 7.45 to 9. Medium · rooms.*

Croydon La Vida 164 Cherry Orchard Road Surrey
TEL 01-681 3402 *Tue to Thur 12 to 2. Tue to Sat 6 to 10. Vegetarian · wholefood · medium.*

Cupar Ostlers Close Restaurant 25 Bonnygate Fife
TEL (0334) 55574 *Mon 7 to 9.30. Tue to Sat 12.15 to 2, 7 to 9.30. Medium.*

Derby Lettuce Leaf 21 Friar Gate Derbyshire
TEL (0332) 40307 *Mon to Sat 10 to 7.30. Wholefood · vegetarian · inexpensive.*

Dervaig Druimnacroish Country House Hotel Druimnacroish Isle of Mull Argyll
TEL (068 84) 274 *Dinners daily from 8. Wholefood · expensive · rooms.*

Dormansland Claridge House Lingfield Surrey
TEL (0342) 832150 *Normal meal times. Wholefood · vegetarian · inexpensive · rooms.*

Dublin Kapriol Restaurant 45 Lr Camden Street Dublin 2
TEL 751235 or 985496 *Mon to Sat 7.30 to 12. Expensive.*

Dumfries Opvs 95 Queensberry Street
TEL (0387) 55752 *Daily 9 to 5. Thur 9 to 2.30. Closed Sun. Inexpensive.*

Eastbourne Brown's Restaurant 17 Carlisle Road East Sussex
TEL (0323) 28837 *Lunch 12.15 to 2.15. Dinner 6.30 to 9. Expensive.*

Eddleston The Horse Shoe Inn Peeblesshire
TEL (072 13) 225 *Mon to Sat 11.30 to 2.30, 5 to 11. Sun 12 to 2, 6.30 to 10.30. Wholefood · inexpensive.*

Ellesmere The Grange Shropshire
TEL (069 171) 2735 *Daily 7 to 9.30. Wholefood · medium · rooms.*

Farnham The Viceroy Restaurant 23 East Street Surrey
TEL (0252) 710949 or 716054 *Daily 12 to 2.30, 6.30 to 11.30. Medium.*

Glastonbury Rainbow's End Cafe 17a High Street Somerset
TEL (0458) 33896 *Daily 10 to 4.30. Closed Wed and Sun. Vegetarian · wholefood · inexpensive.*

Hanmer Buck Farm Clwyd
TEL (094 874) 339 *Daily 7 to 3, 7 to 11. Wholefood · inexpensive · rooms.*

Harlech The Cemlyn High Street Gwynedd
TEL (0766) 780425 *Daily 7 to 9.30. Wholefood · medium.*

Harrogate Hedleys Wine Bar 4 Montpellier Parade North Yorkshire
TEL (0423) 66881 *Mon to Sat 11.30 to 3, 6.30 to 10.30. Medium.*

Harrogate Maddicks Seafood Restaurant 4 Montpellier Parade North Yorkshire
TEL (0423) 66881 *Mon to Sat 12 to 2.30, 7 to 12. Medium.*

Haslemere Crown and Cushion Weynill Surrey
TEL (0428) 3112 *Daily 10.30 to 3, 6 to 11. Inexpensive.*

Hastings Number One 1 Brook Street East Sussex
TEL (0424) 444383 *Bookings all year round any time. Vegetarian · wholefood · medium · rooms.*

Haverfordwest Wolfscastle Country Hotel and Restaurant Pembrokeshire Dyfed
TEL (043 787) 225 *Daily 12 to 2.30, 7 to 9.30. Medium.*

Holford G. Perry Smith and Partners Riverside Cornwall
TEL (032 623) 443 *Apr to Oct daily 7.30 to 9.30. Expensive.*

Herstmonceux Sundial Restaurant Gardner Street East Sussex
TEL (0323) 832217 *Tue to Sat 12.30 to 2.30, 7.30 to 9.30. Sun 12.30 to 2.30. Expensive.*

Higher Disley Moorside Hotel Mudhurst Lane Nr Stockport Cheshire
TEL (066 32) 4151 or 3000 *Mon to Sat 12.30 to 2.30, 7 to 11. Wholefood · expensive · rooms.*

Hindon The Lamb Nr Salisbury Wiltshire
TEL (074 789) 225 *Daily 12 to 2, 7 to 10. Medium.*

Hinton Charterhouse Homewood Park Hotel Bath Avon

TEL (022 122) 2643 *Daily 12 to 1.30, 7 to 9.30. Sun 7 to 8.30. Wholefood · expensive · rooms.*
Hope End Hope End Ledbury Herefordshire
TEL (0531) 3613 *Mar to Dec Open. Dinner 7.30. Wholefood · expensive.*
Horton Gower The Hollies Swansea South Wales
TEL (0792 390) 423 *Daily 9 to 11.30, 12 to 3.30, 7 to 12. Wholefood · inexpensive · rooms.*
Hove Figs 81 George Street East Sussex
TEL (0273) 776776 *Mon to Sat 9.30 to 5. Vegetarian · inexpensive.*
Huddersfield Shabab Restaurant Ltd 37–39 New Street West Yorkshire
TEL (0484) 49514 *Daily 11.30 to 2.30, 6 to 11.45. Closed Sun Lunch. Inexpensive.*
Huntingdon The Old Bridge Hotel 1 High Street Cambridgeshire
TEL (0480) 52681 *Daily 12 to 2, 7.30 to 10.30. Inexpensive.*
Ilkley Craig End Lodge Vegetarian Guest House Cowpasture Road Yorkshire
TEL (0943) 609897 *Open Easter to Nov. Daily 8.30. Lunch 1. Dinner 7. Wholefood · vegetarian · inexpensive · rooms.*
Ipswich Marno's Food Reform 14 St. Nicholas Street Suffolk
TEL (0473) 53106 *Mon to Sat 10.30 to 2.30. Vegetarian · wholefood · medium.*
Isle of Iona Argyll Hotel Baile Mor Argyll
TEL (068 17) 334 *Daily Easter to Oct 8.30 to 9, 12.30 to 1.30, 7. Wholefood · medium · rooms.*
Keighley Ponden Hall Stanbury West Yorkshire
TEL (0535) 44154 *Meals usually for residents only. Wholefood · vegetarian · medium · rooms.*
Kendal Waterside Wholefoods Kent View Cumbria
TEL (0539) 29743 *Mon to Sat 9 to 4. Vegetarian · wholefood · inexpensive.*
Kenmare Park Hotel Co. Kerry Ireland
TEL (064) 41200 *Apr to Nov 8 to 10, 1 to 2 and Dinner 7 to 10.45. Wholefood · inexpensive.*
Keswick Orchard House Borrowdale Road Cumbria
TEL (0596) 72830 *Daily. Dinner from 6.30. Must book. Vegetarian · medium · rooms.*
Keswick Underscar Applethwaite Cumbria
TEL (0596) 72469 *Daily all day. Closed 2 weeks Christmas. Wholefood · expensive · rooms.*
Kingham The Mill Hotel and Restaurant Oxfordshire
TEL (060 871) 8188 *Daily 7.45 to 11. Medium · rooms.*
Kingussie The Osprey Hotel Highlands
TEL (054 02) 510 *Daily 8.30 to 9.30, 7.30 to 8. Wholefood · medium · rooms.*
Langbank Gleddoch House Hotel and Restaurant Renfrewshire
TEL (047 554) 711 *Daily 12.30 to 2, 7.30 to 9.30. Expensive · rooms.*
Ledmore Shepherds Cottage By Lairg Sutherland
TEL (085 484) 243 *Bookings only from Oct to May. Daily 8 to 9.30, 7 to 8. Closed Christmas. Vegetarian · wholefood · inexpensive · rooms.*
Leighton Buzzard The Swan Hotel and Restaurant High Street Bedfordshire
TEL (0525) 372148 *Daily 12 to 2, 7 to 10. Wholefood · expensive · rooms.*
Lelant Woodcote Hotel The Saltings St Ives Cornwall
TEL (0736) 753147 *Daily Mar to Oct 6.30 to 10. Vegetarian · wholefood · medium · rooms.*
Leswalt Lochnaw Castle By Stranraer Wigtownshire
TEL (077 687) 227 *Open for all meals. Wholefood · medium · rooms.*
Letterfrack Rosleague Manor Connemara Co. Galway Ireland
TEL Moyard 7 *Open Easter to Nov. Wholefood · expensive · rooms.*
Lincoln Straits Wine Bar 8/9 The Strait Lincolnshire
TEL (0522) 20814 *Mon to Sat 12 to 2.30, 7 to 11. Inexpensive.*
Llandudno Junction The Queens Head Glanwydden Gwynedd
TEL (0492) 46570 *Daily 11 to 3, 7 to 10.30, 7 to 11 Summer. Wholefood · medium · rooms.*
Llanelidan Leyland Arms Hotel Ruthin Clwyd
TEL (082) 45207 *Daily 12 to 3, 7 to 12. Medium · rooms.*
London Ajimura Japanese Restaurant 51/53 Shelton Street WC2
TEL 01-240 0178 *Mon to Sat 12 to 5, 6 to 11. No lunch Sat. Wholefood · expensive.*
London Athenaeum Hotel 116 Piccadilly W1
TEL 01-499 3464 *Daily 7 to 10.30, 12.30 to 2.30, 6 to 10.30. Expensive.*
London Govindas Vegetarian Restaurant 9 Soho Street W1

TEL 01-437 8442 *Mon to Fri 11.30 to 8. Sat 12 to 6. Vegetarian · inexpensive.*
London L. S. Grunts, Chicago Pizza Co. 12 Maiden Lane WC2
TEL 01-379 7722 *Daily 12 to 11.30. Inexpensive.*
London The Hat Shop 11 Goldhawk Road Shepherds Bush W12
TEL 01-740 6437 *Daily 12 to 11. Inexpensive.*
London Kalamaras 76/78 Inverness Mews W2
TEL 01-727 9122 *Mon to Sat. Dinner 7 to 12. Medium.*
London Mandeer 21 Hanway Place Tottenham Court Road W1
TEL 01-323 0660 *Mon to Fri 12 to 3. Vegetarian · inexpensive.*
London Nature's Way 140 High Street Penge SE20
TEL 01-659 0814 *Mon to Sat 10 to 4. Vegetarian · wholefood · inexpensive.*
London Neals Yard Soup and Salad Bar 2 Neals Yard Covent Garden WC2
TEL 01-836 3233 *Mon to Sat 11 to 5. Vegetarian · wholefood · inexpensive.*
London Royal Garden Hotel Kensington High Street W8
TEL 01-937 8000 *Lunch Mon to Fri 12.30 to 2.30. Dinner Mon to Sat 7 to 1. Wholefood ·*
expensive · rooms.
London Sabras 263 High Road Willesden Green NW10
TEL 01-459 0340 *Tue to Sun 12.30 to 9.45 Summer. Winter close 8.30. Vegetarian · medium.*
London The Sun Wheel 3 Chalk Farm Road NW1
TEL 01-267 8116 *Daily 12 to 12. Medium.*
London Swiss Centre Restaurants 10 Wardour Street W1
TEL 01-734 1291 *Daily 12 to 12. Medium.*
Lostwithiel Trewithen Restaurant 3 Fore Street Cornwall
TEL (0208) 872373 *Mon to Sat 7 to 9.30 Summer. Winter Tue to Sat. Medium.*
Lynton Chough's Nest Hotel North Walk Devon
TEL (0598) 53315 *Week prior to Easter to mid-Oct 7 to 8. Wholefood · vegetarian · medium ·*
rooms.
Machynlleth Plas Dolgrog Hotel Powys
TEL (0654) 2244 *Daily Dinner 7 to 9. Sunday Lunch 12 to 2.30. Wholefood · vegetarian ·*
medium · rooms.
Malvern (West) Runnings Park Hotel and Conference Centre Croft Bank Worcestershire
TEL (068 45) 3868 *Daily 8.30 to 9, 12.30 to 2, 7 to 7.30. Wholefood · vegetarian · medium ·*
rooms.
Manchester Body 'n Soul 23 Whittle Street Left off Oldham Street Greater Manchester
TEL 061-832 6834 *Wed to Sat 5 to 10.30. Sat 12.30 to 10.30. Vegetarian · medium.*
Manchester Greenbourne 331 Great Western Street Rusholme Greater Manchester
TEL 061-224 0730 *Daily 12 to 2.45, 5.30 to 11. Vegetarian · wholefood · inexpensive.*
Manchester Kosmos Taverna 248 Wilmslow Road Fallow Field Greater Manchester
TEL 061-225 9106 *Daily 6.30 to 11.30. Fri/Sat 6.30 to 12.30. Medium.*
Manchester Wild Oats 88 Oldham Street Greater Manchester
TEL 061-236 6662 *Wed to Sat 5 to 11. Wholefood · vegetarian · medium.*
Mayfield Old Brew House Restaurant High Street Sussex
TEL (0435) 872342 *Tue to Sat 7.30 to 9.30. Sat Lunch 12.30 to 1.30. Wholefood · vegetarian ·*
medium.
Minstead Honeysuckle Cottage Restaurant Nr Lyndhurst Hampshire
TEL (0703) 813122 *Wed to Sat 7.30 onwards. Wholefood · expensive.*
Newton Tabuteaus Restaurant Newton Grange Rugby
TEL (0788) 860348 *Tue to Sat 7.30 to 12. Lunch parties by arrangement. Wholefood · medium.*
Northallerton McCoy's Restaurant The Tontine Staddlebridge North Yorkshire
TEL (060 982) 207/427 *Open Mon to Sat all day. Wholefood · vegetarian · expensive · rooms.*
Northam Grays Restaurant 4 Fore Street Bideford North Devon
TEL (023 72) 6371 *Tue to Sat 7.30 to 9.30. Closed 2 weeks Oct. Wholefood · medium.*
Norwich Bagley's Barn Pancake Restaurant 3 Bagley's Court Pottergate Norfolk
TEL (0603) 26763 *Mon to Sat 12 to 2.15, 6.30 to 11. Inexpensive.*
Norwich The Coffee Bar Sainsbury Centre for Visual Arts University of East Anglia
Norfolk

TEL (0603) 56161, Ext. 2468 *Tue to Sun 12.30 to 4.30. Wholefood · vegetarian · inexpensive.*
Oxford Cherwell Boathouse Bardwell Road Oxfordshire
TEL (0865) 52746 *Daily 2 to 10.30. Sun Lunch 12.30 to 2. Lunch Weekdays 12.30 to 2,
Sun all year 1 to 2; dinner 8 to 10.30. Summer. Wholefood · vegetarian · medium.*
Peebles Sunflower 6 Bridgegate Borders
TEL (0721) 22420 *Mon to Sat 10 to 5.30. Half-day Wed. Vegetarian · inexpensive.*
Penrith In Clover Poets Walk Cumbria
TEL (0768) 67474 *Mon to Sat 9 to 5. Wholefood · vegetarian · inexpensive.*
Perranuthnoe Ednovean House Hotel Nr Penzance Cornwall
TEL (0736) 711071 *Daily 6.30 to 8. Wholefood · vegetarian · medium.*
Pershore The Angel Inn and Posting House 9 High Street Hereford and Worcester
TEL (0996) 552046 *Daily 8 to 9, 12 to 2, 7 to 9. Wholefood · vegetarian · expensive.*
Pilton Long House Pylle Road Somerset
TEL (074 989) 283 *Open Daily 8.45 Breakfast. Dinner 7.30. Nov to Feb advance bookings.
Wholefood · vegetarian · medium · rooms.*
Pinner La Giralda 66 Pinner Green Middlesex
TEL 01-868 3429 *Tue to Sat 12 to 2.30, 6.30 to 10.30. Wholefood · vegetarian · medium.*
Pontfaen Tregynon Farmhouse Nr Fishguard Pembrokeshire
TEL (0239) 820531 *Daily, dinner 7 onwards. Wholemeal · vegetarian · inexpensive.*
Poole Inn and Nutshell 27 Arndale Centre Dorset
TEL (0202) 673888 *Mon to Sat 9.30 to 5. Vegetarian · inexpensive.*
Poole The Mansion House Hotel Thames Street Dorset
TEL (0202) 685666 *Mon to Sat 12.30 to 2.15, 7 to 10. Wholefood · vegetarian · expensive ·
rooms.*
Ripon The Old Deanery Restaurant Unster Road North Yorkshire
TEL (0765) 3518 *Mon to Sat 12 to 2, 7 to 10. Wholefood · vegetarian · vegan · medium.*
Robeston Wathen Robeston House Hotel Nr Narberth Dyfed
TEL (0834) 860 392 *Closed Jan. Daily 7 to 9.30. Lunches during summer months. Wholefood ·
vegetarian · medium · rooms.*
Ross-on-Wye Pengethley Herefordshire
TEL (0989) 87 211 *Daily 8 to 10, 12.30 to 3, 7 to 12.30. Wholefood · vegetarian · expensive.*
St. Austell Boscundle Manor Tregrehan Cornwall
TEL (0726) 81 3557 *Mon to Sat 7.30 onwards. Wholefood · vegetarian · expensive · rooms.*
St. Breward Shap Hundred Shap Hundred Higher Penquite Bodmin Cornwall
TEL (0208) 850659 *Open at times convenient to guests. Wholefood · vegetarian · vegan ·
inexpensive · rooms.*
St. Martins Itati Le Varclin Guernsey
TEL (0481) 38754 *Open 20th May to 20th Sep. Breakfast and evening meals only. Wholefood ·
vegetarian · inexpensive · rooms.*
Salisbury Mainly Salads 18 Fisherton Street Wiltshire
TEL (0722) 22134 *Mon to Sat 10 to 5. Vegetarian · wholefood · inexpensive.*
Scarastavore Scarista House Isle of Harris Western Isles
TEL (085 985) 238 *Mon to Sat dinner only. Non-residents must book. Wholefood · vegetarian ·
expensive · rooms.*
Scotsdyke March Bank Country House Hotel via Longtown Cumbria
TEL (0228) 791325 *Open Jan. to Nov. Lunch and dinner bookings. Wholefood · vegetarian ·
medium · rooms.*
Seaford Trawlers 32/34 Church Street East Sussex
TEL (0323) 892520 *Mon to Sat 10 to 2, 5 to 9 restaurant. 11.30 to 2, 5 to 9/10 take-away.
Inexpensive · vegetarian.*
Sedbergh Oakdene Country Hotel Garsdale Road Cumbria
TEL (0587) 20280 *Mar to Dec daily 8 to 8. Wholefood · vegetarian · medium · rooms.*
Sevenoaks Alpinia Patisserie 1 Tubs Hill Parade Kent
TEL (0732) 454669 *Daily 8.30 to 6.30. Half-day Mon. Inexpensive.*
Southport Casa Italia 517 Lord Street Merseyside
TEL (0704) 33402 *Wed to Mon 12 to 2, 6 to 11. Inexpensive · vegetarian.*

Ston Easton Ston Easton Park Bath Avon
TEL (076 121) 631 *Daily 12 Lunches. Dinner from 7.30. Wholefood · vegetarian · expensive · rooms.*

Stratford-on-Avon The Vintner Wine Bar 5 Sheep Street Warwickshire
TEL (0789) 297259 *Daily 10.30 to 11. Wholefood · vegetarian · medium.*

Studley Interesting Things 8 Marble Alley Warwickshire
TEL (052 785) 3964 *Tue to Sat 10 to 5. Inexpensive · vegetarian.*

Sudbury The Coffee Shop 36 King Street Suffolk
TEL (0787) 73632 *Mon to Sat 8 to 4.30. Inexpensive · vegetarian.*

Sunderland Raffles Coffee Lounge 24 Frederick Street Tyne and Wear
TEL (0783) 40623 *Mon to Sat 9 to 5. Inexpensive · vegetarian.*

Swansea Home on the Range Ltd 174 St. Helens Avenue West Glamorgan
TEL (0792) 467166 *Mon to Sat 10.30 to 3.30 and Wed to Sat 6 to 10. Inexpensive · vegetarian.*

Talsarnau Hotel Maes-Y-Neuadd Gwynedd North Wales
TEL (0766) 780 200 *Daily 12.30 to 2, 7.30 to 9. Medium · rooms.*

Tetbury Gentle Gardener Hotel Long Street Gloucestershire
TEL (0666) 52884 *Wine Bar Mon to Sat 7.30 to 10. Dinners Wed to Sat 7.30 to 10. Medium · rooms.*

Thornden Dowlands Eye Suffolk
TEL (037 971) 262 *Open daily from 6.30. Vegetarian · wholefood · inexpensive · rooms.*

Thurlestone Thurlestone Hotel Nr Kingsbridge Devon
TEL (0548) 560382 *Open daily breakfast and dinner. Expensive · rooms.*

Tintagel House on the Strand Trebarwith Strand North Cornwall
TEL (0840 770) 326 *Open Easter to Nov 10.30 to 9.30. Inexpensive.*

Tintern The Nurtons Chepstow Gwent
TEL (029 18) 253 *Open Mar to Nov. Breakfast 8.30. Dinner 7. Vegetarian · wholefood · medium · rooms.*

Tiverton Hendersons Restaurant 18 Newport Street Devon
TEL (0884) 254256 *Tue to Sat 12.15 to 2 and dinner from 7.15. Medium · vegetarian.*

Torquay Brookesby Hall Hotel Heskeith Road Devon
TEL (0803) 22194 *Open Apr to Nov 8.30 to 9.30, 6.30 to 7.30. Vegetarian · wholefood · inexpensive · rooms.*

Torquay Feist's Restaurant 59 Abbey Road Devon
TEL (0803) 26081 *Open daily in summer. Tue to Sat 12 to 2, 7 to 10. Medium · vegetarian.*

Torrington Rebecca's 8 Potacre Street Devon
TEL (0805) 22113 *Mon to Sat 9 to 9.30. Wholefood · vegetarian · inexpensive · rooms.*

Tweedsmuir The Crook Inn Biggar Lanarkshire
TEL (089 97) 272 *Daily 12.15 to 2.15, 7 to 9. Wholefood · medium.*

Ullapool Altnaharrie Ross-shire Highland
TEL (0854) 83230 *Open Apr to Oct lunches, dinners. Wholefood · medium · rooms.*

Wadebridge Pityme Restaurant and Bars Rock Road St. Minver Cornwall
TEL (020 886) 2228 *Daily 11 to 2.30, 6 to 11. Inexpensive.*

Warminster Jenner's 45 Market Place Wiltshire
TEL (0985) 213385 *Daily 9.30 to 5.30. Winter closed Sun. Vegetarian · wholefood · inexpensive.*

Watford Pizza et Pizza 129 High Street Hertfordshire
TEL (0923) 44841 *Daily 11.30 to 12. Inexpensive · vegetarian.*

Wellingborough Tithe Barn Restaurant Burystead Place Tithe Barn Road Northamptonshire
TEL (0933) 78764 *Mon to Sat 10 to 4.30. Wholefood · vegetarian · vegan · inexpensive.*

West Mersea Blackwater Hotel 20/22 Church Road Essex
TEL (0206) 383338/383038 *Daily 12 to 2, 7 to 10. Closed Tue lunch and Sun night. Expensive · vegetarian.*

Wetheral Fantails Restaurant The Green Carlisle Cumbria
TEL (0228) 60239 *Tue to Sat 12 to 2, 6 to 9.30. Closed Feb. Wholefood · vegetarian · medium.*

Windermere Roger's Restaurant 4 High Street Cumbria
TEL (096 62) 4954 *Mon to Sat 7 to 10. Closed Mon Jan to Mar. Wholefood · medium.*

Worcester Natural Break 4 The Hopmarket Hereford and Worcester
TEL (0905) 26654 *Mon to Sat 10 to 4. Wholefood · vegetarian · inexpensive.*
Worthing Hannah 165 Montague Street West Sussex
TEL (0903) 31132 *Mon to Sat 9 to 5 and Fri and Sat 7 to 10. Wholefood · vegetarian · inexpensive.*
Worthing Vega 17 Warwick Street West Sussex
TEL (0903) 32920 *Mon to Sat 10 to 5. Wholefood · vegetarian · inexpensive.*
York Daily Wholefood Guest House 3 Scarcroft Road North Yorkshire
TEL (0904) 39367 *Daily from 6.30. Inexpensive · rooms · vegetarian · wholefood.*
York Gillygate Millers Yard North Yorkshire
TEL (0904) 24045 *Mon to Sat 10 to 5.30. Vegetarian · wholefood · inexpensive.*
York York Wholefood Restaurant 98 Micklegate North Yorkshire
TEL (0904) 56804 *Mon to Sat 10 to 3.30 (3 on Wed). Thur to Sat 7.30 to 10. Vegetarian · wholefood · vegan · inexpensive.*

SHOPS

Neal's Yard, London

Ambrosia Wholefoods Ltd, 160 King Street   TEL Aberdeen (0224) 639096

Customers from far and wide, from the higher reaches of the scenic Dee and Don valleys frequently call at this co-operative. Behind the counter it's women only; in the shop they are not short of male customers for their good wholesome food at reasonable prices. A good deal of their flour is milled for them by Green City in Glasgow, the remainder by Pimhill. Apart from bread, which comes from Newton Dee Village Bakery and includes a fine rye loaf, ready to eat foods are hardly stocked. Good natural produce is: all flours and grains are organic and so too are pulses, whenever this is possible. There are nearly always fine quality, unsulphured Afghan apricots, and organically grown Moroccan dates. They have goats' cheese, natural yoghurt, and free range eggs. 'Campaign Coffee' (unexploited estate workers) using Tanzanian and Nicaraguan beans is a particular favourite. Otherwise expect to find the usual range of juices—Lindaria, Volonte, and Aspel—as well as herbs (including some medicinal), spices and teas.

Open: Mon, Tue, Fri, Sat, 9.30 to 5.30; Wed, 9.30 to 1; Thur, 9.30 to 7.

Health and Dietary Food Stores, 81 Rosemount Place
TEL Aberdeen (0224) 630845

A little north of the centre (that is Union Street) but handy for Robert Gordon's, the art gallery, library and cathedral, John Gray's store, below a granite tenement block, has been established some eighteen years. They are practitioners of alternative medicine, but also basic foods and loose goods. Mr. Gray claims to stock over 3,000 lines some 200 of which are herbs. No fresh fruit, vegetables or bread are available but there is a full range of grains, flours, pulses and dried fruits.

Open: Mon to Sat, 9 to 5.

Cornucopia Health Foods, 13 Market Street   TEL Abergavenny (0873) 5346

The Dinsdales are new proprietors of this shop (established eight years) and their philosophy is to attract and educate anyone interested in wholefoods and to cater for vegetarians and vegans. Herbal and homeopathic remedies and the needs of those with food allergies are other matters with which they are concerned. Specialities are a balance between herbs (just short of a century—from allspice to yarrow), teas, honeys, dried fruits and nuts, soya products (Bean Machine tofu—plain, herb and smoked), and vitamins and herbal remedies. A take-away service includes filled rolls, pies, homemade paté and yoghurts from Leasowes but no breads, fruit or vegetables are available. As a matter of principle no form of meat product is stocked. Eggs are from Mr. and Mrs. Rolfe's farm just outside the town.

Open: Mon to Sat, 9 to 5.30; Thur, 9 to 1.

ABERYSTWYTH   Gwent   Map 2
Frost's Fruit and Flower Stalls, Market Hall, Great Darkgate Street
TEL Aberystwyth (0970) 615980

Restaurateurs and private shoppers alike have an affection for David Frost's stalls. They are really run to sell Mr. Frost's own nursery and market garden produce (organic standard flowers too!) but, in his own words, 'we aim to offer a complete range of fresh produce for which we are popular with locals, farmers, students and professionals.' All the soft fruits and a high proportion of the vegetables are organic. When his own home grown supplies fall short of the demand, more are brought in from Aeron Park and Blaencamel. Butter is farm made and there is also buttermilk. There are yoghurts from Aeron Vale and Rachel's Dairy as well as cottage cheeses. Non-battery eggs are his own home produce. Home grown, fresh cut flowers, pot plants and a large selection of the dried variety always available.

Open: Mon to Sat, 9 to 5.30.

ABERYSTWYTH   Gwent   Map 2
Maeth y Meysydd Wholefood Shop   TEL Aberystwyth (0970) 612946

Aberystwyth is a town which takes causes seriously. From Mr. Frost the organic greengrocer; Ceredigian the wholefood baker; to Mr. Engelkamp.—Maeth y Meysydd— who is virtually corn-chandler, from his Upper Town premises. The wholefood trade, one might say, is shared on the basis of an informal tripartite agreement, with Mr. Engelkamp selling dried goods. Cereals, principally flour from a growers' co-operative, and oats—both organic, like the muesli and rice—are often sold by the sack. 'We seem to move tons. Everyone is happy because it is organic and locally grown.' There are useful reductions on bulk purchases. Moroccan dates are organic too but not so the other dried fruits, from all around the world—except South Africa. They are keen to sell more organic foods but find them rather difficult to come by. Apart from a local smallholder's non-battery eggs, the shop is vegan. All kinds of teas and coffees are a feature and some of the former, from India, Ceylon and China, are offered loose.

Open: Mon to Sat, 9.30 to 5; Wed, 9.30 to 1.

ALDEBURGH   Suffolk   Map 3
Aldeburgh Health Food and Delicatessen, 183 High Street
TEL Aldeburgh (072 885) 2234

According to Felicity Bromage, clients aged from five to 90 turn up on her doorstep for 'a little bit of what you fancy, together with advice on diet and cooking.' Of course, they're the regulars: a little sunshine and a festival brings the crowd to 'the only place round about where the message is understood'. Felicity Bromage, here three years, sees her customers 'seasonally divided and probably peculiar to a seaside town', but there are tales of 'winter leanings towards unhealthy luxury and self-indulgence'. So much for Aldeburgh! One begins to wonder what the message was. Mr. Smith, the baker, makes the bread which is both granary and wholemeal though it only comes on Tuesdays, Thursdays and Fridays. Don't try Felicity for cakes, scones or pastries. Fresh fruits and vegetables she stocks when local residents have surplus crops. The sugar-reduced jams and preserves are from Whole Earth, the marmalade is homemade. A wide variety of cheeses, including Blue Cheshire, Maasdam, Quark, Brie and Stilton are stocked as well as a small supply of local, non-battery eggs and dried fruits—a wide selection but always bought in small quantities so reliably fresh. There are loose teas by Hankow and Batchelor, and Twinings do the others. Aspall, Copella and James White are apple juices from conveniently local sources, along with Volonte juices and some de-alcoholised wines. Coming shortly: fruit sorbets with no additives. Finally, there are cosmetics, cookery books, and fresh pasta.

Open: Mon to Sat, 9 to 1, 2 to 4.30; Wed, 9 to 1.

ALDERSHOT Hampshire   MAP 3
Melfoods, 235 High Street   TEL Aldershot (0252) 28927

Little more than a year ago, Simon Avey, with no small amount of family backing and
encouragement, took over Melfoods, but there's been a shop here much longer. Reports
suggest that previous standards are being maintained and probably improved. Mr. Avey
carries a wide-ranging stock, and, in addition to cereals, nuts and grains, there are health
foods and supplements. Although not all products are free from additives or organically
grown, whenever possible unadulterated food is stocked, and, what is more, competitively
priced; the assistants helpful and knowledgeable. All the take-away foods are 100%
wholefood, supplied by Link. They include items as diverse as aduki-burgers, rum truffles
and bread pudding. Cakes include apricot, date and almond slices, and flapjack. Doves
Farm, Allinson and Jordan supply the flours; ice creams and yoghurts are from Loseley;
breads, baps and granary rolls from Manna. Also available: wines, punches and dog foods.

Open: Mon to Sat, 9 to 5.30.

ALFRETON Derbyshire   MAP 6
Herbs, Spices and Wholefoods, 6 High Street   TEL Alfreton (0773) 836363

They've been in the attractive High Street of this one-time mining town for thirteen years
'supplying locals who know what they want'. Customers head straight for the Thomson,
Lexian or Muscat raisins—according to individual preference—and other dried fruits,
which are untreated as far as possible. Otherwise there is a good range of packaged foods,
jams and juices. Herbs are, of course, the house speciality as this is how the shop came into
existence. Mr. Hathaway is a qualified herbalist, and will prescribe, if required. He also
sells cheeses and goats' milk, yoghurts but no eggs. After his original baker closed down
there were difficulties, now happily resolved, with bread, scones and baps delivered fresh
daily—to specification—from the Royce bakery in a nearby village.

Open: Mon to Sat, 9 to 5.30; Wed, 9 to 1.

AXMINSTER Devon   MAP 2
Ganesha Wholefoods, West Street   TEL Axminster (0297) 33957

After six years here (and graduating from a restaurant) the Eastons are now confident
enough to have opened a second branch in Honiton. They draw customers from a wide
surrounding area most of whom speak warmly of the quality of service, the helpful
friendly staff, the variety and competitive prices, and the notable absence of advertising
and sophisticated packaging. Others mention their enthusiasm to promote healthy eating
and the 'beauty without cruelty industry'. Limited supplies of fresh fruit and vegetables
come from local people and the Blakes at Flax Drayton Farm, South Petherton. There are
Loseley yoghurts and ice creams, goats' and sheep's yoghurt and Quicke's vegetarian
cheddar. Turners Rose Farm at Stockland and Dares Farm Dairy, Colyford between them
provide the non-battery eggs. In addition to wholemeal bread, there is coarse wheatmeal,
malthouse and wheatmeal French sticks from John Robinson at Charmouth. As well as
wholefood flapjack, apricot and date slices, there are scones and spiced buns. A good
many of the dried fruits come untreated with sorbates or mineral oil and there are
organically produced apricots and prunes. Take-away foods are all cold (from the same
bakery as the bread in addition to the Wholefood Kitchen in Charmouth).

Open: Mon to Sat, 9 to 5; Wed, 9 to 1; Sun, 9 to 12.

AYLESBURY Buckinghamshire   MAP 3
Counterpoint, 38 Buckingham Street   TEL Aylesbury (0296) 85275

Increasing emphasis is being placed on the retail shop side of this restaurant (see entry) so
in due course look forward to free range eggs, teas, coffees and perhaps grains, flours and

pulses. Homemade, inexpensive wholefoods are available as take-aways.

Open: Mon to Fri, 9 to 3; Sat, 10 to 3.

AYLESBURY   Buckinghamshire   MAP 3
Hampers of Aylesbury, 56 Kingsbury Square   TEL Aylesbury (0296) 23487

Mr. Addison's long established delicatessen is not the first to flourish within the shadow of bigger brother, Sainsbury, in a fragment of the town which has escaped redevelopment. A specialist food store, Mr. Addison's stock is one of exceptional variety, with genuine examples of items such as York ham bought in from J. Adamson in London. Cheeses come in as many as seventy varieties, live, low-fat, goats' milk and buttermilk among them. There are free range eggs from local farmer, Mr. Toome. Coffees from several continents—Columbian, Continental, Jamaican, Kenyan and teas are well represented. Most of his take-away foods are baked on the premises, and are of particularly good quality. Chicken and ham quiches are made up in both white and wholemeal cases, the fats used are vegetable so that other varieties—cheese and asparagus, spinach, mushroom—are acceptable to vegetarians. Samosas and pasties of several kinds, some with tofu fillings, are made locally. A mark of distinction is made with bread, wholemeal from three sources: Goswell and Springhill, and a local Italian bakery which makes a matozza, together with caraway, rye and the increasingly popular kolos. The strong local Polish and German community accounts for the sharp interest. Flours, some organic, are Prewett's, Allinson's, Jordan's and an expensive—about £1 for 1½kg—Canadian white version. They have been known to carry organic vegetables but supplies are irregular. As they are licensed, they stock a range of popular wines including champagnes and ports, and Polish lager.

Open: Mon to Sat, 8.30 to 4.30.

BARNSTAPLE   North Devon   MAP 2
Linacre's Wholefoods, 19 Pilton Street   TEL Barnstaple (0271) 75776

Roughly speaking, Mr. Linacre does the pottery part, sensible domestic wares 'not twee stuff' using local clay in a centuries old tradition hereabouts, while Mrs. Linacre oversees the shop. They like to think that they are the best in North Devon for their large range of plump, succulent dried fruits. 'At this time of the year this is what we make our living from. The finest are American; slightly less so, though still excellent, are the Australian.' As many as possible are additive free, except for some which are sulphur dioxide treated, and are clearly marked so. 'We cannot go too far, otherwise it all finishes up rotten and bug ridden. But, they are not treated with mineral oil, as is much fruit in the trade—in America and Australia it's forbidden by law.' Nuts and loose muesli are the other specialities, which established the shop's individual character. They concentrate on low-salt, low-sugar, low-fat, high-fibre products and diet foods. You can find: Stapleton Farm produce (cottage cheeses, live yoghurts); appetising herb sausages (hormone and additive free) from Ann Petch at Hele Farm; and, not surprisingly, the improved margarines such as Vitaquell and near relation, Vitasieg, along with a complete range of teas, coffees and herbs.

Open: Mon to Sat, 9 to 5.30; Wed, 9 to 1.

BARNSTAPLE   North Devon   MAP 2
Sunfood, 5 Bear Street   TEL Barnstaple (0271) 43476

George, Karen, John and Julie are partners in this spacious old town shop, a little out of centre but close enough to bring in lunchtime shoppers and office workers here and to Heavens Above, the upstairs restaurant run by friends (see entry). Other customers are scattered in the surrounding unspoilt countryside. Wholemeal bread is available and sour dough rye which is homemade daily (someone else's home, not theirs) mostly to a consistently high standard using an organic flour. When they can get them fruit and vegetables are naturally grown. Cheddar and Double Gloucester are both made with vegetable rennets. Yoghurts come in a whole range—natural, sugar-free, fruit flavoured, supplied by Stapleton's and Loseley while free range eggs come from a variety of reliable people. No meats of any kind are stocked. They bag up a lot of their own flour, and sell it alongside the proprietary bagged ones from Doves Farm and Jordan. A big 'L'-shaped counter is divided up into glass fronted compartments for the dried fruits, and all the things like rice and the muesli mixes of which they do quite a lot themselves. Morning Glory (52p lb, and there is a cheaper version at 42p) rates as exceptionally tasty and has people coming in from miles around. Fresh ground coffee, farmhouse cider (still and made locally by Hancocks, 'down the road') and real ale, complete the fare.

Open: Sun to Sat, 9 to 5.30; Wed pm closed.

BATH Avon MAP 2
Allen's Wharf Stores, 2 Prior Park Road, Widcombe   TEL Bath (0225) 316696

The Wharf's first claim to fame was through its links with Ralph Allen who commissioned John Wood to design the magnificent 18th century Prior Park nearby. Tim Bruce is celebrated for opening his corner store just a year ago in the historic area (presently enjoying a reprieve from the planner's axe) where the river and the Kennet and Avon meet. 'Pragmatic not dogmatic' is Mr. Bruce's guiding philosophy; 60% of the fresh fruits and vegetables sold here are organic, coming from Blakes at South Petherton and Charles Dowding's lush Shepton Montague oasis (he supplies the better known Neal's Yard too). Travel on the Indian sub-continent, noting how well vegetarians kept themselves and 'some years of disillusionment as a National Health Service food buyer' brought Mr. Bruce to this enterprising corner store, which actually started life as Ralph Allen's foreman's house. 'Home baked goodies are something of a speciality' made up for him by local people who 'do the dishes they know best'. Breads come from Cobbs of Bath who use vegetable fats for their 'scoffers', rye and wholemeal breads and eggs come from Martin Pitt at Marlborough. Grains, cereals and pulses are out of the wholesale section of Harvest Wholefoods in the city, with more bought in from Nature's Store's range. Fruit juices are Aspalls, Copella, Del'Ora and Stute.

Open: Sun to Fri, 9 to 6.30; Sat, 9 to 4.30.

BATH Avon MAP 2
Broad Street Bakery, 14 Broad Street   TEL Bath (0225) 62631

Rachel Demuth and Donald Butler who trained in Neal's Yard, which they like to think was the most lasting influence, bake their bread daily using a hitherto unknown hand kneading operation, to which they welcome school groups and parties to watch. They will also experiment with customers' own recipes. They begin to be their own people when it comes to the selection of variations on the theme. For the courageous—an excellent accompaniment with cheese—the garlic and onion special finds favour. The cheese and herb loaf is strictly in the Marshall Street mode, the savouriness baked into the loaf. The tea loaf of raisins, dates, orange, lemon, honey, malt and sweet spices is sumptuous. Soya bread offers a meal in a slice—a mix of soya and wholewheat flours, it is full of protein. Equally satisfying is a filling, dark, heavy, rye with caraway seeds. Naturally there is plain 100% stoneground, including large and small loaves, cottage, flats, split tin, and French sticks, pittas, baps, and rolls. Crunchy wheat bread is still wholemeal, slightly lighter with 'kibbled grain for extra fibre and nutty crunch'. A German recipe is used for the sour dough. Flour and Elizabeth David's Bread Book are sold so you can even try yourself! Their range of specialities includes cheese breakfast muffins, tempting (meatless) Cornish pasties, savoury croissants and sandwiches and pittas, 'full of interesting things'. For the sweet tooth there is fruit custard cake, a melt-in-the-mouth combination of fresh fruit and custard, juicy brandy cake, crunchy cookies, gingerbread men and homemade ice creams for the summer. Everything is entirely vegetarian, made on the premises and free from any refined ingredients, artificial flavours, colours or preservatives. Eggs are free range and vegetables locally grown.

Open: Mon to Fri, 9.30 to 6; Sat, 9 to 4.

BATH   Avon   MAP 2
Harvest Wholefoods, 37 Walcot Street   TEL Bath (0225) 65519

More formally known to the many old, regular customers, as the Bath Wholefood Co-operative, consensus is that the basic range of wholefoods here is excellent value. Parents of young children appreciate the large playpen with assorted toys that leaves them free to browse in peace. Given the style of the operation this can mean grazing, studying or both. Others, from outback grazings just arrive monthly or seasonally, to stock up economically and 'keep the housekeeping bills at bay'. At the back, where the shop widens, most of the space is devoted to large hoppers for self-service rice, pastas, peas, beans, oats, lentils and various own grades of muesli. Many in the wide range of flours are both organic and stoneground. Herbs too are from self-service bins and in wide variety. Bread is from Stoneground in Bristol who do wholemeal, fruit and herb varieties. There are various locally made vegetarian pasties, quiches and samosas, which do not break new ground gastronomically. There is also a range of non-animal tested products which includes washing-up liquids, lavatory cleaners and cosmetics. The vegetarian frozen 'chilli' in foil containers is spoken of highly, and there is appreciation for the range of soya products, including milk and tofu. Yoghurts and cheese come in cows', goats' and sheeps' milk forms, and there are Martin Pitt non-battery eggs. Wines and ciders are not carried but there is a wide choice of juices and apple juice concentrate. Fresh fruit and vegetables and a decent corner for a good in-house read.

Open: Mon, 11.30 to 5.30; Tue to Sat, 9.30 to 5.30; Fri, 9.30 to 7.30.

BATH   Avon   MAP 2
Scoff's Wholefood Bakery, Kingsmead Square   TEL Bath (0225) 62483

A bakery, shop and small eat-in—a few stools around a counter top—the inspiration and design come from Cranks. Colin Jenkins, his wife and her sister all once worked there. Savouries and cakes are one of their major strengths including vegan food. In addition, pizzas, nut rissoles, homity pies, pitta breads with fillings which are all cooked fresh daily. Salads are numerous. The cakes are typical Cranks type recipes—apricot, apple and date slices, banana and walnut fruit loaf. The carrot kind has a cream cheese and honey topping. Scones are cheese, fruit and plain. Colin only uses unrefined ingredients and stoneground flour from small mills such as Pimhill, Doves Farm and Shipton which is also used for the granary, wholemeal and oat and rye breads, hand-kneaded from a Hobart machine. His pastry is made using an extra fine 100% flour, just flour, fat and water blended his style. The pizza have a wholemeal, cheese and herb base.

Open: Apr to Sep, 8 to 8; Oct to Mar, 8.30 to 6.

BAUGHTON   Hereford and Worcester   MAP 2
Vine Cottage, Baughton, Earls Croome   TEL Baughton (068 46) 2568

In this tiny village store the owners try to stock as much wholefood as is possible in the space available, eschewing other foodstuffs. In addition to dried goods (which are available in small quantities) they provide free range eggs and goats' milk. Their range of food is gradually increasing as people get to know of their goods.

Opening hours are irregular.

BECCLES   Suffolk   MAP 3
The Hungate Health Store, 4 Hungate   TEL Beccles (0520) 715009

Teaching, publishing and a surfeit of over-rich meal sampling for the Good Food Guide
brought Catherine Dowding to Beccles, and 'the healthier wholefood way'. Victorian
work and more recent rendering partly obscure the 17th century origins of this Listed
shop in the yachting centre on the Waveney. Mrs. Dowding likes to feel that friendliness,
personal attention, and advice are the hallmarks here, 'where stock is top quality'. They
are renowned for the herbs and spices which line all of one wall in sweet jars. 'Customers
help themselves to these and come from a long way around to get them.' Lack of bakers'
goods (except for a recommended honey and lemon cake) and 'samosas, quiches, and
vegetable balls which would never make the headlines' are weaknesses. Fresh vegetables
from Marion and Anthony at Fressingfield and Katie and Desmond at Halesworth are
sporadic but are organic and there are non-battery eggs. A 10 % discount comes with
anything over 5 lb in the flour line which includes one from Garboldisham Windmill
(organic), as well as all the usual pulses and grains. Dried fruits include all the regular
varieties and the very popular seedless Lexia raisins. 'We are an antidote to supermarket
uniformity—and very popular with regulars and visitors.'

Open: Mon to Sat, 9 to 1, 2 to 5; Wed, 9 to 1.

BEDALE   North Yorkshire   MAP 6
Bedale Bakery, Allerton House   TEL Bedale (0677) 22195

In a small firm of Swiss patissiers, a younger generation has an obvious commitment to
alternative food. Well known for their cream cakes and other shameless things, their
Ripon and Bedale bakery shops yield a fantastic range of zealously correct stoneground
wholemeal delicacies. In York's Gillygate (see entry) is a small mill where the flour is
ground while someone from their Ripon bakery looks on. Quiches take on new meanings
with the leek and Gruyère, the broccoli and mushroom or spinach and Gruyère making
choice difficult. Fresh fruit pies are just that; tinned fruit is never used. There are
combinations of raspberry and orange, blackberry and apple, bilberry, gooseberry and
more according to season. Fruit cakes draw equal acclaim and as a sideline 5,000 or so are
exported each year. But beware, 'the sloe gin', 'honey liqueur' and 'old peculiar' (all fruit
cakes); butter goes into all of them, including the wholemeal version. Safer is the bran loaf
made with goats' milk or a moist carrot cake adapted from a Cranks' recipe.

Open: Mon, Tue, Wed, Fri, 8.30 to 5; Thur, 8.30 to 1; Sat, 8.30 to 2.

BEDFORD   Bedfordshire   MAP 3
Sunflower Wholefoods, 103 Castle Road

Established six years, the stock of this co-operative is largely limited to dried goods such
as grains, fruits, nuts and mueslis which are available in bulk. They are perhaps a little
unusual too in that they trade seven days a week, even opening until 8 pm weekdays. A
local group of Friends of the Earth was responsible for establishing the non-profit making
enterprise and staff are a combination of paid servers and volunteers. A neat published
price list is an attraction, running to just under 250 items, though it gives no indication of
the economies made with bulk purchases (be prepared to haggle is probably the best
advice), neither is there any indication of which stock is organic. Jordan's are the only
proprietary brand flours but they do offer their own pack stoneground (at a higher price)
along with rye, brown rice, buckwheat and carob versions. A range of wholemeal pastas
includes shells, tagliatelle and lasagne, as well as the more regular macaroni and spaghetti.
There is a local goats' yoghurt and non-battery eggs from Mr. Rozman at nearby
Wootton Green. Otherwise there is a notable absence of fresh foods.

Open: Mon to Sat, 9.15 to 1, 2 to 8; Thur, 9.15 to 1, 6 to 8; Sun, 10 to 1.

BIDEFORD   North Devon   MAP 2
Arcadian Wholefoods, 4 Cooper Street   TEL Bideford (023 72) 3243

Garry Wharton and Sue Arnold have been scarcely two years in this good old fashioned shop with nothing added and nothing removed, in the quaint narrow street. Everything is squeezed in, including the wholefood café at the back. It just seats fourteen. They are wholefood rather than vegetarian. Summer time brings visitors; in winter they have a faithful local following. Richard Kerswell sends a few vegetables from South Devon, which is odd when there are closer suppliers. Non-battery eggs come from a farm at Fairy Cross, and there are nine different flours (one organic) and rather more dried and vine fruits, and organic dates. Jams are Whole Earth, Harmony, Stute and diabetic; milk is soya and goats'. Coffee is ground to order and is daily fresh 'in the back' to go with the shortbreads and scrumptious fruit cakes. They are not strong on afternoon teas but the light lunch menu offers baked potatoes, with a choice of fillings including tuna and mushroom, which are cheap, at 75p.

Open: Mon to Sat, 9 to 5; Wed, 9 to 1.

BLACKBURN   Lancashire   MAP 6
Lovin Spoonful, 76 King William Street   TEL Blackburn (0254) 675505

Jean Noble and John Banks go from strength to strength with their seven-year-old combined wholefood and restaurant premises, now at the hub of matters in the prestigious King William Street. Having moved from Mincing Lane someone long had the mistaken idea they traded in securities! 'We test everything' is the by-line in a store trying to stock only natural products and foods untreated by chemicals. Foods are mostly vegetarian, many vegan, many suitable for diabetics. A refrigerated display is stocked with homemade pizzas, flans and savouries, even take-away, convenience homemade soups. Blairs at Pilling maintain vegetable supplies, not fruit, and non-battery eggs are bought from a Ribchester farmer. Bread is bought in from Hargreaves' in the town. Preserves are 100 % fruit/sugar concoctions, the emphasis on the high fruit content. Only non-alcoholic wines and lagers are stocked. Sugar-free soya ice cream, teas, coffees and (too many to mention) grains, flours and dried fruits are all available.

Open: Mon to Sat, 9 to 5.30.

BLACKPOOL   Lancashire   MAP 6
The Health Food Store, 7 Newton Drive   TEL Blackpool (0253) 33959

Stores specialising in vitamins and sportsmen's supplements are not one of this *Guide's* enthusiasms but as the present owner of this old established shop does a marvellous range of flours—Prewett's, Jordan's, Allinson's, Norfolk Organic, Marriage's and Granary— what else can one do but forgive. There is nearly as good a range of dried fruits too, and among fruit juices, blackcurrant, cherry and prune are listed. The only fresh foods are live yoghurts, vegetarian cheeses and non-battery eggs.

Open: Mon to Sat, 9 to 5.30; closed Wed.

BRAINTREE   Essex   MAP 3
James Bowtell, Bank Street   TEL Braintree (0376) 24046

Coming up towards their centenary (their doors first opened in 1890), this family delicatessen and provision merchants is increasingly turning towards wholefoods. It is a place for specialities, like the locally made Fuller's Jersey Yoghurt and local goats' cheese. Bread comes from the Bakehouse in Bocking, and among numerous kinds of flour are Marriage's, Allinson's, Prewett's and Garboldisham Mill. Eggs are from Fishes Farm, Blackmore End.

Open: Mon to Wed, 8.30 to 5; Thur, 8.30 to 4; Fri, 8.30 to 5.30; Sat, 8.30 to 5.

BRIDGNORTH   Salop
MAP 6
Acorn Natural Foods, 64 St. Mary's Street   TEL Bridgnorth (07462) 61896

This co-operative began nine years ago and still has the same three founder members. Their aim is to supply good food without additives and organically grown vegetables. As part of that policy they offer customers sugar-free muesli, wholemeal bread (delivered three times weekly from the Wedge Bakery in Brosley) and unadulterated yoghurts. The yoghurts and cottage cheese are from Dunsters Farm. Vegetables, including potatoes are grown by Chris Mclean at Pattingham. Vegetarian and diabetic foods are specialities, so they stock animal rennet free cheese (Prewett's) and a good line in shelled nuts, dried fruits and give some special emphasis to flour. Theirs is Mayall's organic 100% stoneground, who are, of course, based close at hand, at Harmer Hill.

Open: Mon to Sat, 9.30 to 5.30; Thur, 9.30 to 1.

BRIDGWATER   Somerset
MAP 2
Country Harvest Natural Foods, 29 Eastover   TEL Bridgwater (0278) 422147

This family business goes from strength to strength. Jean Dovey recently enrolled on an advance cookery course, so a restaurant could be in the offing. Not that there is much wrong with present culinary performances; some of the dishes have been star quality even if the Scotch eggs did get a pedestrian coating of Savormix, only salvaged by good stock and some sesame seeds. The customers always go back for more. Nut roasts are lots of crumbled nuts, mushrooms, onions and tomatoes compounded, baked and sliced. They go for supper or on to lunchtime sandwiches. A different nut mixture goes into the crumbly cheese pastry sausage rolls. Two of the pâtés have cheesy bases, another cashew nuts. Homity pies have a strong vegan following. Carrot cake is made to their own recipe although Alan Dovey and daughter Joanne Chrisoforides have a preference for the Cranks' version, given an orange butter icing and walnut topping. A lot of effort went into finding a good baker, and the outcome is an alliance with John Allen at Keinton Mandeville. Mr. Allen uses a traditional oven and his loaf is reckoned to be the best for a good many miles around. His rye loaves, usually bought in bulk, go direct into freezers. The scones, like everything else from 100% flour, are baked on their premises. Wyvern Organics fill in any gaps in the vegetable supplies from Flax Drayton. Goats' milk is Staplelawns Farm and organic. Cows' and goats' yoghurt is Meadowsweet while Stapleton Farms do the fruit and Greek types. Heavens Gate Animal Rescue Centre has grateful hens which send eggs. Sometimes the extensive list of prepacked wholefoods is overshadowed by their other enthusiasms. Mr. Dovey wholesales as well and lists 180 items in 400 sizes, a sprinkling of which is organically grown. There is olive oil amongst the four cold-pressed kinds. All of the Johannus biodynamically grown juices are stocked. Ice cream is the Cricket St. Thomas 40% dairy cream type.

Open: Mon to Sat, 9 to 5.30.

BRIDGWATER   Somerset
MAP 2
Natural Food Centre, 31 High Street   TEL Bridgwater (0278) 56545

One of the old High Street shops in the town, where the Duke of Monmouth was proclaimed King in 1685, these are larger newly refurbished premises for Jill and Peter Kunzli. Crisp bright paintwork, careful lighting and even more stock seems to be going down equally well with old and a whole lot of new customers. At the back is their own wholefood bakery. Another Kunzli is the Thursday Cottage man, well-known for his speciality jams and chutneys. Perhaps surprisingly, they are also a registered egg packing station but it seemed a sensible answer to the erratic supplies of non-battery eggs. The bakery side is a considerable strength. Quiches are made with soya milk instead of cows'; which accommodates the needs of various allergy sufferers and keeps the saturated-fats level down. Origin of the eggs is guaranteed, and the mixture is frequently thickened with rice or potato flour. Pastry flour is mostly Doves Farm organic grade, delivered fresh. The vegetables used are Flax Drayton. Given advance notice they will also bake to special requirements, omitting perhaps the onions but carefully flavouring in the manner of Swiss forebears. The approved flavourings are passed on to cheese and potato and to vegetable pasties. Although it is tricky to get the rye bread to rise without putting in some wheat (as most bakers do), this is being managed. Summertime brings salads. A staggering 150 different lines in grains, flours and pulses are stocked along with cold-pressed oils, cows' yoghurt (South Field Farm), goats' yoghurt (Stone Mill), a local goats' milk brie and vegetarian Cheddar. Jams are the agreeable Ethos (no sugar made by the National Association of Health Stores) and Thursday Cottage to the new format of half the previous raw sugar content.

Open: Mon to Sat, 9 to 5.

BRIGHTON   East Sussex   MAP
Infinity Foods, 25 North Road   TEL Brighton (0273) 690116

Now one of the landmarks in wholefooding, Infinity Foods began modestly enough as small retail shop. The bakery and wholesaling operation came as afterthoughts. Judging from the large, cheery and well detailed price list, publishing could be next! All the items they list as labelled organic are certified organically grown to the minimum standard set by the British Organic Standards Committee. Some foods are imported from the U.S.A. so, as they point out, many are grown to the even higher standards set there. When it is matter of cereals, flours or pasta, the organic versions easily outnumber the regular. Ten out of fourteen grains meet with this standard. No less than ten pastas do the same. The pasta is from Italy but made with durum wheat. The organic grains include couscous (France), bulghur (China), whole yellow millet and buckwheat groats (U.S.A.). Only two out of ten cereal flakes are without an organic guarantee, so there are sufficient to make up an entirely conventional muesli base. Flours offer even more encouragement, as not only is a choice of organic stonegrounds—Elbridge Farm, Boathouse Farm and an 85% Mayall—but they embrace rye, barley, millet and rice also. Pulses are on a weaker from but even here they can rustle up brown beans and lentils, cannellini bean, chickpeas, red kidney and the soya kind. They depend on Spain for some plump almonds, Italy for hazelnuts, with sunflower seed from the U.S. and home grown alfalfa. Apart from Greek currants—and supplies are not always certain—organic prunes and raisins are American. An interesting recent development is their own label jam, using maize syrup, lime pectin and naturally grown fruit, which puts it a complete category ahead of Whole Earth. 'It gives the palate a break from apple concentrate sweeteners,' they claim. Only three varieties at present (apricot, blackcurrant and strawberry) but more may follow and the price is very competitive. On the subject of sweeteners, the barley malt extract is to B.O.S. Apart from the approved Aspall apple juice and cider vinegar, consider another own label range of pear, grape (red and white) and seven or so blended versions. Parents of young babies might consider the Demeter, ready-to-eat babyfoods under the Johanus label, as well as their children's juice. Organic tofu is 'Full of Beans'; sauerkraut and gherkins, two of some of the Eden range carried, one no-salt. All the oils are unrefined, first pressings, all (except the dark style Greek olive) French with the sunflower organic standard.

Open: Mon to Sat, 9.30 to 5.30; Wed, 9.30 to 2; Fri, 9.30 to 7.

BRIGHTON   East Sussex   MAP
Simple Supplies, 11 Princes Street   TEL Brighton (0273) 694600

Aiming to provide good food as cheaply as possible, in trading terms, deserves to pay off. In the course of ten years Ivan, Bas and Andy—and their predecessors—have proved does, moving up from a market stall to two shops and warehouse. Their other outlet at 167 Lewes Road. It's a co-operative of people who seek worthwhile work within a non-hierarchical structure. They are not by any means entirely vegetarian: non-battery chicken meat is sometimes stocked and can also be obtained to special order. Eggs are from the same source. The small, crowded shop has something of an air of Aladdin's Cave with grains, pulses, rice, organic vegetables and a wide range of herbs and spices, and their staple stock. The latter are sold loose and, indeed, there is minimal packaging on all their goods. Vegetables are from over the hill, so to speak, grown by the Reynolds at Barrow Hill Farm, Henfield. 'We sell everything you would expect to find in a wholefood shop, and more, but there is not enough room on your sheet to list them all!' they claim. The usual dried fruits like raisins, sultanas and currants are stocked. Others—figs, prunes, dates, bananas, apples, peaches and pears—are well represented, with 10 % off 10 lb, 15 % off 20 lb and special rates for whole sacks or cases. Daily bread deliveries are from Needham's in Preston, once upon a time a village, now a town suburb. Cheese is made with vegetable rennet. Along with this and goats' yoghurt are water filters, vegetable steamers, recycled paper, seed sprouters and shampoos.

Open: Mon to Sat, 9.30 to 5.30; Thur, 9.30 to 1.30.

BRIMPTON   Berkshire   MAP 3
Jane's Bakery, Oak Cottage, Hyde End Lane   TEL Brimpton (0734) 713814

Handmade bread made the 'money' for Jane to go to college and with that objective behind her, boyfriend John Rhodes carries on with equal dedication after a two year interval. It has got to be the most idiosyncratic bakery. Oak Cottage is an old drovers' inn, and the baking is done in an old-fashioned range. At one stage an energetic Jane had a weekly output of more than three hundred loaves, all hand kneaded. John still lags well behind this record but will make batches to order, to go into deep freeze. 'We set out to make the bread absolutely as pure as possible, for people who are fed up with processed food.' The business grows by word of mouth and John will deliver. The cost for this uniquely textured food, which finds ready buyers, is around 80p a loaf. He will also do rolls and scones, but the latter are made with baking powder. Using Michael Marriage's Doves Farm organic flour, there are claims 'it can be eaten fresh after a week'. 'Malt extract is used instead of sugar which gives the sought after slightly bitter flavour.' Grape oil is used for shortening and just sufficient salt to bring out the taste.

Open: Mon to Fri, 8 to 10, 5 to 8.30.

BRISTOL   Avon   MAP 2
Beanos Natural Foods, 12 Chandos Road, Redland   TEL Bristol (0272) 731147

People from all walks of life crowd into the little Victorian shopping centre store for their brown rice, mueslis and take-aways. Stella Turner, ex-home economics teacher, confidently dispenses vegetable and bean pies, rissoles, bhajis and Scotch eggs from reliable suppliers like Stoneground, Wholesome Foods and Stokers. These same suppliers produce the rye, granary and garlic breads or the muesli loaf and wholemeal which both find greater favour. Carrot, apple and apricot muesli cakes are a speciality. Cheeses include a best-selling genuine farmhouse Cheddar and regulars like Somerset, Blue Stilton and Brie, an authentic Caerphilly, and a Cheddar with garlic. Discounts for quantity off the organic rice and flour. Also on sale are dried fruits free from mineral oils, and teas sold loose.

Open: Sun to Sat, 9 to 1, 2 to 5.30; closed Wed pm.

BRISTOL   Avon   MAP 2
Moores Health Foods, 267 Lodge Causeway Fishponds
TEL Bristol (0272) 651221

A modern suburban shop decorated in Real Fare colours, Alan Moore first opened up here eight years ago. The Real Fare link is to take advantage of group purchasing discounts, keeping prices competitive. That this works can be judged from the fact that he crossed over Lodge Causeway just about a year ago into larger premises. Raw foods, wholefoods and health foods suggest the general style, with a decent representative stock of most lines. Mr. Moore's staff weigh up all the grains, nuts, dried fruits and muesli. Cricket St. Thomas full-cream ice cream is an indulgence while tofu, cows' and goats' cheeses with vegetable rennet are more conforming items. Cottage Bakeries do a granary and a wholemeal loaf in addition to a moist carrot cake, light or textured scones and various fruit slices. All vegetables are organic, and an amazing number of books—over five hundred titles—are stocked.

Open: Sun, 9.30 to 12.30; Mon to Fri, 9 to 5.30; closed Sat.

BRISTOL   Avon   MAP 2
Nova Wholefoods Co-op, 14A St. Thomas Street, Redcliffe
TEL Bristol (0272) 211902

Principally, this is a wholesale operation but the ten member co-operative which has been trading with a spectacular growth record is particularly interested in encouraging smaller co-ops, of say, four or five people to buy, but, in fact, anyone who can put together a reasonable order is welcomed. It is buyer Sanjoy Das' proud boast that their four trucks now turn round in excess of £2m a year. Their origins, as they freely admit, were humble. They would go round to likely shops, take an order on the basis of a price list then, after hiring a truck, would head for London and Whole Earth or Community Foods. Followed by a quick dash back to get the cash! They were lucky to be in a growing market. 'Now we are into brokerage, importing and commodity dealing,' says a proud Mr. Das. 'Since starting to hold stock we have absorbed an 8,000 sq. ft former Coca Cola warehouse.' When buying items such as dried fruits or nuts, minimum purchases of 2½ kg and 5 kg respectively, must be made. All the regular wholefood items are stocked—buckwheat (roasted and raw), couscous, organic flours and oat flakes. The range is wide: herbs alone amount to about 200 lines. Most dried fruits are organically grown; cheddar is curdled with vegetable rennet and the jams are sugar-free or diabetic varieties. Minimum orders of £40 will be delivered within an 80 mile radius of Bristol, for further afield, the order must be £80.

Open: Mon to Sat, 9 to 6.

BRISTOL   Avon   MAP 2
Redland Wholesome Foods, 29 Zetland Road, Redland   TEL Bristol (0272) 46505

'The oldest established health food shop in Bristol—as far as we know, and no one has leapt to contest the claim,' say the Shellabears whose faithful clientèle has been returning for fifty years. How many of them are genuine originals, if any, is not stated. The health food vitamin supplement side of the business has to face strong competition from the wholefoods, so there is a gradual change of face. Helen Shellabear cooks from the back of the premises, the output going to twenty or so other shops in the Bristol area. 'We turn out flapjacks by the thousand, and in variety.' Brownies and carrot cake are other favourites and there is a reasonable demand for the samosas, beanburgers and bhajis. Bread is imported from Bedminster, Miles Kirk's Stoneground Bakery (see entry) which does an interesting range of 100% and 85% extraction loaves. Among the Cheddar and Cheshire, yoghurts and goats' milk, there is a vegan cheese.

Open: Mon to Sat, 9.30 to 1, 2 to 5.30; closed Wed.

BRISTOL   Avon   MAP 2
The Rowan Tree, The Triangle, Berkeley Place   TEL Bristol (0272) 277030

Four shops in one—gifts, books, wholefoods and vegetarian café—has a prime trading position close to House of Fraser, with food the theme. Fresh additive-free foods are the speciality and supplies come from some impressive sources. Bread from Bristol's specialised high quality Stoneground Bakery (see entry) in East Street, who make cakes and pasties as well. Organically grown vegetables from Cherry Orchard (in Bristol), the reliable Camphill Village Trust at Newnham and the Blake family at Flax Drayton Farm, South Petherton. Jams are Whole Earth and there is live yoghurt. They also sell dried fruits, flours (Doves Farm), teas and coffees. Small take-away service in the food shop. Coffee all day in the café.

Open: Mon to Sat, 9 to 5.30.

BRISTOL   Avon   MAP 2
Stoneground Bakery, 78−82 Bedminster Parade   TEL Bristol (0272) 634666

A combination of stone and roller ground wholemeal flour is used to get the larger bran particles which Mr. Kirk feels gives a better, more beneficial loaf. The rye bread is natural rise, made without yeast and there is also a granary version. All their breads are fermented for twice the time of a standard loaf using much less yeast than the normal commercial bakery. Cakes come with a difference too: carrot, apple, natural fruit and coconut are the most sought after kinds. Totally vegetarian, only vegetable fats are used in bread and cakes. Sweeteners, as far as possible, are honey, apple juice, and unrefined sugars—never white sugar and only sea salt is used. Outlets are in Bristol and Bath, mainly to wholefood shops though some are sold to delicatessens and the like.

Open: Mon to Sat, 9 to 5.30; Wed, 9 to 1.30.

BRISTOL   Avon   MAP 2
Wild Oats Wholefoods, 11 Lower Redland Road   TEL Bristol (0272) 731967

Practically a supermarket (for better or for worse) is often the reaction to Mike Abrams' huge range of products which even has a babyfood section. Grains and pulses are self-weigh so you can have exactly the right amount which matters a good deal given undergraduate cash-flow and storage dilemmas in this, the centre of studentland. With all the staff vegetarian and knowledgeable about the subject, cooking utensils, and good prices, it is a sensible place to embark on a cookout. It is another delivery point for Stoneground bread and a selection of pastries, among them the sugar-free variety. Customary dried goods, organic if possible, are available with discounts for large packs. Yoghurt is Langmans, the organic kind (cows' and goats'), Meadowsweet, territorial cheeses, vegetable rennet and eggs Martin Pitt. No meats, fresh fruit or vegetables. Organic wines, cider and ale on the way. Take-aways are from several sources. Macrobiotic diets a speciality.

Open: Mon to Fri, 9 to 5.45; Sat, 9 to 5.30.

BROADSTAIRS   Kent   MAP 3
Good Health, 42 Albion Street   TEL Broadstairs (0843) 62130

Victorian Albion Street (Dickens once stayed in the Albion Hotel here) is in a conservation area, and between the shop and the 13th century former St. Mary's chapel (next door) is the space where 'broad stairs' are said to have once led down to the shore. Hayden and Kay Whiley's timber lined and wooden shelved shop is historic in its own way, retaining the 19th century seaside atmosphere. The old 'breakfront' with the apothecary's shelving is a store for the herbs. Goods are weighed up on the old-fashioned scales while you wait in a corner shop atmosphere. Older customers are happy because they can rely on a greeting and will not be ignored. Bakers' products perhaps do not stand out as being specially good but there is decent bread from Claris in Ramsgate, which brings back many customers daily. Eggs come from people called Voisey-Youldon at

Alkham (FREGG-registered). Organically grown wholewheat flour is grown at Perry Court Farm (near Petham), a Steiner school, where it is also milled. Sugar-free bulk muesli, cheeses, yoghurts and a few take-away items are also available.

Open: Mon to Sat, 9 to 5; Wed, 9 to 1.

BURFORD   Oxfordshire   MAP 3
The Foodsmith, The Forge, High Street   TEL Burford (099 382) 3594

Susan Wood's tiny former blacksmith's is at the bottom of the steep main street, near the almshouses and the Victorian restored church which prompted William Morris into founding the Society for the Protection of Ancient Buildings. The attractive shop (crisp and fresh with genuine period features) is everything that can be wished. Delicatessen foods are a speciality, meeting general small town needs. Six home honey roast hams are likely to be despatched, slice by slice, in the course of a week. She tries to stock as many unpasteurised cheeses as possible. These include Cheddar, single and Double Gloucester, Brie and, when the goats have a high yield, a local one of theirs with chives. Yoghurts are made with untreated Jersey cream on Sir John Langman's Perrotts Brook Farm, together with his Greek style ewe, and the familiar low-fat versions. Another unpasteurised cheese comes from Sir John's Dorset-based sister's farm. Exemplary French bread and croissants are on sale Sundays only, when there is time for baking. Small quantities are readily catered for and there are delicious Scotch eggs which are vegetarian, in a substantial wrap of ground hazels and flaked almonds. Flans and salads are made up in the sparkling kitchen, the former using a lighter fifty/fifty mix of wholemeal and white flour—some with vegetarian fillings, others with chicken and ham. Hot take-away soup is in a class of its own, favoured by impecunious locals. Seasoning can be over-lavish but the mushroom variety is all dark edible fungi, not flavoured flour sauce; chicken noodle, elegant, with fine pasta strands; the carrot robust and tasty. Rombouts coffees are ground to order, and Blue Boar teas are on sale together with an own label house wine.

Open: Mon to Sat, 8.30 to 6.30; Sun, 8 to 1.

BURTON JOYCE   Nottinghamshire   MAP 6
The Drug and Wholefood Store, 49B Main Street
TEL Burton Joyce (060 231) 3672

This drug store was in decline and experienced a renaissance only a few months ago. 'We once knew a marvellous place in Pickering, which sadly is no more because the owner went to Chelsea for some unknown reason. However we were inspired and decided this was the thing for us,' says Mrs. Jean Ford. Actually it was just the thing for her; husband is the local G.P. and in a village of several thousand souls, he is quite busy with his own calling. The byword for the store is a natural healthy diet, nothing added, nothing removed. The drug store side brings in the buyers who might be otherwise reluctant to enter. They rely on Henry Brown, a Nottingham baker, for savouries, breads and sweeter things. Cheese and onion pasties, tvp Cornish pasties are a popular line but might benefit from a more generous hand with the filling. Custard tarts, in a light short wholemeal pastry case have a very short shelf life. Of course they do all the loose mueslies, grains, pulses, nuts and flours as well—reserves at the back of the shop. One of the flours is Pimhills organic. Norfolk Punch—in high demand—is available and fruit juice sales are mainly Volonte, Prewetts, Suma or Jedwells but there are also the St. Clement's fruit squashes approved by the Hyperactive Children's support group.

Open: Mon to Fri, 9 to 12.30, 2 to 5; closed Wed, Sat pm.

CAMBORNE   Cornwall   MAP 2
Health Foods, 62 Trelowarren Street   TEL Camborne (0209) 714242

The A30 (the fast bit, before Penzance) skirts the town and with less mining going on here is more time to let thoughts dwell on the good quality healthy foods sold by the Bowdens. Theirs is a useful stock of dried goods—oat, rye, barley and wheat flakes, and culinary herbs. Mr. Sell's free range eggs and wholemeal bread from Marks, one of the town bakeries, are stocked along with Zimbabwe goats' yoghurt (plain and fruit), and raw and sugar-free jams.

Open: Mon to Sat, 9 to 5; Thur pm only; Fri, 9 to 5.30.

CAMBRIDGE   Cambridgeshire   MAP 3
Arjuna, 12 Mill Road   TEL Cambridge (0223) 64845

Extremely successful traders, as shown by their recent expansions into a warehouse where bulk orders can conveniently be collected, Arjuna like 24 hours' notice and offer price reductions. Slightly faceless (they are an eighteen strong co-operative), it is no place for personality cults, but more importantly, as admirers say, they put principles before profits. Started in 1973 as a macrobiotic shop and restaurant, the style is now more simply that of a wholefood store and packing factory. Unlike most small shops, the policy is to buy direct from manufacturers, importers and growers, not wholesalers and distributors. Baking and convenience dishes are done on the premises; all eighteen members bake from time to time which, some claim, explains the occasional inconsistencies. Chapmans and Maskells, both local, do a really good loaf, 'some of the customers hanging about waiting for delivery' because it sells out quickly. French sticks, soda bread, and croissants are all made with wholemeal flours. Mr. Baker, Michael and Mr. Brookman do the organic vegetable growing and a 'nice lady', Mrs. Swaines, does the really beautiful eggs. It is the good food she gives her chickens which makes the rich brown colour. A little surprisingly she is also a small-time home miller, so her flour is sold too. Goats' yoghurt is Corkhill. No-mineral-oil dried fruits include organic dates and Hunza apricots. Traidcraft teas and coffees are available as well as herb plants in season and the dried kind on a weigh-your-own basis.

Open: Mon to Fri, 9.30 to 6; Thur, 9.30 to 2, Sat, 9.30 to 5.30.

CARDIFF   South Glamorgan   MAP 2
Cardiff Wholefoods, Fitzroy Street, Cathays   TEL Cardiff (0222) 395388

Ashley and Betty Bovan are 'committed to holistical living' at this shop established for the needs of new consciousness' they have been running for eleven years. They opened simply because there was nowhere to get food needed for themselves, and felt there must be others in the same plight. They are no longer macrobiotic themselves, but there is support and interest here for those who are. Dyfed Organic Growers bring regular vegetable supplies from Llandyssul along with live Welsh Farm Yoghurt. Non-battery eggs are from Gwar Hynnon Farm, near Lampeter. A full range of grains, flours and pulses (some organic) with bulk stock on most lines or orders as required. Herbs come ready packed, very cheaply and in great variety. Try them for peanut butters, refrigerated pasties, samosas, burgers (all vegan), from the Bean Machine and Cauldron Foods. Cardiff's huge young vegan population, whose tenacity and commitment is remarkable, buy them voraciously.

Open: Tue to Sat, 9 to 5.30; Fri, 9 to 6.

CARDIFF   South Glamorgan   MAP 2
Pulse Wholefoods, 171 Kings Road, Canton   TEL Cardiff (0222) 25873

Homely, small double-shop premises in downtown Canton are Rosy Thompson's base for a combined food store and alternative therapy centre. Dr. Thompson, a physician (she qualified at Cardiff Medical School) opened up here four years ago. Conventional medicine was just not working so now she directs a friendly, impressive organisation with twelve or more therapists in disciplines ranging from acupuncture, through psychotherapeutics to sex therapies and homeopathy. Naturally there is dietary advice from a nutritionist able to suggest adjustments to lifestyle and diet. Those who found their own way turn up for the breads and other homemade goodies carried on the long racking all down the shop's left hand side. Small scale, local, wholefood caterers do the baked goods. Farmhouse cheeses, brought in weekly from West Wales, are among the highlights. Tyn-y-Grug, Pantyllyn and Waungron, 'done with peppers, garlic, onions' and other unspecified 'things', may turn up in the savoury pastries. Memorable sour dough loaves are done by the same West Wales couple. Gluten-free and strong white unbleached breads are baked in the City's 'Hot Pantry', the same source for wholemeal croissants and a 100% loaf that puts other brown breads to shame. Weekly shop cook-ins provide the lovely lentil bakes, root vegetable pies, or the popular leek and mushroom pie, and the beany bakes. Gooey, sticky gingerbread, fruit cake (made with goats' butter) are among the shop kitchen successes. Summer only, brings a ewes' milk yoghurt. There are fresh fruit and vegetables, origin not disclosed on account of extremely limited supplies which they value. Unconventionally there is bed linen, duvet covers and pillowcases of a special kind and thought to be good, made up by Matthew and Derry, old Banbury friends with a good eye for fantastic colours. The same pair apply skills to dyeing cotton shirts, all cut from heavy Indian cottons. Anytime now, there will be hand-knitted jumpers!

Open: Mon to Sat, 9.30 to 6.

CARMARTHEN Dyfed MAP 2
Aardvark Wholefoods, 2 Mansel Street TEL Carmarthen (0267) 232497

The Barnetts, here nearly eight years, are refugees from teaching and London. Theirs is a comprehensive range of wholefoods and they also wholesale to local buying groups, market stalls and co-ops. Prices are generally reckoned to be low with discounts for bulk purchases. They try as far as possible to buy organically grown foods. Annie Cogan, a local friend with a stall on Cardigan market, does wholemeal baking, mostly take-away savouries. Vegan pasties come from the Bean Machine at Crymych. Basic breads are made from a locally milled and baked wholemeal flour. Rye bread, the very popular sour dough and a raisin loaf (the last two organic and to a vegetarian standard) are from another small bakery at Glynhynod, made by Dutch people who do cheeses as well. There are small supplies of organic standard vegetables from various local growers. Cheeses are in considerable variety, including goats', ewes', Caerphilly and Cheddar along with non-battery eggs, third world coffees.

Open: Mon to Sat, 9 to 5.

CARMARTHEN Dyfed MAP 2
The Covered Market

The hard-hit dairy farmers of Dyfed have resorted to selling their produce the old fashioned way from public market stalls. This is one way out of the difficulties imposed on them by E.E.C. quotas. John Savage-Onstwedder—he is Dutch born—sees it as 'the dairy farming communities non-violent answer. More and more of those with smaller farms have turned to producing their own cheeses and butter the traditional way. Using raw milk as the basic material enhances the flavour and taste.' Mr. Savage-Onstwedder farms at Ffostrasol, and his own Glynhynod Farmhouse Cheese is made using Jersey and Friesian milk, guaranteed free of antibiotics. A mild cheese, it resembles the texture of Dutch Leiden and Swiss Gruyère, in plain and herb varieties (the latter are grown organically). A low-salt version, weighing two to three pounds is also made. In this case a low-sodium salt solution is used in place of the conventional brine bath. Nine different farms send their produce to this stall so there is an excellent choice. Wednesday is market day when there is a good selection of other produce from West Wales growers.

CHALFONT ST. PETER Buckinghamshire   Map 3
Only Natural Wholefoods, 41 St. Peter's Court
TEL Chalfont St. Peter (0753) 889441

'Our latest addition,' Nicki proudly announces as if they had just added to the family, 'is a peanut butter-making machine, making peanut butter while you wait with just peanuts, no added salts or oils.' She is also enthusiastic about their frozen vegetarian meals, burgers, hot dogs, kebabs which are apparently very popular but their warm endorsement so far remains unconfirmed by local herbivores. Nicki and Geoff Hale specialise in organic and vegetarian foods, 'learning the hard way through bad health and opening a wholefood shop seemed the right thing to do'. Bread is organic and made to their own recipe by Horwoods at Bovingdon. Patrick Holden delivers the Soil Association standard vegetables, all the way from Pembrokeshire. Loseley yoghurts and ice creams; Prewitts animal rennet free cheese. Eggs from Manor Farm, Cressenham, Norfolk. For the non-vegetarian, Nicki Hale can recommend a source for organically produced meats, similarly with chickens, but she declines to have anything to do with it at the shop. There is a 5 % discount from bulk purchases of grains and pulses. Attempts are being made to get better supplies of organic fruit juices. A pure, good quality New England ice cream is also available.

Open: Mon to Sat, 8.30 to 5.30.

CHARMOUTH Dorset   Map 2
Robinsons of Charmouth, The Bakery, The Street   TEL Charmouth (0297) 60213

John Robinson bought out this old established private bakery seven years ago after being in senior management with one of the large national bread producers. He is convinced the future of this business is in wholefood. 'Not that there can be anything more nerve-racking than getting up at four on the first morning and doing it yourself.' His aim is to make all breads—white as well—from entirely natural ingredients using English organically grown flours without added chemicals. A rye bread is made up in small quantities. It is a whole rye, not the sour dough type. Because he uses small volumes, Mr. Robinson 'manages to get by with a standard dough, leaving it to ferment three hours or so, not the customary sixteen. No wheaten flour whatsoever is added. Around thirty loaves a week are produced, to order. All the bread is acceptable for vegetarians. Shortly he plans to experiment with lower salt levels. Wholemeal bread, however, is the speciality, going into local wholefood shops as well, and fast gaining ground are the wholemeal pizzas, quiches and cakes, especially the Dorset apple cake.

Open: Sun to Sat, 8.45 to 5; closed Wed, Thur pm winter.

CHATHAM Kent   Map 3
Solastor Health Foods, 272A–274 High Street   TEL Chatham (0634) 811223

The owner of this smart Medway town shop had fifteen years supermarket experience behind him before coming into wholefoods five years ago. Dried goods are mainly packed under their own label in an ethical health food shop where help and advice is given for vegetarian and vegan diets. Link supply most of the convenience foods now, since an arrangement with local ladies was terminated. A Gravesend baker, Smiths, does the rye, cracked wheat, and wholemeal breads, Loseley and Herdgate supply the cheese, the latter eggs as well. Fruit and vegetable supplies are still anxiously being sought.

Open: Mon to Sat, 9 to 5.30.

CHESTER Cheshire   Map 6
Alternatives, 26 Frodsham Street   TEL Chester (0244) 313074

Christopher and Katie Quartermaine are, by wholefood standards, big in the local scene, with another shop in Northgate Street, a warehouse in Ewart Street and yet a further shop, albeit tiny, in Wrexham, after starting off in a back street living above the shop. Somewhere in between came a market stall. After building up a good stock and a reputation for wholefoods in the bright airy, green carpeted shop, there is promise of more and better convenience and take-away foods. Like a good many other shrewd wholefooders they have recognised the latent talent amongst local housewives, who tend to do this sort of thing with more loving care than the commercial baker. P. and A. Davies in the city do them decent wholemeal and rye loaves. Occasionally they manage free range eggs. Soured cream goats' cheese is Neilsons. Organic fruit and vegetables are new to them and under trial. Pills abound—they can pretty well guarantee to find any one cares to name.

Open: Mon to Sat, 9 to 5.30.

CHINNOR   Oxfordshire   MAP 3
Celestial Foods, 4A Thame Road   TEL Kingston Blount (0844) 51556

Miss Connor steers a careful course between the day-to-day demands of a village store and those of admirers travelling increasing distances for her real food specialities. It is this which for her, makes it all so worthwhile. Enthusiastic reporters see her as their delicatessen and particularly recommend the delicious crusty wholemeal from Wrights in Thame, the free range eggs and the soya milk, all big surprises and enterprising stuff for a little place just below the Bledlow Ridge. Meats and cheeses are regular standbys. Expansion—so far as space will allow—is coming with vegetable lasagne, 'in a foil pack just like a Chinese take-away'. Curries and risotto are also in the pipeline. Vegetable, chilli and nut burger are already established favourites—baked beans taking a back seat. A keen village cook is being coached, so more appetising dishes could be on the way. It is just the sort of place to stock up the freezer from.

Open: Mon to Wed, 8 to 7; Thur, Fri, 8 to 8.

CIRENCESTER   Gloucestershire   MAP 3
Great Western Wholefoods, 69 Cricklade Street   TEL Cirencester (0285) 61360

The Prices come up with the quality one would expect in a town such as this where the Bathurst Estate still holds sway. A spacious, tiled-floor shop has individuality in that fresh foods get more than customary emphasis. They happily dispel the notion that whole-fooders must evermore conscientiously munch oats. The highlight is the tiny take-away booth engineered at the back. Luscious, nutty wholemeal baps, sized to suit the appetite, come with delicious vegetable and mayonnaise fillings. There are egg and cottage cheese versions, each with a generous allocation of crisp greenery. Cheese and onion, cheese and tomato and peanut butter are less prosaic than they might first sound, given the quality of the Prices' baking. Salads in cartons come in at least eight varieties daily, all made up from fresh vegetables, nuts and pasta. There is always a rice salad of sorts, perhaps combined with peppers or peas. Fruit salads done out with chopped nuts—natural and fruit yoghurts to accompany. Vegetarian pasties are crumbly savoury jobs which might partner well the regular curry dish. Quiches are whole or by the slice. Vegetarian wedges—bought in from a vegetarian cook—have lentil and spinach bases. The newly launched sausage roll (vegetable filling) has been well supported. Carrot cake of the type that would make the donkey ask for more, almond slices and apple doughnuts. Vegetable fats in everything including the breads, which are of first order. Just a touch of sugar to start the yeast working, no more. Some loaves find their way, wrapped, into the town Waitrose, presented so only the alert make the immediate distinction between them and less substantial bedfellows. A few loaves are known to reach surrounding villages. Hatherop Gardens, Quenington, with help from local gardeners ensure decent seasonal vegetable supplies, sometimes fruit. Cheeses are English and foreign. Woeful Dane Farm, Minchinhampton are the egg suppliers.

Open: Mon to Sat, 9 to 5.

CLITHEROE   Lancashire   MAP 6
E. H. Booth & Co., Station Road   TEL Clitheroe (0200) 27325

Just one of a twenty-one store chain with branches in Lancashire and Cumbria, they claim
to be 'the oldest established multiple grocers in England'. Actually it is an enormous
supermarket with large car parking facilities, 8,000 grocery lines and ten check-out points.
Perhaps not an obvious choice for a *Guide* entry but a good many of the Booth shops
have regular organic produce supplies, grown and delivered by Blair's of Pilling. When
shopping here remember to ask for Blair produce by name. Watch for their tomatoes
(April to November), cucumbers and peppers (June to October) and lettuce (May to
October). September to February there should be carrots, onions, leeks and courgettes.
Wholemeal bread is from three local bakers, all sorts of flours and pulses (not organic),
goats' milk cheese and ice cream are also on offer. Enthusiastic reports speak of superb
cleanliness, attractively displayed foods and excellent service.

Open: Mon to Wed, 9 to 5.30; Thur, 9 to 7; Fri, 9 to 8; Sat, 9 to 5.

CORWEN   Clwyd   MAP 6
Simon's, 4 Edyrnion Terrace   TEL Corwen (0490) 2296

Rosie Prime's and Tony Speirs' cheerful store is part grocery and delicatessen as well.
They need to be to survive in this little Deeside town with a population of only 2,000.
'Many years ago there were six railway turntables here.' Now the town is stabilised in its
decay, with visitors coming for the fishing, the partly 13th century church and the curious
6 foot high monolith set in its east wall. Rosie actually runs the shop while Ray Roberts, a
master baker, produces the popular organic wholemeal, rye and granary loaves on the
premises. When not busy with breads he has an increasing output of pastries, rolls,
samosas and other vegetarian savouries. Only vegetable fats are used. Before long there
should be more convenience wholefoods. They have a full range of soya produce—tofu,
milk, mayonnaise, cream and ice cream. The tofu is homemade and goes into their pasties.
These are supported with a good range of yoghurts and cheeses and local non-battery
eggs. There are random supplies of locally grown vegetables but no fruits. Herbs are
reckoned to be a speciality, numbering 120 or so from stock. Andrew Jedwell, who has
moved on to bigger things—wholesaling and own label cold-pressed oils, peanut butters
and yeast extract—launched the shop seven years ago.

Open: Mon to Sat, 9 to 5.30.

COVENTRY   West Midlands   MAP 3
Drop in the Ocean Wholefoods, 17 City Arcade   TEL Coventry (0203) 25273

Teacher turned businessman, Richard Morris has quickly graduated to two shops (see
entry—Walgrave Road) and is already making significant inroads into ready-to-eat foods
and dishes for the freezer market. Much of the food is homemade for him by locals and he
sets high standards: 'Casseroles find themselves quite quickly making the journey back
home if below par.' Ingredients are free range eggs, 100 % flour, vegetable fats. Some
delighted customers commend the vegan samosas, others rate the superb, extremely tasty
vegan pasties in a light wholemeal pastry. The organic stoneground loaves come minus
any improvers, with a good firm texture done to specification by his nearby baker.
Cheeses are by Singletons in Lancashire, with yoghurts and cottage cheeses from
Huddersfield's progressive Longley Farm. In all there are twenty-four varieties of frozen
vegan meals under the Mr. Chef label from Birmingham—chilli con carne, Mexican chilli,
vegetable pilau, and the less highly spiced but acceptable spaghetti romano are some
getting good ratings. 'A wholefood diet provides all the vitamins and supplements
needed by the normal person,' Mr. Morris observes. 'Anyone promoting tablets and pills
beyond that is simply helping to empty your pocket.'

Open: Mon to Sat, 9 to 5.30; Thur, 9 to 3.

COWBRIDGE   South Glamorgan   MAP 2
L'Epicure, 42 High Street   TEL Cowbridge (044 63) 2387

First appearances might suggest one may be at the wrong end of the town but this quaint shop full of old dressers and tables of interesting displays is something of an attraction in its own right, stocking only the best quality natural products: cheeses, fruits, smoked salmon, prawns, pulses and fresh pasta. Homemade cakes and buns they make themselves, on the premises, though they are not always entirely wholemeal as the lady who makes them prefers to use the hard Canadian wheat she can get in the rival Tesco outlet— proprietor Sue Wadham is working on her. A plus point, vegetable fats are used. Organic fruit and vegetables from Dyfed Organic Growers; non-battery eggs from Mrs. Hayes at Llansannor; ewes' and goats' milk foods from Mrs. Wren at Peterston Super Ely.

Open: Mon to Sat, 9 to 1, 2 to 5.30: closed Wed pm.

CRYMMYCH   Dyfed   MAP 2
'The Bean Machine', Station Road   TEL Crymmych (023 973) 610

Tradition dies hard, so in this admirable organisation—to make commercial sense—they feel obliged to promote and name their range of soya produce as facsimiles of better known foods made with ingredients of animal origin. They are also packaging conscious. Paraded together soysage, soyannaise, tofu and well-formed pasties might well be front line foods on one of Fortnum's counters. Now a co-operative with a national distribution network through wholefood shops in Wales, London and the West Country, Zorah and Jon Groom were responsible for launching the enterprise three years ago. After a spell in the west of Ireland, at an offshoot of the Tennessee farm run by Stephen Gaskin, the Grooms returned to Wales to launch the factory. Born of soya technology, the tofu soysage is just a variation of the soya theme, as is soyannaise which is an agreeable dressing for salads, baked potatoes, or even for adding to soups. The 'factory' where it is manufactured is no less remarkable than the product itself. In a Crymmych side street (Crymmych is so small it doesn't have many side streets), it adds to the character of the mid-west.

Open to traders only.

CUPAR   Fife   MAP 7
Compleat Foods Wholefood Victuallers, 63—67 Bonnygate
TEL Cupar (0334) 53018

To this late Georgian market town, Maureen Tinsley came partly for the simple unspoilt nature of the place. She has been cautious not to do anything to the interior of the shop to detract from the fine traditional Scottish character. Though erring towards pine and wicker, the Georgian style is retained. Untraditionally hereabouts, salads are a high point, with vegetables as varied as the market allows, and often quite unusual because of that. The menu includes cheesy things like salads and flans, homemade soups to ward off draughty days, but no meat. 'A lovely, satisfying, firm textured wholemeal loaf is made at the back, where the two places meet'—shop and snack bar. For customers the rich chewy carrot cake with orange icing on top is a firm favourite. Greek cows' and ewes' yoghurt, eggs from local small farmers, intermittently homemade jams are available. Flours, grains, pulses, coffee ground while you wait and herbs 'of every description she can lay hands on'. Miss Tinsley's goal is to get people eating to a higher standard, making sure they are aware of what they are eating. Reductions for bulk.

Open: Mon to Sat, 9 to 5.30.

DAWLISH   Devon   MAP 2
Poppadums, 39A The Strand   TEL Dawlish (0626) 863128

In this retirement area, Poppadums are popular with older people for their good all round
range of wholefood groceries. During the summer they get lots of younger people down
for a healthy break by the sea and on the sandy beaches. It is a place where one can
confidently come for a representative range of teas and coffees—Hag, Melitta, Ridgeways
and others. They are not licensed but try them for fruit juices which include the Prewett
and Copella brands. Cheeses and yoghurts are from Blackmore Vale, Quickes and
Stonemill, and the latter (they are in Paignton) deliver the non-battery eggs. Flours are
Jordans and some of the less usual stoneground organically grown grains from Doves
Farm. Wholemeal, granary and wheatmeal breads and a seedy loaf made up from
sunflower and sesame seeds come from the Black Swan Bakery in Dawlish—but these are
not made to a vegetarian standard—no one in the area can be persuaded to do this at
present. Other bakers' lines are just a few locally made quiches, flapjack and cakes.

Open: Mon to Sat, 9 to 1, 2.15 to 5.30; Thur, 9 to 1.

DIDCOT   Oxfordshire   MAP 3
Nature's Best, 122a Broadway

Linda Christie, it could be said, grew into the shop, after working a number of years for
the previous owner. Lack of space means she does not stock fresh foods but mueslis, apart
from the fine one bought in, are mixed on the premises. Mrs. Christie mixes a very
popular coarse one. Didcot's doctors tend to send their patients down to her for this and
'in no time at all we are away, into beans, lentils, herbs—there is no stopping them.' An
acceptable wholemeal loaf comes from Shepherds of Chievely, made in their traditional
bakehouse—for knowledgeable tastes perhaps erring towards the light and spongy (in
the nicest possible way) but good for new converts to wholefood. Flours in various grades
are from Doves Farm. Useful range of dried fruits, grains, pulses, herbs, teas, coffees are
stocked and during November and December a wholemeal Christmas cake is available.

Open; Mon to Sat, 9 to 5; closed Mon and Wed, 1 pm.

DISS   Norfolk   MAP 3
The Natural Food Store, Norfolk House, St. Nicholas Street
TEL Diss (0379) 51832

Nicola Kempston's was the first wholefood shop in this part of the world, in a huge former
brush factory tucked away in the prettiest corner. 'We meet the needs of a wide range of
people not just Wholefoodies,' says Nicola, who has a firm policy. 'Our purpose is to
educate the public on the value of food with a high life force and to supply the same
organically grown wherever possible.' The sleepy town of old Diss was not the most
obvious place to go on a food reform mission but Nicola's view was pragmatic: 'if things
did not go well we could always eat the food ourselves, over a period of years!' This last
resort has not, so far, been necessary. The girls are kept busy serving the town needs with
Peter Hibberd's excellent bread (though it only comes in twice weekly), and a year-round
supply of vegetables, and apples in season, all organically grown. Savoury goods are in a
very limited supply but they are absolutely top quality and sell out very early. By devious
means they come from Christine Ryecroft, via Harlesden and the bread van. Eggs are
delivered from Rettery Cottages, Dragon Hill, Eye. She claims to stock every type of
flour, together with some organic flakes, rice and pulses. Just good quality teas—Earl
Grey, Lapsang, Darjeeling, Luaka—but a representative stock of dried fruits. Nicola is
happy to give her advice on gluten and sugar-free diets and the like.

Open: Mon to Sat, 9 to 5.30; closed Tue, 1 and Mon, Wed, Thur, 1 to 2.

DONCASTER   South Yorkshire   MAP 6
Naturally, 10 Market Hall   TEL Doncaster (0302) 832907

This stall in the covered market is the town's only outlet that is devoted entirely to
wholefoods. Dried, prepacked goods are the speciality. There is a ready sale for Jean
Roberts' dried fruits, nuts, nibbles, rice, pasta and beans. She also does herbs, spices, grains
and flours. A good many items are organically grown, particularly the dried fruits. Other
regular stock items are peanut butter, tahini, malt and molasses. Muesli, mixed by Suma in
Leeds, is her best-selling line.

Open: Tue, 9 to 4.30; Wed and Thur, 10 to 2: Fri and Sat, 9 to 4.30.

DORKING   Surrey   MAP 3
Haggers Natural Foods, 348 High Street   TEL Dorking (0306) 880302

'Not the usual run-of-the-mill health food shop,' John Hagger insists and this seems to be
borne out by his customers who come in from Redhill and Reigate 'to a poor old town like
this, without an M. & S.' Usefully, his wife studies dietary therapy and, both having been
vegetarians for 12 years, they feel confident about offering advice on diet and nutrition.
Vegetarian fast-foods include ready made meals, 'which taste as good as home cooking'
(their claim not the *Guide*'s, such as some amazing vegetarian sausages, burgers, salami
and kebabs, imported from Israel. 'The hens which produce the eggs are not fed chemical
feed.' Paul Brown, their keeper, is FREGG registered. The cows and goats supplying milk
for sundry yoghurts are from the Herdgate herd. Cereals and pulses packed on the
premises offer considerable savings in amounts of 5 lb and upwards. Apricots come in five
grades with or without the sulphur dioxide; prunes are unsorbated and the raisins, currants
and sultanas are all without mineral oils. Nothing has been added to the dried bananas,
figs and dates, the last mentioned organic into the bargain. Indian spices they reckon to be
a speciality along with the other ingredients, poppadums (five types), basmati rice,
chutneys, pickles and 'joss sticks for the atmosphere, spiritual day incense for the soul'. No
fresh fruit but their vegetables grown by the Willcox's at Henfield are organic. Barleycup
is their cheapest tea—around £1.05 for a large packet. Paul's tofu is a fine, bland version;
take-aways include just a limited range of burgers and pasties.

Open: Mon to Sat, 9 to 6; close Wed, 1; Fri, 9 to 8.

DOVER   Kent   MAP 3
Dover Health Food Centre, 16 Charlton Centre, High Street
TEL Dover (0304) 210970

First catch your customer was a thought uppermost in the Prevetts' minds when they
came to a unit in a precinct close to Sainsbury, having previously had another town store
on a franchise arrangement. Independence has brought a stock of natural foods, as far as
possible, free from all preservatives. A good many lines are entirely natural. Eggs are from
the Elham Free Range Egg Farm. No chicken meat is stocked but Mr. Prevett recommends
Jordans at Capel-le-Ferne, Folkestone for their non-battery poultry. Anyone seeking other
meats free from hormones or implants are guided to Mrs. Smith's Cliffend Farm, near
Hawkings. He recommends their own stock of goats' yoghurt and cheese which they get
from Whitefits Goat Farms, near Verwood in Dorset, along with the goats' milk. Grains,
flours and pulses come with 5 % reductions for bulk purchases. Wholemeal bread, flapjack
and carrot cake, fast-selling oat and date slices, and some savouries are from Watsons
Bakery in St. Margaret's Bay. The nut rissoles and cheese savouries are usually those of
C. & S. Enterprises in Folkestone, and less anonymous than they sound.

Open: Mon to Sat, 9 to 5.30; Thur and Fri, 9 to 7.30.

DUNDEE   Tayside   MAP 7
Tayside Health Food Stores, 36 Albert Street   TEL Dundee (0382) 405 15

It is many years since Mr. Comstable became a refugee from a multi-national confectionery
company to open his wholefood store beneath a Victorian tenement block. Albert Street
turns its back on the broad Tay Firth but it would be worthwhile visiting the town to see
the famous two mile Tay railway bridge, successor to an earlier one which collapsed in a
gale. Mr. Comstable draws comfort from the fact that the food sold is what the customers
need to keep healthy. So he stocks high-fibre, low-sugar, low-salt, low-fat foods. Some is
suitable for allergy sufferers, some is organic, everything is vegetarian and sometimes
vegan. His is really a dried goods stockist though there are occasions when fruit and
vegetables trickle in, usually customers' own surplus, and the renowned raspberries. A
decent commercial loaf from Goodfellowe or Stevens in Broughty Ferry, eggs from local
farmers and smallholders and as much organic food as possible (sacks to order, 10 % off
whole cases), make up the fare.

Open: Mon to Fri, 9 to 5.30; Wed, 9 to 1; Sat, 9 to 5.

DURHAM   Durham   MAP 6
Maggie's Farm, 6 New Elvet   TEL Durham (0385) 731920

Maggie's Farm is the home of the Durham Wholefood Co-operative. For Tony Curtis,
'one of the workers' it is a flight from another organic activity, archaeology. The shop is
not exactly centrally placed but 'as everything is small scale here anyway this is no
problem'. It is another enterprise which started life as nothing more promising than a
market stall before blossoming into a shop with back up from their own warehouse. 'Our
aim is to provide good cheap, unadulterated food together with information on food and
diet. We are the only wholefood shop in the city so most of our goods are specialities. We
have our own muesli blends and a wide range of herbs and spices. We also wholesale
herbs and spices from our warehouse to other shops throughout the north of England.'
Their stock list is impressive and a delight to peruse for its own sake. In addition to the
conventional range of cooking oils, they carry cold-pressed safflower, sunflower, sesame
and corn germ, though no cold-pressed olive oils. Fruit juices are fairly standard but
mineral waters include Allendale and Highland Spring. They are stronger on teas than
coffee, the range including Assam, Keemun, Darjeeling and Lapsang and a dozen or so of
the herb varieties. Campaign instant coffee is carried. One could scarcely quarrel with the
selection of nuts, grains, beans and convenience items such as pâtés—Golden Harvest,
mushroom and tropical. Dent's, a local baker, provides the bread, while a village bakery at
Melmerby (see entry), across the Pennines sends pastries and scones. Langley Farm and
Bottom Village both supply cheeses and yoghurts, and Singletons a vegetable rennet
cheese. Eggs are free range from Mrs. Beckett at Holywell Hall and Mrs. Sedgewick at Hill
Top Farm.

Open: Mon to Fri, 9.30 to 5.30; Wed and Sat, 9.30 to 5.

EAST DEREHAM   Norfolk   MAP 3
Guy's Health Store   TEL East Dereham (0362) 3402

Ghulam Murtaza's vegetarian school has been an unusual, lasting influence. Guy's is
flourishing. They virtually limit themselves to lines that traditional grocers used to sell,
only missing out on meat items. Bakery goods are eschewed apart from the twice weekly
visit from Norman Olley's North Elmham bakery to bring wholemeal bread. Regulars
know the days when it is due. Lines that are stocked—pulses, rice, barley, flours, dried
fruits, teas and coffees—are well represented along with live yoghurt, fruit and natural,
cottage cheeses and animal rennet free Cheddar. No bulk purchases or concessions.

Open: Mon to Sat, 9 to 1, 2 to 5; closed Wed pm.

EDINBURGH Lothian MAP 7
The Breadwinner, 20 Bruntsfield Place TEL Edinburgh 031-229 7247

The red plush curtains, pelmets and lacy tablecloths are all aimed at 'creating a genteel atmosphere in which customers can buy their wholefoods or sit down to eat curried vegetable dishes or a vegetable pie'. It seems a successful recipe, for this is the McVeys' second retail outlet, after long being a bakery only enterprise. The shops are primarily designed as outlets for their own range of convenience foods and breads. They pioneered a nutty loaf which seems to have been taken up by every other baker, so there is much head scratching in the race to keep ahead with tasty healthy food. Wholemeal bread is made with just a little sea salt, no other additives. More details are given in a leaflet handed out to customers. Wholemeal pastry is used for the apple strudel, banana and nut, or raisin and sultana slices and the honey and walnut and date and walnut varieties. It is also used for the cheesecakes, Danish pastries, fruit, cheese and plain scones, all of which have a vegetable fat shortening. Garlic, onion and cheese topped wholemeal rolls are nearly as popular as the wholemeal quiches, pizzas, lentil burgers and nut roasts to take away.

Coffee shop open: Mon to Sat, 9 to 4.30.
Bakery open: Mon to Sat, 8 to 6.

EDINBURGH Lothian MAP 7
Real Foods, 37 Broughton Street TEL Edinburgh 031-557 1911

This (dare one say) unique organisation—'the largest U.K. distributor'—crosses distributive boards. They are wholesalers throughout Scotland; mail order throughut Britain and the offshore islands; and retail through two city shops in the New Town. 'We are interested in natural diets and attract everyone,' defines their confident mood. Though that may mean middle and upper-class (social divisions never lightly abandoned) cooks, OAPs get a look in too, with discounts. Students come for their cheap prices; the kids for sugar-free snacks; office workers for the take-aways. Local manufacturers make up very acceptable wholemeal pies, flans, sugar-free cakes and tofu cheesecake to their special requirements. Bread is wholemeal and organic. Available too is wholemeal, rye, cracked wheat and tea loaves, all baked by the Garvald Training Centre using polyunsaturated fats. Many packaged foods—pear and apple spread, peanut butter, muesli mixes or local delicacies like wholemeal shortbread—are made to their own standard and have their own labelling. As 'wholesale victuallers' their impressive easily-read list accounts for much of the self-assurance. Prunes, for example, are offered in no less than seven different grades, apricots in no less than ten. The unsulphured Chinese apples in stock are a new variety, lightly preserved in sugar which can be washed off. Corn, olive, sesame, safflower and ground nut oils are carried in cold-pressed grades, some virgin and the olive as extra virgin. One of the seven gluten-free flours is suitable for babies. All the massive range of flours are free of additives, bleach and bromide. Among the stoneground flours are Springhill, in coarse and fine grades; their own house label Special Bread; British Bread and Biscuit (coarse and fine) and Malthouse. The last is a blend of wheat, rye and malt flours and added malt grains, and a new line to Real Foods. Thirty-two pulses and beans are sold at a U.K. recleaned standard. Over sixty nuts and seeds, all sizes of new crop walnuts and a new hazelnut butter. Apricot kernel butter is sold in 12 oz jars, blended with 30 % raw cane sugar. Fresh fruit and vegetables arrive mainly from friends who bring in their surplus. Bulk prices are the same on the separate wholesale and retail mail order price lists, discounts as high as 15 %.

Open: Mon to Sat, 9 to 6; Wed, 9 to 5.30.

EDINBURGH   Lothian   Map 7
Roots Wholefoods, 60 Newington Road   TEL Edinburgh 031-668 2888

Customers are enthusiastic about the larger shop Fiona Horsbrugh has just acquired. Searching winds were bad for customers morale at the old place, when they had to queue outside. Mrs. Horsbrugh believes she is a service to the community, 'be it a little old lady buying a pound of lentils, because we're cheaper than the supermarket.' She has all of the dried packet goods elsewhere and a better than average take-away/convenience food section stocked by Edinburgh's enterprising Breadwinner bakery and Garvalds. Expect to see samosas, pakoras, falafels, salads, quiche and filled rolls, and a variety of wholefood scones and pastries. Jams are Whole Earth and Thursday Cottage, animal rennet free cheeses plus the usual Cheddars, Brie, Stilton. Non-battery eggs from Simpsons at Innerleithen.

Open: Mon to Fri 9 to 5.30; Sat, 9 to 5.

ELGIN   Grampian   Map 7
Kinbro Health Foods, 40 South Street   TEL Elgin (0343) 49318

This is just a little shop in the pleasing Moray Firth Royal Burgh. There is not the space to stock all that Mr. Brown would like so, with the exception of Walker's Aberdour wholemeal, muesli and rye breads, there are few fresh foods, which is disappointing for a town in the fertile Laigh of Moray, near the pioneering Findhorn Community. Eggs are an exception, from Speyside Poultry, Archiestown, a district better known for distilling. However there is an extensive range of grains, flours and pulses, with reductions on bulk purchases. Discounts made known on request. A similarly representative range of apple rings, apricots, bananas, cherries, dates, figs, pears, peaches, prunes and fruit salads.

Open: Mon to Sat, 9 to 5.15; closed Wed pm.

ELY   Cambridgeshire   Map 3
Horizon Health, 29 Forehill   TEL Ely (0353) 61600

Closer to the river than the Cathedral (though nothing in the little town is any great distance) Susan Dovey's and George Lange's stock is limited to inexpensive dried goods, apart from their live natural yoghurts, cheese selection and non-battery eggs. A good range of flours includes soya, brown rice, and Doves Farm organically grown wholemeal. There are dried fruits bought in from Community Foods in London. Herbs are from the same source and Whole Earth. Cakes are baked with 100% flour, vegetable shortening and demerara sugar or honey. Bread, including a rye, from Wrights of Haddenham. Butter can be used in the cheesecake, if requested. Non-alcoholic wines, cider vinegars, soya ice cream complete the stock. Wholefood take-away menu cooked on the premises, as for the café upstairs (see entry).

Open: Mon to Sat, 9 to 5.30; Tue, 9 to 2.

EXETER   Devon   Map 2
Peck and Strong, St. Anne's Well Brewery, Lower North Street

The home kitchen here (soon to give way to larger premises) is operational Sundays to Thursdays for the production of savoury and sweet things. A wholemeal, or a mixture of wholemeal and 85% flours, is always used for their special pastry style savouries and desserts. Customers approve of the attention paid to presentation as well as flavouring of dishes which, with the exception of cheesecake, are neatly sliced and ready to serve. Savoury spiced vegetables come in a flaky pastry case; spinach and cream cheese appears to be a consistent favourite amongst quiche addicts, while the use of mature Cheddar as a topping for the pizzas is popular. Some like it sweet and the traditional treacle tart is unmistakable for a syrupy sweetness offset by the added flavour of tangy lemon. The totally decadent enjoy the dark moist chocolate sponge covered in chocolate fudge icing. More everyday, an apple flapjack that is set apart from the ordinary by a broad seam of puréed apple sandwiched in the middle.

Open: Mon to Fri.

EXETER   Devon   MAP 2
Seasons, 8 Well Street   TEL Exeter (0392) 36125

'Wholefooding is as good as anything one can do with a degree in philosophy,' feels Mr. White after six years in this turn-of-the-century store just off the main street, that is probably the principal outlet for organic fruit and vegetables in the area. Exclusively vegetarian, emphasis is on wholefoods free from additives. Bread comes from the Roseland Dairy, Topsham and Country Bumpkins, Exmouth. Organic standard fruit and vegetables from Flax Drayton Farm and the lesser known Wood-Roberts at Winkleigh. Non-battery eggs from the Joyces at Chideock. Cheeses (farmhouse ones are a speciality) are goats', cows' and ewes', always using vegetable rennet. Curried vegetable pasties and apple flapjacks are best-sellers among the limited bakers' lines stocked. Own brand muesli is sugar-free.

Open: Mon to Sat, 9.30 to 5.30.

EXMOUTH   Devon   MAP 2
Country Bumpkins Bakery, 23 Albion Street   TEL Exmouth (0395) 275004

After home baking in steamy cottage kitchen (working into early hours and alarming neighbours) the Joyces moved into their seaside shop and bakery. 'The necessity of making a living means we are not a white flour-free enclave'—much as they would like to be—'if it doesn't sell, we don't make it.' Good commercial sense, but they do have principles. Bread is a 100% loaf, fat-free and no improvers at all. Their pies, pizzas and buns are of a 'homely' character, and find their way on to the market stalls in Topsham and Exeter, in addition to their own two outlets and five other shops. They also sell their own flour.

Open: Mon to Sat, 8.30 to 5.30.

EXMOUTH   Devon   MAP 2
Round the Bend Wholefood Shop, 53 The Strand   TEL Exmouth (0395) 264398

In one of the narrow streets in the town centre, Sue Glanville's wholefood store started out as a very modest concern selling just a few wholefoods but has grown with the passing of the years and several moves, to this former grain merchants. 'We sell more muesli, wheatgerm, bran and honey than anything else. Recently both the soya and the goats' milk have become very popular.' Country Bumpkins in the town, do the bread. Other things—cakes, biscuits, hummus, and pasties—are made in her restaurant kitchen (see entry). Apple juice is organic from the pastoral Budleigh Orchards, soya sauce, apple concentrate and cider vinegar are on draught. Ice creams and sorbets are Loseley. Eggs are from Hembury's, Woodbury Salterton and Pearsons, Woodbury, both up by the Common of the same name with the marvellous view taking in the coast from Berry Head to Portland Bill. Vegetables—and occasionally fruit—from Flax Drayton and Wood-Roberts Farm, Winkleigh, are used in the shop and restaurant.

Open: Mon to Sat, 9.30 to 5.30; closed Wed pm.

FALMOUTH Cornwall   MAP 2
Harvest, 16 High Street   TEL Falmouth (0326) 311507

For Gina, John and Marie coming down to the town and establishing their cosy community shop was something of an adventure. They like to think of it as 'a place people look forward to visiting'. Perhaps it is as well they are venturesome for although number 16 manages to survive, shops and houses further along have suffered subsidence. Jars and sacks are favoured for storing the muesli, wholegrains, the bran and the dried fruit. Rollings (they are in the town) bread is rated absolutely wonderful, baked in one of the few surviving old stone ovens. Wholemeal is good strong stuff; and the rye is not at all bad, distinctively floured with caraway seeds. No convenience foods but good friends make flapjack and chocolate cakes. During the summer they stock fresh fruit from local growers and householders. Vegetables come from the Menadues whose produce is approved by the Soil Association. Huge stocks of pulses, herbs (with vignettes alongside saying what they are good for medicinally) and grains. Goats' milk, yoghurt and cheeses, bean sprouts, tinned water chestnuts and Mexican delicacies make up a small stock of delicatessen items.

Open: Mon to Sat, 9 to 5.30.

FRAMLINGHAM Suffolk   MAP 3
Carley and Webb, 29 Market Hill   TEL Framlingham (0728) 723503

Grocers have traded from this address since the year Victoria came to the throne, but not for as long as there has been a moated castle which has hazy origins dating before 1150. A specialist shop, there is a particularly fine selection of hams, pâtés and over a hundred cheeses. Ice creams and sorbets are homemade. Chocolates are handmade and continental. All very decadent but they gain marks for their fresh fruit and organically grown vegetables, and breads, in no less than twenty varieties from two local bakers. There are no non-battery eggs but there is non-battery chicken meat. Grains and flours come from a local granary. Dried fruits of all types are bagged by themselves, when they are not grinding coffee or weighing out loose teas. For take-home or a picnic, sample the pasties, quiches and salads.

Open: Mon to Sat, 8.30 to 5.30; Fri, 8.30 to 6.

GLASGOW Strathclyde   MAP 7
Forrest and Niven, 73 St. Vincent Street   TEL Glasgow 041-221 7865

Mr. Niven has been twenty years in the Victorian city centre commercial area where the shop first opened its doors as a health food store some fifty years ago. This busy place sells breads from four bakers—Star, Diggens, the Glasgow Co-operative Wholefood Bakery and Gardners in Prestwick. Supplies from the last are usually breathlessly awaited around 11.00 am in time for the lunchtime onslaught. Along with their organic bread they send the sought after savouries, scones, croissants, tarts, and fruit treats which bring the people into the shop. Sugar-reduced preserves are Slonon and Country Basket as well as the better known sugar-free Whole Earth. Among the many grains only the brown rice is organic. Cheeses are made with vegetable rennet. Yoghurts are ewes' and goats' milk.

Open: Mon to Sat, 9 to 5.20.

GLASGOW Strathclyde   MAP 7
Grassroots (Wholefoods and Herbs), 498 Great Western Road
TEL Glasgow 041-334 1844

Far from being the oldest established outlet but, strategically close to Byres Road and Kelvingrove's ivory towers, the future augurs well for this hard-working co-operative. Occasionally there is worry and tension, but they enjoy the challenge and appreciate the fact that they take direct responsibility for earning their living. Every task from floor scrubbing, bagging, and making coffee when not selling Traidcraft, to top executive decision-taking, is done turn about by each with shared responsibility. There are home brew supplies alongside the herbs and spices; standbys are beans, rice, breads from Glasgow Co-operative Wholefood Bakery, nuts and stoneground flour imported from England. For take-aways the menu is predictably samosa, quiche, wholewheat pizza and—mild uplift—the more inventive pakora.

Open: Mon to Sat, 9.30 to 5.30; Tue, 9.30 to 2.

GUILDFORD   Surrey   Map 3
Earthbound Wholefoods, 10 Madrid Road   TEL Guildford (0483) 69611

This small, downtown store steers clear of the chain-store image, and has a clientèle that is, by and large, the locally well-informed. After twenty-five years as a home economist, Isabelle Glynn has no urge for further cooking and has contracted a private caterer to provide all her convenience foods. Hammonds, a small family baker in Milford, does her lighter than average breads. A date and walnut cake is wheat-free. Cakes and pies are all wholewheat, and so good that Mrs. Glynn has been known to pretend they are her own! She also cleverly discovered Groves Farm at Puttenham as a source of vegetables, but by mid-winter there are only supplies of potatoes. Cheese is vegetarian standard; eggs are from Plaistow. Ice cream is nearby Loseley, along with cheese and the new Greek-style yoghurt. An even newer line is stoneground flour carrying the Loseley label. Load up here with bulk purchases because being out of the centre the parking is marvellous.

Open: Tue to Fri, 9.30 to 5.30; Sat, 9.30 to 5.

GUILDFORD   Surrey   Map 3
Food for Thought, 17 North Street   TEL Guildford (0483) 33841

Apart from Lifestyle, their 5,000 sq. ft Frimley 'superstore', there are six further branches in this progressive organisation. At Frimley it is Richard Ramsden and his partner's ambition to offer everything essential to a healthy lifestyle in addition to a full range of foodstuffs. Predominantly it is an outdoor sports and leisure store. They even bear a thought for the sedentary, stocking Ballands, a range of Norwegian chairs which encourage the sitter in a kneeling rather straight sitting position. 'Many who have had back problems find them very useful,' they claim. 'You can sit at a desk for hours on end without discomfort.' They enjoy advising customers here, and selling foods at the best prices high street rent and rates will allow. Goswells do the bread in most of the stores using Doves Farm organic flour. Other lines are from local bakers, among them some very good breads, but they are not yet serious about the take-away market and won't be until there are more reliable supplies of a better quality. They are showing the same caution with organically grown fresh produce. 'Poor stuff, even if organic, will not do anything useful for our reputation.' Mr. Ramsden is on the lookout for a grower able to bring regular supplies, prepacked and to a guaranteed quality. Frozen convenience foods, including the uneasily labelled Pedco—a new proprietary line from Israel—are well represented. Pedco do a very tasty vegetable burger and their scrumptious sausage rolls easily outpace most of their meaty counterparts. Frozen goats' milk and the increasingly popular soya ice cream (from Foundation Foods)—vanilla and carob flavours—are other cold cabinet items. Martin Pitts has for some time carried the imperial mantle abandoned by the Egg Marketing Board with his own brand of stamped, free range eggs from his Wiltshire farm. Mr. Pitts is recently back from a European tour (on a Nuffield Scholarship) studying free range production. But the keen shopper should beware. He already has some questionable imitators!

Open: Mon to Sat, normal shop hours.

HADLEIGH Suffolk   Map 3
Sunflower, 101 High Street, Hadleigh, Ipswich   TEL Hadleigh (0473) 823219

In a street of exceptionally fine buildings in this former wool town, Mrs. Hilder's small shop stocks a better than average wholefood range and also has a wine and beer making section. Unpasteurised milk, cheese and yoghurts and specialities from the Merlaid Jersey Dairy in Sudbury are sold and the same dairy provides pork meat. Flour is milled (using organic wheat) at the Layham Watermill, a mile or so downstream from the town. She can also offer fairly reliable vegetable supplies grown by Vernon Richards at Justice Wood near Polstead. Rice, oatflakes and a muesli base are offered in organic grade, sometimes dried fruits too along with local Copella apple juice and the organic Aspall kind. Bread from Sparkings in Lavenham and eggs from Deaves Farm, Lower Layham.

Open: Mon to Sat, 9.30 to 5.30; Wed, 9.30 to 1.

HARROGATE North Yorkshire   Map 6
The Cheeseboard, 1 Commercial Street   TEL Harrogate (0423) 58837

Joan Chantler and Brenda Crosbie run a constantly air-cooled, marbled slabbed shop, so their cheeses—and patés—are always in prime condition. Your requirements are cut to order from this fine display of infinite variety that includes a lovely selection of goats' and ewes' milk types from this country and abroad, a boon to those allergic to cows' milk products. Saturdays tend to be frantic so it is worth thinking of a weekday visit for a leisurely inspection and more than breathless advice.

Open: Mon to Sat, 9 to 5.30.

HASSOCKS West Sussex   Map 3
Nature's Corner, 34 Keymer Road   TEL Hassocks (079 18) 5400

What was once Utopia in the Downland village is now more modestly Nature's Corner, since the Allens took over several years ago. Customers come for the interesting variety of basic dried goods, dried fruits and some of the 100 or so herbs stocked. As many again are here for the bakers' goods, at one stage made on the premises but now from Dunfords in Henfield. Everything is made with vegetable oils. The only cheese is a vegetarian grade. Live, natural low-fat yoghurt—only natural flavours—and their ice cream is by Loseley. Eggs are categorically free range, from Barrow Hill Farm.

Open: Mon to Fri, 9 to 5.30; Wed, 9 to 1; Sat, 9 to 5.

HAY-ON-WYE Hereford and Worcester   Map 2
Hay Wholefoods and Delicatessen, 1 Lion Street
TEL Hay-on-Wye (0497) 820708

With the counter attractions of so many books and bibliophiles, not to mention a Norman castle looming above, Jan Shivel and Paul Goldman have to try hard in this beautifully located Wye town. 'Unless the weather is horrible' they even open on Bank Holidays, except for Christmas. With so many entrepreneurs cropping up in the Welsh Borders there are compensations. Pru Lloyd with her wonderful dairy products (from her Hereford cows) is not too far away in Weobley and they are handy for the cider orchards, especially the trail blazing Dunkertons at Pembridge with their unadulterated old-type cider apples. Specialities range from corn on the cob and cobnuts to taramasalata and natural live yoghurt. There is a variety of English and continental cheeses (twenty to thirty traditionally made English varieties at a time), among them several local ones and a vegetarian farmhouse Cheddar. Pru Lloyd sends the skimmed milk, medium and full fat cream cheese, double cream and cheesecakes. Pâtés (from Ros Fry, Boatside Farm) are meat, vegetarian and vegan, without fillers, colours or preservatives. Marmalades, jams and chutneys are local makes and the proprietary sugarless kind. Pasties are filled with spinach and walnuts, and other interesting delicacies go into vine leaves and brioche. More rudimentary, but wholesome, vegetable and bean pasties from Crymych's Bean Machine. Sandwiches made on the premises and fruit cakes are supplied by Gaffers Wholefood Café in Hereford. Rye bread is to their own recipe, strong white plaits have poppy seeds, all by Neville Jones in the same street who also makes the batches of treacly gingerbread (another own recipe). Vegetable fat is used in all of them. Fresh fruits and vegetables, all organically grown, come more seasonally. All the fruits, except lemons, free from sprays.

Open: Mon to Sat, 9.30 to 5.30.

HAY-ON-WYE   Hereford and Worcester   MAP 2
Specialité Foods, Boatside Farm   TEL Hay-on-Wye (0497) 820108

Ros Fry emphatically stresses, 'My dishes are not meant to last as long as plastic ham and mummified pork pies.' Hers is a home-catering enterprise where she caters for parties, weddings, picnics, deep freezes or any other purpose, 'as long as I am allowed to use natural, healthy ingredients.' In the process she gently advocates meatless dishes and is trying hard to put over to her more traditional customers the idea that a healthy vegetarian dish can be just as good as a meaty one. It is uphill work, but she persists. Striving to keep costs to a minimum, she adheres to the principle that quality ingredients must be used.' Tinned mushrooms should never be used, for example. Fresh are always available, and if not, then an alternative recipe using local ingredients in season should be substituted. When she does cook meats, the organic kind is sought, preservatives are never added—only slow thorough cooking, garlic and cayenne. Her cookery courses do not mean preparing endless nut roasts, nice though they can be. She is interested in showing people how to cook delicious food, often adapted from traditional cuisine, bridging the gap between the processed and the whole.

HEREFORD   Hereford and Worcester   MAP 2
The Good Food Shop, 3 Bridge Street

Michael Snell is really a farmer and happier with gum boots and tractor, the shop only came into being to retail his farm produce. 'Our selling points are fresh produce delivered daily from the farm, fruit too whenever this is seasonally available.' Teas, coffees and delicatessen lines are gradually being introduced, cheeses and terrines are a speciality. The home grown fruit and vegetables do not fully meet with organic growing standards but they are moving quickly that way. Some pesticides are still used but no artificial fertilisers; they use farmyard manure.

Open: Mon to Sat, 9 to 5.30.

HERTFORD   Hertfordshire   MAP 3
The Good Food Shop, 4 Old Cross   TEL Hertford (0932) 550101

Customers without exception commend the Burtons' courteous smiling service here, as well as the wholefoods and homemade take-aways. The window display's competitively priced tofu burgers, quiches, chocolate and walnut cake, and Bakewell tart are all made to a high standard by their good local cook. The enormous demand is supplemented by Link Wholefoods. There is no preservative or colouring in the local baker's bread which is used for sandwiches.

Open: Mon to Sat, 9 to 5.30; Thur, 9 to 2.

HOLT   Norfolk   MAP 3
Larner Brothers, 10 Market Place   TEL Holt (026 371) 2323

A market town of 2,000 or so and with a school like Gresham's is probably just large enough to support a quality delicatessen wholefood type shop such as Larners, which opened here in 1873. They are of interest to the *Guide* on account of the vast variety of cheeses, Indian, Mexican and European foods, attracting customers from a wide surrounding area. Flours are Prewetts and Allinsons, stoneground, in wholemeal and granary grades. There is excellent dried fruit representation. Even figs are from five sources, apart from good ranges of more general dried fruit lines. Bread is from Lushers at Sheringham. With several hundred captive customers, it comes as no surprise that ice creams, Loseley plus the popular Bertorelli, Prospero (local) and even Walls, are taken very seriously!

Open: Mon to Sat, 8.30 to 5; Thur, 8.30 to 1.

HORNCASTLE   Lincolnshire   MAP 6
Country Kitchen, 15 North Street   TEL Horncastle (065 82) 6578

Mrs. Dunford and Mrs. Ball, who launched this shop, are friends with a common interest in good wholesome food. A local signwriter has demonstrated his skills, lending their two shops (see entry Louth) individuality with a bold wheatsheaf to decorate the windows. Concern about additives and colourings put into food, not to mention their apparent effects on the allergic, first alerted them to the need for wholefoods. Friends with hyperactive children actually clinched the matter. All foods are sold with the proviso they are free from additives, which includes free range pork from the Manor House at Kirkby on Bain. Yoghurts and cream from Longley Farm, hard cheeses by Prewett's vegetarian, plus Brie and Stilton. Bread is granary style, wholemeal, with a nutty flavour of added malt and cracked wheat to a not particularly strong texture, by Horncastle's general bakers, Myers and Sons. Non-battery eggs from the Bentons at the delightfully named Mareham-le-Fen. An interest in diets is a speciality and there are flours (including Truefree) and biscuits for those on a gluten-free regime.

Open: Mon to Sat, 9 to 5; Wed, 9 to 1.

HUDDERSFIELD   West Yorkshire   MAP 6
Peaceworks Co-op, 58 Wakefield Road, Aspley
TEL Huddersfield (0484) 23915

This is really a buyers' co-operative which 'just got out of hand', so the shop is a natural sequel. According to spokesman, Charlie Brooke, a special effort is made to stock organic grade produce. To this standard they can do rice (long and short grain), oats, bread and pastry flours, non-wheat flours, and some grains. Similarly dates from Iran, Morocco and Afghanistan and sometimes vegetables from an undisclosed source, along with animal rennet free red and white cheeses. Wholemeal bread comes from Heeleys of Huddersfield, and 'Dawn's mum—Dawn is a co-operator—(using shop's food) does the vegan pies, bhajis, almond tarts and flapjack.' They sell all manner of cooking herbs.

Open: Mon to Sat, 10.15 to 6.

ILMINSTER   Somerset   MAP 2
Ilminster Health Foods, 15 Silver Street   TEL Ilminster (046 05) 2712

Mike Finberg's little shop (next door to his pharmacy) operates with the fraternal feelings that the shopkeeper of old had. He does not stock bread as the baker next door does; he does not do fruit and vegetables because the greengrocer, the other side, does. And you get your free range eggs from some good people a few doors further down. All this is generous and gratuitous information and he will gladly tell you where the most promising pub or caff is—that is for wholefoods and the like—over a twenty mile radius. Actually there are more than one might imagine. His little Listed shop now has a health clinic attached to it. Wholefoods are packed on the premises. Preserves are Thursday Cottage and Whole Earth. Goats' and ewes' yoghurt. Rushall's organic flour comes from a revived mill of the same name, close into Upavon, on Salisbury Plain's northern edge.

Open: Mon to Sat, 8.30 to 5.30.

LAMPETER   Dyfed   Map 2
Mulberry Bush Wholefoods, 2 Bridge Street   TEL Lampeter (0570) 46380

This shop was launched by Josie and Brian Smith in January 1974 with 'just £200 capital, much hard work, and a lot of love. We started because we eat wholefoods which were difficult to get in those days. We even travelled to London to get our brown rice. Interest and support in wholefoods is spreading throughout the community. Now it is not just the younger people: there are as many in the upper age ranges and not just for economic reasons. We offer good food at reasonable prices and a lot of advice about diet and alternative medicines. Customers are not just till fodder.' The Smiths supply a wide range of herbs, their own muesli (bulk supplies, if necessary), teas, coffees, and goats' milk and soya dairy produce. There are quiches and pastries—though supplies can be erratic—from the Bean Machine at Crymych. Charles and Carolyn Wacher send their excellent fresh vegetables from Aeron Park but supplies tend to dry up by February or March. A firm attitude is taken towards bread: no nonsense with this 85 % extraction—they get wholemeal from Tegwens in Llanybydder. Any reasonable requests for teas, good coffee, nuts and herbs can usually be met. Up to a point they err towards being a delicatessen, though strictly vegetarian. There are generous discounts on grains and flours in bulk.

Open: Mon to Sat, 9 to 5.30; Wed, 9 to 1.

LANCASTER   Lancashire   Map 6
One Earth, 1 King Street   TEL Lancaster (0524) 32916

Barry Male feels his may be an aspiring social group's substitute to the Alternative Co-op, his longer established town rivals in Penny Street. One Earth sell food but the herbal and homeopathic remedies are just as important. Much of the stock is prepacked. They pride themselves in the organically grown flour (from the Watermill) which is also used to make the bakery goods in the shop. Bread, baps, scones, croissants and wholefood confectionery are regular and popular lines. Admirers commend the 'first class wholemeal bread, scones and pies'. There is approval for the health foods of all kinds that are well displayed. Free range eggs.

Open: Mon to Sat, 9.30 to 5.15.

LANCASTER   Lancashire   Map 6
Single Step Co-operative, 78A Penny Street   TEL Lancaster (0524) 63021

Alternative books here come close to being as important as the food. Self-caterers down from the campus make up the majority of their customers. Single Step's spokesman, Steve Miller, is a graduate of the university. The hundred-year-old cheese warehouse was launched on its new lease of life with support and encouragement from the local council. Shortage of space rather than supplies limits the number of convenience foods, so they tend to concentrate on big hoppers of self-weigh dried goods. This means savings in handling costs for the Co-op, which are passed on to the customers. A useful range of herbs is on offer from stock—about 50—and many more are available on special order. Dried fruits can be supplied treated with vegetable oil, some unsulphured, and a wide selection are sold loose. Cheeses, cows', ewes' and goats', are vegetarian, in fact there is a strict policy on vegetarianism. They like to think their wide range of gluten-free foods are a speciality, including a rye bread, local like the wholemeal croissants, 'they are rather special', and other organic loaves. The flour for these, traditionally ground, comes from the entertaining little Salkeld Watermill (see entry), just out of Penrith on the Alston Road. So far the bakers have not managed to cope very well with the Granarius flour. They manage a fairly steady supply of free range eggs from several local poultry keepers. Seasonal supplies of salad stuffs are sent by Blairs who are only a few miles from Pilling near Fleetwood. Vegetables come from other local growers, and more supplies 'veering towards the pricey for some pockets' come from a London distributor. Cruelty-free cosmetics are also available.

Open: Mon to Sat, 9 to 5; Fri, 9 to 5.30.

LEAMINGTON SPA   Warwickshire   Map 3
House of Goodness Ltd, 98 Warwick Street   TEL Leamington Spa (0926) 35006

Run by a Christian community (the Jesus Fellowship Church), they aim to supply good wholefood at competitive prices. 'All kinds of people from health food fanatics to pub landlords turn up here,' says Nick Everard who manages this branch, one of a group of nine stores around the Midlands, as well as a warehouse cash-and-carry. This is a bubbling enterprise which started out as something of an experiment; progress has been swift. The service is friendly; 'though we have our off days, like anyone.' A bakery doing breads, cakes and savouries forms a part of the operation but the output is sometimes less than wholefood. They rate well however with regulars and the style is popular. Try their tasty pizzas or well-filled samosas. At lunchtime there are always several other hot take-aways like vegan pasties, conventional burgers and the tofu variety, coming from several outside suppliers including Nouvelle Cuisines. The range of English and Continental cheese is excellent. You can also get foods for athletes and bodybuilders. There is a very large range of honeys at good prices and the jam range is nearly as good with Whole Earth, Stute and the excellent value Balkan preserves. Most dried goods are packed under their own label and they reckon to be cheaper than the other chains. Eggs are from the deep litter poultry on their own farm. Doves Farm organic flour may be bought in bulk. No alcoholic drinks but they sell a goats' milk ice cream.

Open: Mon to Sat, 9 to 5.

LEEDS   West Yorkshire   Map 6
Beano Wholefoods Co-operative, 36 New Briggate
TEL Leeds (0532) 435737

After cutting the umbilical link with Suma Wholefoods, this pace-setting establishment is entirely independent. Labour though is unremitting for current co-operators Marcia, Martin, Gordon, Suzanne, Jill and Jane, as they are newly installed in larger premises so that there will be more juices, vegetables, fruit, take-aways and advice. And more and more will be organic. The list they publish is an impressively long affair but it does leave out details like place of origin. Probably the best shopping advice is to get their list first, peruse it carefully, then buy your choice. There are no deliveries. Herbs — in 260 varieties — are a speciality, like their books and take-aways. A very wide range of wholefoods includes some unusual items, for this part of the world, like miso (Japanese soya bean paste), genmai miso with brown rice or hacho miso, which is soya beans only. Tempeh is a more recent addition to the range. Cold-pressed vegetable oils are well represented but again leaving the shopper at a loss for any detail. One hundred per cent wholewheat pastas include a buckwheat spaghetti and two are organic. Wheat flours include three which are organic. In addition to a muesli base (32p for 500 g), the house style muesli is an economical 54p, neither is organic but then there are enough other cereal flakes stocked to make up a pleasing mix to satisfy individual tastes. The only jams are Whole Earth, suitable of course for diabetics as the sugar-free mixed fruit pickles and chutneys should be. Since moving they have increased their range of bakery items (all wholewheat and the breads all organic flours) with things like sesame bread cakes, cheese and thyme, cheese and garlic, or cracked wheat—all delivered daily from David Fawcett's Headingley Bakery. As yet fresh produce supplies are still erratic but vegetables are filtering through from Meanwood Urban Farm. Their miscellaneous non-food list finds customers for pure vegetable candles, recycled paper products, rice paddles, washing up liquids, and other random articles. All dried goods attract a useful 5 % discount on bulk buys '2 kg and above'. They are well worth a trip.

Open: Mon to Sat, 9.30 to 5.30; Wed, 9.30 to 2.

LEICESTER   Leicestershire   MAP 3
Wholemeal, 18 Queens Road   TEL Leicester (0533) 703617

'Service here is friendly, the food weighed and packed frequently so its always fresh,' comments one enthusiastic regular, a view categorically shared by another who, with some dedication, travels in from Coalville once in a while. Organic vegetables are available, the eggs are free range and the bread is delivered daily. The choice of herbs and spices is wide and there are teas, barley cup and other beverages. Grains, brown rice, flours, cereals, nuts and seeds are in sufficient variety to cater for most preferences. A selection of yoghurts, fruit juices and sea vegetables are also available.

Open: Tue to Fri, 9 to 5.30; Sat, 9 to 5.

LEIGH-ON-SEA   Essex   MAP 3
Mother Earth Wholefoods, 108 Broadway   TEL Leigh-on-Sea (0702) 713547

If they were to be frank, they have really long been firmly embraced by Southend-on-Sea, but the spirit of independence dies hard and a Mother Earth admirer likes to think of this as their own small town wholefood store. Into what is a very small shop a great deal of stock is crammed and they are highly commended for own package grains, flours, nuts and beans. Cruelty free cosmetics and the small array of cookery and health books are also available. Beyond the shop, a tiny café serving hot vegetarian and vegan lunches, with take-away service if preferred.

Open: Mon to Sat, 9 to 5.30.

LEOMINSTER   Hereford and Worcester   MAP 2
Barber and Manuel, Victoria Street   TEL Leominster (0568) 3381

There have been some acid observations that Mr. Hurley's is merely a convenient grocer who has joined the wholefood bandwagon in a casual sort of way. But others heartily approve of his personal service and his delicatessen goods, and the choice of quiches and convenience dishes has greatly expanded. Furthermore Mr. Hurley tries very hard with breads—garlic, granary, rye and the now inevitable wholemeal—from both Howe and Bosbory. He also has a demand for soya milk, soured cream, local dairy yoghurts (fruit and plain), goats' and ewes' milk cheeses, and cheese cakes. Early Bird Poultry are a local non-battery egg supplier; Clun Farm eggs are from further afield. The local stoneground flour is Dr. Lear's, ground in his mill at Tenbury Wells. Local ciders and wines are also available.

Open: Mon to Sat, 9 to 5; Thur, 9 to 1.

LEOMINSTER   Hereford and Worcester   MAP 2
Nitty Gritty Wholefoods, 9 School Lane   TEL Leominster (0568) 611610

After nine years, Pamela Horsley has her principles steadfastly sorted out at this strictly vegetarian wholefood establishment. Bakers do her bidding: there is excellent brown shortbread; luscious wholemeal lemon cakes (sold by the slice or as cakes); pasties are melt-in-the-mouth affairs, with a herby organically grown vegetable filling. Somewhat erratically there are supplies of homemade burgers, together with more regular supplies from Cauldron Foods in Bristol. Mostly tofu-based with brown rice, and in three flavours— chilli, vegetable, and nut—these burgers are sold in packs of two for reheating and home consumption. During the summer they will sell fruit and vegetables from the shop on behalf of anyone, providing they are organically grown and the quality is up to her standards. Otherwise it is more customary for her local growers to bring them in just for busy Friday market days. Bread is made with flour ground by Dr. Lear on his Newnham Bridge Farm (organic and 100% extraction of course) which is always used within two weeks of grinding so it has a reliably high vitamin content. Cheeses are Leasowes, from cows' and goats' milk, and among them the quark skimmed milk type so useful for smooth sauces, or other cooking as a substitute for cottage cheese. Any purchase of flours (some non-wheat), grains and pulses attracts a 10% reduction on buys of 7 lb and over; 25% comes off unsplit sacks, and any not in stock can be specially ordered. There are various vine and other fruits with several known to be organic. Mrs. Horsley is worth seeking for her speciality jams and homemade pickles. No colourings or preservatives of any kind are added, only fruit and sugar goes into the jams. Good local ladies accord the same respectful treatment to the cabbages (a special sauerkraut), onions and gherkins that they pickle and bottle, sometimes using Simmonds' cider vinegar which can be bought in the shop. Non-battery eggs are also available.

Open: Mon to Sat, 10 to 5; closed Thur pm.

LETCHWORTH   Hertfordshire   Map 3
Fairhaven Wholefoods, Unit 9, Letchworth Market Hall
TEL Letchworth (046 26) 4588

Robin and Wendy Sternberg are pioneers in their own way; their friendly efficient service to the door has now been running four years. Their origins stem from within the flourishing local branch of the Vegetarian Society, strong in the district, which might be attributed to the influence of St. Christopher's School (see entry). Each month every home (in Welwyn, Hitchin and Wheathampstead as well) gets their list delivered with the local free newspaper. That way they now have upwards of 1,200 regular customers using their very personal wholefood delivery service. If your requirements are not large enough to take advantage of their larger packs they can—and often do—find you a food mate. No other commitment! Like-minded people are introduced to each other (if they wish) if there are particular allergy problems or hyperactive children, or cancer sufferers on the Bristol approach, gentle diet. The list is helpfully annotated. Few questions are left unanswered: if your food must be gluten-free, sugar-free, organically grown, it is marked so. One can also pick out the new season's crop and lines 'new this month' from the 240 strong list of popular wholefoods. Pot barley (organic) at £1.35 the $2\frac{1}{2}$ kg pack (85p regular); long grain brown rice (organic) at £2.40 (£1.70 regular); and organic buckwheat flour at 90p for 1 kg, are random prices. Yoghurt coated peanuts and raisins, and Lym Valley fruit bars are popular treats. Among several savoury spreads, Telma vegetable pâté, two $3\frac{1}{2}$ oz packs for £1.05 is the most interesting; Granose margarine is £3.90 for five 500 g. Wholemeal bread from the retail shop in the market together with Allen's vegetable rennet cheeses and sometimes fresh vegetables. There are plans for modest expansion. With a little luck there may soon be the much needed restaurant for the area. Free range eggs.

Open: Mon, Tue, Sat, 8.30 to 5; Thur, Fri, 8.30 to 6.

LEWES   East Sussex   Map 3
Full of Beans, 96–97 High Street   TEL Lewes (0273) 472627

'We are both very, very keen on oriental cooking,' says John Gosling, and this is confirmed in their rather special range of Japanese and Indonesian soya foods. John makes the tofu, miso and tempeh (all organic) himself. 'Tempeh does not seem to be made in any quantity round at this side of the globe. People travel just to eat this alone.' The miso starts its long maturation period in a small manufacturing area they have in part of an old brewery. Sara Gosling gives talks and occasional demonstrations to help spread the message. The two dark blue shops in a 400-year-old building are full of sacks and beans with an entire wall still lined by the former owner's fitments. Paton & Baldwins have given way to packet beans and dried fruits. Vegetable rennet cheeses are in 20 varieties and as many of the grains as possible are organically grown. Brighton's Infinity Foods are an obvious choice for bakery lines, a well flavoured loaf among them, but more scones, fruit slices and a fruit and nut loaf come from Durnferas. Take-away pasties, filled wholewheat rolls and salads are made on their own premises. There is a wealth of fresh interesting produce available and advice is freely given, and there are always new and exciting cookery books. This is indeed a shop to recommend! Non-battery eggs; Loseley ice creams; own brand organic ices; coconut milk; fresh coriander and occasionally fresh limes, are available.

Open: Mon to Fri, 9 to 5.30; Sat, 9 to 5.

LEWES   East Sussex   MAP 3
Lansdown House Health Foods, 10 Lansdown Place   TEL Lewes (0273) 474681

Cindy Holmes has only just taken over the reins in this long established health food store where she hopes to continue providing a good range of reasonably priced basic commodities. There are also plans for expansion. Organic produce is likely to be a feature before long so that she can cater for those with special dietary needs—allergies, coeliacs, the Bristol Diet. Several bakers already supply her cold baked goods such as vegetable pastries, savoury rolls, and breads at several extraction rates. The latter include a rye bread and a peanut loaf. One of her plans is to expand this range to include homemade snacks of a style which will tempt the local school children to eat sensible wholesome things offered at reasonable prices. The deep litter egg supply comes from the organically fed poultry at Chailey. In the dairy cabinet there is goats' milk alongside Loseley yoghurt, Prewett's vegetarian cheese and mature English Cheddars. Flour is locally milled and organically grown, in sacks at reduced rates to special order. Dried fruits are in a fairly wide range, the raisins usually organic and the apricots unsulphured. There are teas and herbal teas, and four sorts of coffee beans which are ground to order, as required:

Open: Mon to Fri, 9 to 5.30; Sat, 9 to 1.

LINCOLN   Lincolnshire   MAP 6
Greens Health Foods, 175 High Street   TEL Lincoln (0522) 24874

The shop name is gained from a good lady of that name who, with courage and foresight in 1910, opened her doors at this address as a vegetarian and wholefood establishment. Though not quite in the forefront today, popular selling lines are honey, snack foods, herbal and homeopathic medicines, but they also have a great variety of other stock from apple juice to ionisers. Bread is 100% wholemeal, baked locally each day using an Allinsons flour, scones are only 85%.

Open: Mon to Sat, 8.30 to 5.30.

LINCOLN   Lincolnshire   MAP 6
Pulse (Pure Foods), 25 Corporation Street   TEL Lincoln (0522) 28666

Gordon Leek is commended for his well-run dry goods and book shop. Macrobiotic staples reflect the orientation here together with a strong emphasis on the DIY. Yoghurt is homemade (also homemade goats' cheese to order), so are most of the take-aways, and vegetables will frequently be backyard surplus. All the burgers, pâtés, pasties and sandwiches, cakes and teacakes are vegan standard (all vegetable oils). Not so the scones.

Ginger parkin, fig squares, cashew and coconut slice add variety to the range of better known recipes. Showing admirable attention to detail, all the cooked foods carry a display card listing the ingredients. None of the snacks contains sugar and there is very little in the way of other sweeteners like honey. Wholemeal bread is from a small local baker. Free range eggs, when available, are from Ella's Dairy in Willingham. When vegetables are bought in from commercial sources, it is always from local Soil Association growers. Dried goods have 10 % off for 5 kg or more, with a sack or case rate by arrangement. Dried fruit varies from crop to crop; Moroccan dates are organic but all are mineral oil coated. In season some fresh herbs.

Open: Mon to Sat, 9 to 5.30; Wed, 9 to 2.

LISKEARD Cornwall MAP 2
Ough & Sons, 10 Market Street   TEL Liskeard (0579) 43253

This is an old fashioned shop, established in 1846. Pulses are kept in the drawers, 'in the original mahogany fittings at the back where they weigh and serve from'. As yet they are as much an old style grocer selling home cooked gammon, side of bacon and farmhouse cheese, 'people down here are only slowly moving towards wholefoods' but 'they will get anything people want to order'. Some of the cheeses are already the vegetable rennet variety, particularly the Cornish ones which include a nettle-coated semi-hard version, a black pepper, and a herb and garlic. Salads, pies, quiches and pizzas are all popular lines, 'some I make, some I have baked and some I buy in'. The same lady who 'bakes the wonderful quiches for Jeff and Edwina Markham does wholemeal cheese scones and spinach pies whenever there is time. It's a soul search, she is always baking.' Home-grown (actually from a local farm) smoked chicken is in the inventive patter of a short conversation, 'hypodermic-free'. Sounds safe enough. Fresh non-battery chickens and free range eggs are other lines. Wholemeal bread deliveries come daily along with bloomers, 'like a short fat French stick, edges rounded and paler, and 100 % bread rolls. They are an outlet for that fast-gaining-ground preserve manufacturer, Cartwright and Butler, who are doing chutney and pickles as well. Balkan jams are popular, 'cheap and just fruit and sugar'. Own blend teas (straight and herbal) and coffee also available.

Open: Mon to Sat, 8.30 to 5.30; Wed, 8.30 to 1.

LIVERPOOL Merseyside MAP 6
Dancing Cat Trading Co-operative, 107 Lodge Lane
TEL Liverpool 051-733 5205

If you are in Liverpool and it has got to be organic, then Dancing Cat's high street shop is the only place. Not that they scorn modern technology, their healthily long list, issued only for customer guidance, as prices and varieties of many items change from day to day, is computerised. Their name was born of frustration, drawn from a hat after failure to agree on anything else. Fruit and vegetables sent up by Organic Farm Foods include (astonishingly) imported Italian parsley. Otherwise a comprehensive vegetable list, fewer fruits but lemons and oranges are both untreated. Fruit juices are mainly the Volonte range. The cider vinegar is organic as is the pot barley, wheat grain and porridge oats. Prices quoted are normally for lb multiples, except for 25 and 50 kg sacks, in all instances with the 1 lb unit cost helpfully shown. Flours would benefit from additions to the range, at present limited to wholemeal in coarse, fine and pastry grades. Best bread—rye, barley, organic granary and wholemeal—is to own recipe by the local Robinson's Bakery, and a cheaper wholemeal version from Chalkin and Dodd. Goats' and soya milk ice creams in vanilla and strawberry flavours, with the first also in 'lolly' form. Saturdays here tend to be chaotic, Monday morning is staff training, sometime in between you should get the benefit of their enthusiasm for food and customers.

Open: Mon to Sat, 9 to 5.30.

LONDON   Map 4
The Aetherius Society Health Foods, 767 Fulham Road, SW6
TEL London 01-736 8848

An efficient up-to-date food store, it trades on the basis that 'there is a definite relationship between food and health, and if you put low-grade fuel in your tank, your engine is likely to stall even before out of warranty.' Dr. Valerie Lawford (of the Spiritual Brotherhood) and her trained staff set out to make certain that customers are serviced according to specification, and they have been established twenty years. They are a reliable source for prepacked foods especially grains, dried fruits (around 25 kinds) and a choice of ten or so flours. Tisanes come in nearer 30 varieties, along with regular types. Bread by Goswells, Hampton and Hicks. No wines, but there is Norfolk Punch in bottles and, for a real thirst, pitchers. For a sweeter treat, Norfolk Delight and around 30 juices, are available bottled and cartoned, FREGG approved eggs come from two farms, distributed by Mr. Pine. Goats', ewes' and cows' yoghurt and a selection of cheeses are stocked. The Society goes to town with cosmetics, herbal remedies and books, 200 or more in each of the first two categories.

Open: Mon to Sat, 9 to 6; Fri, 9 to 7.

LONDON   Map 4
Barbara's Health Food Centre, 113 Turnpike Lane, N8   TEL London 01-348 5000

Barbara Green, an exiled Celt, runs this thoughtful enterprise with her cosmopolitan clientèle's enthusiastic support. 'It is a busy shop catering for the intelligent and food conscious, looking for more natural and healthier ways of eating. No animals have been involved in either the testing or manufacture of the stuff sold in our shop,' says Ms. Green. The large freezer cabinet bulges with vegetarian salamis, sausages, dumplings, burgers, nut roasts, pancakes. Alongside are organic cold-pressed oils for cooking and baking. Gluten-free items like rice cakes and Granose proprietary stock finds a ready market. Acidopholus milk, fruit quarks, Rivendell (plain and fruit) and goats' milk yoghurts take up much cool cabinet space. Own pack mueslis, grains, fruits and nuts are usually organic. Herbs are from comfrey to valerian, and numerous spices include saffron which, with herb teas, are much sought after by knowledgeable ethnic groups. Large cakes are sold by the slice—banana and walnut, apple and sultana, apple and coconut, and a cinnamon and carrot speciality without eggs—are made by a West Indian caterer doing so well she has just opened her own restaurant. John Coleman's Norfolk Specialist Eggs are non-battery. The battery of books on alternative therapies, health and vegetarian cooking (it must be the largest hereabouts) has about 800 titles.

Open: Mon to Sat, 9 to 6; Thur, Fri, 9 to 6.30.

LONDON   Map 4
Bushwhacker, 59 Goldhawk Road, W12   TEL London 01-743 2359

Conspicuously placed by Goldhawk Road Underground Station, Sunita and Chris Shipton carry an interesting stock of fresh foods among the open wooden shelving and soaring Japanese paper lampshade spheres. With a strictly enforced no-sugar rule operating, Loseley ice creams are the only item to pass through the net. Organic produce is well represented with British grains and flakes, some of which are used in their special, own brand muesli. The fresh fruit and vegetable stock from Organic Farm Produce rates quite well. South London Bakers Co-operative, who use organically grown wholewheat flour, supply most of the bread. Smaller quantities come from Natural Rise (the unleavened variety) and their pies, pasties and crumbles are stocked too. Good Life do the burgers, tandoori and nut, and the curry pasties. Two local ladies bake the date and walnut cake and the spinach savoury. Tofu burgers and tofu, tempeh and hummus sandwiches (fresh daily on Ceres bread) come from Universal Sandwiches. Yoghurts are from all sorts of sources including Greece, Langman's Dairy and Rozbert Dairy, with sheep's yoghurt from the second. Free range eggs and Aspall's organic apple juice are also stocked.

Open: Mon to Sat, 10 to 6; closed Thur 2.30.

LONDON   Map 5
Clearspring Natural Grocer, 196 Old Street, E1   TEL London 01-250 1708

Peter Bradford's traditional grocery, specialising in organically grown staples, is tucked into part of the lower ground floor of what was formerly St. Luke's Parochial School, now housing a comprehensive range of packed, principally organically grown foods and fresh vegetable counter. Two-way traffic is difficult between closely spaced fixtures. Mr. Bradford knows what he is doing and enjoys successful retailing on his own. At first he was a partner in the Sunwheel health foods enterprise, who manage to find shelf spaces for their foods in most wholefood stores. Whenever possible, he steers well clear of refined products—no sugar and he firmly excludes vitamins and supplements. The mail order list has the edge on most, for helpful explanatory notes on unusual products, many of which he has pioneered. Japanese sea vegetables are a catalogue speciality. 'Mineral-rich traditional foods are rapidly regaining popularity as a regular daily food,' he claims. 'Agar flakes are a natural sea vegetable gelatin for desserts and savoury aspics. Women divers harvest the mild tasting arame, from the famous Ise peninsula, whilst the more strongly flavoured Hiziki is a favourite with macrobiotic cooks.' *Japonaiserie* is familiar for soya bean fermentations (eleven are listed) perhaps less so for pasta. Soba (or spaghetti) is offered in styles varying between 40% and 100% buckwheat content, no other ingredients; it is gluten-free and salt-free. Bonito dried fish flakes (a special grade of mackerel) are steamed, dried, wood smoked and then shaved wafer thin, usually used as a garnish. In all, Mr. Bradley can probably claim 400 or more food items for his intriguing list. Pottery, cookware and kitchen gadgets account for another 100. Nevertheless, more familiar wholefoods still fill large areas of shop shelf space. Breads include several varieties of traditional sour dough (natural rise without yeast). Cakes without sugar or honey, only cereal malt sweeteners; similar criteria are in force when it comes to take-aways which are in imaginative variety—rice balls, sushi, sandwiches, and salads; tofu and tempeh dishes; desserts, rolls and muffins. 'Guaranteed' FREGG eggs only.

Open: Mon to Fri, 10.30 to 7; Sat, 10.30 to 5.

LONDON   Map 4
Dandelion Natural Foods, 256 Battersea Park Road, SW11
TEL London 01-223 9211

It would please the grocery magnate to know that in at least one shop Lipton's fitments including marble slabs, counters and glass jars survived—and to serve their original purpose. And as if to emphasise the old world atmosphere they still weigh up in 1 lb bags (actually 450 g to satisfy the alert trading standards man). The 150 herbs and spices are sold by the ounce. The dairy counter has seen changes since the days of the steam yacht with vats of butter usurped by Greek-style yoghurt, Canadian Cheddar by goats' cheese. Eggs are Martin Pitt. Cooking is done on the premises, homemade soups, samosas, main dishes of the day, and pecan pie. Breads are bought in daily from Goswells, South London Bakery Co-operative and Natural Rise. The muesli is made up of entirely organic flakes.

Open: Mon to Sat, 9.30 to 6.

LONDON   Map 4
Di's Larder, 62 Lavender Hill, SW11   TEL London 01-223 4618

Local office workers and a lot of teachers descend at lunchtime to this neighbourhood shop in the high street parade. Bill Kilpatrick bakes bread on the premises, all hand-kneaded, for the quite modest charge of 68p and 72p a loaf respectively, wholemeal and granary. Enthusiasts come from as far as Greenwich. His wife achieves fame through lending her name to the organisation. Her hot dishes of the day—for take-away—may be a lasagne or casserole, quite often a pizza or tortilla, fairly certainly a quiche or two, always homemade. Innovatively there are several hot salads, based on savoury rice. The cheese counter is quite large and carries their own yoghurt, made from half-skim, half-whole milk, a very thick Greek one, a soya version, all backed up by the more regular Cheddar, Double Gloucester, and Leicester. On dried goods there is 10% off for 5 lb, bigger discounts negotiable for larger purchases. They buy organic when available. Plurableu is a more unusual brand name on the juice scene, sold alongside Epicure white cox and russet apple juices, and the familiar Copella, Aspall and Lindavia. Eggs are Robert Pyne. Fresh fruit and vegetables not sold but Organic Farm Foods supply the kitchen.

Open: Mon to Sat, 10 to 6.

LONDON   MAP 4
Earth Exchange Collective Ltd, 213 Archway Road, N6   TEL London 01-340 6407

This one-time derelict house in a garden is, with the passing years, now looking marginally more prosperous though it seems unlikely it would ever (or they would ever want it to) rate as smart. Members of the collective are more concerned to promote wholefoods and natural healing for all those interested in improving their health. Real estate standards are scarcely a priority. Long shop shelves are stocked with principally organic foods packed by themselves. They rejoice in being one of a handful of places where foods containing sugar are not sold as a matter of policy. Only honeys and apple juice concentrates are used as sweeteners. All the jams and preserves fall into this category, of course. They are also one of a small group of London shops privileged to be able to offer orthodox baking from so many different sources: Ceres, South London Co-op and Bamboo Grove. Other things they happily tackle in their own kitchen, but standards can fluctuate with cooking roster changes. As with bakery goods it is their good fortune to be within delivery distance of Organic Farm Foods so greengrocery never presents problems. Neither do eggs, from Peter Tamlyn at Dunmow, or yoghurts, natural low and full fat, plain and flavoured. Vegetable rennet cheeses are in fair array too. Though they recently sought and obtained a licence, fruit and vegetable juices are still a main line. Panther non-alcoholic beers are still drawn, now in competition with Aspall's organic cider. 'Soyboy' is the soya milk ice cream.

Open: Fri to Tue, 11 to 7.

LONDON   MAP 5
Friends Foods, 113 Notting Hill Gate, W11   TEL London 01-221 4700

'We are on the wrong side of the street,' says Ann Fowler, manager for a co-operative associated with the Friends of the Western Buddhist Order, yet they appear to be flourishing after a short spell as a market stall. They specialise in wholemeal breads (South London Bakery Co-operative and Ceres), free range eggs (Martin Pitt) and untreated wholefoods, 'entirely vegetarian in accordance with our non-violent aims. We prefer products which promote the health of our customers, while not damaging the earth.' These include the popular Rose and Antoine savouries and cakes made from wholemeal flour and no sugar. More meatless burgers, pasties, sandwiches come from a variety of small businesses, some of whom are also co-ops. Organically grown fruit and vegetables are not part of their stock though 1985 sees them launching into ecologically sound products, such as bio-degradable detergents and recycled paper products. Otherwise there is a stock of figs, dates, raisins, currants, bananas and such: decaffeinated coffee— not the pure stuff; Eden organic fruit juices; grains, beans and flours (some organic).

Open: Mon, 11 to 5.30; Tue, Wed, Fri, 10 to 6.30; Thur, 10 to 5.30; Sat, 9 to 5.30.

LONDON MAP 4
Haelan Organic Food Centre, 37—39 Park Road, Crouch End, N8
TEL London 01-340 4258

In 1971, Mr. Booth pioneered 'one of London's original wholefood shops'. No food containing sugar of any extracted type is ever sold and as much as possible is organically grown. An incredible range of breads—about twenty-two types—are a speciality coming from an astonishing variety of sources: Ceres, Bamboo Grove, South Bakers Co-operative, Infinity Foods, Natural Rise and Springhill. Rose and Antoine, starting some years ago with a stall on Camden Lock have recently become a wholesale operation and a good many of their recipes, using organic, stoneground English 100% flour but no sugar, are stocked here. Cakes and sweet pastries dominate: 'a nice carrot cake, the popular lemon poppy seed and a vegan date-topped apple cake.' A year ago the four or so foot run of greengrocery was lengthened to an entire shop side—plus window display—and since then that side of the business has flourished. Deliveries on most days from various suppliers. In the course of a year, there is the choice of a hundred different vegetables and there could be as many as twenty varieties of apple, mostly English. Dairy produce— non-animal rennet cheeses, up to ten types, goats' milk yoghurt (plain and fruit up to biodynamic standard). Non-battery eggs are from Robert Herd's. All the foregoing enthusiasms should not overshadow the fact Mr. Booth's stock of grains is the equal of his peers, all of which are organic. This includes some beans too, though only a few of the dried fruits reach this standard. On balmy summer days the variety of herb plants runs into three figures and three times as many again in dried form. Apple, grape (red and white) and pear juices are organic, from a total of twenty juices which can be followed by vegetable soya ice cream.

Open: Mon to Fri, 10 to 6.30, Sat, 9.30 to 6.

LONDON MAP 4
Haynes, Hansom & Clark, 17 Lettice Street, SW6 TEL London 01-736 7878

With the advantage of warm endorsement by Elizabeth David, Zyw Tuscan cold-pressed extra virgin olive oil is imported by this Kensington firm of wine merchants. Alternatively those further north may find it convenient to contact Adam Zyw whose address is 1 Hawthornbank Lane in the picturesque Dean Village, Edinburgh, with an approach as steep as any Tuscan hillside. Mrs. Lesley Zyw has produced a helpful little pamphlet outlining the special merits of particular grades of olive oils, and the pitfalls for the unwary. It is worth reading for, as Elizabeth David notes, *'the little article answers all of my queries and some others I did not know I needed to ask. I can with certainty say that information about how to choose these fine oils is almost as much sought after as the oil itself. Again as with wine, the only certain way to find out which you like and which you don't is by trial and error, and errors come expensive. So it does help to have a sound idea of what you are looking for and of what the label means, if anything. Is there, for example, a significant difference between an oil labelled cold-pressed and one with no reference on the label to pressing method? Is there such a thing as hot pressing and if so what is its effects on the oil? What distinguishes Extra Virgin Oil from Soprafino, Fine Virgin and unqualified Virgin? What is the importance of First Pressing as opposed to Second Pressing? Why are some olive oils green and others golden? Why have some a strong smell and taste of the fruit and others little of either?'* Olives are harvested in winter, beginning when they are almost ripe, usually in November. The Zyw olives are then taken to a press at a local farm where they are ground into a paste, flesh stones and all. The paste is then pressed hydraulically to extract the oils and liquids. These then pass to a centrifugal separator, which yields pure oil on one side and gets rid of water and wastes on the other. That is all. That is how First Pressing, Cold Pressed Olive Oil is made. The residual dryish pulp goes to a factory where it is pressed again with heat and boiling water, yielding a fattier and more acid oil.

Open: Mon to Sat, 9.15 to 7.

LONDON   MAP 5
Holborn Bakery, 50 Lambs Conduit Street, WC1   TEL London 01-405 4542

In reality Bloomsbury's village baker, for their best wholefoods' clients, known to drop by
for chats, are Quacks in Theobald's Road and Alara in nearby Marchmont Street. It is not
a specialist wholefood bakery but a place to go for a range of stoneground wholemeal
loaves in light and dense textures (according to preference), a high fibre version, a French
stick and wholemeal fruit breads and ginger cakes. There is also a rye loaf and a spiced
fruit granary bun is another line. Their's is a fairly standard commercial bake but they have
readily adapted to demands for natural foods. Wholemeal is made to a recipe of flour,
yeast and water, no sugar, shortening or salt. The high fibre loaf is just the same with the
addition of bran. All other recipes are made using a vegetable fat, which includes all their
white breads. Eastertime brings a wholemeal hot cross bun.

Open: wholesale only.

LONDON   MAP 4
Kamakarsini Health and Beauty Centre, 34 West Green Road, Tottenham, N15
TEL London 01-802 8082

Irving and Patricia Bailey have given their small family store a new Georgian front and
fitted out the interior with mahogany and teak shelving. P.E. teacher and beautician
respectively, they seem well qualified to undertake body care. Advice on different diets is
willingly given. A fairly new organisation in Stoke Newington, the Rainbow Co-op make
traditional West Indian type breads, hardow, made from sweetbreads and another—only
to be taken in moderation—sugar cake, just as its name implies a concoction of sugar,
coconut and honey. Bamboo Grove do their regular wholemeal, rye and crispbreads. Both
kosher and vegetarian needs are jointly met with tasty salami, sausages and hot-dogs
imported from Israel. There are several yoghurts, among them the Loseley Greek style
(and their ice cream) and the hard cheeses are made with vegetable rennet. Non-battery
eggs from Robert Herd; no fresh fruit or vegetables but a selection of brans, pulses and
grains with discounts up to a generous 20 % on quantity.

Open: Mon to Sat, 9 to 7.

LONDON   MAP 4
Lewisham World Shop, 88 Sydenham Road, SE26

Founder members of this group concerned with education were a thirty-five-strong group
meeting in a Lewisham church hall. Now an incorporated voluntary association, besides
wholefoods they have taken to books and Third World crafts. Keeping life fairly simply,
stock is largely represented by brown rice, millet, buckwheat, bran, muesli mixed
themselves, oats, peas, beans and lentils of various types. Fresh bread reaches them
Mondays and Fridays only—wholemeal, rye, fruit—from the South London Bakers
Co-operative. Mr. Barber delivers his eggs weekly from Stonham Parva.

Open: Mon to Sat, 9.30 to 5.30; closed Wed.

LONDON   MAP 5
Neal's Yard Shops, 1 Neal's Yard, Covent Garden, WC2
TEL London 01-836 1066

These trend-setting shops hidden away from the street are not entirely original. In fact, far
away St. Augustine, Florida and Salem, Massachusetts offer equivalents. Their prices may
be unimitated when the humble vegetable pasties (even if appreciated) are marked up
at 85p, when the meat equivalent elsewhere hovers around 35p. That much said, it
remains a bright stimulating place. They are an inspiration for their sharp attitude to
food reform, in a series of small enterprises grouped around the leafy green triangular

courtyard, and to prove they mean what they say, conservation-minded staff bicycles are neatly stacked in one corner. Farm shop proprietor Sean McArdle is up from Dorset three days a week to re-stock with organic garden produce, some collected from other growers en route. The shop is not entirely organic but there is nothing remotely ambiguous about the labelling so you may buy in confidence. Supplies are from Charles Dowding at Montague Organic Gardens, Wincanton and the Moorfoot Organic Garden at Denbury near Newton Abbott. Citrus and other vegetable supplies are from Israel, the Western Galilee State Agricultural Service and the Yodfat Agricultural Community. So there is not too much dependence on the vagaries of the short British growing season. Also the variety is well ahead of that of most organic produce shops, with fresh produce prices that are not quite so shattering. Bananas at 55p per lb cannot be a bad buy for organic quality in mid-winter when regular supplies are fetching 45p. The Yard bakery shop was possibly the prototype for the High Street Hot Bread shop. Similarities end here. High street encounters with wholemeal, rye and sour dough of this standard are rare. That goes too for the scrumptious hot savouries and cakes, but for shoppers there may well be a delicate balance between the needs of the tummy and the priorities of the budget. Above the bakery is an equally wholesome, if rudimentary, tea-room where the same goods are available along with tisanes, coffee and fruit juices. Back at ground level the dairy offers take-away vegetable soup, chilli and rice, millet and vegetable rennet cheese, baked potatoes (with imaginative garnishes), crisp fruit salads, apple crumble and vanilla custards, Greek-style yoghurt with its creamy golden crust and their exquisite *fromage blanc*. It is a place to call in for more traditional English varieties, some made using the increasingly popular vegetable rennets. The Apothecary's Store carries literally hundreds of herbs and it is well worth seeking their printed list for leisurely reading. There are a few more not listed so remember to ask if something rare is sought. Soaps are another basic stock item, made exclusively of natural, glycerine and buttermilk.

Open: winter, Mon to Fri, 10 to 6.30; summer, Mon to Fri, 10 to 7.30; Sat, 10 to 6.30; Sun, 10 to 5.30.

LONDON   Map 5
Neal's Yard Wholefood Warehouse, 21–23 Shorts Garden, WC2
TEL London 01-836 5151

Geographically it is outside the limits of Neal's Yard proper even if within calling distance, and is part of the same successful tenacious empire. They have been long-hour, seven-day trading for years while others still go on thinking about it. A warehouse by the old definition of the word, outside and in, it is infinitely more appetising than the modern prefabricated anonymous counterpart. Inside an Aladdin's Cave of variety is one enthusiastic and really quite appropriate assessment. One only begins to quibble, just a little, after getting sight of their list. They manage to carry an enormous stock but for some reason there is an uncharacteristic reluctance to give more than bare details. Too many questions are really left unanswered by these undoubted flagwavers. Less reticence would do the establishment—the cause and the customer—much more justice. Flours are exclusively from Doves Farm and five types of that dependable mill's eight variations are kept. All (including a rye) are stoneground, the wholewheat is organically grown and the maize meal is both gluten and wheat-free. Doves Farm also supply the wheatgerm and bran. A trifle surprisingly all the flours are only mentioned in standard 1.5 kg packs when a variety of sack sizes can be obtained. They begin to display their potential with dried fruits running a forty-four different packs' types. Nine of them are apricots, including a hefty £6.67 for 2kg size best quality wholefruits. There are two grades of the unsulphured kind. The only organic dried fruits are dates. It is not really a place for margarines (only Granose is represented) nor for the large Eden-Waren range of wholefoods though the latter's organic carrot juice is stocked. Bread is a great strength hereabouts for not only can you get the in-house specialities (across in the Yard) but also an excellent range from Ceres, Pema and Springhill. From the last range there is pumpernickle, sprouted grain (both sliced), rye, malt, gristy, sour dough and a Country

Bran. Pema do a linseed loaf. Ceres supply natural leavened and sour dough, as well as sesame baps and sticks and wholemeal. Honeys are from Simon Weir (Hampshire, Heather and English Honeycomb), Rowse, and under their own label wildflower, orange blossom (7 lb size £5.77), acacia, Mexican and Australian (both 7 lb for £4.19). Louisiana organic rice is £1.69 a kg and, for those well heeled or on a special binge, wild rice £1.24 for 50 gm. The Petropoulos olive oils are unrefined, whilst at four times the price (25 cl size only £2.31) is Taylor and Lakes walnut oil.

Open: Mon to Sat, 10 to 6.30; Sun, 10 to 5.

LONDON   MAP 4
Only Natural Wholefoods, 108 Palmerston Road, Walthamstow, E17
TEL London 01-520 5898

Derek Norris runs this excellent wholefood shop which has a modest vegetarian café and restaurant attached, called 'Le Soleil'. A take-away service is also available. Bakers' goods include wholemeal bread, homemade cakes, pasties and quiches. Many of these are made by local people and range from cheese and potato savoury to apple shortcake or wholewheat bread puddings. There is a choice of organic mueslis which are available in quantities from ½ lb to 20 lb, with bulk discounts. These are also available for pulses of which there is a wide range. A good range of flour including organic buckwheat and rye is on offer and an equally wide range of rice (organic, Italian, Thai, etc). Bring your own bottle for apple juice, cider vinegar, soy sauce, tamari and peanut butter, or buy the cartons of pure fruit juice. Among the preserves, the local Epping Forest honey is a speciality, and there is a particularly useful free delivery service of the organic fruit and vegetables (good choice) for orders over £10.

Open: Mon, Tue, Sat, 9 to 5.30; Wed 9 to 1; Thur, 9 to 7; Fri, 9 to 6.

LONDON   MAP 3
Rawel's Super Foods, 12 Hampden Square, Southgate, N14
TEL London 01-361 2180

After holding the fort for twenty-eight years Mr. Rawel's can fairly be considered a long term commitment. He makes a speciality of stocking items not found in his competitors' shops and in his largish premises carries a fair sprinkling of provisions, delicatessen, frozen foods and possibly the largest selection of non-animal fats in North London. Discrimination is needed when selecting bread, for alongside his wholemeals from Goswells and a reputable Greek source he has less desirable popular kinds. The fruit and vegetables are not organic. Milk includes soya; flours Allinsons and Jordans. Pulses in about 15 kinds and eight kinds of rice but no bulk stock. Some tinned fruits are in natural juices. Frozen vegetarian convenience foods in around ten varieties.

Open: Mon to Sat, 9 to 6; Fri, 9 to 6.30.

LONDON   MAP 5
Sesame, 128 Regents Park Road, NW1   TEL London 01-586 3779

Problems with the lease overcome, for the time being at least, they can now devote their energies to the serious business of selling food. After Ceres, they like to think they were one of the very first wholefood shops to move away from the old health food image. For Peter Haxton it is a recent move from Amersham Wholefoods where they also made their own bread and cakes, the flour actually milled on the premises. Here Mr. Haxton manages to cook daily but it is more likely to be soups or hot main dishes to satisfy voracious lunchtime appetites. Some think they do a hot-pot rather well. Residents of smarter households round about come for suppertime quiche, salads and pizza, otherwise serious lunchtime buyers are people who work in the vicinity. A few are picnickers in the park or at the zoo, summertimes that is. Ceres and South London Bakery Co-operative have been hauled in for bread deliveries, and, more recently, Bamboo Grove now enjoying a renaissance. Fruit loaves, tea loaves, currant buns or whatever attract praise. A few organic vegetables 'the prices and quality better than they were until recently'.

Open: Mon to Sat, 9.30 to 6.

LONDON   Map 4
Towards Jupiter, 191 Mare Street, E8   TEL London 01-985 5394

Richard and Letitia Costain are anthroposophists so they run the shop according to the principles laid down by Rudolf Steiner earlier this century. Basic foods are a priority and the absence of additives and preservatives a matter of more than average importance. Fortunately they have useful links with Tableshurst Farm (Sussex) and Oaklands Park (Gloucestershire), both Steiner schools with home farms offering reliable and fairly regular fruit and vegetable supplies. However there is a rather restrictive proviso for shoppers, everything must be ordered in advance. Casual shopping will not do! For bread they are fortunate again with daily deliveries from the South London Bakers Co-operative. For ready-to-eat savouries and a few pastries they depend on Natural Rise and a reliable local girl. Cows' and goats' yoghurts are Leasowes, and the eggs Martin Pitt. Plain things like teas, coffees, grains, flours and dried fruits are stocked in great variety. Ice cream is soya.

Open: Mon to Fri, 10 to 5.30; Sat, 10 to 5.

LONDON   Map 5
Universal Sandwiches, 188 Old Street, EC1   TEL London 01-250 0096

After an uncertain start, Joe Simpson's sandwich service has taken off, which forced the recent move to larger premises under the wing of the East West Centre at this address. Tempeh, traditional to Indonesia as an alternative to meat protein (good on vitamin B12 too) is being prepared for kebabs, burgers and sandwiches. Cooking for the sandwiches means pan frying in olive oil and seasoning with shoyu. Hummus, tofu and seitan (the so-called wheat meat) are also popular sandwich fillings. Mr. Simpson's is a wholesale service to shops and other take-away outlets which include Neal's Yard, Clearspring (at 188 Old Street), Friends Foods, Bushwhacker, Open Sesame and Les' Natural Foods.

Wholesale only.

LONDON   Map 5
La Vie Claire, 31 Monmouth Street, WC2   TEL London 01-836 4842

The staff came with the stock so you will get 'a taste of France' more readily if you can speak the language, otherwise there is charming diffidence, preferring talk amongst themselves. This first British branch was launched only a year ago but has quickly found favour among health-conscious consumers recognising the potential dangers from fertilisers, pesticides and herbicides. A cool clean interior is decorated in the company's cheerful emerald green and white graphics, the back way in leading from the Neal's Yard shops. The two are an interesting contrast. There is no resemblance to the latter's bucolic earthiness: they are their own men. Part of a two hundred chain, where all the products are French, on home ground it is company philosophy to keep the shops well supplied with fresh organically produced fruit and vegetables year round. In France this presents no problems, with the growing number of small farmers using organic methods of production in preference to others. So, the shops are never starved of quality produce in a condition which the customers will not hesitate to buy. Proudly they claim 'we sell what we tell you to eat'. Bread has a special importance and in Paris there are three bakeries turning out 7,000 loaves daily. Until a suitable British baker is found Monmouth Street remains breadless. When it does come it will probably be in some of the lighter grades preferred back home, 80%, 85% and 90% extraction. Meanwhile try their biscuits. Only natural ingredients go into them. Fats are either palm oil or non-hydrogenated vegetable fat. Flours are from cereals cultivated without chemicals and synthetic pesticides. At no time are artificial colours or flavours used but they do succumb to raw sugar. Fruit and vegetable juices are bottled without ascorbic acid though several of the berry type and rhubarb do have added sugar. Jams and marmalades are made with fresh fruit, immediately on harvesting, without resort to sulphur dioxide and the like; neither are pectins or acids added. In accordance with an E.E.C. directive they rate as first class jams as far as the fruit content is concerned, which puts them on a par with our own supermarket 'low sugar' preserves but with the additional advantage of no additives of any description. Apart from all the familiar fruit, there is jam with a difference, banana, creamed prune, cassis and myrtle some of them. Ravioli, gourmet vegetable mix or Ethiopian lentil and tomato are convenience foods entirely sugar-free. A variety of nut purées make tempting sweet and savoury spreads. Public relations are good, with a well prepared stock list and more detailed explanatory handouts dealing with particular food categories. It is worthwhile considering their mail order operation if unable to make a personal visit.

Open: Mon to Sat.

LONDON   MAP 4
Vitality Eats, 143 Greenwich South Street, SE10   TEL London 01-692 1626

Vegans, people on special diets, the animal-care conscious, vegetarians and locals on the bran, form the clientèle at Brian Foulds' new shop. His energies run to whisking up burgers, quiches, wholefood savouries, take-away salads and, on request, vegan dishes, all from the shop's own kitchen. Otherwise it is a place featuring good breads, Greek yoghurts, organic cereals and flours. The first are from Carleys, his local 'home baker'. The dairy cabinet carries Quark cheese, soya milk and cream, a ewes' yoghurt and vegetarian type cheeses. Organic Farm Foods' South London base is handy for an organic fruit and vegetable supply. Non-battery eggs are laid at Upton Farm, South Altham near Dover. The range of dried fruits and nuts is wide, but Mr. Foulds has not come across any that are organically grown. The low tannin tea is without added dye too, the loose teas Lapsang, Darjeeling and B.O.P. For different kinds of thirst, alcohol free wines and lagers.

Open: Mon to Sat, 9 to 6; Thur, 9 to 8.

LONDON   MAP 5
Wholefood, 24 Paddington Street, W1   TEL London 01-935 3924

Lilian Schofield does not really like to be reminded that she has been directing this 'food mission', along with Mary Langman, for nigh on a quarter-century. Actually the shop is the property of Soil Association members, founded in 1960, hoping it would become a model of its kind. Onlookers feel they have succeeded fairly well. From among the myriad pale imitators established since, only a handful even try to meet all the exacting objectives they set themselves. Now a charitable trust, 'Wholefood of Baker Street'—to give them their more familiar name—has become a misnomer. Rent revisions by their first landlord have meant abandoning the prestigious Baker Street address in favour of a less crippling rent round the corner in Paddington Street. Not everything is wholefood but it is better to express it the other way round, few foods are not. No white sugar or white flour is used. No food is stocked which contains chemical additives. The same prohibition is applied to colourings, artificial flavourings, and extenders. From two shops (the butchery department is several doors away) a total food service is offered. Most of the year there is a representative stock of fresh produce from various global sources. Watch out for the red price tickets: they are the organic guarantees. Sometimes they stock the next best, bringing in oranges and lemons guaranteed sunripened and untreated with the usual fungicides and wax after picking. When nothing meets their standards they go without. There may be times for instance when there are no onions or tomatoes in the shop. Many fruit and vegetable juices and purées carry Demeter and Soil Association guarantees. Apricots from Lower Galilee are particularly good value. Untreated against pests, Yodfat dry them right down, so when soaked they swell to a much heavier weight than regular stock. French prunes of dessert quality, otherwise California and the Argentine provide most of the dried fruit stock. Jersey milk, cream and yoghurt comes from a biodynamic farm. Other dairy produce is in great variety from cows', goats' and ewes' milk. Breads from all the main specialist bakers, one range baked using natural leaven. Oils are cold-pressed; baby foods are organic from a Swiss source. Meat and poultry is from animals reared without antibiotics, sex hormones or other artificial stimulants to growth. Aberdeen beef, Dorset lamb and pork; free range chickens; naturally reared turkeys, geese and ducks and kid meat. In season game and venison. Beef and pork sausages, pâtés and cold roasts are all prepared on the premises. They stock one of the most comprehensive lists of health books in Britain.

Open: Mon, Wed, Thur, 8.45 to 6; Tue, Fri, 8.45 to 6.30; closed Sat pm.

LONDON   Map 4
Wild Oats, 210 Westbourne Grove, W2   TEL London 01-229 1063

Admirers recommend them for friendliness, nice produce and reasonable prices. In an area of antique shops, a food shop of any type is something of a welcome rarity. Even dealers have to eat, quite a number finding their way here. Gareth Zeal himself carries a now valuable collection of enamel signs (picked up for a song, and a marvellous investment) firmly fixed to the shop's walls. A variety of suppliers are used: Natural Rise for a rice loaf and a Japanese couple for tofu pockets with rice, arame, Japanese pickles; Justin de Blank for a softer loaf and South London Bakers Co-operative for something firmer. Once a competitive 'power lifter', subtly different from weight lifting, Mr. Zeal has moved on to martial arts and given up all meat eating on his trainer's advice.

Open: Mon to Fri, 9 to 6.30; Sat, 9 to 5.30

LONDON   Map 5
Wilkins Natural Foods, 53 Marsham Street, SW1   TEL London 01-222 4038

After seven years, they are firmly part of the Marsham Street scene with a reputation for imaginatively prepared fresh food: even the cleanliness of the place and the courtesy of the staff is sufficient in itself to attract complimentary comment. Pizzas, salads, quiches and the like, prepared in their restaurant kitchen (see entry) are available as take-away items, along with the homemade scones and sugar-free cakes and regular bread lines from Goswells, Ceres and Bamboo Grove. Vegan Christmas and birthday cakes can be made to order. Fruit and vegetables guaranteed organic are all supplied by Organic Farm Foods. Yoghurts are Leasowes, Loseley and—probably the best—Miracle Herd. There is a full complement of the other foods expected of a shop of this kind, including non-battery eggs from Countryside Products, Fakenham.

Open: Mon to Fri, 8 to 6.

LONDON   Map 4
Windmill Wholefoods, 486 Fulham Road, SW6   TEL London 01-385 1570

Having been brought up on a farm, then having a farm of his own, Noel McDonald's life has somehow always revolved around food. What is more he has 'been eating this sort of thing all my life so it just seemed the logical thing to go into.' Tucked in behind his restaurant (see entry), his is more of a small warehouse than shop, for all kinds of grains, mueslis, pulses for which there is 10% off bulk purchases. Room is found for Lancashire, Cheddar, and Double Gloucester to accompany the Quark, the yoghurt (goats' and ewes') and the cottage kinds. Pick up bread here, from Ceres, South London Bakers Co-operative and Bamboo Grove, crispbread, sour dough, grain and rye. Cakes are made on the premises. Fruit juices in considerable array are extended with the organic vegetable types.

Open: Mon to Sat, 9.30 to 6; Fri, 9.30 to 7.

LOUTH   Lincolnshire   MAP 6
The Wholefood Co-op, 12A Mercer Row

Derek, Jan, Janet, John, Ian, Lucy, Rebecca, Ruth and Wendy banded together to form this co-operative because they held strong views on food, and have speedily consolidated their forces with a new Grimsby branch. A newsy list is helpful. Serious customers however should demand more information than they offer so far, but it's a start. They give a lot of thought to mueslis. It is one commodity on which they are prepared to be expansive, naming the ingredients. Herbs and spices are a reasonable line and, if the list is not open to misinterpretation, prices derisively low. Coriander a mere 2p for 10 grams. Tumeric, mixed sweet spices, fenugreek and chilli all only 3p. Either they keep slave labour or others are racketeers. Most of the curry blends are only 5p. Decaffeinated and coffee substitutes get more than normal representation; juices include Aspall's organic kind (their organic cider vinegar as well) and pear concentrate; cooking oils in an array of cold-pressed grades. Pasta: the lasagne, macaroni and wholewheat spaghetti are organically grown. The first and last mentioned in bulk cases up to 25 kg. Ask for current prices. Grains, of which five mentioned are organic, in sack sizes up to 50 kg. Lincolnshire honey is a speciality though only the botanically knowledgeable would have known that there was a heather nectar in the district waiting to be collected!

Open: Mon to Sat, 9 to 5.

MACHYNLLETH   Powys   MAP 6
National Centre for Alternative Technology   TEL Machynlleth (0654) 2400

Actually out of town, three miles up the road towards Dolgellau, this enterprise in an unpromising former slate quarry was established ten years ago when sceptics thought it was due for a short life. Not so! They flourish. The residential part (for visitors) has been abandoned but interest never wanes for natty solutions to some environmental problems. Some of them attract those curious about their money saving ideas too. To the captive audience, they take the opportunity to demonstrate the range and scope for the use of wholefoods. The menu is completely vegetarian and, like the related café in the town, very acceptable soups, vegetable bakes and salads are the main lunchtime dishes. Everything is prepared and cooked on the premises. Home baked rolls and cakes especially good and prices modest. This is one of the incredibly rare places that also offer a polyunsaturated margarine at table in lieu of butter. The eggs used are free range and the vegetables organically grown when available.

Open: daily, 11 to 5.

MACHYNLLETH   Powys   MAP 6
The Quarry Shop, 13 Maengwyn Street   TEL Machynlleth (0654) 2624

The brightly painted shop (red, green and black) is not easily missed in the little town centre. Inside cream paint and functional timber fittings give a mellower effect in this neatly kept place. Annie Lowmass has a general overseership in this outstation of the dauntingly named Centre for Alternative Technology (three miles north along the Dolgellau Road). Alternatives are more apparent in the dairy cabinet offering tofu, soya milk and yoghurt. They pack a lot into limited space. A selection of fresh foods is cooked in the café kitchen behind (see entry), mainly pizzas, quiches, salads and their well-filled rolls. No time or room for bread making so there is improvisation with a decent enough loaf from Arvonia bakery. No room for fruit and vegetables so they put customers in touch with Aber Nant Garfan organic growers, who are not too far away. Non-battery eggs are sporadic, coming, as available, from various small suppliers. Their enthusiasm runs to making a special effort to be helpful to tell people how to make the most of alternative foods.

Open: Sun to Sat, 9 to 5; closed Sun, Thur pm.

MAIDSTONE   Kent   MAP 3
Honesty Wholefoods, 71 Union Street   TEL Maidstone (0622) 677713

This is Michael Clark's 'animal-free, smoke-free patch', opened eight years ago after Infinity in Brighton passed up his hint that they might bring the gospel to north Kent. Mr. Clark, part-time disc jockey, can offer all the usual packed grains and flours, a more than decent selection of herbs and an equally representative dried fruit stock. Salt and sugar-free goods include the Whole Earth preserves range. There are free range eggs from Mr. Kerry at Aylesford. Tofu and a conventional stock of vegetable rennet cheeses. No bread or fresh fruit but occasionally some vegetables.

Open: Mon to Sat, 9.30 to 5.30.

MANCHESTER   Greater Manchester   MAP 6
The Green Door Bakery and Wholefood Shop, 72 Hamilton Road
TEL Manchester 061-224 3382

This all women's co-operative has survived the vicissitudes of nine years and admirers insist they are still the city's best bread makers. Others speculate that judging from the regular turnover of co-operators, there must by now be a good many diploma bread makers hereabouts lying low. Perhaps the greatest testimony to their skills is the fact that the cakes and pizzas get on to the shelves of that mixed movement 'On the Eighth Day', where the Oxford Road cognoscenti gather. There is no formal stock list, but they improvise with a cartoon handout, which could be either an amusing idea or presumption that some of us are less literate than themselves. Watch out for their bread in some of the city restaurants. All the baking goes on behind the shop except for Indian savouries brought in the front way by a local woman. Zest and imagination account for the herby garlic, honey and sesame, malthouse, rye and granary breads. Cakes are sugar-free. Frozen lentil and nut bakes and vegetable crumble are new lines for the freezer. The shop is well stocked with general wholefoods, herbs and spices, Pimhill's organic flours, organic oats and potatoes, a few other vegetables to Soil Association standards but fruits only if specially requested. They are good on gluten-free cereals, alternative papers, Women's Liberation and Link-up. They also throw their energies into catering for parties and conferences. Just at present they are 'working like the clappers to match the funds being put up by a grant aiding body to carry out major improvements.'

Open: Mon to Fri, 10.30 to 6; Sat, 10 to 5; closed Wed.

MANCHESTER   Greater Manchester   MAP 6
On the Eighth Day Co-operative, 111 Oxford Road
TEL Manchester 061-273 4878

Opposite the college, a good many coming here are students with a sprinkling of families doing monthly shopping. Some think that they are the best wholefood shop in the North West and with shameless immodesty they are known to be of that view themselves. Beans are a speciality, stocking every type (their claim) in organic and regular grades. Flours and rice all have their organic versions and all of this stock is available by the sack given a week's notice. This is a southerly outlet of Little Salkeld watermill flour. All dried fruits are dressed in vegetable oils. Coffees and teas are Traidcraft Barleycup, Caro, Swisscup Whiteheads and Twinings. Apple juice is Aspall's first pressing. Fruit and vegetables are not stocked but they do have free range eggs and wholemeal bread from an Altrincham baker, Christies. Customers appreciate the goats' milk cheese (there is also yoghurt and regular cheeses), tofu and tofu burgers, seafood vegetables and the various miso mixes. One keen macrobiotic customer travels from Barrow-in-Furness for the Japanese sea vegetables. As with their café, trading under the same name (see entry), there are pastries from Manchester's Green Door (all done without sugar). The popular samosas (from Chunis Chaat House Restaurant) rate well. Eighty are sold daily. Enthusiastically sought mushroom, cheese and onion, and vegetable pastries travel from Ellesmere (Deeside Bakery) in Shropshire. Pies from Sunrise Bakery.

Open: Mon to Sat, 10 to 5.30.

MELMERBY   Cumbria   Map 6
Village Bakery, Melmerby   TEL Melmerby (0768) 81575

Foods from the unique wood-fired brick oven are the specialities from this unlikely-situated Pennine bakery-cum-shop-cum-restaurant (see entry). Ambitiously Lis and Andrew Whitley have made pure food their cause, daily producing bread, pies, cakes and biscuits mostly using their own organic produce—there is a smallholding at the back. All the flour is stoneground at Little Salkeld's watermill, just a few miles back towards Penrith. The shop stocks sixty or so varieties of cheese, salamis, cooked meats, their own paté and meatloaf as well as the regular lines of a wholefood grocer. Vegetarian specialities are a feature. Hummus, mincemeat and savouries with meatless fillings are all made in the kitchen. Take-away salads are available along with sandwiches with an almost unlimited range of fillings. Whenever possible the smallholding's freshly picked fruit and vegetables are used. Look for their foods too in their other shop in Angel Lane, Penrith and a number of other wholefood shops within daily commuting distance.

Open: Mon to Sat, 8.30 to 5.

MILLBROOK   Cornwall   Map 2
J. P. Widdicombe, 4 West Street   TEL Millbrook (0752) 823193

They are out of sight of the sea but John Widdicombe still gets plenty of summer visitors to his surprising village vegetarian greengrocery and wholefood store. The greengrocery bit is the key to survival. Vegetarian/wholefood customers are fewer, though they can sometimes expect fruit and vegetables to be the organic kind from Keveral Farm, Downderry. Farm fruit yoghurts healthily lack colouring or preservatives. Among the grains are organic rice and oats. Juices are Copella and Volonte; coffees decaffeinated and coffee substitute.

Open: Mon to Sat, 9 to 1, 2.15 to 5.

MOSSLEY   Lancashire   Map 6
Mossley Wholefoods, 10 Stockport Road   TEL Mossley (045 75) 67743

Pauline Clifford and Andrew Waide's shop, on the edge of the Peak (Black Hill behind rises to 1,900 feet) makes a minor bit of history. In the modest little former mill town there is no record of any establishment—shop, restaurant, hotel or wine bar—having previously appeared in any guidebook. Their all-vegetarian food is as near as natural as circumstances permit, organically grown whenever available. Muesli is sugar-free. Fruit and vegetables are bought from Manchester Organic Foods, all grown to Soil Association standards. Yoghurts and low-fat cheeses come from the enterprising Langley Farm, handily placed over the hill at Huddersfield. Rennet free (really meaning vegetable rennet) hard cheeses are Singletons. Mrs. Brownley of Charlesworth produces the non-battery eggs. Breads (including a rye), scones, apple slices, and wholemeal fruit cake come from Buckleys of Uppermill. There are 19 pulses, 9 grains, 15 flours (only one white) and among them are rye and barley versions. All 30 varieties of dried fruits are washed and in vegetable oil though some of them come with the customary sulphur dioxide. Dates are organic. The seven coffees are freshly ground to order, supplemented by six regular and ten herb teas, 90 % of the 100 or so herbs are for culinary use, fresh stock and competitive in price. First pressing organic fruit juices should be with them very soon. Ready to eat pies and pasties are also available.

Open: Mon to Fri, 9 to 1, 2 to 5.30; closed Tue pm; Sat, 9 to 4.30.

MULLINGAR   No Map
William J. Graham Ltd, 34 Greville Street   TEL Mullingar (044) 48454

Evolution from tea merchant (with experiments in delicatessen and self-service groceries in between) to wholefoods took nearly twenty years. However, having found a true vocation, John Fitzpatrick enters into the spirit of things enthusiastically. No less trenchant are the customers from the castles and studs, the barracks and hotels of his native Westmeath, some emigrés from the European mainland. Even were it not rye, gluten-free and wholemeal there would be Celtic compensations in breads from the likes of Dusty Miller, or more prosaically from Downes in Dublin. As might be expected there are numerous kinds of tea which they will blend as required. Coffee they will freshly grind or supply the decaffeinated and dandelion versions. Grains and pulses are in wide variety and the organically grown flours come in wholemeal and cake grades. The dairy section can offer yorlait, yoghurt (farmhouse natural), Irish factory cheeses including Cheddar rolls, as well as the genuine Irish farmhouse product. Local non-battery eggs, no vegetables but sometimes organic local fresh fruit.

Open: Mon to Sat, 9 to 6; closed Wed.

NEWCASTLE-UPON-TYNE   Tyne and Wear   Map 6
Mandala Wholefoods, 43 Manor House Road
TEL Newcastle-upon-Tyne (0632) 810045

The reformist nine-year-old collective, with six members, exists to provide vegetarian foods, household items, animal-free cosmetics and to act as a local nutrition information centre in the Jesmond area. Their regular stock list (neat but scarcely informative in spite of laudable crusading aims) is designed as a kitchen memory jog, with, less helpfully, no prices. Olive, sunflower, sesame, safflower and corn germ are all cold pressed cooking oils, alongside regular versions. Fruits and nuts offer an average choice and some of the former will prove to be of organic origin, apricots unsulphured and all fruits vegetable oil sprayed. Freshly milled flour, to Soil Association standards and in conservation grades, comes from the popular Watermill, Little Salkeld, whose flours find their way into most of the better shops and restaurants in Cumbria and Northumberland. Watermill flour comes in 100 %, 85 % and their own special coarse grade. The excellent list of specialist flours includes brown rice, barley, carob, gram, maizemeal, buckwheat, rye and potato. Expect substantial wholesale reductions on flours and their other organic and non-organic grains and pulses. Customary Tradecraft and Barleycup coffee substitute are on offer alongside a wide selection of teas and the conventional kinds. Occasionally non-battery eggs, always curd cheese, animal rennet free cows' and goats' cheese, the first with or without herbs. Greek yoghurts, tofu, goats' milk and unpasteurised cows' milk. Fresh fruits and vegetables only when local residents' productivity turns to surpluses. With local resident kitchen support, there are commendable wholemeal, 85 %, rye, rosemary and garlic breads every day except Monday. The same baking buffs do the carob cakes, oat bars, bean and vegetable pasties, pizzas, onion bhajis. Some of the biscuits and cakes are sugar-free. Herbs and spices are weighed to order, whole or ground according to need and vegetarian pâtés are stocked.

Open: Mon to Sat, 9.30 to 5.30.

NEWCASTLE-UPON-TYNE Tyne and Wear MAP 6
Milburn Health Foods, 42 Newgate Shopping Centre
TEL Newcastle-upon-Tyne (0632) 329091

This long established suburban store has the benefit of Mr. Milburn's twenty years' experience in the trade. Staples are the speciality, grains prepacked or bulk, similarly with the dried fruits. Fresh food is scarcer, limited to Calthwaite plain and fruit yoghurts, and the Greek variety (cows' and ewes') alongside Prewett's vegetarian hard cheese. Fresh wholemeal bread daily. Delicia and Sunwheel jams and marmalades are stocked along with fruit juices in better than average variety from Volonte, Copella, Eches (West German grape), Schloss (more unusually) and Aspall.

Open: Mon to Sat, 8.30 to 5.30.

NEW MILTON Hampshire MAP 3
Scottocks Health Foods, 35 Station Road, New Milton
TEL New Milton (0425) 619090

Phil and Yvonne Tiley's 'strictly ethical stock' specialises in vegetarian foods. Eggs are local from picturesque Burley in the nearby New Forest. The Tileys are refreshingly frank about their large range and perfectly good dried fruits: 'It is difficult to state with any certainty and truth whether they are organically grown or not.' They feel happier asserting that the Aspall and Ethos fruit juices are. And they enthuse over the Cricket St. Thomas ice creams, made in Chard. Case and sack lots of flours, or grains, or pulses will bring a 10 % discount. Goats' cheeses are Zimbabwe and 'Vicarage'! Standard wholemeal bread.

Open: Mon to Sat, 9 to 5.30.

NEWPORT Isle of Wight MAP 3
Newport Health Food Centre, 102 High Street
TEL Newport (IoW) (0983) 522121

A small market town drug store, gradually moving towards wholefoods and herbs, has recently moved shop to cope with enthusiastic local demand. After fourteen years David and Angela McKinley have found it worth their while also to open a second store in Shanklin. Bread in variety comes from the island's old watermill at Calbourne. Goats' milk cheese is in regular supply; goats' yoghurt is only seasonal. Non-animal margarines are another speciality. Bulk reductions on the large range of flours, among which are some organic brands. A range of dried fruits—none known to be organic—and Whole Earth sugar-free jams are available.

Open: Mon to Sat, 9 to 5.

NEWTOWN Powys MAP 6
Sparrow Wholefoods, 13 High Street TEL Newtown (Powys) (0686) 27002

Extensions and alterations are under way which are going to increase the shop's scope here. With support from housewives to hippies they have already graduated from smaller premises. Cheese (some West Wales farmhouse types) and herbs are specialities which are all offered in variety. Tannants of Bishops Castle do the bread baking, there is rye and wholemeal alongside lighter types, and local girl Valerie Jones the carob slices and savouries. Cevnant Farm eggs make a devious cross-country journey from Pont Robert. Discounts for bulk purchases of dried goods and flours.

Open: Mon to Sat, 9 to 5.30.

NORTHAMPTON   Northamptonshire   MAP 3
Daily Bread Co-operative, The Old Laundry, Bedford Road
TEL Northampton (0604) 21531

Taking their name from the Lord's Prayer—'we mean not only bread to eat, but also all things needed for people to live a fulfilled life.' They like to stress that they are not a consumer/retail co-operative (owned and controlled by the customer), instead those who work here own and control the business. It is ten years since 'a cell of nine Christians began meeting in each others homes fortnightly to celebrate Eucharist, their beliefs and aspirations.' The surprise is who would have thought, a decade hence, the enterprise would manage a £¼ million turnover, all achieved in a redundant out-of-town hospital laundry! There are links with MIND and each worker holds a £1 share and in this only mildly hierarchical organisation where Roger Sawtell is manager. Apart from the sheltered employment offered, many feel 'they deserve patronage for the quality of their food list and competitive pricing.' DBC Special (no, it is not the Danish Bacon Company)—house label muesli—has eleven ingredients and is offered at 80p per kg, with the 5 kg pack at £3.70. The more modest Anne's Muesli (six ingredients) is at a very inexpensive 67p, and even greater savings, at £3.10, for the 5 kg. Flours are equally economical. A Canadian wholewheat at £1.98 the 1.5 kg bag is about average but Doves Farm stoneground organic, 59p the 1.5 kg size shows a distinctive saving over most outlets. Holywell Farm stoneground organic flour, with an only recent Soil Association seal of approval, is an out-and-out bargain at 46p. Surinam/Thai more chewy thin grain brown rice is recently up to 70p a 1 kg pack. Porridge oats are only 44p per kg against 60p or so for their supermarket counterparts. Butter beans are Madagascan, red lentils (Turkish) and the green (Canadian) creeping towards £1 per kg against a difficult exchange rate. American red kidney beans also reflect the cascading value of sterling. The high quality Tanzanian coffee, not cheap, is sold to draw attention to the social aspects of coffee growing in the Third World. 'After oil, coffee is the largest commodity market!' Traidcraft, who import it, return 10 % of the proceeds to Third World projects. First pressing olive oil is Greek. Otherwise there is regular sunflower—half the price—£1.05 a litre. Kenyan pineapple and mango are sugar-free. Bulk orders are put together on request, ready to load straight into your vehicle, but a couple of days' notice is sought.

Open: Mon to Fri, 9 to 5.30; Sat, 9 to 4.

NORWICH   Norfolk   MAP 3
Natural Food Store, 4 Exchange Street   TEL Norwich (0603) 613228

'A clean, bright, efficient shop—always with a smile—in fact the best shop of its kind for miles around,' is a partisan view. The Stephensons have been here from the outset to offer a stock of mainly dried goods. Most of the grains and fruits have their organic versions and most of the foods prepared in Höfels Suffolk warehouses are stocked. Bread is from Vignaux. Eggs are from the Bink's at Pulham Market. There is goats' milk, cheese and ice cream. Herbs are in vast variety.

Open: Mon to Sat, 8.15 to 5.30.

NORWICH   Norfolk   MAP 3
Norwich Health Foods, 8 White Lion Street   TEL Norwich (0603) 26493

In 1914 life for wholefooding vegetarian shopkeepers seems to have been tough. History tells us that the Mr. Manthorpe who opened this shop was a 'crank'. Nowadays customers of all ages and types dare to come to Mr. Roberts in this little shop operating only a few yards outside the castle walls. He sells 'all that one would expect to find in a shop of this kind and—for those not yet convinced that good food is generally sufficient for most—vitamins and supplements.' Vignaux bread is stocked.

Open: Mon to Sat, 9 to 5.30.

NORWICH   Norfolk   MAP 3
Rainbow Wholefoods, 16 Dove Street   TEL Norwich (0603) 25560

The narrow pedestrian street is usually thronged with shoppers and tourists, and a good many must spill over into the shop for a regular customer feels 'the shop would benefit from being physically larger'. They manage to surprise with the bread, for it is delivered at least three times daily by Bob in Queen Street. And it is organic with rye and granary options. Malt loaves for a teatime treat. Jams: (they refuse to sell with any sugar in) a pot of blackcurrant (organically grown and Dutch) is encouragingly more blackcurrant than the added apple juice base syrup and lime pectin. 'Richard at Rainbow' and his team exist to sell only wholefood, no pills, no instant food, no chemicals, preservatives or colourings. Foods are organic. Whenever possible they positively discriminate pricewise in favour of organic foods. Cereals include a lot of organic produce and there are claims that the currants, raisins and prunes are the same standard. Fruit and vegetables (from Mangreen, outside the city), dairy cabinet, but no eggs are available.

Open: Mon to Sat, 9.30 to 5.30.

NORWICH   Norfolk   MAP 3
Renaissance, 4 St. Benedict's Street

They succeed in giving the appearance of wholesome pre-forties' provision merchants, even if the result is mildly chaotic. Burgeoning window displays show off their excellent variety of bakery goods one side, the local (organically grown) garden produce the other. A printed notice thoughtfully explains 'What's the point of buying organic?' Graham Hughes at Mangreen and Jeremy Kent at Arninghall jointly grow most vegetable lines though in season Rainthorpe Hall send massive pumpkins. Fruit is not organically grown but it has not been sprayed or treated. Prices are modest, as they are not committed to making a profit. Medicinal and culinary herbs are priced much less than the conventional prepacked sort. Parson's Pantry bake the cakes and pastries (sugar-free), whilst samosas and the like (many vegan) are from a private source. Most of the staff are off the campus, Ludi with a Ph.D. in development studies!

Open: Mon to Sat, 9 to 5.30.

NORWICH   Norfolk   MAP 3
Taylor's Wholefoods and Herbs, Norwich   TEL Norwich (0603) 21831

The old fashioned shop overlooks the diminutive cobbled, tree shaded square at the foot of the hill in this historic quarter. A full range of wines, coffees and delicatessen goods is offered, in addition to pulses, nuts and an exceptionally good selection of dried fruits. There are dried peaches, apricots, bananas, apples, prunes and dates in great variety, some prepacked, some sold loose. Cheeses are English and Continental; coffee ground to order.

Open: Mon to Sat, 8.30 to 5.30.

NOTTINGHAM   Nottinghamshire   MAP 6
Ouroboros Wholefood Collective, 37A Mansfield Road
TEL Nottingham (0602) 419016

From their shop opposite the bus station, it would be optimistic to expect scenic value or fresh air, but they do have the attraction of offering good food cheaply. They adhere strictly to the no sugar, no additives or preservatives principle. Happily the six strong partnership will provide all your brown rice, nuts, muesli, bean and grain needs. The first organic grade, sometimes the others. Tofu and tofu burgers from the Regular Tofu Company, authentic samosas, bhajis and the potato pakora from their Indian lady friend who does them rather well. Wholemeal flour, yeast and water is the recipe for a variable, good strong textured loaf by Gearys of Ratesby. The rye and malt type, polythene packed, from another source, are decent enough but will not bring awards. Whole Earth do their jams; Maythorne the honey and marmalades. Mr. Howard of Radcliffe-on-Trent fetches the eggs. Traidcraft and Campaign tea and coffee are stocked along with honey sweetened soya ice cream and Aspall's organic apple juice. Willingly they will advise on how to cook or sell you cookery booklets published by Leicester Cookery School.

Open: Mon to Sat, 9 to 5.30; Wed, 9 to 6; closed Thur.

OSSETT   West Yorkshire   MAP 6
Funny Foods, 42 Station Road   TEL Ossett (0924) 273255

Mrs. Cockroft takes business life more seriously than her shop name might imply and she deals shrewdly in bulk purchases. Locals know her well and reckon they get good value. Most of the foods offered in more prestigious establishments will be found and there is space for a few convenience foods from Nouvelle Cuisines. This same firm does the one wholemeal loaf. A local farmer produces the eggs and chickens, and although there is no fresh fruit and vegetables, herbs are in endless variety.

Open: Mon, pm; Tue to Sat.

OSWESTRY   Salop   MAP 6
Honeysuckle Wholefood Co-operative Ltd, 53 Church Street
TEL Oswestry (0691) 653125

Established seven years, a sycamore counter, put in by earlier grocery tenants, runs the length of the shop. The smart list with the nice typeface was done on a Smith-Corona, borrowed from friends. The listed herbs, filling all of the back page, intrigue with names like slippery elm powder, scullcap and galangol root. Flours usefully include potato, chick pea, polenta and kibbled wheat. Two grades of rice and the porridge oats are organically grown but none of the fruit and nuts come up to this standard. Morreys of Chirk bake a non-commercial loaf of individual, if not always consistent, character. The Sunrise Bakery (they work from the kitchen in an isolated farmhouse at Sodyllt) prepare the vegetarian picnic rolls, vegetable pasties or samosas to a good standard. Anna Doggart, just out of town, maintains wonderful vegetable supplies—reliable quantities and commendable quality. Goats' cheese and Langley eggs are available. Look them up for brewing grains, wine kits, sweet lime chutneys, hot mango kasaundi along with basic ingredients for an Indian supper.

Open: Mon to Sat, 9 to 5; Thur, 9 to 1.

OXFORD   Oxfordshire   MAP 3
Uhuru Wholefoods, 48 Cowley Road   TEL Oxford (0865) 248249

This well established women's collective sets its sights on selling only whole and organic foods. Their bread is something of a disappointment; do they not know that the city can offer better things? Fresh fruit and vegetables hold out more promise with, in season, vegetables, salad crops, gooseberries, redcurrants, raspberries, and strawberries sent by North Sydmonton Nursery. The autumn brings greengages, plums and apples from the same source. There is live yoghurt and goats' cheese, and eggs from the confusingly similar Syndenham. Recently a few of the flakes, wheat, rye and oats have come into the organically grown category—a new line from Morning Foods. They can now put together an entirely organically grown grade muesli. No ready-to-eat foods, but a lasagne now carries an organic tag. Coffee, mostly comes from Tanzania and Nicaragua. Discounts for bulk buys.

Open: Mon to Thur, 10.30 to 6; Fri, Sat, 9.30 to 6.

PENARTH   South Glamorgan   MAP 2
Beanfreaks Health Food Centre, 3 Victoria Bridge   TEL Penarth (0222) 706632

Kevin Bowles feels their success is due to their general knowledge of what they sell, and belief in what they do. Apart from wholefoods there is a keen interest here in special diets, rice cakes, gluten-free wafers and even a gluten-free muesli mix, for the allergic but equally popular with a good many others. There is a not bad wholemeal loaf and in another baker's loaf, sodium salt was replaced with a potassium based salt; organic flour, orange juice, sunflower oil and honey (in place of customary additives) may be introduced soon. Non-battery eggs. Discounts for quantity.

Open: Mon to Sat, 9 to 5.30.

PETERSFIELD   Hampshire   MAP 3
The Bran Tub, 20 Lavant Street   TEL Petersfield (0730) 64208

Really three shops in one, the last is in old fashioned style retaining original wooden shelves and quarry tiled floor, and acts as the grain shop. More akin to a modern health food shop, the remainder carries the regular packed lines. It is the town's only wholefood outlet and is slowly adjusting to become a significant stockist of organics. It is a firm run by vegetarians for vegetarians, and customers find 'a good many products are, in practice, vegan, with some emphasis on those foods containing B12 important to a vegan diet'. Dairy cabinets and deep freezers contain the selection of take-aways and convenience dishes, some from Link Wholefoods, the remainder by the Roberts' resourceful daughter— some reckon Gillian's heart and soul is in all this, though she is not the only one baking. Others help and 'as quickly as things go on display they go.' The range takes in nutburgers, soyaburgers and a textured soya variety. Links do a tofu type. There are cheese and onion pasties not forgetting, of course, quiches. Ready-packed salads handily come on small trays, suitable for office lunches or picnics. Real bread is made by a local chap in East Meon using 85 % and 100 % flours, along with minor back-up lines such as apple tarts. They guarantee the eggs as free range from the Windmill Hill Farm at Horndean. Loseley and Zimbabwean yoghurts (named after the goat herd long before the nation of that name came into being), goats' and vegetable rennet cheese. No reduction on bulk buys due to lack of demand. Soya and Loseley range ice creams. Through their connection with Compassion in World Farming, which functions from offices above, the Roberts were recently featured in a film, syndicated through the American TV network to eleven states.

Open: Mon to Fri, 9 to 5.30; Sat, 9 to 4.

READING   Berkshire   MAP 3
Reading Wholefoods, 7 London Road   TEL Reading (0734) 55175

'Simple foods and reasonable prices' is the directive favoured by Mrs. Craddock and her 'cook by inclination' daughter. Homemade convenience foods—pizzas, quiches, vegetable rissoles and burgers—are quickly growing in importance. Any cakes around will be homemade and muesli and granola is own brand. Specialities are gluten-free flours, vegan and macrobiotic foods. Scott's Caversham bread is both fat and additive-free. No fresh fruit or vegetables but fresh tofu, Loseley yoghurt and Marigold vegetarian cheese. Non-battery eggs are from Martin Pitt (Marlborough). Among the oats, millet, corn, barley, rice and flours are organic versions. There is 10 % off bulk orders, which means buys of 10 lb and over. Traditional grocery lines include grain coffees, Jacksons, Bancha and green teas. Local hospitals, trying to put more fibre into diets, come for grains and beans.

Open: Mon to Fri, 9 to 5.30; Sat, 9 to 5.

RICHMOND   Surrey   MAP 4
All Manna, 179 Sheen Road   TEL Richmond 01-948 3633

The plain little shop, pretty inside, optimistically once had an outdoor restaurant. Owner and general labourer, Elizabeth Garton, only recently the incumbent and known to hide her laurels under a bushel, operates more practically. Ardent admirers expect hand-kneaded loaves on several days of the week (when she can keep up with demand) and substitutes on other days, Natural Rise unyeasted breads. She uses Rushall or principally Shipton Mill organic flours. Mrs. Garton's style is macrobiotic 'becoming more and more purist as the supermarket competition hots up. Everything must be untreated especially the apricots and other dried fruits.' She makes irresistible mushroom tarts. Devotees selfishly wish she found even more time for this cooking. Her buns and oatmeal slices are kept low-fat and she gets away without using any sugar; apple juice concentrate went into the Christmas puddings, extra ripe bananas and spices often go into other recipes. Admirers comment: 'the shop needed someone to take it over: now we have a real enthusiast.'

Open: Mon to Sat, 10 to 6.

ROGERSTONE   Gwent   MAP 2
Starbake, The Star Bakery, Wern Avenue   TEL Rogerstone (0633) 895797

The Kears family are into bread in a big way from their South Wales bakery, strategically placed for distribution through the motorway network to all points in the South Midlands and South West. At present Bournemouth is their most south-easterly destination. As a mass production unit they have taken a big innovative step with the introduction of a new brand name, Heart of Gold. It comes in both white and stoneground wholemeal varieties and its big attraction is that it is to a formula 'possibly beneficial to certain heart conditions and high blood pressure'. The normal sodium salt has been replaced with a potassium based salt. Giving more reason for enthusiasm is their recently introduced organic wholemeal loaf, from which they have left out all unnatural additives. Orange juice, sunflower oil and honey replace the customary ingredients. Altogether they have something like 2,000 outlets and if your local supermarket or wholefood store is not stocking the particular loaf you want it is worthwhile asking the shop manager.

Wholesale only.

ROSS-ON-WYE   Hereford and Worcester   MAP 2
Fodder, 46 High Street   TEL Ross-on-Wye (0989) 65830

Jonathan Seddon-Harvey began his career as an itinerant trader, until he bought his first shop in Hereford—'warmer in winter than a stall.' Here in Ross all the usual grains and pulses and a good variety of flours including local grown and milled, with 10 % to 20 % discounts for bulk, depending on size. An extensive range of dried fruits starts from a modest 45p per lb (sultanas, raisins, currants) for which they seem to be well known. A good range of yoghurts and cheese are stocked but less well represented are the fresh fruits and vegetables—just a few seasonally sent in by customers—and breads are not sold at all. Reliance on customers again for non-battery eggs. Apple juice is local. What else would one expect from where the cider apples grow? Herb and garden plants are also on sale. In nearby Capuchin Yard (Church Street) is his bistro (see entry).

Open: daily, 9 to 5.30; Wed, 9 to 1.

ROTHWELL   Northamptonshire   MAP 3
Ladywell Wholefood Bakery, Market Hill   TEL Rothwell (0536) 710713

Older people still remember the quality of this particular bakery before it closed after the death of an earlier owner in 1975. There is a happy sequel, however, as it was re-opened in the autumn of '84 after extensive renovation by Mervyn Ishmael. To survive in a hard world, Mervyn is obliged to use ordinary commercial grade white flour in some of his products that are for the local trade. His sights though are set higher and most of his food is made using conservation and organic grade 85 % and 100 % flours. Furthermore he has a good source of free range eggs from a nearby village. Consequently animal exploitation in his venture is minimal. Vegetable oil is used for shortening in the bread, and his flour is stoneground from Holywell for the wholemeal loaf and the garlic herb bread. Malt loaves are made using a non-chemical malt crystal and 85 % conservation grade flour. A good many customers stock up their freezers with Ladywell Savouries, which are gaining a useful reputation. The buckwheat knish, arame round and vegetable pie are all made with pure wholemeal. A Mexican bean pie and one of the pizzas have the lighter 85 % grade. Actually before now some mention should have been made of the oven: it is the original brick built one, overhauled and now gas fired.

Open: Mon to Sat.

SAFFRON WALDEN   Essex   MAP 3
Nuts in May, 32 King Street   TEL Saffron Walden (0799) 23573

In Anthony Gill's fairly small premises a good deal of listening goes on as they hope to give advice and help whenever required. It is a self-service layout, the 'staff are not locked up behind counters'. An appropriately named Mr. Miller in the town bakes bran, rye and wholemeal loaves. Far away in Leighton Buzzard an enthusiastic young professional cook—at Harvest Time—cooks the take-aways, sold cold. Specialities are sugar-free mueslis, dried fruit, nuts, herbs and spices (sold by weight), honeys, herb teas, flour and fresh eggs, the last from Rozbert Dairy at Mildenhall. Low-fat Jersey milk yoghurts (fruit and plain), the goats' milk variety and cheeses, and only organic rice and flour are stocked. Discounts for bulk purchases of all catalogue items.

Open: Mon to Fri, 9 to 5.30; Thur, 9 to 1; Sat, 8.30 to 5.

SCARBOROUGH   North Yorkshire   MAP 6
Sarah Brown's, 13 Victoria Road   TEL Scarborough (0723) 360054

The better known restaurant at this address is the outcome of publicity received following Sarah's popular television cookery demonstrations. The shop occupies the ground floor of a small Victorian house among a row of other shops. The difference is this one has never been altered so one might well be entering the front room of a private house. Sarah Brown's policy is to buy stock in bulk, pass the savings on to the customer and, at the same time, spread the vegetarian gospel by means of her cookery classes. In the last she is obviously succeeding. Anyone who has viewed the deft handling of the dough (in the TV programme) can come and witness the reality. One hundred per cent wholemeal is baked nearby by Hall's to her own recipe. The recipe is worth passing comment: it is part wholemeal, part soya flour, with soya oil for shortening and molasses in lieu of sugar to get the yeast working. Amazingly, her tiny restaurant kitchen finds room—and time— to turn out samosas, pizzas, pasties, burgers, salads, quiches and cakes. Saturdays are special days, this is the day the savoury cheese and garlic and cheese and thyme loaves are baked. The cakes are worthy of a second glance too, or better still a taste—apricot and coconut, carrot and cinnamon, tassajara and the date and oat slices. Bob Sergeant (see entry), not far away at Flixton, grows all her vegetables organically. Animal rennet free cheese comes from the Camphill Village Trust at Danby to the north of the National Park. Naturally as much as possible of the other stock is organically grown too—rice, oats, flour, field beans, wheat grains and flakes.

Open: Mon to Sat, 9.30 to 5.30; Wed, 9.30 to 2.

SHEFFIELD   South Yorkshire   MAP 6
The Flour Bin, 36 Exchange Street   TEL Sheffield (0742) 24842

Mr. Marsden's specialist retail flour shop continues to thrive after seven years. Mr. Marsden speculates that as long as M-th-r's Pr-d- keep churning out white sliced bread he will stay in business. Over forty different varieties are stocked, at the last count, from gluten-free wheat to wholemeal, and all types in between. His list probably has no equivalent, and he sells with the home baker particularly in mind and the larger the bag you buy the cheaper it becomes. Not all the flours are mentioned on his helpfully annotated list, among which is Cauldwell's medium coarse wholemeal, ground in the old water-powered mill in the Derbyshire village of Rowsley. He takes the greater part of their small output. This flour is arguably the best of the four bread wholemeals that he does. Gold Crest is a fairly smooth wholemeal made almost entirely from North American wheat for a lighter than usual textured loaf. The standard wholemeal is medium coarse, nothing added, nothing removed. La Baguette is useful for a good pizza base as well as the more customary French 'baguette' bread, while Cobber is not unlike Granary but not so powerful. For a nutty type texture consider his Scottish Wheatmeal. There are, of course, regular lines like the Hovis, biscuit or strong whites, and amongst several wheatmeals a Scotch version with small bits of ground wheat to give a distinctively nutty type texture. Oatmeal comes in all grades, something fairly uncommon so far south of the border. Naturally in a range such as this there is gram, or chick pea, maize cornmeal, rye (two grades), and soya. Wheat and gluten-free come under the Truefree label in brown, white and self-raising styles. The range of dried fruit is useful and there are nuts, but the latter are scarcely a speciality. New lines are sago flour and rice bran at £1.35 per $\frac{1}{2}$kg and 63p per $\frac{1}{4}$kg respectively, as a guide to prices.

Open: Mon to Sat, 8.30 to 5; closed Thur.

SHEFFIELD   South Yorkshire   MAP 6
Wicker Herbal Stores, 174 Norfolk Street   TEL Sheffield (0742) 24572

As the name implies, they are predominantly a retail herbalists, long established in the city. Chris Hartley is now giving increasing attention to the growing wholefood side of their family business. From their warehouse they pack mueslis and the 200 or so culinary herbs carried. A good many of the dried fruits are mineral oil free and most grains, flours and pulses can be offered at organic standard. No bread, eggs or fresh foods, apart from yoghurt and cottage cheese from Chatsworth and Loseley. A mail order service is a speciality.

Open: Mon to Sat, 8.30 to 5.30.

SHREWSBURY   Salop   MAP 6
Crabapple, 1–2 Castle Gates   TEL Shrewsbury (0743) 64559

A clean welcoming shop with pine shelves and an open fire in winter, which stocks every conceivable kind of wholefood and, claimed by some, the best wholefood bread in town. Seasonally there are organically grown fruits and vegetables. The friendly staff are happy to give advice on diets and wholefood cooking.

Open: Mon to Sat, 9.30 to 5.45.

SOUTHAMPTON   Hampshire   MAP 3
Danaan Wholefoods, 6 Onslow Road   TEL Southampton (0703) 36881

This is not a pretty shopping area, but regulars travel in from Winchester or Hampshire countryside for a service they like, the knowledgeable staff and the low prices. A pound of oats is 21p. Prohibition (of sugar that is) is strict. Geoffrey Atheron and his partner pack their own mueslis. Other goods are weighed up as they go along—the big bags are an appeal of the place. They cook on the premises—an all vegan bake of pasties, cookies and cake—and no sugar, of course. Bread is bought in but made privately 'in preference to the commercial stuff'. It is to a no salt, no sugar recipe, difficult to find elsewhere which is why they do it. Organic fruit and vegetables may be started again, meanwhile they confer with greengrocer neighbours to avoid toe treading. The former vegan standard has been relaxed, just a little, so they now sell cheeses and milk. Granose, Vitaquell and Vitasieg margarines are stocked in the new cool cabinet. Also tofu and the soya milk which has taken off so well as the price becomes more realistic. Wheat flours, organic and non-organic, 85 % and 100 %; rye, barley, soya, and chick pea are some others. A better than usual range of cold-pressed oils—sunflower, safflower, corn germ, soya, peanut.

Open: Tue to Sat, 10 to 5.

SOUTHSEA   Hampshire   MAP 3
Time for Change, 167 Fawcett Road   TEL Southsea (0705) 697313

Fawcett Road cannot lay any claim to the architectural distinction of the town's marvellously restored Regency period Crescent. Instead 167, newly opened by Michael Perrymont, is identified by its enormous emblematic sunflower, freshly painted on to the window. All traces of the earlier tenant's preambulators have been wheeled away to make way for an entirely vegan stock. In addition to decaffeinated coffees and a good selection of herbal teas, they stock a low-tannin tea and Traidcraft teas and coffees, both loose and bagged. Negotiate for discounts on bulk purchases of grains, flours and rice. Try them for an imaginative variety of fruits. So far no fresh fruits and vegetables; they are still scouring the countryside on the look out for suitable supplies. All the herbs and spices are very cheap as they bag their own. Scotts are a local baker in Devonshire Avenue whose bread, with vegetable shortening is thought by those who know it of old to be 'wonderful, really good—a grainy taste and close texture'. A nicely textured fruit loaf too and occasionally pastries. Frozen convenience foods are planned and there are vegan alternatives to regular cheeses and ice cream.

Open: Mon to Sat, 9 to 5.30.

SOUTHWOLD   Suffolk   MAP 3
Nutters, 11 East Street   TEL Southwold (0502) 723645

Jean Page's and Diana Spring's bow-fronted shop is just beyond the triangular market place and handy for the shore. Their little town, once described as having more refined gaiety than some of its larger neighbours, naturally brings in lots of summer visitors. Consequently wintertime stock is at a more modest level. No substitutes are used in the quiches, fruit pies, almond, date and apricot slices and flapjack. Ingredients are those found in the shop, the cooking delegated to local people. Customers especially approve of the ginger cakes, light sponges, heavier fruit cakes and a nicely flavoured date and walnut. Liver and mackerel pâtés they make themselves. Cheeses are English and Continental, sometimes even a local goats' cheese, also, when they can get it, goats' yoghurt and milk. Lots of homemade jams and marmalades come from a friend and contain just sugar and fruit. A fairly good bread comes from Mr. Read of Framlingham, using Bardwell Mills stoneground wholemeal flour. Cereals and pulses are in variety but no eggs or fresh fruit and vegetables.

Open: Mon to Sat, 9 to 5; closed Wed winter.

STEYNING   West Sussex   MAP 3
Steyning Health Foods, Steyning   TEL Steyning (0903) 815953

In one of the pretty small Sussex towns, John Evans (a dab hand at working a pump after seventeen years a publican) keeps an exceptionally well stocked shop—and independence, despite the association with a trading group. Mr. Evans' baker is 'Master B' in Worthing, a normal commercial bake but Tuesdays and Thursdays rye is delivered which goes straight into the freezer. It is a matter of transferring it from there to his customers' own freezers. Convenience foods are from Link. Bulk purchase of grains and pulses, by the case or sack, with negotiated discounts—Mr. Evans is always open to a deal. Half the shop is entirely devoted to vegetarian foods. Meat products are not stocked.

Open: Mon to Fri, 9.30 to 1.30, 2 to 5.30; closed Thur pm; Sat, 9 to 5.

STOW-ON-THE-WOLD   Gloucestershire   MAP 3
The Wholefood Shop, The Square

Pleasantly set out in a space scarcely more than a ten foot square, the mellow pine-panelled room with casement doors to the street is part of what was once the manor house. Quite a few wondered whether it would survive—as so few non-antique shops do! So far Stow has been lucky. The shop has, or tries to get, just about everything necessary for a varied vegetarian diet. There is emphasis on good quality branded goods, which sell readily to visitors. Excellent homemade fare is in better supply during vacations, when the owner's daughter and her boyfriend are active cooks. What happens following graduation day is not entirely clear! Moist sultana cake, middling weight wholemeal scones and fruit slices are all beyond criticism. Bread is from Colletts at the old mill in nearby Lower Slaughter, tasty with a good firm texture which holds together well. More occasionally than one would like, there are tasty locally made peanut savouries and vegetable burgers. Dried fruits, seeds and grains, prepacked and in quite an array are on offer.

Open: Mon to Sat, 9 to 5; closed Wed midday.

STRATFORD-UPON-AVON   Warwickshire   MAP 3
Country Health, 29 Henley Street   TEL Stratford-upon-Avon (0789) 296256

The Bard was born in this street—in 1564, for those who have forgotten—and Rob Yellowhammer's quaint timber-framed store (with later Georgian front) is only a hundred yards away and still within sight. Mr. Yellowhammer, factory managership behind him, specialises in organically grown foods, vegan and milk and sugar-free products. Sentiments here are towards compassion for both human and animal suffering so he is very choosy about food sources. It is a shop, like his other branch, for prepacked products rather than fresh foods, nevertheless an interesting stock, where dried fruits, herbs and grains are well-represented. The latter, so far in thirty varieties, are all organically produced. The bread makes an interesting story as the flour (organic too) is from the newly re-opened Charlecote Mill, two miles from the Park of the same name where Shakespeare was fined by Sir Thomas Lucy for poaching. Browns, in Stratford, bake the bread. Dairy products are strictly limited to those of soya origin, including the milk. Only the Whole Earth and Nature's Store exclusively sugar-free preserves are stocked. Costs are kept down by weighing up and inexpensive packing on the premises. One customer feels that 'as the owner has only two shops this accounts for the particularly personal friendly service.' And, 'as a shop with a conscience a vegan may buy anything from soap to packed frozen food with confidence.'

Open: daily, 9 to 6 summer; 9 to 5.30 winter.

STREET   Somerset   MAP 2
Country Harvest Natural Foods, 136c High Street   TEL Street (0458) 42108

Begetter of the flourishing Bridgwater offshoot (see entry), the Dovey family's stock (from their prepacked wholefood warehouse based in the town) is much the same. Filled rolls are the only take-away item so the sparkle given off by Jean Dovey's enthusiasm for cooking is absent. It is still one of the best sources hereabouts for basic foodstuffs.

Open: Mon to Sat, 9 to 5.30.

STURMINSTER NEWTON   Dorset   MAP 2
Foodwatch, Buttspond Industrial Estate   TEL Sturminster Newton (0258) 73356

This is a unique service. More and more have a need for pure foods for either allergies or conditions necessitating a special diet. No ordinary shop anywhere, so far as the *Guide* is aware, is able to offer even a small proportion of the specialities for which this firm has become renowned. They are also sufficiently experienced and knowledgeable to answer queries about food labelling, composition of food, rotational diets, and in addition have the facilities for carrying out some basic food allergy testing. Those seemingly sound in heart and general health may find the food list of as much interest. It is invaluable simply as an aid to adding variety to the ranges customarily carried in ordinary wholefood stores. Many of the products offer an answer to the needs of those trying to avoid foodstuffs to which ingredients of animal origin have been added. It is essentially a mail order service, and the mailing-on-cost can be quite hefty. However considerable economies can be made by personal collection (by arrangement) at the warehouse. Alternatively it may be worthwhile exploring the possibility of forming a small buying group. Freight charges on a good sized order are proportionately less. Even a 'food mate' scheme, similar to the scheme used by Letchworth's Fairhaven Foods, could show a useful saving. Fortunately the Campbells, husband and wife team, issue a thoughtfully prepared list. With one or two exceptions all the stock is carefully described and the advisory notes are easily understood. So there is no need to struggle with the small print in supermarkets. Following recent media promotions, some of the stock is looking less specialised than it would have done a year or so back. Milk-free margarines, for instance, are now fairly generally available in good wholefood shops. Vitaquell and Vitasieg, imports from West Germany, like Granose (Danish), do not have any added whey powder. Furthermore, the first do not include hydrogenated oil of any form, which Foodwatch's own brand does. But it is always worthwhile studying their specification because their formula may well be better suited to your special needs. The flours they sell are completely free of bleaches and 'improvers' though they do contain additives required under the Bread and Flour Regulations. Other cereals may be gluten and/or grain-free—maizemeal, millet flakes and flour, or buckwheat flakes and flour, in addition to chick pea (gram), sago, tapioca, potato, arrowroot and chestnut. Egg white replacer is completely inert having been a specially purified form of ethylmethyl-cellulose (E465), which sounds deadly but actually has no known harmful effects as it passes through the body unchanged. It is very useful in baking. They recommend the Epicure brand of South African marmalade as the fruit is not chemically treated. Some people who normally cannot eat oranges can eat this marmalade without ill effects. Their Mexican set honey is guaranteed to be produced by bees that are not fed on sugar. Robusta coffee beans are stocked because studies have revealed that this African variety of bean has a great deal less of the chemical rejoicing in the general name of atractyloside glycosides, than the South American arabica varieties. There is nothing proven but this chemical is regarded with suspicion by some. The fruit juice concentrates do not have additives of any kind. Consequently they must be kept refrigerated but under these conditions remain usable for three to six months. A wheat-free baking powder is suited to those on gluten-free diets. Puffed rice cakes are salt-free. Anyone studying the list might usefully do so in conjunction with the inexpensive *Foodwatch Alternative Cookbook* (£1.95), designed to assist customers in the use of the more unusual flours and other foods that they sell.

Open: Mon to Fri, 10 to 1, 2 to 5.

SWANSEA   West Glamorgan   MAP 2
Curds and Whey, 64 Swansea Market   TEL Swansea (0792) 3471

Thor Ekevall brings a Scandinavian influence to this 'cheese only' market stall he runs in partnership with John Driver. They came together through involvement in organic vegetable distribution, when they started buying cheese from farms. 'We had similar roles to those of pedlars in the Middle Ages, except that we had a Dormobile, they had a donkey.' They were suppliers to a predecessor with a stall here, which really explains how this nomadic pair came to settle as market traders. Basically they do three kinds, the very cheap block cheese, higher quality English and continental cheeses and their forte (what they really like doing), buying the genuine Dyfed farmhouse kinds. 'In the hills round about old-fashioned farming practices have never been abandoned.' In varying degrees these cheeses are about 90 % organic, from animals generally treated homeopathically by the farmer. 'Vegetable rennet is most likely to be used and notable absentees are extenders, blenders and additives. Few, if any, will have the Soil Association symbol which is incredibly hard to get for animal products but it is the closest thing to an organically produced cheese,' they say. Some will be low-salt or bio-salt and labelled so. Explanatory leaflets and labels have been printed for some as an initiation aid. John enthuses over their single most popular kind, Tyn-y-Grug (House on the Heather), from near Lampeter, a Cheddar of which they will sell three whole cheeses (around 100 lb) in a week: an extremely nice mature cheese, six to eight months old. Pantyllyn (roughly translated, Spring on the Lake) is 'a high-class Caerphilly—it is not true that you cannot get a genuine Caerphilly any more.' And that is only one out of three of that character which, of more than passing interest, are low-salt too. Altogether there are at least ten local cheeses. An Ayrshire kind is low-fat. The cottage cheese position has been more difficult, though there is an Italian Ricotta, a whey type. For one with no fat at all there is always the German Quark.

Open: Mon to Sat, 9 to 5.30.

SWANSEA   West Glamorgan   Map 2
Ear to the Ground, 68A Bryn-y-Mor Road   TEL Swansea (0792) 463505

Some suspect that the tide has an influence over the ebb and flow of their enthusiasms. There were ambitious plans for a restaurant which did not come to pass, leaving followers disappointed. Homes have been moved in west Swansea, stalls in the covered market changed and in between a palace revolution. However sincerity, consistent good value and friendly faces please a good many. It should be no surprise that dairy produce and baked goods are specialities. Though—as they are vegetarian—cheeses are limited to the non-animal rennet kind, with some ewe and goat types. There is also ewes' and goats' yoghurt and frozen goats' milk. A wholemeal loaf made to their specification is, with its pleasing chewy texture, in a class of its own. They put up a respectable performance with rye, sour dough, herb and spice versions. Welsh cakes are not quite the standard of wholemeal fruit scones. This is a good lunchtime pick-up place for salads, quiches, and vegetable pastries erring towards the substantial. Subject to availability (meaning erratic) fruit and vegetables. Local eggs. Discounts—10 % to 15 %—off flours, pulses and grains, some of which may be organic. Apple juice is organically grown and unsulphured apricots are available.

Open: Mon to Sat, 9 to 6; Sun, 10 to 4.

SWANSEA   West Glamorgan   Map 2
Mumbles Health Fayre, 622 Mumbles Road   TEL Swansea (0792) 69624

This is Mrs. Osborne's second term in office at the homely little store looking on to Swansea Bay. She launched it sixteen years ago, then sold, only to buy her way in again in '79. Hers is a touching concern for customers' poor diet and good health. A favourite maxim goes, 'Look after the customer and the till looks after itself.' In such a tiny place she surprises with at least thirty varieties of tea, though only a few herbs. Dried fruits are a fairly strong line and flours include Prewetts and Marriages. Wholemeal bread but only once weekly deliveries. Yoghurts, cheese and eggs supplied by Clive Jenkins, from Carmarthen.

Open: Mon to Sat, 9.30 to 5.30; Wed, 9.30 to 1.

SWINDON   Gloucestershire   Map 3
Swindon Pulse Wholefoods Co-operative, 105 Curtis Street
TEL Swindon (0793) 692016

Essentially this is a shop to come to for dried goods and herbs, although free range eggs
are sold. There is also a cold cabinet for bean curd, fresh yeast, vegetable pâtés and peanut
butters. Otherwise their stock—apart from herbs, a speciality—is summarised on a single
sheet handout. Sometimes prices edge rather high, but they can surprise with bargains like
Rushall's organically grown wholemeal flour, 60p a 2 kg bag, £6.92 the sack. For the
Doves Farm variety add 33 % to this price. In all, flours are quite a good line here, running
the gamut of most known to specialist shops, with the less easily found potato, soya,
carob and pea versions.

Open: Mon to Sat, 9 to 5.15.

TAUNTON   Somerset   Map 2
Country Harvest, 8 The Courtyard, St. James Street   TEL Taunton (0823) 52843

Mr. Masterton-Smith sees this as 'more of a health and remedy shop, servicing patients of
local practitioners and providing for special diets.' However he helpfully carries the
Cauldron range of convenience foods. Nut burgers and vegetable burgers come hot ready
to eat immediately. Encouragingly the choice can only improve as he searches for new
supplies, which could in due course include pastries. A wholemeal and a granary loaf by
Pullen, a local source, are already stocked. Preserves are Stute, Thursday Cottage and
Whole Earth. There are the usual yoghurts, animal rennet free cheese and eggs from
Chilcombe Farm. Doves Farm is one of several stoneground flours.

Open: Mon to Sat, 9.30 to 5.30; Wed, 9.30 to 6.30.

TAUNTON   Somerset   Map 2
Natural Foods, 18 Station Road   TEL Taunton (0823) 88179

Elaine Mendola and Colin Wavell have found their feet after four years and managed
to pinpoint local sources of good unprocessed foods. There are now better supplies
of vegetables, from Tindon Home Farm and from Flax Drayton, all organic grade of
course. Now there is plain and fruit yoghurt from the local Coombs in addition to the
regular animal rennet free cheeses. Bread, wholemeal and granary, is Pullens of Lydiard
St. Lawrence. Some of the grains and dried fruits are also organically grown.

Open: Mon to Sat, 9 to 5.30.

THURSO   Caithness   Map 7
Health Food Centre, 5 Princes Street, Thurso   TEL Thurso (0847) 63561

Marion Shaw, who pioneered the district eight years ago, is admired for her knowledgeable
concern about pure foods, and gains approval for the wholesome shop standards she
maintains, not always synonymous with wholefooding. She stocks pretty well everything
mentionable one would find further south and for bulk purchases of grains and pulses,
offers useful discounts—a good idea in more ways than one when snowbound. Savouries
and sweeter things are baked in wholewheat pastry cases, not forgetting shortbreads,
which may be served up as snacks on the premises. For reasons unknown bread deliveries
are irregular, so pick up some yeast while you're there. She supports local growers of
organic produce, which does not include fruit, and stocks vegetarian cheese, no eggs but
local suppliers will be recommended.

Open: daily, 9.30 to 1, 2 to 5; Thur 9.30 to 1.

TONBRIDGE   Kent   Map 3
Healthy Living, 126A High Street   TEL Tonbridge (0732) 361170

Maureen Whiteman's bright shop is a welcome addition to the small town high street
shopping scene. A comfortable, small café above is equally appetising and imaginative.
Shop stock is limited to packaged goods with the exception of Sillitoe's bread from
Tunbridge Wells and whatever might appeal on the upstairs take-away counter. She also
stocks Herdgate eggs. This apart, a good range of flours (including an organic rice), ten
or so types of beans, up to twenty teas and coffees and eight coffee substitutes as well as
yoghurts, plain and fruit, with or without sugar.

Open: Mon to Sat, 9 to 6.

TOTNES   Devon   Map 2
Charles Riggs, Weston House   TEL Totnes (0803) 862066

The Riggs sell produce from a gate stall and supply two local markets. (For details see
Growers' section.)

Open: Totnes market, Fri; Newton Abbot market, daily.

TOTNES   Devon   Map 2
Sacks, 80 High Street   TEL Totnes (0803) 863263

In season, among the home-grown vegetables which flourish so willingly hereabouts there
will be at least a choice of garlic, potatoes, tomatoes and peppers and pumpkin in slices,
Chinese leaves, onions and root stuffs like parsnips, carrots and beet. As the garden
responds to flashes of rain and warmth, lettuces (in variety), radishes and spring onions.
Other stock—unprocessed cereals, nuts, dried fruits, pulses—are always bought in bulk
and sold loose.

Open: Sun to Sat, 9.30 to 5.

TREGARON   Dyfed   Map 2
Tregaron Foods, Station Road   TEL Tregaron (097 44) 8944

This company is the only manufacturer of spray dried goats' milk powder in Britain, a
claim which seems likely to be disputed before very long. Production was commenced to
meet the growing demand and interest in goats' milk products, especially from those with
an allergy to cows' milk. It is of particular interest to those who have difficulty in
obtaining fresh supplies. Additive and preservative free, it is sold in packs of five sachets
which will each reconstitute to a pint of milk. The powder is excellent for cooking, making
superb yoghurt, sauces and ice cream. Most branches of Waitrose and Holland and Barratt
are stockists.

Wholesale only.

TRURO   Cornwall   Map 2
The Granary, 36 St Austell Street   TEL Truro (0872) 77686

John and Shirley Carley's establishment drew more spontaneous letters of commendation
than any other *Guide* entry. John Carley says, 'Our policy is to be extremely choosy,
selling food rather than vitamins, offering organic foods whenever possible, and selling no
sugar of any colour, and no foods containing sugar. We are still working hard to make
The Granary a sugar-free zone! Daily we bake wholemeal and malthouse breads, using
naturally leavened organic wholemeal twice weekly, and always cold-pressed oils. Our
apple and raisin slice, much sought from among a dozen or so cakes, is made without
sugar. We pride ourselves on stocking only unsprayed lemons, oranges and grapefruit,
from Organic Farm Foods along with some of their vegetables. Organically-grown citrus

will be available shortly. Our main vegetable supplier is Carl Soper at St. Michael Penkivel. In summertime there are several hundred jars of our own sugar-free marmalades. Fruit juices include the Infinity range of first pressings, no concentrates and from organically grown fruit. But we do stock fruit concentrates and our own blends of blackcurrant and apple and passion fruit and apple. Wines and cider available only by the case, are all organic. There is a discount for very large bulk orders.

Open: Mon to Sat, 9 to 5.30; Fri, 9 to 7.

TUNBRIDGE WELLS   Kent   MAP 3
Natural Life, 66 Grosvenor Road   TEL Tunbridge Wells (0892) 43834

Suzanne and Philip Castleton are from Canada, successfully finding fame and fortune in the old country with their warm friendly approach. There is a lot of emphasis on foods of organic origin. This includes some of the grains and flakes; the fruit and vegetables from Organic Farm Foods. Even organically grown grade breads, which include rye and sesame loaves from Cyrnel Bakery, Forest Row, and more from Rosbridges and Bell's Bakery, Heathfield, and a variety of pastries and cakes from these places. Raw milk yoghurt, quark and animal rennet free cheese, as well as Loseley ice cream, are stocked.

Open: Sun to Sat, 9 to 5.30.

TUNBRIDGE WELLS   Kent   MAP 3
The Pilgrims Health Food Shop, 37 Mount Ephraim
TEL Tunbridge Wells (0892) 20121

High up, back turned to the common, this one-time small shop has grown at a slower pace than the popular sibling restaurant behind (see entry). Vegetarian delicatessen is a more apt description than either wholefood or vegetarian store. Gabrielle Higgins worked in France when she was young and it shows. The shop keeps marvellous hours, better even than the restaurant's whose cooked dishes are all available here as take-aways in foil packs. Granary rolls have generous fillings; pasties come in several kinds, including cheese and vegetable and a mild curry version. Much sought after is the cheese and spinach puff pastry. Cakes are all made on the premises too. Bread—sold in vast quantities—is bought in, the straight loaf in two textures—medium and gourmet close texture. Granary is very popular, more so than French sticks, other fancies and rolls with an 85 % flour. Two of the ladies who work there have smallholdings and their produce finds its way into the shop. Otherwise this busy section is kept well-stocked with a wholesaler's supplies. More of macrobiotic standard are grown by the Steiner School at Forest Row. Free range eggs are from private suppliers, the yoghurts, ice cream and cream from Loseley. There is a large variety of grains, pulses and flours, reductions for bulk but non-organically grown. Carrot and beetroot juices are organic.

Open: Mon to Sat, 8.30 to 8.

WARE   Hertfordshire   MAP 3
Down to Earth Wholefoods, 7 Amwell End   TEL Ware (0920) 3358

Beamed backquarters are hidden by the later Victorian front of this largish shop. For lunchtime there are delicious sandwiches with a choice of at least twenty fillings. Hot items, like pizzas, are all made on the premises. There are six or so types of cake, two always sugar-free. Contrary to popular belief loaves are not homemade, but from Walkers of Standon. They are fairly light but made with a 100 % organic stoneground flour. Barwick Ford Farm—fifteen acres under organic cultivation—provides constantly improving vegetable supplies, and there are more from Latchford Organic Farm. All kinds of grains and flakes, organic rice, Rozbert goats' yoghurt, Loseley cow yoghurt and ice cream are on offer. Organic blackcurrant and raspberry juices.

Open: Mon to Sat, 9 to 5.30; closed Thur midday.

WATFORD   Hertfordshire   MAP 3
Crystal Harvest, 172 High Street   TEL Watford (0923) 20962

Katherine Simpson's shop is one of the few surviving old buildings in Watford. The most
popular stock here is the fresh dried fruit and nuts which sell in large quantities. There are
also many different pulses and lentils. All the ready-to-eat foods are homemade—flapjacks,
occasionally cakes and quiche. The Yorkshire Bakery, in town—a one man band—does a
medium heavy wholemeal, French sticks and rolls. There is ewes' yoghurt and cheese;
non-battery eggs from Norfolk Egg Suppliers, and Japanese sea vegetables. Bulk
purchases qualify for a discount.

Open: Mon to Sat, 9.30 to 5.30; Wed, 9.30 to 1.30.

WEEDON   Northamptonshire   MAP 3
Goodness Foods, 40 High Street   TEL Weedon (0327) 41137

This is another case of 'we're smaller so we try harder'. Goodness Foods can for instance
offer up to sixty kinds of cheese, quite apart from yoghurts in variety, and goats' milk ice
cream. With less certainty there are vegetables grown by Mr. Lancebery at New
Gresham Farm. There's real enthusiasm for taramasalata, coleslaws, salads, savoury
pastries and cakes, some homemade, some vegan. Mr. Lancebery supplies the free range
eggs. Wholemeal flours are organically grown. Around twenty kinds of pulses are not. An
apple press is expected shortly to make juice without preservatives from apples in the
orchard. Bulk purchases qualify for a discount.

Open: Mon to Fri, 8.30 to 5; Sat, 8.30 to 4.30.

WELLINGBOROUGH   Northamptonshire   MAP 3
Wellingborough Health Foods, 22 Silver Street
TEL Wellingborough (0933) 76703

Much of the packed goods and honeys are under Wellingborough Health Foods' own
label, packaged on the premises. Bran and granary loaves come from Kinloch; pasties and
pies are· vegetarian. Summertime specialities include salads on trays. Cheese is goats',
animal rennet free, as well as traditional French and English varieties. There are discounts
for bulk purchases of pulses, lentils and dried fruits. Eggs are non-battery, but there are no
fresh fruits or vegetables.

Open: Mon to Sat, 9 to 5.30.

WELLINGTON   Somerset   MAP 2
Sunseed, 24 High Street   TEL Wellington (082 347) 2313

Since 1980, Mr. Bourne has introduced a full range of wholefoods, organic vegetables,
home-brew, tofu and for good measure, vitamins, herbal and homeopathic remedies.
Bread is local and a fairly ordinary commercial bake, but is 100% flour. Organic
vegetables are fairly reliable, most are from local gardens and small growers. Suppliers
include Bindon Agricultural Collective, County Garden Products and Huish Organic
Growers. The shop offers ewes' and goats' yoghurts and a whole range of dried goods,
including organically grown dates. Bulk purchases qualify for discount.

Open: Mon to Sat, 9 to 5.30.

WELSHPOOL   Powys   MAP 6
Sparrow Wholefoods, Hopkins Passage, Broad Street
TEL Welshpool (0938) 4918

In a little passage of shops off the main street, a great deal is packed into a small space.

Ingrid Maughan finds room for twenty-five to thirty cheeses (including animal rennet free Cheddar), plain and fruit yoghurts and thirty-four sorts of flour include 100 % and 85 % extraction kinds. Herbs and spices number about seventy. Wheat, oat, barley and millet flakes are in variety, and there is a fair choice among lentils and peas. For the freezer, there are sausages and pasties, and four sorts of tofu from the Bean Machine, parathas (lightly curried lentils and potatoes) made by a friend, and on Fridays only a muesli loaf and wholemeal scones. Oven-baked bread comes from Morrays of Bishops Castle, there is a choice of four (no whey powder) vegan margarines and Aspall's apple juice.

Open: Mon to Sat, 9.30 to 5.30.

WELSHPOOL   Powys   Map 6
Welshpool Herbs and Spices, 24 High Street   TEL Welshpool (0938) 3180

Most of the herbs sold are grown in Rita Wyatt's own garden at Cathen's Inn between Guilsfield and the town. In season there are fresh herbs from the garden, otherwise they are dried, in special foil-lined bags with a two year shelf life, and protected from the light, they retain their full flavour and colour. All are organically grown, like the onions, garlic and seasonally available vegetables. Other lines are locally-made mustards, chutneys and honeys, without preservatives or additives. Honey comes from an area unpolluted by spraying.

Open: Mon to Sat, 9 to 5; closed Thur.

WEMBLEY   Middlesex   Map 4
Bridge to Health, 25 Bridge Road   TEL Wembley 01-904 1370

A better than average selection of fresh breads from Vienna Bakeries is available from breakfast time. Vienna Bakeries also supply wholemeal pasties, cakes and soya burgers. Sugar-free jams come from Whole Earth and Ethos. Yoghurts, vegetarian cheeses and eggs from Neal's Yard farm shop. Most common grains are supplied by Whole Earth and Marriages Flour. There is Loseley ice cream and a non-sugar soya variety too.

Open: Sun to Sat, 8 to 6.

WICKEN BONHUNT   Essex   Map 3
The Brewhouse Traditional and Wholefood Company, The Brick House, Wicken Bonhunt, Saffron Walden   TEL Wicken Bonhunt (0799) 40348

After five years occupation, the Cornfords have de-grassed the old vegetable garden and orchard to put back pear and apple trees, followed by plum, cherry, peach and quince. From the new vegetable garden there is more than enough fresh produce and soft fruit (in season, of course) for family, friends and customers. There is also a fine collection of herbs and everything is organically grown. In the meadow, five dozen Warren Studler free range hens and six Jacob ewes and their lambs work hard to keep down the grass. In the orchard three colonies of bees may provide close on 200 lb of honey. All foods are free from chemical additives and minimally processed. The Cornfords do not sell bread but there is fresh yeast. They sell Whole Earth sugarless jams and their own traditional preserves, chutneys and mustard. In the autumn there are organically grown potatoes from Marcus Ridshill's Newhouse Farm in neighbouring Radwinter. A local goat herd can come up with yoghurt, milk and cheese. Egg supplies are supplemented by the Wellers at Thaxted and the Dixons at Quendon. Some of the meat is the Cornfords' own and they can put people in touch with other suppliers of naturally reared animals. Bulk purchases qualify for a discount.

Open: Thur to Sun, 10 to 6.

WINDSOR   Berkshire   Map 3
Oasis Wholefoods, 96 Peascod Street   TEL Windsor (075 35) 60618

This shop has 1,500 sq. feet of selling space and with space like this the Coxs can indulge
their fancy with pack sizes of grains ranging from 500 mg to 50 kg, some organic. Dried
fruits get the same treatment. Goswells supplement the offerings of a local baker, so
expect rye, fruit, vogels and organic loaves. Convenience and take-away food are
homemade or bought in from Link. Eggs are bought in from Martin Pitt. There are
vegetarian cheeses, yoghurts and Loseley dairy foods. Bulk purchasers are given a
discount.

Open: Mon to Sat, 9 to 5.30.

WISBECH   Cambridgeshire   Map 3
Brian Hardy, 50 Hill Street   TEL Wisbech (0945) 582437

Reports speak of very helpful service and excellent choice for such a small shop, however
most of the pastries and cakes contain animal fats, even where wholemeal flour is used.
Mr. Hardy's is essentially a stock of prepacked grains, flours and dried fruits. The cheese
counter is a feature.

Open: Mon, Tue, 9 to 5.30; Wed, 9 to 1; Thur, Fri, Sat, 8.30 to 5.30.

WITNEY   Oxfordshire   Map 3
Beanbag Wholefoods, 48 High Street   TEL Witney (0993) 73922

The Osgerbys will go to a great deal of trouble to get special items and they have
recently introduced some organic produce. Cereals are sold from sacks until such time as
they can be weighed and bagged. Wholemeal bread is an interesting line, baked in long
narrow tins, with or without a caraway seed topping. Savoury pasties and sweet pastries
quite an important line. There are free range eggs and goats' milk.

Open: Mon to Fri, 9 to 5.30; Sat, 9 to 5.

WIVENHOE   Essex   Map 3
The Wholefood Shop, 5 Station Road   TEL Wivenhoe (020 622) 3723

Pat Smith started this tiny shop in her front room. Jennie Gladwin, her partner, does all the
baking. Trading philosophy here is to offer a selection of basic wholefoods at rock bottom
prices by buying in bulk and re-packing. The shop will loan out cookery books, pass on
favourite recipes, run courses and hold open days. Maltflake and muesli are additions to
the wholemeal bread range, hand-kneaded by Jennie, only the third hand-bread-maker in
the *Guide*. Fruit cakes, puddings and pies are her other specialities, the second is sugar-free
cooked in the bottom of a slow oven for a couple of days. She will do maize and other
breads for those on special diets. Twelve or fifteen kinds of biscuits are sold, using Cranks'
recipes as a basis. Savouries are mainly flans. Organic tofu comes from Bramble in
Braintree. There is still a search for a free range egg supply. On offer are twenty-one
different pulses, grains—whole ground and flaked, potato and chick peas, gluten-free
flours. Small amounts are packed for the elderly and discounts to anyone for quantity.

Open: Mon to Sat. Closed lunchtime and Wed and Thur pm.

WORCESTER   Hereford and Worcester   Map 2
Millwheel, 22 The Shambles   TEL Worcester (0905) 23353

This shop is in the same style as the Southport namesake (who in turn modelled
themselves on Cranks). Phillip Coward's policy is to sell only natural foods, nothing
added and nothing removed. Convenience food and take-away service are specialities as

are homemade pâtés, nut roasts, wholemeal flans, cheese and millet croquettes. No meat is used in any of the recipes, but occasionally there is a little fish. There are no fresh fruit and vegetables—they will recommend a local grower. Roberts and Lane rate quite highly for the home-baked bread, even if there are days when they don't get it to rise consistently. Wholemeal scones are more reliable. Natural and fruit yoghurts, and natural cottage cheese come from Dunster's Farm. Goats' milk is frozen. From the village of Throckmorton, there are non-battery eggs. The hens are kept in the open, but according to the recent court ruling they do not rate as free range. Grains and flours are Dove's Farm and there is a fair variety of vine fruits. Cider vinegar is organically grown. See entry for café in adjacent premises.

Open: Mon to Sat, 9 to 5.30.

WREXHAM   Clwyd   MAP 6
The Granary, 7 Church Street   TEL Wrexham (0978) 261615

A miniature version of the bigger Chester relation. The Granary thrives in the cramped oldest building in town, with beamed ceilings. Like the other shop, this has a fairly representative range of packed wholefoods.

Open: Mon to Sat, 9 to 5.

YORK   North Yorkshire   MAP 6
Alligator, 104 Fishergate   TEL York (0904) 54525

A modest enterprise just outside the city centre, Alligator is perhaps overshadowed by the York Wholefoods and the Gillygate Bakery, whose breads they stock. Bulk wholefoods, sold loose as far as possible, are their particular speciality. Organically grown stoneground wheat flour, again from Gillygate, is sold by the sack. Bulk discounts.

Open: Mon to Fri, 10 to 6; Sat, 9 to 6.

YORK   North Yorkshire   MAP 6
Gillygate Wholefood Bakery, Miller's Yard   TEL York (0904) 24045

The speciality here is organically grown, stoneground, English wholewheat flour (from Organic Farmers and Growers) which is used in their own baking and is supplied to other specialist bakers. Flour is used within 24 hours of milling to ensure the greatest nutritional value. Wholewheat, cheese and garlic, and cheese and thyme loaves are baked daily. Thursdays bring a nutty farmhouse, and malted fruit version, the former on Tuesdays too. There is rye (sour dough) on Wednesdays and Fridays. Wholewheat or cheese and garlic baps have the same appealing texture. Sugar is not used, just soya oil and a little salt. Peas, potatoes and spices in a pancake parcel are the substance of a light samosa. Tofu burgers or cheese and potato pies cost the same or there is a tasty pizza for a little more. The same quality is upheld with traditional Yorkshire parkin. Try the tempting banana sponge, or apple cider cake, just as bad for you though with Aspall's Organic Cider. Fresh fruit cake is made without sugar or fat. Vegans miss out on the pastry—there is butter in it. Their pastry slices are loaded with apricots, sugar, honey and banana. All the food can, of course, be sampled in the adjacent café (see entry). Wholefood grocers, Marriages', Pimhill's and Jordan's flours are stocked, alongside their own. Other flours are carob, chapati, rice and potato. Cold-pressed oils take up space alongside miso, genmai and hatcho, shoyu and soyabean curd. Dairy stuffs come under Calthwaite, Bottom Village and Longley Farm labels. Honey from Mexico is organic (clear and set). Apple chutney is homemade. Brown rice (Italian), pot barley (U.K.) and wheat grain (U.K.) are organic wholegrains. Teas are in variety but coffee is blended Campaign. Mrs. Londsdale's Damhills Farm provides non-battery eggs.

Open: Mon to Sat, 9 to 6.

YORK   North Yorkshire   MAP 6
York Wholefoods, 98 Micklegate   TEL York (0904) 56804

From the top floor a team of four is always busy stocking the shop below with their
baked goods. In between is the self-sufficient restaurant, with its own kitchen (see entry).
There are dependable savoury and sweet dishes, many vegan and/or sugar-free. Quite
delicious croissants are made, as well as carrot cake and sweet munches. Sometimes there
are éclairs with a carob dressing. Year round vegetable supplies come from several sources
in the Vale of York and Humberside (including tomatoes, cucumbers and peppers).
Seasonally they can offer raspberries, strawberries and currants. Another local grower
offers organically grown herb and vegetable seeds. Non-battery eggs are so popular that
it takes three suppliers to keep up with demand. There is a good range of whole grains,
plus bulgar and couscous. A wide variety of flakes and flours takes in gram (besan),
buckwheat, soya and semolina. All dried fruits, among them dates (pitted, whole and
chopped), are free from mineral oil. South African produce is not stocked. Aspall's
organically grown and their freshly pressed apple juices, and red beet juice (biodynamic
Demeter standard) are listed. Among the yoghurts and cheeses are animal rennet free,
biodynamic, as well as traditional farmhouse types, from suppliers like Longley Farm and
Calthwaite. There is goats' yoghurt, goats' cheese, spray dried goats' milk, soya milk and
tofu. Other foods include arame, nori, wakame, kombu seaweed; low sodium salts and
baking powders; vegetarian tinned and packaged convenience foods free from artificial
colours, flavours and preservatives. Bread in some of its finest forms comes from York's
Gillygate Bakery (see entry).

Open: Mon to Sat, 9 to 5.30; Wed, 9 to 3; Fri, 9 to 9.30.

OTHER RECOMMENDED
SHOPS

Aberystwyth Ceredigion Wholemake The Toll House 1 Llanbadarn Road
TEL (0970) 611174 *Open Mon to Sat 8 to 6.30.*
Abingdon Frugal Food 17 West Saint Helen Street Oxfordshire
TEL (0235) 22239 *Open Mon to Sat 9 to 5.30.*
Accrington Natural Food Store 10 Bridge Street Lancashire
TEL (0254) 77331 *Open Mon to Sat 9.15 to 5.15, closed Tue.*
Amersham Amersham Wholefoods 156 Upper Station Road Buckinghamshire
TEL (024 03) 6752 *Open Mon to Sat 9 to 5.30.*
Ashburton The Ark Wholefood Shop 38 East Street Devon
TEL (0364) 53020 *Open 9 to 5.30 except Sat and Wed afternoons, closed 1 to 2 lunchtimes.*
Aylesbury Tantadlin Wholefoods (Tipi Workers Co-op) Friars Square Buckinghamshire
TEL (0296) 23430 *Open Mon to Sat 9 to 5.30.*
Bangor Harvest Wholefoods 23 Wellfield Court Gwynedd
TEL (0248) 364518 *Open Mon to Sat 9 to 5.30, half-day Wed.*
Bangor Peter Winstanley 2 Chapel Road Pentraeth Gwynedd
TEL (0248) 351562 *Open Mon to Sat 9 to 5.30, half-day Wed.*
Bath Health Foods 6 Green Street Avon
TEL (0225) 62449 *Open Mon to Fri 9 to 5, Sat 9 to 1.*
Bedford Bedford Health Food Centre 104 Bromham Road Bedfordshire
TEL (0234) 50947 *Open Mon to Wed 9 to 5.30, Thur 9 to 2.30, Fri to Sat 9 to 6.*
Belfast Jack McClelland Naturally! 327 Antrim Road Northern Ireland
TEL (0232) 744590 *Open Mon to Sat 9 to 5.30.*
Belfast Sassafras Wholefoods 102 Gt. Victoria Street Northern Ireland
TEL (0232) 224549 *Open Mon to Sat 9 to 5.30.*
Bingley Fodder Wholefoods 2 Norfolk Street 6 Mornington Road West Yorkshire
TEL (0274) 560790 *Open Mon 10 to 5, Tue 10 to 1, Wed 10 to 5, Thur 9 to 5, Fri 9 to 6, Sat 9.30 to 4.30.*
Birchington-upon-Sea Spice of Life 87 Station Road Kent
TEL (0843) 43610 *Open Tue 9 to 5.30, Wed 9 to 1, Thur 9 to 5.30, Fri 9 to 6, Sat 9 to 5.*
Birmingham Dandelion Wholefoods 12 Coton Lane Erdington West Midlands
TEL 021-382 4393 *Open Mon Tue Thur Fri 9.30 to 5.30, Sat 9 to 5, closed all day Wed.*
Birmingham Sage Wholefoods 148 Alcester Road Moseley West Midlands
TEL 021-449 7921 *Open Tue to Sat 9 to 5.30.*
Blandford Blandford Wholefoods 7 Georgian Passage East Street Dorset
TEL (0258) 54070 *Open Mon to Sat 9 to 5, Wed 9 to 1.*
Bodmin The Bran Tub 12 Market House Arcade Fore Street Cornwall
TEL (0208) 6625 *Open Mon to Sat 9 to 5.30, Wed 9 to 1.*
Bolton Impulse Wholefoods 102 Newport Street Lancashire
TEL (0204) 391 672 *Open Mon to Sat 10 to 5, Wed 10 to 1.*
Bournemouth Earth Foods Ltd 75 Southbourne Grove Dorset
TEL (0202) 422465 *Open Mon to Sat 9 to 5.30.*
Bournemouth Just Natural 573 Wimbourne Road Winton Dorset
TEL (0202) 526562 *Open Mon to Sat 9.15 to 1, 2 to 5.30, Wed 9.15 to 1.*
Brightlingsea 'Cornflower' 49 High Street Colchester Essex
TEL (020 630) 4854 *Open Mon to Sat 9 to 1, 2 to 5, Thur 9 to 1.*
Brighton Herb and Healthfood Stores 106 Trafalgar Street East Sussex
TEL (0273) 607704 *Open Mon to Sat 9 to 5.30.*

Bristol Foda Foods 224 Cheltenham Road Avon
TEL (0272) 425997 *Open Mon to Sat 9.30 to 5.30, Wed.9.30 to 3.30, Fri 9.30 to 6.*
Bristol Health Foods 16 North Street Bedminster Avon
TEL (0272) 634292 *Open Mon to Sat 9.30 to 1, 2 to 5.30.*
Bristol Manor Farm 259 Gloucester Road Bishopston Avon
TEL (0272) 47696 *Open Mon to Sat 9 to 1, 2 to 6, closed Wed.*
Bristol Spa 60 The Mall Clifton Avon
TEL (0272) 560103 *Open Mon to Sat 9.30 to 5.30.*
Bristol Sunflower 359 Gloucester Road Horfield Avon
TEL (0272) 40833 *Open Mon to Sat 9 to 5.30, Wed 9 to 1.*
Bromley Bromley Health Centre 54 Widmore Road Kent
TEL 01-460 3894 *Open Mon to Sat 9 to 5.*
Budleigh Salterton Cornucopia 30 Fore Street Devon
TEL (039 54) 3003 *Open Mon to Sat 9 to 1, 2 to 5, closed Thur at 12.*
Bury St. Edmunds Marpa Wholefoods 56 St. John's Street Suffolk
TEL (0284) 68436 *Open Mon to Sat 9 to 5.30, closed Thur afternoons.*
Cambourne Sunflower Wholefoods 16a Cross Street Cornwall
TEL (0209) 715970 *Open Mon to Sat 9 to 5.30.*
Cambridge Fitzbillies 52 Trumpington Street and 50 Regent Street Cambridgeshire
TEL (0223) 352500 and 64451 (Regent Street) *Open Mon to Fri 8.30 to 5.45, Sat 8.30 to 4.45.*
Cambridge Natural Selection (Wholefoods) 30 Regent Street Cambridgeshire
TEL (0223) 65819 *Open Mon to Sat 9 to 5.30.*
Canterbury Gateways Bulk Store 21 The Borough Kent
TEL (0227) 69839 *Open Mon to Sat 9 to 5.30.*
Canterbury Gateways Wholefoods 15 St. Dunstan's Street Kent
TEL (0227) 69839 *Open Mon to Sat 9 to 5.30.*
Canterbury Oasis Wholefoods 24 Palace Street Kent
TEL (0227) 463941 *Open Mon to Sat 9 to 5.30.*
Cardiff Cathays Wholefoods Crwys Road South Glamorgan
TEL (0222) 34822 *Open Mon to Sat 9.30 to 6.*
Cardiff Spice of Life (Wholefoods) Inverness Place Roath South Glamorgan
TEL (0222) 487146 *Open Mon to Sat 9.30 to 5.30.*
Cardigan Community Wholefoods Upper Market Hall Dyfed
TEL (0239 74) 503 *Open Mon to Sat 9 to 4.30, closed Wed.*
Carmarthen Waverley Healthfoods Lammas Street Dyfed
TEL (0267) 6521 *Open Mon to Sat 9 to 5.30.*
Cheltenham Barley Corn 317 High Street Gloucestershire
TEL (0242) 41070 *Open Mon to Sat 9.30 to 5.30, Wed 9 to 1.*
Chesterfield The Happy Nut House 19 Glumangate Derbyshire
TEL (0246) 75928 *Open Mon to Sat 9 to 5.30.*
Chichester Beanfeast 25b Southgate West Sussex
TEL (0243) 783823 *Open Tue to Sat 9.30 to 5.30, closed Mon.*
Chorley Chorley Health Foods 23 Cleveland Street Lancashire
TEL (025 72) 76146 *Open Mon to Sat 9 to 5.15, closed Wed.*
Codsall The Bran Tub 6 Birches Bridge Shopping Centre Wolverhampton Road
West Midlands
TEL (090 74) 2646 *Open Tue to Sat 9.30 to 5.30, closed Mon.*
Colne Greens Wholefoods 25 New Market Street Lancashire
TEL (0282) 867971 *Open Wed to Sat 10 to 5.30.*
Cranham Cranham Bakery Front Lane Essex
TEL (040 22) 26735 *Open Mon to Sat 9 to 5.15.*
Crediton Aduki Wholefoods 4b High Street Devon
Open Mon to Sat 9.30 to 5.30.
Crediton Windmill Foods Devon
TEL (036 32) 4305 *Open Mon to Fri 9 to 5.30, closed Sat.*

Croydon The Wholefood Store 96 High Street Surrey
TEL 01-688 2899 *Open Mon to Sat 9.30 to 5.30.*

Crymmych Bwyd y Byd Station Road Dyfed
TEL (023 973) 537 *Open Mon to Sat 9 to 6.*

Dartford Food for Living 46 Lowfield Street Kent
TEL (0322) 78790 *Open Mon to Sat 9 to 5.30, Wed 9 to 2.*

Deal The Delicatessen 49 The Strand Kent
TEL (0304) 2028 *Open Mon to Sat 9 to 1, 2.15 to 5.30.*

Derby Ambridge Fare 30 Green Lane Derbyshire
TEL (0332) 385909 *Open Mon to Sat 9 to 5.30.*

Dorchester Cornucopia Whole Foods 34a High West Street Dorset
TEL (0305) 62586 *Open Mon to Sat 9 to 6.*

Dorchester Health Foods at Trinity Street Georgian House Trinity Street Dorset
TEL (0305) 3979 *Open Mon to Sat 9 to 5.30, Thur 9 to 1.*

Downham Market Capricorn Wholefoods 1c High Street Norfolk
TEL (0366) 387123 *Open Mon Tue Thur 9 to 1, 2 to 5.30, Wed 9 to 1, Fri 9 to 5.30, Sat 9 to 5.*

Dublin Naturesway 33 Ilac Centre Eire
TEL 0001 728 391 *Open Mon to Sat 9 to 6.*

Dublin Naturesway 51 Blackrock Centre Blackrock Eire
TEL 0001 056 27372 *Open Mon to Sat 9 to 6.*

Dublin Phil Guiney's Food Shop 9 Fleet Street Eire
TEL 0001 710 880 *Open Mon to Fri 10 to 6.*

Dublin Tony Quinn's Health Store 67 Eccles Street Eire
TEL 0001 308 588 *Open Mon to Fri 9 to 10, Sat 9 to 6.*

Dundee Wholefood Co-operative 10 Constitution Road Tayside
TEL (0382) 28265 *Open Mon to Sat 9 to 5.30, half-day Wed.*

Erith Food for Living 'Superstore' Town Square Kent
TEL (0322) 346554 *Open Mon to Sat 9 to 5.30.*

Exeter City Ditch Wholefoods 14 South Street Devon
TEL (0392) 50925 *Open Mon to Sat 9.30 to 5.30, half-day Wed.*

Folkestone Nature's Way 80 Sandgate Street Kent
TEL (0303) 43646 *Open Mon to Sat 9 to 5.30.*

Forest Row Cyrnel Bakery Lower Road East Sussex
TEL (034 282) 2283 *Open Mon to Sat 8.30 to 5.30, half-day Wed.*

Gateshead Jo Thunderbolt's Pulse Emporium Unit 3 Lower Floor Gateshead Indoor
Market Tyne and Wear
TEL (0385) 69135 *Open Mon to Sat 9 to 5, half-day Wed.*

Glastonbury Sunrise Wholefoods 4 High Street Somerset
TEL (0458) 31004 *Open daily 9 to 5.30.*

Grantham Catlins Grocer/Shop/Café High Street Lincolnshire
TEL (0476) 65428 *Open Mon Tue Thur Sat 8.30 to 5, Wed 8.30 to 2, Fri 8.30 to 5.30.*

Gravesend Good Health Wholefoods 142 Pelham Road Kent
TEL (0474) 58192 *Open Mon to Sat 8.30 to 5.30, Wed 8.30 to 1.30.*

Gt. Yarmouth Health Foods 43/44 Central Arcade Norfolk
TEL (0493) 855316 *Open 9 to 5, half-day Thur.*

Greystones Nature's Gold (Wholefoods) 1 Killincarrig Road Co. Wicklow Eire
TEL 01 0353 404 876 301 *Open Mon to Sat 10 to 6.*

Hay-on-Wye Hay Garden Shop 5 Market Street Powys
TEL (0497) 820047 *Open Mon to Sat 9.30 to 5 summer months, Thur and Sat only during
winter.*

Hebden Bridge Aurora Wholefoods 54 Market Street West Yorkshire
TEL (0422) 844505 *Open Mon to Sat 9.30 to 5.30.*

Helensburgh Healthcraft 62 West Princes Street Strathclyde
TEL (0436) 4993 *Open 9 to 5.30, half-day Wed.*

Hereford 'Fodder Wholefoods' 27 Church Street Hereford and Worcester
TEL (0432) 58171 *Open 9 to 5.30.*

Hereford The Marches 24–30 Union Street Hereford and Worcester
TEL (0432) 55712 *Open Mon to Sat 8.30 to 5.30.*
Hessle Mayes Fresh Foods 25 The Square North Humberside
TEL (0482) 648571 *Open Mon to Fri 9 to 5, Sat 8.30 to 5.*
High Wycombe Better Health Shop 19a High Street Buckinghamshire
TEL (0494) 22893 *Open Mon to Sat 9 to 5.30.*
Hull What Comes Naturally 513 Anlaby Road North Humberside
TEL (0482) 564676 *Open Mon to Wed 9 to 5.30, Thur 9 to 6, Fri 9 to 7.30, Sat 8 to 5.30, Sun 12 to 4.*
Ilford Food for Thought 4 Cameron Road Seven Kings Essex
TEL 01-597 4388 *Open Mon to Sat 10 to 5.30, closed Thur.*
Ilkeston The Sunflower Shop 51a Bath Street Derbyshire
TEL (0602) 304750 *Open Mon Tue Thur Fri 9 to 5.30, Wed 9 to 1, Sat 9 to 5.*
Inverness Brambles Wholefoods 45 Huntly Street Highland
TEL (0463) 223550 *Open Mon to Sat 9 to 5.30.*
Inverness Gordons Health Store 20 Baron Taylor Street
TEL (0463) 233104 *Open Mon to Sat 9 to 5.30.*
Ipswich Marno's Food Reform 14 St. Nicholas Street Suffolk
TEL (0473) 53106 *Open Mon to Wed 10 to 2.30, Thur Fri Sat 10 to 5.*
Kendal 'Waterside' Wholefoods Cumbria
TEL (0539) 29743 *Open Mon to Sat 9 to 5.*
Kings Lynn The Whole Food Shop 50 Norfolk Street Norfolk
TEL (0553) 68379 *Open Mon to Sat 9 to 5.30, half-day Wed.*
Kington Spread Eagle Foods 5 Church Street Hereford and Worcester
TEL (0544) 230355 *Open Mon to Sat 9 to 5.30.*
Lancaster Spice of Life 5 Marine Drive Hest Bank Lancashire
TEL (0524) 822655 *Open Mon to Sat 9 to 1, 2.15 to 5.30, Wed 9 to 1.*
Leamington Spa The Corn Mother Regent Place Warwickshire
TEL (0926) 29334 *Open Mon to Sat 9 to 5.30.*
Leicester Downey's Wholefoods 143 Evington Road Leicestershire
TEL (0533) 736108 *Open Mon to Fri 9 to 5.30.*
Letchworth Squires Dairies 49 Leys Avenue Hertfordshire
TEL (046 26) 3281 *Open Mon to Sat 9 to 5.*
Liverpool Lancashire Pure Foods Blacklers Stores Great Charlotte Street Merseyside
TEL 051-708 9561 *Open Mon to Sat 9 to 5.30, Thur Sat 9 to 6.*
Liverpool The Wholefood Shop 6 Ashfield Road Aigburgh Vale Merseyside
TEL 051-728 8536 *Open Mon to Sat 9.15 to 1.15, 2.30 to 5.30, Wed Sat, 2.30 to 5.*
Llandrindod Wells Van's Good Food Shop Middleton Street Powys
TEL (0597) 3074 *Open Mon Tue Thur Sat 9 to 5.30, Wed 9 to 1, Fri 9 to 6.*
Llantwit Major The Country Food Store 8 Church Street South Glamorgan
TEL (044 65) 2533 *Open Mon to Sat 9 to 5.30.*
London Alara 58–60 Marchmont Street WC1
TEL 01-837 1172 *Open Mon to Fri 9 to 6, Sat 9.30 to 5.30.*
London Bread and Roses 316 Upper Street N1
TEL 01-226 9483 *Open Mon to Sat 10 to 5.*
London Bumblebee Natural Foods Stores 30 and 33 Breckock Road N7
TEL 01-607 1936 *Open Mon to Sat 9.30 to 6.30.*
London Cornucopia 64 St. Mary's Road W5
TEL 01-579 9431 *Open Mon to Sat 9 to 5.50.*
London Cranks Health Foods Marshall Street W1
TEL 01-437 2915 *Open Mon to Fri 9 to 6, Sat 9 to 4.30.*
London Cranks in the Market Unit II Covent Garden Market WC2
TEL 01-379 6508 *Open Mon to Sat 10 to 8.30.*
London Culpeper 21 Bruton Street Berkeley Square W1
TEL 01-629 4559 *Open Mon to Sat 9.30 to 5.30.*

London Golden Temple 246 Belsize Road NW6
TEL 01-328 4781 *Open Mon to Sat 9 to 5.30.*

London Highgate Granary 17 Highgate High Street N6
TEL 01-341 2337 *Open Mon to Sat 9 to 6, Sun 10 to 6.*

London Moguls Health and Wholefoods 31 Goodge Street W1
Open Mon to Sat 9 to 5.30.

London Quacks Wholefood and Takeaway 33 Theobold's Road WC1
TEL 01-405 4542 *Open Mon to Sat 8.30 to 5.*

London Terrapin Station 76 Effra Road SW19
TEL 01-543 3999 *Open Mon to Sat 9 to 5, half-day Wed.*

London The Lima Shop 65 Station Road Winchmore Hill N21
TEL 01-360 7143 *Open Mon Tue 9.30 to 4.30, Thur Fri 9.30 to 5, Sat 9.30 to 2.30, closed Wed.*

London The Orange Tree 16 Inverness Street Camden Town NW1
TEL 01-267 6586 *Open Mon to Sat 9 to 5.30, Wed 9 to 4.*

London The Spice House Unit 65–67 Market Hall Shopping City Wood Green N22
TEL 01-881 1471 *Open Mon to Sat 9 to 5.30, Thur 9 to 8, Fri 9 to 6.*

Loughborough Elf Foods 47 Market Street Leicestershire
TEL (0509) 212424 *Open Mon to Sat 9 to 5.30, half-day Wed.*

Ludlow Broad Bean 60 Broad Street Salop
TEL (0584) 4239 *Open Mon to Sat 10 to 1.15, 2.15 to 5, Thur 10 to 1.15.*

Newbury Sunstore Marsh Lane Berkshire
TEL (0635) 30825 *Open Mon to Sat 9 to 5. Closed Wed pm.*

Newquay The Pure Thing 4 East Street Cornwall
TEL (063 73) 6772 *Open Mon to Fri 9 to 5.30, Wed 9 to 3.30, Sat 9 to 5.*

Northampton Backs Fine Foods 12 St. Giles Square Northamptonshire
TEL (0604) 36558 *Open Mon to Sat 8.30 to 5.30.*

Northwich The Happy Nut House 20 Market Way Cheshire
TEL (0606) 3585 *Open Mon to Sat 9 to 5.30, closed Wed 12.*

Oakham Tuppenny Rice Wholefoods 8 Northgate Rutland
TEL (0572) 2078 *Open Mon to Sat 9 to 5.*

Orpington Food Reform 111 High Street Kent
TEL (0689) 37172 *Open Mon to Sat 9 to 5.30, closed Thur 12.*

Oxford Leaders Suffolk House Banbury Road Summertown Oxfordshire
TEL (0865) 52528 *Open Mon to Sat 8.30 to 5.30.*

Paisley Hill's 9 New Street Strathclyde
TEL 041-889 4669 *Open Mon to Sat 9 to 5.30.*

Parkstone Earth Foods 113 Commercial Road Lower Parkstone Poole Dorset
TEL (0202) 733393 *Open Mon to Sat 9 to 5.30, half-day Wed.*

Penzance The Granary 15d Causeway Head Cornwall
TEL (0736) 61869 *Open Mon to Sat 9 to 5, closed Wed.*

Peterborough Peterborough Health Food Centre The Arcade Cambridgeshire
TEL (0733) 66807 *Open Mon to Sat 9 to 5.30.*

Plymouth Barbican Wholefoods Citadel Ope The Barbican Devon
TEL (0752) 660499 *Open Mon to Sat 9.30 to 6.*

Plymouth Beggars Banquet 5a Regent Street Devon
TEL (0752) 28449 *Open Mon to Sat 9 to 5.30.*

Portsmouth Seasons Wholefoods 24 Marmian Road Hampshire
TEL (0705) 825319 *Open Mon to Fri 9.30 to 5.30, Sat 9 to 5.*

Poulton-le-Fylde Natural Choice 2–6 Market Place Lancashire
TEL (0253) 893952 *Open Mon to Sat 9 to 5.30.*

Preston Amber Wholefoods Canon Street Lancashire
TEL (0772) 53712 *Open Mon to Sat 9 to 5.30.*

Reading Harvest Wholefoods Harris Arcade Friar Street Berkshire
TEL (0734) 580649 *Open Mon to Sat 9 to 5.15.*

Ringwood Scoltocks 20 Lynes Lane Hampshire
TEL (042 54) 3787 *Open Mon to Sat 9 to 5.30.*

St. Austell The Good Food Shop 6/10 East Hill Cornwall
TEL (0726) 73548 *Open Mon to Sat 9.30 to 5.*
Scarborough Victoria Health Food Centre 142 Victoria Road Yorkshire
TEL (0723) 369895 *Open Mon to Sat 9 to 5.30.*
Scunthorpe Health Food Store 11 Oswald Road South Humberside
TEL (0724) 3983 *Open Mon to Fri 9 to 5.30, Sat 9 to 4.*
Spalding Eggstasy Wholefoods 25 New Road Lincolnshire
TEL (0775) 61927 *Open Mon Wed 9.30 to 5, Tue Sat 9 to 5, Thur 9.30 to 1, Fri 9 to 6.*
Spalding Holbeach Wholefoods 16 Fleet Street Holbeach Lincolnshire
TEL (0406) 362426 *Open Mon Tue Thur Fri 9 to 5.30, closed Sat 5.15, closed Wed.*
Surbiton Surbiton Wholefoods 20 Claremont Road Surrey
TEL 01-399 2772 *Open Mon to Sat 9 to 5.30.*
Tavistock Kilworthy Kapers 11 King Street Devon
TEL (0822) 5039 *Open Tue to Sat 9 to 5.30.*
Torquay Lynnell's 120 Reddenhill Road Babbacombe Devon
TEL (0803) 37102 *Open Sun to Sat 8.45 to 6.*
Totnes Cranks 35 High Street Devon
TEL (0803) 862526 *Open Mon to Sat 9 to 5.30.*
Towcester Goodness Foods 109a Watlington Street Northamptonshire
TEL (0327) 51653 *Open Mon to Sat 9 to 5.30, Fri 9 to 6.*
Wareham The Purbeck Wholefood Store 17 West Street Dorset
TEL (092 95) 2332 *Open Mon to Sat 9 to 5, Wed 9 to 1.*
Wells Good Earth Priory Road Somerset
TEL (0749) 78600 *Open Mon to Sat 9 to 5, Wed 9 to 1.*
West Wickham Farrington Health Foods 7–9 Beckenham Road Kent
TEL 01-777 8721 *Open Mon Tue Thur Sat 9 to 5.30, Wed 9 to 1, Fri 9 to 6.30.*
Wimborne Goodness Gracious 6a Leigh Road Dorset
TEL (0202) 882172 *Open Mon to Sat 9 to 5.30, closed Wed early.*
Wooler The Good Life Shop 50 High Street Northumberland
TEL (0668) 81700 *Open Mon to Sat 9 to 5, open Thur 12.30.*

SUPERMARKET SURVEY

Although supermarkets are not yet as good as specialised wholefood shops for variety of real food supplies, many of them are stocking more and more real food items. This survey compares the major supermarket chains with each other, and with the Holland and Barrett and Great Western Wholefoods chains. Harrods is included to show the range carried by an up-market food store and Wholefoods of Baker Street as one example of a wholefood shop, as a control.

- ● available in all branches

- ○ available in major branches

	BOOTS	BRITISH HOME STORES	BUDGEN	CO-OP	INTERNATIONAL	LITTLEWOODS	MARKS AND SPENCER	SAFEWAY	SAINSBURY	TESCO	WAITROSE	HOLLAND AND BARRETT	GREAT WESTERN WHOLEFOODS	HARRODS	WHOLEFOODS OF BAKER STREET
Bread															
Wholemeal—commercial bakes	•	•	•	•	•	•	•	•	•	•	•			•	
Wholemeal—special bakes	•								•		•	•	•	•	•
Organic															•
Other		•	•					•	•	•	•		•	•	•
Breakfast cereals															
Sugar-free muesli	•	•			•		•	•	•		•	•	•	•	•
Other sugar-free cereals		•	•	•	•	•		•	•		•		•	•	
Organic cereals															•
Cakes															
Wholemeal flour	•								•		•	•	•	•	•
Low-sugar or sugar-free	•											•		•	•
Gluten-free	•								•					•	
Other	•						•	•	•				•	•	•
Cheese															
Animal rennet free		•						•	•	•	•	•		•	•
Goats', ewes', quark	•	•				•	•	•	•	•	•	•	•	•	•
Coffee															
Decaffeinated	•	•	•	•	•		•	•	•	•	•	•	•	•	•
Cooking oils															
Cold-pressed grades				•				•			•	◐	•	•	•
Other non-regular grades	•		•	•				•	•	•	•			•	•
Cream															
Untreated														•	•
Soured		•		•				•	•	•	•			•	•
Vegetable substitutes								•	•		•			•	•
Eggs															
Non-battery		•						•	◐	◐	•			•	•
Fish															
Fresh						•	•	•	◐	◐	•			•	
Flour															
Stoneground wholemeal	•	•	•		•			•	•	•	•	•	•	•	
Organic stoneground wholemeal												•	•	•	•
Gluten-free	•								•				•	•	•

	BOOTS	BRITISH HOME STORES	BUDGEN	CO-OP	INTERNATIONAL	LITTLEWOODS	MARKS AND SPENCER	SAFEWAY	SAINSBURY	TESCO	WAITROSE	HOLLAND AND BARRETT	GREAT WESTERN WHOLEFOODS	HARRODS	WHOLEFOODS OF BAKER STREET
Fruits															
Canned in natural juice	•		•	•	•	•		•	•	•	•		•	•	
Dried natural		•		•				•					•	•	•
Semi-dried											•			•	•
Fresh		•	•	•			•	•	•	•	•		•	•	•
Juices—natural	•	•	•				•	•	•	○	•		•	•	•
Juices—organic											•		•	•	•
Game								•	•					•	•
Herbs															
Fresh							•	•	•	•	•			•	•
Ice cream															
Soya														•	•
Jams and preserves															
Low-sugar	•	•		•	•		•	•	•		•	•	•	•	•
Sugar-free	•			•							•	•	•	•	•
Using untreated fruit									•		•				
Other		•							•		•	•	•	•	
Margarine															
Vegetable (including whey powder)		•	•	•	•	•	•	•	•	•	•	•		•	
Vegetable (excluding whey powder)											•	•	•	•	•
With cold-pressed oils (excluding whey and hydrogenated oils)											•	•	•	•	•
Other		•						•		•	•		•		•
Mayonnaise (special recipe)	•							•			•	•		•	•
Meat															
Organically reared															•
Milk															
Ewes', goats', soya	•						•	•	•		•	•	•	•	•
Pasta															
Wholemeal	•	•	•	•	•			•	•	•	•	•	•	•	•
Fresh wholemeal							•	•	•	•				•	
Pickles and chutneys															
Without colour or preservatives		•												•	•
Poultry															
Fresh chicken		•	•	•	•	•	•	•	•	•	•			•	
Free range chicken															•
Other			•		•	•	•	•	•	•	•			•	•

	BOOTS	BRITISH HOME STORES	BUDGEN	CO-OP	INTERNATIONAL	LITTLEWOODS	MARKS AND SPENCER	SAFEWAY	SAINSBURY	TESCO	WAITROSE	HOLLAND AND BARRETT	GREAT WESTERN WHOLEFOODS	HARRODS	WHOLEFOODS OF BAKER STREET
Pulses															
Under 10 varieties	•	•	•					•		•	•				
10 to 20 varieties				•	•				•						
More than 20 varieties												•	•	•	•
Salt															
Low-sodium	•	•	•	•	•				•	•	•	•	•	•	•
Snacks															
Sugar-free	•	•					•		•			•	•	•	•
Soya foods															
Tofu	•											•	•	•	•
Bean curd	•											•			•
Textured soya bean protein		•		•				•			•	•	•	•	•
Take-away wholefoods							•					•	•	•	•
Tea															
Herbal, China	•	•	•	•	•		•		•		•	•	•	•	•
Vegetables															
Sugar-free baked beans	•											•	•	•	•
Fresh		•	•	•	•		•	•	•	•	•		•	•	•
Juices—natural				•			•		•			•	•	•	•
Natural vegetable stocks and extracts	•											•	•	•	•
Other	•								•					•	•
Vinegar															
Wine, cider	•	•	•	•	•			•	•	•	•	•	•	•	•
Wines															
Organic															•
Yoghurts															
Natural		•	•		•	•		•	•	•	•		•	•	•

GROWERS

MAP 6

ARKHOLME   Lancashire
Ferrocrete Farm, Arkholme   TEL Hornby (0468) 21965

On the B6254, midway between Carnforth and Kirkby Lonsdale. Approaching from the former, turn right at the village crossroads. The farm is next to the shop.

Simple, basic foods without additives are produced in Sim and Geoffrey Fowler's dairy. Most of the time they make yoghurt using milk from their own goats. The goats are fed minimal amounts of high protein food, the remainder of their diet is made up of roughage in various forms. Cows' milk is bought in for ice cream and the old fashioned curd cheese, a dairy speciality, to which nothing is added, but the whey is extracted to give a semi-hard cheese which can be sliced. Low-fat cheeses are made to order; a yoghurt cheese is a regular line. Customers come to the farm shop, others find Arkholme foods in the supermarkets and health food shops in a wide surrounding area, marketed under the 'goat' symbol.

All year   cheese · yoghurt · milk · ice cream · small quantities of non-battery eggs.
Occasionally   goat meat · limited supplies of dairy fed pork, if entire pig is bought by special order.

Open: any hour but telephone first.

MAP 3

ARKLEY   Hertfordshire
Arkley Manor Farm, Rowley Lane, Arkley, Barnet   TEL Barnet 01-449 7944

From Arkley war memorial, take the Rowley Green Road for one mile, past Arkley Golf Club.

The late Dr. Shewell-Cooper who pioneered the Good Gardeners' Association (an international association of organic gardeners) used the gardens here at Arkley to demonstrate his organic no-digging method of cropping. His son, Mr. Ramsay Shewell-Cooper, maintains the 34-year-old tradition. Demonstrations are still regularly given and anyone interested should contact the farm for details. Six acres are cultivated in this fashion and the wide variety of crops grown can be bought on Wednesdays and Saturdays in Barnet Market, or, by appointment, at the farm on Tuesdays and Fridays. Further produce is sold through Organic Farm Foods (Unit 7, Ellerslie Square, Layham Road, SW2).

All year   fruit · vegetables.

Open: farm gate Tue and Fri; Barnet market Wed and Sat.

MAP 2

BERE ALSTON   Devon
Higher Birch, Bere Alston, Yelverton   TEL Yelverton (0822) 840257

Follow signposts from A386 in Yelverton or A386 in Tavistock for approximately seven miles in each case. (Map reference SX 440 655.)

Bere Alston was once a mining settlement on a peninsula between the Tamar and the Tavy, and the jetty from where the ore was shipped downstream to Plymouth is a mile down the road. Farm produce went the same way. Years ago early strawberries were successfully grown here but are now a thing of the past. Mary and Norman Willcocks work 73 acres rearing mainly cattle and sheep, which are fed home-produced, organically grown food. To broaden the diet for their livestock, sugar beet and calcified seaweed is occasionally bought in. Whenever possible, veterinary disorders are treated homeo-pathically. Soil Association symbol holders.

Late June to Nov   beef · lamb.

Open: by prior arrangement.

BESSINGBY   North Yorkshire   MAP 6
Church Farm Gardens, Field House   TEL Bridlington (0262) 603593

Left-hand side of a pair of village houses, off the A166 just inside Bridlington town boundary.

Bill and Ginnie Shaw's four acre holding is mainly used to grow organic produce for the family but surplus yields find a way into the Four Seasons and the Barn Restaurant, both in the town. Their example is used by local schools as an educational model. Half an acre has recently been planted as orchard. All year round, there are free range eggs from organically fed poultry, normally spoken for by regulars. Coming into production shortly: spinach, broccoli, leeks, beans and courgettes.

June   beef.
July to Sep   lamb.
Dec   geese.

Open: Thur to Sat, 9.30 to 4.

BICKER   Lincolnshire   MAP 6
The Gauntlet, Bicker, Boston   TEL Boston (0205) 820327

The village is seven miles south west of Boston, a $\frac{1}{4}$ mile off the A52.

In an almost exclusively farming community in the middle of the Fens, John Butler has been producing organically grown crops for almost thirty years. He has farmed this property for the last twenty. 'It all started one day during the war when father came back from Home Guard duty and reported Dr. McDonald's (an early pioneer in the organic movement) enthusiasm for compost heaps.' They have kept one ever since. Three acres of this incredibly rich soil is cultivated organically and entirely by hand. It has no contact with machinery, artificial fertilisers, pesticides or weedkillers. Mr. Butler sells from the farm gate—contact him directly for details—and makes deliveries to Sheffield and London.

Midsummer   cauliflowers.
Autumn to early winter   carrots · onions · potatoes.
Occasionally   small surpluses of milk and eggs.

Open: phone for details.

BINFIELD HEATH   Berkshire   MAP 3
Pond House, Kiln Lane, Binfield Heath, Henley   TEL Reading (0734) 478511

The village is three miles south of Henley, off the A4155.

Diana Seidz has recently laid down an orchard, rather as some might do for good wines, on two acres of ground. Most of the crop is sold through Marigold Farm Shop in Upper Basildon, but anyone caring to telephone will be given details regarding availability and directions to reach her retreat.

Aug to Jan   apples.

Open: by appointment.

BISHOPTHORPE   North Yorkshire   Map 6
Brunswick Nursery, Bishopthorpe, York   TEL York (0904) 760307

Four miles south west of York, off the A64. Turn into Sim Balk Lane. The holding is on the left-hand side beyond the old railway bridge.

A six woman co-operative intensively cultivate this two and a half acre patch, still within sight of the city. Over a period of eight years they have painstakingly built up the soil fertility to a high standard using vast amounts of compost. Rarely do they use insecticide, even the organic kind. The entire plot is divided into squares, the crops regularly rotated. Their large variety of produce is eagerly sought in York shops—Wholefood in Micklegate, and Millers Yard in Gillygate. Sales from the garden gate.

June to Nov   cut flowers.
July to Sep   soft fruits · apples.
All year   carrots · cabbages · onions · Jerusalem artichokes · salad crops · courgettes · cucumbers · broccoli.

Open: 9 to 5.30 during the summer and 9.30 to 4 in winter.

BODENHAM   Hereford and Worcester   Map 2
Broadfield Court Vineyard, Bodenham, Nr Leominster
TEL Bodenham (056 884) 483

Five miles south of Leominster, on the A49 to Hereford, take a left turn signposted Bodenham. Two miles on, take a left turn for Broadfield Court.

'The '77 vintage is still drinking well,' claims Keith James, saying much for its fundamental quality. Mr. and Mrs. James laid plans in 1968 to revive the Roman tradition of viniculture in the area. Since then, ten acres have been planted, following the success of fifty trial vines in the old walled garden, adjoining the estate's rambling house. Keith James continues, 'A feature of our vineyard is the ability to produce fully ripened grapes even in poor summers, which is why so many vineyards existed in the district during Roman times. The implication for foodwatchers is that sugar is therefore never used as a fermentation aid. Reichensteiner is the leading variety, grown because of its ability to ripen consistently despite our unpredictable weather and still maintain high sugar readings. The alcohol content of Reichensteiner '81 was 11.25 %, which is considerably in excess of many white wines, English and imported. Thus this wine has real body and local character of its own.' Pressing is carried out at Pilton Manor in Somerset; the juice is then siphoned into Broadfield vats for fermentation. Vineyard activities involve only a small part of the estate. At least four hundred cows are milked with a similar number of followers reared. Justerini and Brooks (50 St. James' Street, London) and Tanner's of Shrewsbury are stockists. Otherwise wine may be bought by arrangement at the vineyard during the summer. Pre-booked groups can be given escorted tours.

Open: days in summer.

BORTH   Dyfed   Map 6
Rachel's Dairy, Brynllys   TEL Borth (097 081) 489

At Borth turn off the B4353, uphill then left.

Rachel Rowlands and her husband were the first farmers in the country to carry the full Soil Association symbol for their produce. 'We started out just doing cream. We've been farming here organically—with the Soil Association symbol for the whole farm—for twenty years. We continued the way my parents had done, something we believed in, in the family. And, if it is right for us we believe it is right for the people who eat our food. At long last the message is getting around.' They have a traditional 250 acre Welsh Farm with sheep, pigs and cattle. The meat (lamb and pork) is in great demand and much of it is sold from the premises from April through to August. More is sold through David Frost, a stallholder in Aberystwyth Market where, from October onwards, he takes their vegetables. Cream, butter, buttermilk, cottage cheese and yoghurt are the dairy lines, the yoghurt live and the fruit part-organically grown. Customers speak of produce in first-class condition. Mrs. Rowlands is highly esteemed by those who have discovered the delights and benefits of her organic produce.

All year   milk · cream · butter · soft cheese · yoghurt (plain and fruit).
Apr to Aug   lamb · pork.
Oct onwards   potatoes · swedes · carrots · onions · cabbage · cauliflowers.

Open: farmgate sales any time within reason.

BOXFORD   Essex   MAP 3
Hill Farm (Copella Fruit Juices), Boxford, Colchester   TEL Boxford (0787) 210348

The village lies ten miles north of Colchester, on the A1071, midway between Sudbury and Hadleigh.

'No, Isaac Newton was not a persuasive influence,' Devora Peake affirms but with a little deft thinking along gravitational lines she has found a good use for her fallen apples. Although more famed for its Copella Fruit Juices, wheat, too, is grown here, then stoneground and packed on the farm for sale in the shops under the Prewetts Organic label, or as Boxford Flour. Apple juices, however, have become the mainstay of the 800 acre family farm, in beautiful countryside on the edge of Dedham Vale. Mrs. Peake has good reason to be grateful to the Common Market: it was the fear of a flood of foreign apples which lent impetus to the search for alternative outlets. That was in 1968. In the seventeen years since then, the apple presses at Boxford have worked hard. Much of their success can be accounted for by increasing public awareness of the virtues in unprocessed food. The Peakes have met the need effectively by eschewing juice concentrates. At Hill End these are never used. Their juice is simply freshly crushed English apples — 75 % Cox's Orange Pippin — flash pasteurised, then immediately bottled or carton packed. All sweeteners, preservatives and colourings are taboo. 'Neither do we filter out the fine apple particles which contain so many of the nutrients in the fruit,' which explains the opaque appearance. Demand is now so great that, to keep up with it, they have to buy fruit in from other sources. In smaller quantities Morello cherries and blackcurrants are grown, pressed in the same way, then blended with the apple juice for the cherry with apple or blackcurrant with apple versions. Less well known is their pear juice. To Devora Peake it is a matter of great regret that Copella does not qualify for the organically grown symbol. 'Market forces dictate that dessert apples have unblemished skins' so spraying is necessary. Artificial fertilisers are not used for the Peakes are firm exponents of the organic cause and their enthusiasm is not confined to fruit. The farm carries a Jersey herd; there is a market garden; and poultry are reared.

All year   fruit juices · free range eggs · butter · cheese · cream · vegetables · apples.
July, Aug   soft fruits.

Open: farm shop weekdays, 9 to 4.

BRISTOL   Avon   MAP 2
St. Werburgh's City Farm, Watercress Road, St. Werburgh's
TEL Bristol (0272) 428241

Take exit three (at City Centre) from M32 and follow slip road signposted St. Werburgh's. Continue to end of Mina Road, through railway tunnel, and Watercress Road is the first on the left.

This farm has a two acre plot within the city and a similar area outside the town. Catherine Holden, three years sales manager here, can guarantee 80 % of the produce sold as organic. Concentrates have to be bought in to supplement the waste foods the animals are fed and in the shop, stock is augmented by non-battery eggs, and organic vegetables and meat bought in. They are popular and widely used by children and the handicapped and all farm profits go towards the running of this charitable trust (founded 1980 and funded by Urban Aid, the county council and several charities).

All year non-battery duck and chicken eggs · goats' milk · cows' milk · yoghurt · cream · vegetables in variety, a greater choice during summer.
As available pork · bacon · lamb · chickens.
Aug to Nov apples · pears · homemade chutney.

Open: every day, 10 to 5.

BROADOAK   East Sussex   Map 3
Sky Farm, Swift Lane, Broadoak, Nr Heathfield   TEL Burwash (0435) 882167

The village is three miles east of Heathfield, on the A265.

Mark and Anne Stace's eight acres are isolated, so generally they go to their customers. Thursday mornings find Mrs. Stace at that harbinger of things for the future, Mayfield Organic Market. Other days she will have travelled as far as Eastbourne, replenishing buying groups. Vegetables are their main business. Very occasionally there is beef, more frequently there are free range eggs from their own poultry. They try very hard to maintain a wide variety of vegetables all year round, including potatoes; also, the now rarely grown peas, which they 'just about manage to make pay'. Soil Association symbol has been applied for.

All year vegetables · limited quantities of free range eggs.

Open: telephone before calling in person.

BROOKETHORPE   Gloucestershire   Map 2
Brentlands Farm, Brookethorpe, Gloucester   TEL Gloucester (0452) 813447

North of motorway bridge on A4173.

All the beef supplied by the Warners' 200 acre family farm is produced from stock bought in as calves (normally about 2 weeks old) and reared through to maturity without the use of hormones or growth promoters. Michael Warner, farming organically here for a year, puts his 180 animals out to grass for the summer and feeds them his own silage and barley during the winter. Carcases are properly hung before being boned, cut and packed ready for freezing. Mr. Walker sometimes makes suet, and kidneys and fat are available if required. A joint is usually cut to about 4 lb; steak and minced beef in bags of 1 to $1\frac{1}{2}$ lb sizes. The only precaution: is there room in your freezer for a two and a half cubic feet order! Lamb is produced to the same standard. Mr. Warner requires a deposit in advance for this very personal service and emphasises the need to collect at the time specified. If necessary, he can arrange direct delivery but this may entail freezing the order first.

Open: by prior arrangement.

BROOKETHORPE   Gloucestershire   Map 2
Gilbert's, Brookthorpe, Gloucester   TEL Painswick (0452) 812364

North of motorway bridge on A4173. First house on right 300 yards down the lane opposite Brookthorpe Filling Station.

Only quite small quantities of any kind of food are produced on Mrs. Beer's five acres at the Cotswold edge. A number of cattle, sheep and poultry provide balanced grazing and manure. Most of her produce finds a ready market amongst regulars, though there are occasional surpluses. She also offers bed and breakfast in this beautiful 300 to 400-year-old timbered farmhouse—breakfasts largely organic wholefood. Nearby is a fine gabled manor and an 800-year-old church with a saddleback tower.

Variably   veal · lamb · beef · eggs from free range hens fed wholefood.
Summer to autumn   soft fruit · apples · plums · vegetables in variety.
All year   honey · cottage cheese.

Open: telephone for times.

BROUGHTON   Hampshire   MAP 3
Green Circle Growers, The Anchorage, Salisbury Road
TEL Broughton (079 430) 234

The village is a mile south of the A30, three miles west of Stockbridge.

Julie and Stephen Tidy have been told they could never earn a living from their four acres—but it is early days yet to prove them wrong. Meanwhile they are renting out a cottage and surviving with mother-in-law to make ends meet. They are earnest in their ambition 'to develop an integrated low-input farming system for a small acreage, sustainable for an indefinite period'. Vegetables are their strength, most of which find ready customers at Friday W.I. markets in Andover. Very occasionally there is pork; more frequently poultry. Herbs in pots are a sideline.

All year   eggs.
Aug, Sep   blackberries.
Seasonally   potatoes · carrots · leeks · parsnips · tomatoes · lettuce · peppers.

Open: telephone before calling in person.

CAVERSHAM   Berkshire   MAP 3
Little Bottom Farm, 64 Blenheim Road, Caversham, Reading
TEL Reading (0734) 473157

Callers only by prior arrangement.

Dr. Ellis is gradually building up a fertile plot from a former eight acre pasture. He holds firm views on the question of soil fertility. 'It is the grower's responsibility not only to maintain fertility but, whenever possible, to bring improvements.' Within this small area, paddocks for sheep, a small coppice, a small orchard, fodder crops, soft fruits and vegetables are ingeniously combined. By means of long rotations and by encouraging hedges and wild areas as habitats for predators, Dr. Ellis believes pests can be kept under control naturally. At present all of his crops are spoken for by individuals or groups who collect from the house after ordering by telephone.

Occasionally   rabbits · chickens · lambs.
All year   a little goats' milk · some eggs.
July, Aug   strawberries · raspberries · blackcurrants · gooseberries.
Seasonally   peas (sugar snap, ordinary) · beans (broad, runner French, dried) · kales · carrots · tomatoes · radish (ordinary, Spanish, Chinese, Japanese) · onions · courgettes · salads · leeks · potatoes · spinach · squash.

Open: produce sold privately.

CEFN-Y-PANT   Dyfed   MAP 2
Penrhiw Farm Dairy, Penrhiw, Cefn-y-Pant, Whitland
TEL Whitland (0994) 7351

Cefn-y-Pant is eight miles north west of the M4/A40 at St. Clears, taking an unclassified road signposted Llanboidy.

Paul and Ursula Jackson are working hard towards a high organic standard. After farming this 55 acre holding for six years, and with a reputation now as healthy as their land, an organic symbol should be in the offing quite shortly. All the animals are treated homeopathically whenever possible and no residual chemicals or chemicals have been used since they came. Theirs is basically a dairy farm, the milk sold as yoghurt and cream, but pork and Mrs. Jackson's herby pork sausages, made to her own, undisclosed recipe are also available. It is common knowledge that they find eager customers such as Swansea's Drangway Restaurant, the Waverley Restaurant in Carmarthen and Bwyd-y-Byd, and, perhaps unexpectedly, the Jones' village shop in Crymych. Any surplus might go as far as Clapham's Organic Farm Foods. Their own organically grown fruit flavours the yoghurt. So far vegetables are no more than a sideline.

All year   pork sausages · pork · yoghurt · cream · cheese.

Open: 9 to 6 or by appointment.

CHINNOR   Oxfordshire   MAP 3
Icknield Nurseries, Kingston Stert   TEL Kingston Blount (0844) 52481

The village is on the B4009 between Chinnor and M40 junction 6.

Tania D'Onofria grows vegetables in one field and her parents cultivate in a neighbouring one but she and her husband shoulder the responsibility for all the marketing. She would say she is not organic with a capital 'O'. It just seemed the right way to do things and it took others to remind her that what she was doing was according to the book. Altogether there are eight and a half acres under cultivation. Herbicides and pesticides are never used on their vegetables and fruit, neither are they fed non-organic fertilisers. Indoors her ethics vary slightly: if really pushed she may resort to spraying the pot plants. Early strawberries are a speciality. From mid-May they sell fruit grown under polythene tunnels, finishing in July when the main crop of several, tasty varieties, starts. Blackcurrants are main season. Anyone who missed the summer season soft fruits might try their autumn raspberries. It is not a highly promoted self-pick operation but fruit is usually there for those who wish to gather their own. The salad season commences with April lettuces. From then on there are reliable supplies for the nursery shop. Tomatoes are main crop so none are available until July. A good deal of effort goes into vegetable production, from French and Italian beans, peppers and aubergines through to corn on the cob and some regular root vegetables. Carrots are nearly always grown as the bunching kind. For potatoes they will send you to someone in the village whose crop goes to the organic shops.

May, June   strawberries.
July   blackcurrants.
Sep, Oct   raspberries.
Apr to Nov   salad crops · vegetables.

Open: every day, 9 to 5.

CLYNDERWEN   Dyfed   MAP 2
Glanrhydwilym, Rhydwilym   TEL Clynderwen (099 12) 562

Leave the A40 midway between St. Clears and Haverfordwest, taking the A478 northwards for two miles. On some maps look for the village spelt as Clunderwen.

Edie Wagstaff's ten acres are on a delightfully situated north slope facing the Prescellis. The now fertile soil is the outcome of five years careful husbandry. Mr. Wagstaff has developed a ridge and bed growing system based on low capital equipment and timely cultivations. He manages to work the holding single-handed except for occasional help at peak periods. Strict organic principles are applied and Glanrhydwilym already carries the Soil Association symbol. Wholesale only but a telephone call can secure an order for larger quantities (by the sack) and his produce is available from the Marigold Organic Farm Shop, Upper Basildon or Waverley Food Stores, Carmarthen.

July, Aug   small quantities of strawberries · gooseberries · blackcurrants.
All year   a wide range of vegetables according to their natural season but emphasis on winter crops.

Open: telephone before visiting.

COTTINGHAM   Humberside   MAP 6
York Grounds, Raywell   TEL Hull (0482) 657342

North-western outskirts of Kingston-upon-Hull.

Mr. and Mrs. Thompson have taken self-sufficiency a stage further by installing their own electric mill from which they grind their largely organic standard cereals to order. On 120 acres they also produce potatoes, cabbage, beef and lamb with the minimum of chemical input, a system they have tried to abide by since 1949. By prior arrangement they are happy to sell from the farmgate, but their produce is generally distributed by Hider Food Imports in Hull.

All year   organically grown stoneground flour and stoneground flour grown to Organic Farmers and Growers, 2nd conservation grade.
Oct to Mar   potatoes · cabbage.

Open: by arrangement; closed Sun.

CRATFIELD   Suffolk   MAP 3
Poplar Farm, Silverleys Green, Cratfield, Halesworth
TEL Fressingfield (037 986) 241

Perhaps as remote as it is possible to be in Suffolk, the village is most easily found by leaving the B1123 midway between Halesworth and Harleston (at Linstead Parva), following signs for Cratfield. Then take the left turn at Silverleys telephone box.

Anthony Gaze sees this subject in a more academic light than some and generously feels 'people would be interested to see how a relatively small piece of land can produce a wide range of vegetables, in fact sufficient to provide for a family and to provide a good income for a few months in the year.' Mr. Gaze rotates his crops, feeds his soil compost and manure, occasionally wood ash and seaweed extract. There is a stall at the gate when there is enough produce — but it is best to telephone first.

June to Nov   vegetables of all kinds in season especially garlic · pumpkins · carrots · spinach · chard · lettuce · parsley · French beans · beetroot · courgettes.

Open: June to November callers are welcome any time.

DANBY   North Yorkshire   MAP 6
Bottom Village, Danby, Whitby   TEL Castleton (0287) 6871

Four miles south of A121 (Guisborough to Whitby) close to its junction with B1366.

A purposeful tale of compassion, social conscience and commercial endeavour. Set in the National Park in the Esk Valley, rather remote from anywhere, is the first 'Camphill Village', based on the needs of the mentally handicapped adult. Actually only two in three are handicapped, others are those who take a leading role in running the village together with their families. At Bottom there are 440 acres, 200 of which are under forestry and, in Patrick Ffrench's words, 'we are self-sufficient in clean meat, no hormones or antibiotics. We export a couple of thousand pounds a year to other friendly communities, schools and the like but we can also sell another 1,000 lb wholesale providing we can come to agreement about choice of cuts.' Up here organic fruit is scarce so the six tons of fruit they get through each year—for jams, juices, sauerkraut, pickles and chutneys—comes from commercial growers in the Vale of York. In two years' time they will be able to sell their low-sugar, additive-free products. Just now they have only sufficient for themselves and friends. Creamery and bakery goods are also available. The Bottom Bakery range starts with wholemeal through to banana loaves. Buy it here or sample some in the coffee shop after exploring the gift store or picking up a book from the Camphill Press. Flour is stoneground organic or stoneground organic rye. Vegetables are to biodynamic standard and available to anyone specifically needing them. Selling further afield, they prefer to do so wholesale at harvest time. In this not particularly favourable micro-climate there are cabbages, beetroot, turnips, parsnips and potatoes. Watch out for their foods in wholefood shops within a 20 mile area. All their produce carries the Soil Association symbol. All cheese is made with vegetable rennet.

All year breads · flours · Bottom hard cheese · Bottom Danbydale soft cheese · Bottom natural yoghurt · Bottom fresh curd · butchers' meat by arrangement.
Aug to Mar potatoes · root vegetables.

Produce sold wholesale.

DENBURY Devon   MAP 2
Moorfoot Organic Garden, Woodland Road, Denbury, Newton Abbot
TEL Ipplepen (0803) 813161

Three miles south of Newton Abbot, west of the A381 Totnes road.

Linda Phelps and Gordon Strutt work two acres of ground, the produce finding a ready market. The raised bed technique is solving their drainage problems. What they cannot grow themselves they buy in from Blake Brothers to stock up the garden shop or the van which daily delivers to shops and buying groups in the Torbay area. Six polythene tunnels considerably extend the growing potential in the already mild local climate. The Soil Association symbol is already carried and there should soon be Demeter approval.

In season bunching carrots · parsnips · spring onions · lettuce · courgettes · tomatoes · parsley · peppers · aubergines · kidney beans · cucumbers · melons · strawberries.

Open: Mon to Sat, 10 to 5.

DENHAM Suffolk   MAP 3
Denham End Farm, Denham, Bury St. Edmunds
TEL Bury St. Edmunds (0284) 810653

Five miles south west of Bury St. Edmunds on an unclassified road. Follow sign for Barrow Denham Lane at south end of village.

Caroline Holmes' miniscule plot is primarily a nursery for her interesting collection of herbs which she grows to organic standards. Summertime brings a crop of tomatoes, peppers and aubergines, and sometimes other surplus produce. At any time she will have 150 or more varieties of herbs. Eight species of lavender include Folgate, Spica, Hidcote, rosea and Grappenhall. There is an even more impressive representation with the thymes, nineteen in all including the cultivars Pink Chintz and Silver Posie. Herb orders also available by post.

All year herbs in pots.
Mainly summer vegetables.
Summer, Autumn soft fruits · top fruits.

Open: Sun to Sat, 8 to 8.

DUNMORE EAST   Co. Waterford   No Map
Carney's Organic Farm, Portally Cove   TEL Waterford 83357

From Dunmore East take the Tramore coast road. Farm signposted one and a half miles from Dunmore East.

From the balmy seclusion of their seaside fifteen acres John and Bridget Carney produce vegetables and dairy foods. The cows are a handful of Kerrys to provide the milk for natural yoghurt, cream and hard cheese. During the long growing season a variety of vegetables—tomatoes, courgettes, peppers, aubergines, herbs in variety, the increasingly scarce peas, beans, soft fruits and not forgetting, of course, potatoes—are grown. Those who cannot get down to the farm to buy might try the Full of Beans shop in George's Court, Waterford, or in the same city, the Candlelight Run and the Ship Restaurant.

All year   free range eggs.
Summer, autumn and winter   cheese · yoghurt · salad crops · root vegetables · potatoes.
Summer   strawberries · blackcurrants.

Open: all year during daylight hours.

DUNNINGTON   North Yorkshire   Map 6
Dunnington Lodge, Dunnington, York   TEL Elvington (090 485) 258

About five miles east of York, north of the A1079 Hull road.

Hereabouts organic growing is the fast, food way, to fame. The only trouble is that getting round the studios tends to hinder the milking. Mr. Cochrane's views (eagerly sought by journalists) are summarily, 'I like the taste better and my wife was worried about the excessive variety of chemicals in our diet. Variety is the spice of life but enough's enough. Nowadays we more or less only eat what we've grown ourselves and our stock are certainly healthier.' All 109 Dunnington Lodge acres, mostly dairy with 2 acres of potatoes, are farmed organically. Milk is green top; the eggs are free range. 'Vegetables were a new line last year and now we are trying wheat. Our own potatoes are the only ones we eat with the jackets on.' During June there is an open day, organised through Organic Farmers and Growers Limited—contact them for details. Otherwise visitors are welcome by appointment and shop sales are available at any reasonable time but preferably not Sunday.

All year   green top milk · free range eggs.
From time to time   beef.
Autumn and winter   onions · leeks · carrots · early potatoes.

Open: weekdays.

EAST ALLINGTON   Devon   Map 2
Lipton Farm, East Allington, Totnes   TEL East Allington (054 852) 252

Near Kingsbridge on an unclassified road between East Allington and Slapton.

In this picturesque South Hams district close to the unusual Slapton Ley—a freshwater lake divided from the sea by a gravel ridge—Roger and Rosemary Jones grow grain and milk a Jersey herd. Others languish leisurely on the nearby beaches, while they freshly stonegrind to order—in a modern electric mill—the organically grown grain. The flour sells at £1.30 for an 8 lb bag, ground as you like—fine, medium or coarse. The Jersey milk is all wholesale but in season they sell Dutch white cabbage and cauliflowers.

All year   stoneground flour.
Sep to Apr   Dutch white cabbage · cauliflowers.

Open: please telephone first.

EDINBURGH   Lothian   MAP 7
Gorgie City Farm, Gorgie Road   TEL Edinburgh 031-337 4202

It is really their demonstration flock of deep litter hens which brings the customers, mainly
for eggs. Si Phillips now oversees this particular 'farm' after graduating in agriculture and
disillusionment with intensive rearing. 'We just put up a notice and the business has
grown from there, word of mouth doing the rest. Seasonally we have lamb, pork and
chicken and rabbit meat, all entirely free of additives.' Animal welfare is a priority.
Quantities, it is stressed are small, and it is advisable to contact the farm to see when
produce is actually available. Sometimes they can manage vegetables too. Prices are
reasonable as they are subsidised in part by various charities, such as the Queen's Silver
Jubilee Fund, King George's and John Younger Trusts, and Marks and Spencer.

All year   non-battery eggs.
May to Aug   chickens.
Sep   pork · lamb.
June to Oct   radishes · carrots · marrows · courgettes.
Aug, Sep   tomatoes · berries.

Open: Mon to Fri, 9 to 5; weekends, 11 to 5.

ELLESMERE   Salop   MAP 6
The Orchards Nursery, Greenhill Bank   TEL Dudleston Heath (069 175) 295

Three miles west of Ellesmere on the B5068.

Paul Jennings has a good memory. He read Rachel Carson's *Silent Spring* in 1976 and
cannot get it out of his mind, hence the commitment to organic produce. He has been
growing organically now for twelve years but the nursery is a new venture. Mr. Jennings
does not use any chemicals on his intensively cropped one and a half acres and his
greenhouse plants are fed comfrey liquid or other organic feeds. A little produce is sold
wholesale, some goes through the Tuesday market in Ellesmere, but the bulk is sold from
the nursery gate at any time from dawn to dusk; it's a hard life,' says Mr. Jennings.

All year   potatoes · including earlies · lettuce · broad beans · onions · cabbage · runner
beans · beetroot · tomatoes · cucumbers · courgettes · pot plants
Spring and summer   bedding plants · biennials.

Open: anytime.

FENNY BENTLEY   Derbyshire   MAP 6
The Priory, Woodeaves, Fenny Bentley, Ashbourne   TEL Ashbourne (0335) 29238

Angela Hughes went organic twenty-five years ago. 'The more you think about it, the
more you realise we are not going to die with a nuclear bomb, we will poison ourselves
off well before that. Most people,' she maintains, 'grow things by feeding the plants, while
we feed the soil—and when the soil is right the plants can't help but grow well.' She farms
$22\frac{1}{2}$ acres in the Peak National Park, east of Dovedale. Jacob sheep, pigs and a small
number of hens are kept which find their way to local customers. The beef is sold
through ordinary commercial channels as there is no other way of handling it at present.
Mrs. Hughes' honey is free from oil seed rape.

All year   pork to order · honey.
Summer onwards   lamb to order · hens · ducks—summer surplus · fruits · vegetables—
small surpluses.

Open: by appointment only.

FLIXTON   North Yorkshire   MAP 6
Onaway, Filey Road, Flixton, Scarborough   TEL Scarborough (0723) 890451

Seven miles south of Scarborough. One mile east of the A64 at Staxton roundabout, and half a mile this side of Flixton village.

Mr. Sargent cultivates 9 acres of sandy soil, subject to a good deal of leaching and blowing. A conveniently nearby dairy farm supplies the manure which temporarily gives some body to this hungry, light soil, supplemented by high potash Humber semi-organic fertiliser. In due course he hopes that entirely organic sources may replace the latter. Pasture is an important part of his rotation which is an opportunity to graze lambs. Around here, all roads lead to Scarborough, and most of his output reaches Sarah Brown's restaurant (not her shop) or the Gillygate Bakery in York (see entries).

Winter   lambs, only whole animals ordered in advance.
Spring   rhubarb, not forced.
Late summer onwards   tomatoes · carrots · green vegetables · potatoes · grain · hay.

Open: by arrangement only.

FORDINGBRIDGE   Hampshire   MAP 3
Furzehill Organic Produce, Mocklebegger   TEL Fordingbridge (0425) 53361

Three miles south of Fordingbridge, a mile east of Ibsley on the A338.

Richard and Susan Loader's philosophy is 'if you don't really understand what you are doing, don't do it!' The former botanist and zoologist don't grow everything sold in their organic farm shop. Soft fruits, for instance, may be bought in from Organic Farm Foods, while they in turn export vegetables to London. Citrus are untreated, and occasionally the oranges, lemons and grapefruit are biodynamic. Approximately forty different varieties of vegetables are home-grown. At the appropriate time you can reasonably expect to find sweetcorn, mange-tout, and the well-flavoured black French beans which turn green on cooking. Early potatoes are very popular but their great speciality is the humble lettuce, grown in vast quantities with the main produce crop going to London. Moreover they are sprayed with spring water. What the Loaders particularly like about their family holding is that, being well away from others, they do not get spray drift and the like. Soil Association symbol for the vegetables but not the goats' milk.

All year   goats' milk · vegetables in great variety.
June and July   soft fruit.
June   early potatoes.

Open: Sun to Sat, closed 1 to 2.

GAMLINGAY   Bedfordshire   MAP 3
Rosehaven, 110 Cinques Road, Gamlingay, Sandy
TEL Gamlingay (0767) 50142

Five miles north east of Sandy on the B1040.

Rachel Carson's book, *Silent Spring*, was prescribed reading for Eleanor Hodges and obviously has had a lasting impression. A geography degree has merely fuelled the enthusiasm as—in recent years with her husband—she has 'sought a chance to get some land to grow seriously'. Struggles with onions between the flowers of a Letchworth front garden led her to a registered five acre smallholding. 'It is the only sane way forward,' she says but does not expect it to keep them both. Mrs. Hodges has sensibly experimented with a one acre plot which needs a lot of improving so the geese and sheep earn their keep in more ways than one! Hens and pigs are scheduled to build up the fertility on this hungry land which is going to yield some good carrots and parsnips. Customers already speak highly of the quality and mention the 'delicious taste'. Initially there is commitment to keep Fairhaven Wholefoods supplied (see entry) and supplies are still slight. Do not expect to be able to carry away sacks of potatoes, 10 lb is the limit. At present farmgate sales are only by prior arrangement. Soil Association symbol expected shortly.

Feb to Apr   free range goose eggs.
May to Oct   fresh herbs.
July, Aug   raspberries · blackcurrants.
All year   a fair range of vegetables.

Open: please telephone to arrange visit.

GOXHILL   South Humberside   MAP 6
Roosters Rest, Soff Lane, Goxhill   TEL Barrow-on-Humber (0469) 30827

Leave A1077 at Thornton Curtis, to Thornton Station. Then second right signposted 'Southend and Goxhill'. Farm shop 300 yards on right.

Janet Shephardson sees herself as a guiding light on her father's land. He is involved in commercial egg production, her enthusiasms are for the organic farm shop which she stocks mainly with bought-in organic food, unsprayed citrus and the like. Out on the holding it has been two years of trial and error. A lot of compost of various sorts has gone on to the land and Mrs. Shephardson continues to experiment with 'no dig' plots. 'Most of my growing has been experimental, with many failures! '85 is going to be the start of successful production.' Experimentation hopefully behind her there should be more reliable home-grown supplies from now on.

All year   potatoes · onions · cauliflowers · cabbages · tomatoes · supplemented by a full range of bought-in organic produce.

Open: Mon to Fri, 9.30 to 12, 2 to 5; closed Tue; Sat, Sun, 10 to 12.

GRESHAM   Norfolk   MAP 3
The Stables, Gresham, Norwich   TEL Matlaske (026 377) 468

One and a half miles south of the A148 Holt to Cromer road, down the drive to Gresham Hall.

Anne and Keith Hood attempt to be entirely self-sufficient, which means that even the cows' food is home-grown. They cannot manage wheat (or tea, or coffee) so grain is bought in for the hens. In pre-cow days there were goats, now gone 'since we believe the cows' versus goats' milk issue depends on what they are fed'. Mr. Hood normally manages to place all his surpluses with colleagues at his place of work but they are worthwhile trying.

Dec   geese.
Jan   beef.
All year   unpasteurised milk · unsalted butter · cream · hard cheese · soft cheese.
Spring and summer   free range hen and goose eggs.
June to Dec   honey · vegetables (not potatoes).

Open: telephone to check availability of produce.

HARLOW   Essex   MAP 3
Thrushes Bush Poultry Farm, Nr Harlow   TEL Harlow (0279) 22673

Leave the M11 at junction 7, then take the first right turn from the Harlow road following signs for High Laver or Moreton for two miles. The farm is ¼ mile on the right beyond the Barleycorn Inn.

After fifty years breeding pedigree Rhode Island Reds and White Leghorns, Mary and Frank Edmonds are certainly not novices to the game. Crosses between the two breeds are sold for commercial laying. About 500 laying hens are retained which, along with three goats, supply them and a good many customers with milk, yoghurts and eggs. They are a FREGG approved farm.

All year   free range eggs.
Chiefly summer   goats' milk.
Autumn   apples
July to Dec   fresh roasting chickens and boiling fowl (frozen supplies for the remainder of the year).

Open: weekdays, 8 to 6; Sun, 2 to 6.

HARSTON   Cambridgeshire   MAP 3
Organic Produce, Apple Cottage, Button End   TEL Cambridge (0223) 870443

Harston is on the A10, five miles south of Cambridge.

'What carrot fly with proper maternal instinct will not prefer to lay her eggs on an organically grown carrot rather than one chemically grown,' is Colin Baker's ingenious philosophy towards quality. He makes no claim to freedom from pests and diseases. However he has an encouraging attitude towards freshness. All produce (except for that stored), he promises, is normally picked on the day of sale, certainly never before the day prior to day of sale. More firmly, he guarantees that no chemical sprays or fertilisers have been used for the past five years. Much of the land was previously grazing, having had very little fertiliser for many years. The holding has been 90% organic since 1946. Prices he tries to hold at average Cambridge market prices. Anything of inferior quality is sold more cheaply. Originally Mr. Baker hobby-farmed eight acres for milk and vegetables for an eight strong family, now there are two of fruit and one down to orchard. Saturday mornings he has a stall outside Cambridge's Arjuna (see entry), otherwise sales are from the house by appointment.

Seasonally   vegetables.
Late summer/autumn   apples · apple juice.

Open   Sat only, 9 to 12.

HARTFORD   Cambridgeshire   MAP 3
Michael Paske Farms, Barnston, The Spinney, Hartford, Huntingdon

Asparagus is their speciality. In fact until the recent introduction of smoked salmon it was the only product Michael Paske sold through his unique mail order service. And even that was only for a disappointingly short season, usually May and June but dependent, of course, on the weather. It is not organically grown. However a mention seems justified bearing in mind the special effort Mr. Paske makes to get it fresh to the customer and the limited availability of this delectable vegetable that adds welcome variety. Several years ago Michael Paske astutely noted that the market was undersupplied, hence the mail order sales to both individuals and catering establishments. The asparagus is cut, packed and despatched on the same day by first class letter post. The optimistic will not see any reason then—G.P.O. willing—why it should not arrive in perfect condition at your chosen address next day. The customers keep on returning so the system must work. A good many, private individuals as well as restaurateurs, get the special five kilo packs for freezing, the only way to prolong the pleasure.

May/June   asparagus.
All year   smoked salmon.
Open: mail order only.

HEBRON   Dyfed   MAP 2
Pengelli, Hebron, Whitland   TEL Hebron (099 47) 481

Take the Glandwr turning from the A478, twelve miles south of Cardigan.

Shrewdly, Chris Chaloner acquired three and a half acres of her family farm that had never been harmed by chemical farming techniques. Ms. Chaloner's land metamorphosis is not quite complete; the Soil Association's symbol is still eagerly awaited but as pesticides— artificial fertilisers too—have always been eschewed, her wholesale customers buy here confidently. Artlessly she admits to still being a novice and learning as she goes. Just now she is cultivating an interesting selection of vegetables and herbs.

All year   vegetables · herbs.
Midsummer   strawberries.

Open: daylight hours.

HENFIELD   West Sussex   Map 3
Barrow Hill Farms, Henfield   TEL Henfield (0273) 492733

A mile beyond Henfield village, the A2037 Shoreham road, and on a sharp bend.

Tim May and the Reynolds farm 160 acres of well-wooded land which yields logs for their use and for customers. Ideals here are high but the organic side—for what seem like sensible financial reasons—is slowly being developed. Barley is grown for their own cattle. Twenty-five acres are down to potatoes; only a small proportion of this crop meet an organic standard though all the other vegetables do. A thousand hens are kept free range. Philosophically their aim 'is to produce what is demanded rather than increasing surpluses'. Infinity Foods, Simple Supplies, Food for Friends and In the Pink—all in Brighton—take their produce.

All year   free range eggs · chickens—table ready, live for the back yard, or frozen for the freezer · goats' milk.
Summer/autumn   salad crops · vegetables (some into winter).

Open: daily, 9 to 7.

HORSMONDEN   Kent   Map 3
Small's Farm, Horsmonden   TEL Brenchley (089 272) 2519

On the B2162, three miles north of the A262 where it meets the A21 (north of Lamberhurst).

There are ready local takers for all of Mr. Orbach's limited production from this three-quarter acre kitchen garden, a similar area in an adjacent field and his Cox's and Tideman's Early Worcester apples in a small piece of orcharding. It is a firm requirement that orders must be first placed by telephone for collection by arrangement. Soil Association symbol holder.

July/Aug   gooseberries · raspberries.
Sep/Oct   apples.
May to Oct   courgettes · carrots · lettuce · radishes · beans · leeks · broccoli · pumpkins.

Open: telephone first; closed Nov—Feb.

HUISH EPISCOPI   Somerset   Map 2
Cracknell's Free Range Poultry Farm, Huish Episcopi, Langport
TEL Langport (0458) 250731

Off the B3153 one and a half miles east of Langport, from where the farm is signposted.

After 25 years rearing poultry and selling their free range eggs, Mr. Cracknell is well settled and enjoys a little glory from this seventeen acres. Candidly he puts it, 'All my poultry run out on grass, or primarily mud for six months of the year, from five weeks old until the day they turn up as chicken meat.' His ducks and geese, sheep and goats have equal freedom of movement, thriving on a regime entirely free of growth promoters or feed produced with the aid of artificials. Lamb, locally butchered, can be supplied, if ordered in advance. Chickens are sold by some of the local butchers and private grocers in Glastonbury, Street, Somerton and Yeovil, distinguishable by the Cracknell label.

All year   chickens · goats' milk · free range eggs · lambs to order.

Open; by arrangement, 9 to 5; closed Sun.

ISFIELD   East Sussex   MAP 3
Boathouse Farm, Isfield, Nr Uckfield   TEL Isfield (082 575) 302

Three miles south of Uckfield, east of the A22, and between the Old Ship Inn and Isfield Station.

There are those who claim the place gets its name because ships' timbers were used in its construction but it has never been proved. Reliably there is three-quarters of a mile of fishing at this Saxon holding in the valley of the Ouse from where Mr. Hill sends home-milled wholewheat flour and potatoes to Full of Beans in Lewes, Provender in Forest Hill and Brighton's Infinity Foods. Beef is from a suckler herd, Hereford cross with Simmental. Lamb is from a breeding flock of Border, Leicester and Suffolk. Arable ground is subject to a five year rotation to give spring barley, winter wheat and potatoes. Buckwheat will be an experiment shortly. Customers are welcome reasonable hours any day when they might even be tempted to take the holiday cottage and stay to fish. Soil Association symbol applied for.

All year   freshly ground wholemeal flour.
Autumn and winter   potatoes.
Spring and autumn   beef and lamb, to order only.

Open: daily.

LANGFORD BUDVILLE   Somerset   MAP 2
Bindon Home Farm, Langford Budville, Wellington
TEL Milverton (0823) 400644

West of the B3187 between Milverton and Wellington.

The Bindon Agricultural Collective continues to flourish after thirteen years on this 32 acre holding even though members come and go. Recently they set themselves higher standards and now use biodynamic techniques which finds favour with several London outlets like the Haelan Centre, Wholefoods, Bumblebees and Organic Farm Foods. The Demeter standard has yet to be achieved but hopes are high that this will be managed shortly. Supplies from the farm to order only.

All year   a large selection of vegetables · wholemeal flour stoneground to order.
Late summer/autumn   apples · plums.

Open: telephone before calling.

LEE BROCKHURST   Salop   MAP 6
The Qasid Stud, Moston Pool, Lee Brockhurst, Shrewsbury
TEL Lee Brockhurst (093 924) 695

On the A49, twelve miles from Shrewsbury and six miles from Whitchurch.

The name is taken from the Arabian horses kept on Dorothy Chambers' land, run as a holding since 1840 when the cottage was built, and to which visitors usually get conducted tours. Her champion sire was Mary Chipperfield's circus grey a few years ago. Poultry and pork are sold to order and if a customer only wants half a pig, Mrs. Chambers will find someone to take the other half. At any time there are thirty to forty goats to provide fairly certain milk supplies. All of Mrs. Chambers' animals are fed as much as possible from home-grown produce, and herbal leys or hay is bought in from organic sources. Closed all day Saturday. At other times it is sensible to check by telephone.

All year   pork · calf meat · chickens.
Most of year   goats' milk · fresh and frozen non-battery chicken · goose eggs · surplus vegetables.
Spring   kid meat.
Sep, Oct   damsons · apples · elderberries · surplus honey · herbs.

Open: weekdays, 9 to 5; closed Sat.

LEOMINSTER   Hereford and Worcester   Map 2
Willows Nurseries, Newtown Lane   TEL Leominster (0568) 4041

One step removed from being a food producer, Helen Woodley grows, organically of course, apple, pear, plum and cherry trees on different root stocks. 'It all depends upon how big you want your trees to grow. There are those who put them into hedgerows and for this something vigorous is essential to keep ahead of the hedgerow growth.' Otherwise most with small gardens, looking for an early fruit yield, will likely plump for something on a dwarfing stock. Helen Woodley gained some of her enthusiasms—and expertise—for self-sufficiency while working for the aficionado of the self-sufficiency movement John Seymour, on his West Wales farm. She sells from the nursery or the garden shop in Hay-on-Wye. She stocks a few of the old fashioned apples, the likes of Charles Ross and Sunset and for something more unusual she will put customers in touch with someone suitable.

Autumn through to spring   fruit trees.

Open: summer, Mon to Sat, 9.30 to 5; winter, Thur, Sat, 9.30 to 5.

LEWES   East Sussex   Map 3
Southerham Cottage Kitchen, Southerham   TEL Lewes (0273) 476391

Flirtations with the fresh and frozen vegetarian convenience food market did not pay off, that is in terms of the quality the Wimbush's were trying to achieve. With that experience behind them, their energies and minds are applied to the ewes' yoghurt and cheeses business. Mrs. Wimbush has developed a successful dairy technique distinguishing between the sheep and the goats. Some of the ewes' milk they buy in from Stuart Bell at Calne. Vegetables are grown to Soil Association standards. They distribute all their produce to retailers in Sussex some going to Infinity Foods in Brighton. No farmgate sales.

All year   ewes' milk and yoghurt.
Summer/autumn   vegetables.

Wholesale only.

LINTON   Hereford and Worcester   Map 2
Revells Fruit Farm, Linton, Ross-on-Wye   TEL Gorsley (098 982) 270

The Barters' fruits are all cold-pressed—apples, blackcurrants, blackberries and plums—frequently from deep frozen stocks which allows them to press fruit as they want it without recourse to less desirable means of preservation or extraction. All the juices are entirely free of additives, but not necessarily organically grown. A good deal of the fruit used comes from their own small 150 acre orchard. Long before they started pressing they were producing high grade dessert fruits; it is the second grade fruit which is used for juicing. The juice is normally a Cox and Bramley mix; another version is Golden apple juice made from Egremont russet apples only which gives the quite distinctive nutty flavour. A mixed drink could be Laxton's Fortune, most frequently blended with blackcurrant. They will not use Golden Delicious in any of their juices, on principle, even when English grown. Blackberry and plum juices are also partnered with a suitable apple.

Look for the juices in delicatessen, whole and health food shops. Juices are stored in oak casks stacked in a traditional barn and they are happy to show groups round.

All year fruit juices.

Wholesale only.

LLANDEILO Dyfed   MAP 2
Tyn Grug Farmhouse Cheeses, Tyn Grug Esgerdawe   TEL Pumpsaint (055 85) 400

Four miles south of Lampeter on the A482.

The Antipodean warmth of their birthplace now a distant memory, a cloistered exile a thousand feet up seems to suit brothers Dougal and Alex Campbell. The views are marvellous but with a rainfall like theirs there is not much choice but to stick with permanent grazings, and hope the scenery doesn't pall. It seems to have concentrated minds on cheese production, after a capricious start in engineering and Alpine climbs — sighting Gruyère at close quarters seems to have clinched matters. 'Farmhouse cheeses as we make them mean three things — unpasteurised milk, maturation in a proper rind and, what everyone does not seem to understand, milk always produced on the same farm. It's the consistent milk quality which gives the inimitable quality. Single farm milk,' insists Dougal, 'is vital.' Naturally everything is of entirely organic standard. Cattle are a mixture of Ayrshire and Jersey, all of whose milk goes into cheese-making. 'For us, cheese as a speciality has been a means of making a small farm viable. But it is an everyday cheese which our customers buy in chunks — normally a Cheddar or Caerphilly — occasionally a soft cheese.' From their thriving farmgate, nearly half of the produce is sold during the summer to passing trade. Watch out for the cheese at Curds and Whey in Swansea Market, Glynhynod Farm Cheese in Carmarthen Market, or Dr. Rosy Thomson's Pulse Wholefoods in Cardiff.

All year Cheddar cheese.
Nov to Aug Caerphilly cheese.

Open: telephone to check before calling.

LLANDYSSUL Dyfed   MAP 2
Bryn Saron Farm Produce, Saron   TEL Velindre (0559) 370405

Between the villages of Saron and Rhos on the A484 Newcastle Emlyn/Carmarthen road.

Anne and Charles Griffin are experiencing the problems of many who have the produce but are in the wrong place to find enough local retail customers to make a living. They stick rigidly to the organic principle and they produce meat which they regard as a by-product of this rotation. Garlic here is something of a speciality, both in the fresh and dried powder forms. Mail order enquiries are welcome. As for vegetables they have a wide choice to offer, the season extended with growing tunnels. Farmgate sales or deliveries at any reasonable time but for the former a prior telephone call is desirable. Interested visitors are welcome too but expect to be handed a hoe, unless you have come to camp here or rent the holiday caravan.

All year free range eggs · vegetables · garlic powder · strung garlic.
June, July, Aug soft fruits · in due course there could be top fruits too.
Occasionally meat.

Open: please telephone before calling.

LONGMORN Grampian   MAP 7
Elgin Springs, Longmorn, by Elgin   TEL Longmorn (034 386) 252

The Laigh of Moray is fertile, but the climate fierce, so, since arriving here seven years ago the Bensons sensibly make good use of glasshouses, polythene tunnels and cold frames to prolong their otherwise short, sometimes chilly, summer seasons. The outcome is lettuce, courgettes, cucumbers and pumpkins in a district where they would not normally thrive. Year round there is always a good selection of other vegetables on offer: parsnips, artichokes, curly kale, broccoli, potatoes—early and main crop—together with conventional standbys such as leeks, broad beans, cabbages, onions and the inevitable turnips. In that difficult month of May they start up here with their lettuce. A small herd of British Saanan goats provide fresh milk, some of which goes into making cheese and yoghurt. David Benson prefers large orders at the farmgate but he always looks forward to meeting people and arranging supplies grown entirely without chemical sprays or artificial fertilisers. The Soil Association symbol is carried.

All year   goats' milk · cheese · yoghurt.
According to season   a wide selection of vegetables.

Open: telephone before calling.

LOUTH   Lincolnshire   Map 6
The Old Railway House, Stewton   TEL South Cockerington (050 782) 533

Two and a half miles east of Louth, down Stewton Lane.

Dorothy Mansfield comes from a family where they have always grown organically and they began by producing their own food. Since 1972 they have had this holding, producing vegetables in season, often for people with special dietary needs. They cannot make a living out of it but it is something they strongly believe in. Everything is freshly picked for each customer. All to Soil Association standards.

All year   free range eggs · vegetables according to season.

Open: every day; telephone before calling.

MELMERBY   Cumbria   Map 6
New House Farm, Melmerby, Penrith   TEL Langwathby (076 881) 508

On the A686 midway between Penrith and Alston.

In another daring enterprise in a tough district more familiarly known for sheep runs, snowfalls and fatstock raising, Michael Faith has proved that hard labour is working, after ten years in office, but it usually means protective polytunnels until there is a chance of some fitful English sunshine. Not everything is organic. Some crops are sprayed with a herbicide—never more than once in a season—the remainder, about an acre (as much as he can weed) is entirely spray-free. Mr. Faith's season begins with courgettes and lettuce in June. His problem, he explains, is that he cannot keep up with demand, 'as not many are on to the vegetable job at all round here'. What is not sold at the farmgate goes through the Penrith shop, the Village Bakery in Angel Lane run in conjunction with Liz and Andrew Whitley in Melmerby (see entry). Here, during the summer, everything is organic, and sells because it looks good and fresh, not because it is identified as organic. His produce can be found in the Penrith shop and Brampton market on Wednesdays. Otherwise strictly by previous appointment at the farm.

All year   full range of vegetables.

Open: by appointment only.

MONIAIVE   Dumfriesshire   Map 7
Craigdarroch Gardens, Woodhead Cottage   TEL Moniaive (084 82) 406

Moniaive is 16 miles north west of Dumfries, the Gardens two and a half miles beyond on the B729.

Tim and Fabienne Rapsey sell their output as organic produce in Dumfries and in Glasgow but in the village they are more simply vegetables. Before moving to Scotland they gained valuable experience working the kitchen gardens for the nuns at Stanbrook Abbey. Enlightened parents with young children are among their most devoted customers. Most vegetables are grown in season, along with some herbs and soft fruits. Polytunnels have recently been introduced to extend the season. Everything on these six acres is grown on compost or composted manure and, as far as possible, they work to biodynamic principles. Callers any weekday between 9 and 6 but only by prior appointment.

All year   35 to 45 varieties of vegetables and herbs, according to season. Late winter to spring supplies are more limited.
July, Aug   raspberries.

Open: weekdays; telephone before calling.

NASH   Buckinghamshire   MAP 3
Holywell Farm, Thornton Road, Nash, Milton Keynes
TEL Milton Keynes (0908) 501769

On the B4033, a mile north of the A421 Bletchley to Buckingham road.

Chris and Shirley Phillips now crop 20 acres, increasing annually, using entirely organic methods, after leaving behind a larger family farm. A stone mill has been installed in the loft of one of the traditional farm buildings where the grain is milled to order. Five types of flour are offered — 100 % plain, 100 % self-raising, both in 85 % grades too, and, in addition, a 100 % fine milled plain. All can be made from organic, conservation grade, or conventionally grown high-protein wheat. Pigs are kept to make use of the waste products from the mill, and even the cattle and sheep are only fed farm produced food. A quarter beast is the smallest meat order. Best to telephone before calling. Shop outlets for flour include Wholefoods in Bedford, Rushton and Kettering, Four Seasons in Luton and the Daily Bread Co-operative in Northampton.

All year   various grades of flour, using three wheat types.
Usually available but essential to confirm before required   beef · pork · lamb — all organic.

Open: check before calling.

NEWBURY   Berkshire   MAP 3
North Sydmonton Nursery, North Sydmonton   TEL Headley (063 523) 317

Seven miles south of Newbury between the A34 and A339, signposted Ecchinswell.

From his three acres of crops (half an acre under glass), Peter Rawlinson supplies buying groups in Oxford, Basingstoke, Alton, Farnham and Farnborough, with whom he will gladly put people in touch. Herbs and local honey he carries as regular lines and goats' and green top milk are available to order. Mainly summer crops are grown with a variety of twenty-five or more vegetables during the season, slightly less choice during the winter. But everything is organic, sometimes biodynamic, almost exclusively to Soil Association standards. Do not expect the likes of cucumbers and tomatoes as a result, out of season, although he regularly imports citrus and pears — the unsprayed variety — from North Africa. 'If we cannot provide a variety of produce we cannot advocate eat organic, so during the winter we buy in from other organic growers.' Peter Rawlinson has a benevolent attitude towards his fellow growers. 'It is not an easy way to earn a living and I like to think I manage to pay a little over the going rate.'

All year   goats' and green top milk to order · non-battery eggs · vegetables in variety.
Seasonally   strawberries · raspberries · gooseberries · blackberries · currants.

Open: summer, daily; winter, most days.

NEWNHAM   Gloucestershire   Map 2
The Camphill Village Trust, Oaklands Park   TEL Newnham (059 445) 235

There can be lean times in the year but apart from June and July this West Country Trust 'village' usually manages to offer regular vegetable supplies. Although deep in Gloucestershire, quite a lot of their produce gets through to London, to private buying groups, to the Rudolf Steiner organisation and to the London Bio-Dynamic Food Association. Mr. Grundmann, with a great deal of dedication, directs the horticultural operation from the 'village' and likes to feel they: 'grow everything that will grow in England—it is the variety which makes it work so well.' As a matter of courtesy they will be seeking the Organic Growers symbol, but to them it scarcely matters as those who buy already do so with confidence. Vegetables are limited to about ten acres at any one time on this 150 acre farm (including the old kitchen garden) part of a very wide rotation which minimises pests and diseases. Crops are a real and satisfying project for many of the mentally handicapped adults being helped towards independence and integration within these communities. Everything is grown according to biodynamic principles.

Aug to May   vegetables in variety.
Aug/Sep   plums.
Aug to Mar   apples.

Wholesale only.

NORTH SCARLE   Lincolnshire   Map 6
Red House Farm, Spalford Lane   TEL Spalford (052 277) 224

One mile east of the A1133, approximately eight miles north of Newark upon Trent.

There is nothing remotely ambiguous about Alan and Jean Jones' philosophy towards the quality of farm foods, either on their farm or in the shop. When you are placing your order, Stephen Foster, who does the butchering, will solicitously probe for intimate details: what is the size of your ideal Sunday joint, if this is still a Sabbath lunch-time ritual in your household? Or, how many chops do you want in that bag for a quick supper? Or maybe the capacity of your favourite pie dish? Farming policy at the Red House is spelt out on a specially printed leaflet for all to see. Second best only to some Virgilian landscape, beasts are turned out to graze in spring, summer and autumn, and all their livestock are fed traditional foods. When not outdoors they are bedded on straw. Cockerel purchased at four weeks old (no guarantees before this) are fed a further three months on additive-free feed prior to being offered up for the table. Eggs are from hens similarly fed. Sometimes neighbouring farmers rear stock on their behalf, but always to the additive-free system. Mr. and Mrs. Jones can be quite scathing about modern methods adopted on the majority of farms to save labour, repress disease caused by overcrowding or to tenderise the meat. By the time it gets into the farm shop their beef will have hung for fourteen days to mature naturally in the traditional way. Afterwards it is always cut and packed to individual customer requirements. 'Sausages and haislets are done without fat retainers or so-called safe additives used by most butchers to keep production costs down, increase shelf life and make them appear meaty in spite of a substantial fat content.' Flavourings are all natural herbs; artificial colouring and preservatives, and the textured vegetable extenders firmly rejected. Sausage rolls and Cornish pasties are made to order using organic wholemeal flour. No order is too small, be it a chop or a few sausages. Normally their meat is packed and frozen ready to travel several hundred miles, if required. Everything is sold retail from the farm for personal collection or delivery by road and rail. They are always closed the first week in June and, fortifying themselves for the Christmas onslaught, the first weekend in December.

All year   pork · beef · lamb.
Sep to Dec   chickens · free range eggs (limited winter supplies).

Open: daily, 9 to 12.30, 1.30 to 5; Fri until 7.

PEMBRIDGE   Hereford and Worcester   MAP 2
Dunkerton's Cider Company, Hays Head, Luntley   TEL Pembridge (054 47) 653

Luntley is south of the A44 Leominster to Kington road, at Pembridge.

Cider here is sold from 40 gallon oak casks lining the walls of the Dunkertons' old half-timbered corn barn. One impressed visitor reported, 'It is the equivalent of doing a sherry tasting in Spain.' Susie and Ivor Dunkerton specialise in the strong, full-bodied ciders made from Foxwhelp, Binet Rouge, Yarlington Mill, Cider Ladies Finger and the unique Kingston Black cider apples. These increasingly rare old varieties are pressed separately and blended according to their individual flavours and qualities—that is tannin, sharpness and sugar content. Final blends are strong and aromatic. No water is added, the original specific gravity not less than 1,050—sometimes a great deal more. More apples are bought in from neighbouring Pembridge Farms, other small producers with varieties only found in the district and where sprays never go. There are casks of single apple types taking advantage of the individual character of an apple like Goddard and, of course, Kingston Black. Perry is a sideline, from delicious fruit in an old orchard where vigorous saplings are in the wings, waiting to take over. The matured juice, in four degrees of sweetness, is offered bottled or draught, and for the latter they will fill your own gallon jars or five gallon kegs. Outlets are mainly local, often through wholefood shops.

Open: summer, Mon to Sat, 10 to 7; Sun, 12 to 2; winter, Mon to Fri, 4 to 7, Sat, 10 to 7; please telephone to check availability.

PENRYN   Cornwall   MAP 2
Trenance Fruit Growers, Trenance Round Ring   TEL Falmouth (0326) 74800

May Day, depending a little on the weather, will likely see the start of the Browns' long strawberry season, extended with the aid of polytunnels. Before this, starting in February, there will have been rhubarb. Raspberries follow and by mid-summer an abundance of runner beans. June to October is the serious vegetable season when they can usually offer 'a little bit of everything'. Mr. and Mrs. Brown would never dream of buying in fertilisers, so the Soil Association symbol is being sought. Farmgate sales account for most of their produce but some finds its way into Georges, the Truro wholesaler.

All year   goats' milk · free range eggs.
February   rhubarb.
May onwards   strawberries · vegetables.
June   raspberries.
Late summer   honey.

Open: weekdays, 9 to 5; closed Sun.

POTTON   Bedfordshire   MAP 3
Mr. Brookman, 83 Sutton Mill Road, Potton, Sandy   TEL Potton (0767) 260284

Five miles east of the A1 at Sandy where the B1040 and B1042 intersect.

In a traditional growing district whose chief and only claim to renown is growing vegetables for London, Mr. Brookman intensively cultivates his 15 acres organically. He has worked this way for over twenty years, since being persuaded to try by a Welwyn fruit and vegetable merchant, who was at that time searching in vain for supplies for the then infant Arjuna (see entry) in Cambridge. Potatoes, tomatoes and cucumbers are not Mr. Brookman's favourite crops but bar these he manages to offer a representative selection which still find their way—bearing his name—into Cambridge, the remainder to Organic Farm Foods.

All year   vegetables, especially roots and greenstuffs.

No farmgate sales.

PURLEIGH   Essex   MAP 3
Mill Farm, Purleigh, Chelmsford   TEL Malden (0621) 828280

Five miles south of Malden just off the B1010.

'We grow for those who appreciate the benefits of living with an organic system,' and, inundated with enquiries for their vegetables, the modest adjunct to Helen and Christopher Goldsmith's small dairy farm promises unlimited growth. Their small gently sloping fields on this neck of land between the Blackwater and the Crouch otherwise support sheep and goats, all part of their grand design for a self-sufficient lifestyle. Helen and Christopher manage to cope with a wide range of vegetables to meet their own and general local needs in shops and cafés. It is rare to find either of them without a hoe in their hands during the hectic summer months so regretfully they have to insist that farmgate sales are only by prior arrangement.

All year   goats' cheese · yoghurt · vegetables, but better supplies in summer.
Sometimes   free range eggs.
July to Sep   lamb.

Open: please telephone to arrange visit.

TOTNES   Devon   MAP 2
Charles Riggs, Western House   TEL Totnes (0803) 862066

One mile west of town centre south of A385 in village of Western.

In six acres of garden, some ornamental, Mr. Riggs grows quite a lot of food, some of it root vegetables but mostly salad crops and self-pick strawberries and raspberries. Everything is organically grown and has been since they started ten years ago. Produce is sold daily from stalls in Totnes and Newton Abbot markets along with the crops of others well known to him. Kohlrabi, capsicums, chillis, melons, are some of the less usual items which succeed in this gentle climate. Not all of the stock on the stall is organic—citrus for instance are bought in—but keep a look out for the distinctive labels of which customers speak approvingly and the competitive prices. Produce with green labels are organically grown, the white are not.

Open: produce sold in Totnes market on Fri and Newton Abbot market, Mon to Sat.

OTHER RECOMMENDED
GROWERS

Bickington Oliver Bosence Oxenham Farm Sigford Newton Abbot Devon
TEL (062 682) 609 *Telephone beforehand.*
Billington Staffordshire Organic Growers Newhaven Farm Stafford
TEL (0785) 780253 *Open Fri Sat 9 to 5 from July.*
Broome H. and T. Clement 2 Cottage Farm Stourbridge Worcestershire
TEL (0562) 700147 *Open Fri Sat Sun 10 to 3 or by appointment.*
Cuckfield Laines Organic Farm 47 Newbury Lane West Sussex
TEL (0444) 452663 *Open daily 9 to 6.*
East Dereham David Simmons 2 Scarning Fen Norfolk
TEL (0362) 5947 *Telephone for appointment.*
Ffostrasol Glynhynod Organic Farmers Llandyssul Dyfed
TEL (023 975) 528 *Open daily 10 to 7.*
Glaisdale Giles and Mary Heron Bank House Farm Whitby North Yorkshire
TEL (0947) 87297 *Open daily.*
Glasbury-on-Wye Mrs. D. E. Leitch Wye View Powys via Hereford Hereford and Worcester
TEL (049 74) 354 *Open daily but please telephone first.*
Hatherop Hatherop Gardens Cirencester Gloucestershire
TEL (028575) 326 *Open Thur to Sun 9 to 5.*
Lampeter Patrick Holden Rwllhwernen Fawr Llangybi Dyfed
TEL (057 045) 244 *Open any time.*
Llangeitho Aeron Park Organic Produce Aeron Park Tregaron Dyfed
TEL (097 423) 272 *Open Sun to Sat 9 to 5, closed Tue.*
Llanrhystud David Frost Nursery and Market Garden Tynyrhelyg Dyfed
TEL (097 46) 364 *Open daily 9 to 5.30.*
Malpas Oakcroft Gardens Cross Hill Cheshire
TEL (0948) 860213 *Open anytime.*
Marazion Justin Brooke Chymorvah Vean Cornwall
TEL (0736) 710468 *Open anytime.*
Market Drayton Ford Hall A. Hollins Ford Hall Farm Salop
TEL (063 083) 255 *Open anytime arranged by telephone.*
Mayfield Flintan Farm Enterprises Ltd Clayton Farmhouse Newick Lane East Sussex
TEL (0435) 873476 *Open daily.*
Minto Minto Kirkcudbright Scotland
TEL (055 77) 331 *Open daily—no set times.*
Navan Blackcastle Organic Farm Blackcastle Co. Meath Eire
TEL 046 23363 *Open daily 10 to 6, closed 1 to 2, Sun 3 to 6.*
Newbury Howard Payton and Helen Suttill Beeches Cottage Snelsmore Common Berkshire
TEL (0635) 248606 *Enquiries 8 to 10.*
Newcastle Emlyn Allan Mason Pentre Farm Pentrecagel Dyfed
TEL (0559) 371026 *Open daily.*
New Holland The Poplars Pig Poultry Produce Peploe Lane Barrow-on-Humber South Humberside
TEL (0469) 30180 *Open most of the time.*
North Willingham Ella's Dairy Sandby Lane Farm Market Rasen Lincolnshire
TEL (067 383) 259 *Open by arrangement.*

Nottingham Stonebridge City Farm Stonebridge Road St. Anns
TEL (0602) 505113 *Open daily 9 to 5.*
Oswestry Anna Doggart Organic Vegetables The Poplars Gwern-Y-Brenin Salop
TEL (0691) 652166 *Open weekdays telephone 8 to 8.*
Pattingham Grange Cultivations Grange Farm Hollies Lane Staffordshire
TEL (0902) 700248 *Open collection by telephone order.*
Peaslake Barn Field Organic Produce Franksfield Guildford
TEL (0483) 277127 *Open spring, summer, autumn.*
Pentre Bach Nick and Margaret Smyth Llwyngwril Gwynedd
TEL (0341) 250294 *Open any reasonable time, preferably with telephone call in advance.*
Pen-y-Bont John and Jenny White Organic Smallholders Mountpleasant Carmarthen
Dyfed
TEL (099 48) 315 *Open Sun Wed telephone first, Mon Tue Thur Fri 10 to 5.*
Pilling Blair's Low Carr Nursery Head Dykeln Preston Lancashire
TEL (039 130) 471 *Open only by prior arrangement.*
Prees J. H. and J. Gunton Green Gorse Wood Whitchurch Road Salop
Open Whitchurch Market Fri 8 to 12.
Pwllheli L. and A. Porter Hafodwen Garden Farm Llangwnnadl Gwynedd
Open Mon to Sat anytime.
Radwinter M. F. Ridsdill Smith New House Farm Saffron Walden Essex
TEL (079 987) 211 *Open daily July to Feb.*
Roberts Bridge Scragoak Farm Brightling Road East Sussex
TEL (042 482) 364 *Open Fri to Sun 10 to 5 May to Oct.*
Roche Moorview Strawberry Farm Higher Tresaize St. Austell Cornwall
TEL (0726) 890682 *Open May to early Aug 10 to 8, rest of year Fri Sat Sun 10 to 5.*
Rossinver Eden Plants Eden Co. Leitrim Eire
Open summer 9.30 to 6, winter 10 to 6, closed Wed Sun.
St. Martin Keveral Farm Community Keveral Farm by Looe Cornwall
TEL (050 35) 215 *Open daily—telephone first.*
Scaynes Hill Harry Jenken Ham Lane Farm Cottage Nr Haywards Heath West Sussex
TEL (044 486) 544 *Open 7 days a week all day.*
Sedlescombe Burspin Fruit Growers Battle Sussex
TEL (0424) 751507 *Open daily 9 to 5.*
Sharpthorne Old Plawhatch Farm Old Plawhatch East Grinstead Sussex
TEL (0342) 510857 *Open daily.*
Shepton Montague Montague Organic Gardens Orchard House Wincanton Somerset
TEL (0749) 813319 *Open Apr to Jan.*
Sherborne Organic Growers Beer Hackett Claypitt Farm Beer Hackett Nr Sherborne
Dorset
TEL (0935) 872060 *Open daily but telephone call first.*
Sligo Tir na Nog 4 Wine Street Ireland
TEL 071 62752 *Open Mon to Sat 9.30 to 6.*
South Gorley Hockeys—Naturally Newtown Farm Fordingbridge Hampshire
TEL (0425) 52542 *Open Mon to Sat 9 to 6, Fri 9 to 7.*
South Kilworth Chevelswarde Organic Growers The Belt Lutterworth Leicestershire
TEL (085 881) 309 *Open daily 8 to 9.*
South Petherton F. M. and W. J. Blake Flakdrayton Farm Somerset
TEL (0460) 41062/40855 *Open Wed Thur Sun pm, Mon Tue Fri Sat 10 to 1, 2 to 6,
winter Fri Sat.*
Staplecross Pine Ridge (Organic) Vineyard Robertsbridge East Sussex
TEL (058 083) 715 *Open daily 10 to 6.*
Swardeston Duffield and Hughes Organic Vegetables Mangreen Norwich
TEL (0508) 70295 *Open Mon to Sun 9 to 8.*
Tarbert Achnacarnan Natural Foods Achnacarnan Argyll
TEL (088 02) 440 *Open any reasonable time.*

Thanington Without Orchard View Iffin Lane Canterbury
TEL (0227) 60680 *Open Wed Thur Sat Sun 10 to 5.*
Thornbury Muttons Organic Growers Elm Grove Bromyard Herefordshire
TEL (088 54) 204 *Open Mon to Sat 9 to 6.*
Tintern Medhope Organic Growers Chepstow Gwent
TEL (029 18) 797 *Open daily all day.*
Tynron R. L. Malpas Kirkland Tynron by Thornhill Dumfriesshire
TEL (084 82) 272 *Open daily 9 to 5.*
Uckinghall Rivendell Nursery Gloucestershire
TEL (068 46) 3473 *Open Mon to Fri 9 to 5.*
Wadhurst Old Granary Organic Farm Old Granary Farm Woodsgreen East Sussex
TEL (089 288) 3302 *Open daily 9.30 to 9.*
Westleton Desmond and Kate Brick Kiln Farm Nr Saxmundham Suffolk
TEL (072 873) 600 *Open daylight hours all year.*
Wexford Inisglas Trust Ltd Crossabeg Eire
TEL 28226 053 *Open 10 to 6 except Thur Sun.*
Winkleigh Woodroberts Woodroberts Farm Devon
TEL (083 783) 301 *Open all day, phone first.*
Wisbech St. Mary M. J. Feeney The Elms High Road Cambridgeshire
TEL (094 58) 335 *Open daylight hours.*
Wrexham Mwyaren Wholefoods 19 Bridge Street Clwyd Cymru
TEL (0978) 362046 *Open Mon to Sat 9.15 to 5.30.*
Writtle Anastassis Organic Produce The Causeway Highwood Road Essex
Open July to Sep Mon to Sat 8 to 8, winter Mon to Sat 9 to 5.

MILLS

ALFORD **Alford Five Sailed Mill** Lincolnshire County Council East Street Lincolnshire
TEL (0522) 29931 *An early 19th century windmill.* Sales *stoneground wholemeal flour.*
Visitors *3rd Sat in month July Aug Sep and Bank Holidays. Groups by arrangement.*

AYLESBURY **Springhill Bakery** Gatehouse Close Buckinghamshire
TEL (0296) 25333 *GYO domestic stone mills, hand and electric powered.* Sales *organic grade—Soil Association standard grain · stoneground flour · bread · wholemeal · bran · rye · country malt · pumpernickel · sprouted grain loaves.* Visitors *guided visits by arrangement.*

BARDWELL **The Windmill** Bury St. Edmunds
TEL (0359) 51331 *A tower windmill of 1823.* Sales *stoneground wholewheat · rye · unbleached white flours.* Visitors *conditions permitting.*

BIGGLESWADE **Jordans** Holme Mills Bedfordshire
TEL (0767) 318222 Sales *some organic flours · wholemeal, 85% extraction and strong white · muesli · crunchy bars.* Visitors *Wed after 5 by appointment.*

BLAIR ATHOLL **The Mill** Perthshire
A restored 18th century watermill. Sales *stoneground wholemeal flour.*

BOGNOR REGIS **Elbridge Organic Farm Mill** Chichester Road West Sussex
TEL (0243) 822914 *A modern stoneground electric-powered mill.* Sales *organic grade stoneground wholemeal flour · organic beef · vegetables · free range eggs.* Visitors *customers reasonable hours, groups by arrangement.*

BOTLEY **Botley Flour Mill Company** Botley Mills Southampton Hampshire
TEL (048 92) 2202 *Water turbine driven mill.* Sales *trade and 12 kg packs retail stoneground wholemeal flour.* Visitors *groups by arrangement.*

BROMSGROVE **Danzey Green Mill** Avoncroft Museum of Buildings Stoke Heath Worcestershire
TEL (0527) 31363 *Post windmill from Tamworth-in-Arden.* Sales *stoneground wheat, from a mill run as conditions permit.* Visitors *daily 10.30 to 5.30 1st Mar to end Nov (or dusk, if earlier).*

BURWASH **The Water Mill** Bateman's Etchingham East Sussex
TEL (0435) 882302 *Restored mill with overshot water-wheel.* Sales *very limited supplies ground each Saturday and sold to house visitors (National Trust).* Visitors *Mar to May and Oct daily ex. Fri 2 to 6, June to Sep Mon to Thur 11 to 6, Sat Sun 2 to 6.*

CASTLEFORD **Allinson** Queens Mills Aire Street West Yorkshire
TEL (093 23) 41133 *Largest stone grinding flour mill in world.* Sales *stoneground wholemeal and 81% extraction flour only.* Visitors *individuals by arrangement.*

CHELMSFORD **W. & H. Marriage & Son Chelmer Mills** New Street Essex
TEL (0245) 354455 *A late 19th century roller mill with some traditional French burr stones.* Sales *trade—stoneground wholemeal and 81% extraction.* Visitors *groups by arrangement.*

COALEY **Coaley Mill** Dursley Gloucestershire
TEL (0453) 89376 *13th century, rebuilt in 1977, driven by modern stonegrinding equipment.* Sales *some organic flours, wholesale.* Visitors *by arrangement only.*

CREWKERNE **C. G. Lockyer & Son Clapton Mill** Somerset
TEL (0460) 73124 *Water-powered mill dating from 1870.* Sales *stoneground flour year round.* Visitors *welcome but telephone in advance.*

DISS **Adrian Colman Garboldisham Windmill** Norfolk
TEL (095 381) 593 *18th century post windmill still under restoration. No sails yet!* Sales *cereal products year round · flour · cracked wheat, oatmeal, oatflakes are usually organic.* Visitors *Mon to Fri 9 to 1.*

DRIFFIELD **John Rymer Southern Mill** Southburn Farm North Humberside
TEL (0377) 89264   Sales *stoneground wholemeal flour.*   Visitors *by appointment only.*

EAST LINTON **Preston Mill** Nr Dunbar East Lothian
TEL (062 086) 426   *A water-powered oatmeal mill in working order but not producing flour.*
Visitors *Sun 2 to 6.30, Mon to Sat 10 to 12.30, 2 to 6.30, closes Oct to Mar 4.30.*

GREAT ALNE **O. J. Gray and Sons Great Alne Mills** Nr Alcester Warwickshire
TEL (078 981) 341   *Watermill and turbines restored to use in 1978.*   Sales *organic wholemeal
flour.*   Visitors *Apr to Oct Sat Sun 2 to 5, Teas.*

HAM **Michael and Clare Marriage Doves Farm Mill** Marlborough Wiltshire
TEL (04884) 374   *A modern mill started in 1978 in an old tithe barn.*   Sales *best known for
organic stoneground wholemeal flour, but 22 other types of cereal year round. Soil Association
Standard.*   Visitors *not open.*

HAMPTON LUCY **Charlecote Mill** Nr Stratford-upon-Avon Warwickshire
TEL (0789) 842072   *A working water-powered mill.*   Sales *wholemeal stoneground flour,
some to organic standard; the latter is sold to Brown's Bakery, Avenue Industrial Estate,
Stratford-upon-Avon who bake for several health food shops; flour sold to individuals in 12.5 kg,
25 kg and 32 kg sacks; sometimes bread for sale.*   Visitors *groups by appointment; public
opening on about 30 days in year.*

HARBERTONFORD **Martin Watts Crowdy Mill** Totnes Devon
TEL (080 423) 340   *Water-powered cornmill using original millstones driven by two water-
wheels.*   Sales *stoneground flour year round · wheat and organic rye in packs, sizes from 1.5 kg
upwards; available also in local shops.*   Visitors *flour available weekdays only 9 to 4.30.*

HARMER HILL **S. Mayall and Son Pimhill Mill** Lea Hall Shrewsbury Salop
TEL (0939 290) 342   Sales *stoneground home-grown wholewheat · flour year round · usually
bread too · Sep to Apr, organically grown potatoes, carrots, onions and cabbage.*   Visitors *shop
sales Mon to Fri 8 to 5; mill tours by arrangement.*

HEADLEY **J. Ellis & Sons Headley Mill** Bordon Hampshire
TEL (042 03) 2031   *A working watermill on the river Wey with four pairs of stones.*
Sales *stoneground wholemeal flour year round.*   Visitors *Mon to Fri 9 to 5, Sat 9 to 12.30;
tours of the mill by arrangement.*

HELE BAY **C. L. Lovell Hele Mill** Ilfracombe Devon
TEL (0271) 63162   *A restored working watermill dating back to 1525.*   Sales *four grades of
stoneground wholemeal flour in fine, medium, coarse, and granary grades · kibbled wheat ·
wheatflakes.*   Visitors *Mon to Fri 10 to 5, Sun 2 to 5 from Easter to end of Oct.*

LITTLE SALKELD **Nicolas Jones The Watermill** Penrith Cumbria
TEL (076 881) 523   *A working 18th century corn mill.*   Sales *stoneground organically grown
wholemeal and 85% flour · organic 100% and 85% flour · granarius · cracked wheat · wheat
bran · oat products · muesli · bran breakfast cereals; tearoom, millshop coarse milling, baking and
wholefoods.*   Visitors *Easter to end Oct Sun Mon Wed Thur 2.30 to 5.30.*

LLANSANTFFRAID GLAS CONWY **Felin Isaf Millers Felin Isaf Mill** Colwyn Bay Clwyd
*A recently restored watermill. There is uncertainty about the future of the milling side, as the mill
has changed hands. Until recently, producing wholemeal and 85% extraction flours from locally
grown wheat. Produce was sold in the mill shop where refreshments were also available.*

LONG NEWTON **John Lister Shipton Mill** Tetbury Gloucestershire
TEL (0666) 53620   *A recently restored corn mill.*   Sales *traditional stoneground organically
grown Canadian strong wheats mostly sold to the bakery trade.*

MARLBOROUGH **Wilton Windmill Society Wilton Windmill** Nr Great Bedwyn
Wiltshire
TEL (0672) 870573   *A fully restored 150-year-old working windmill, breezes permitting.*
Sales *usually freshly ground wholemeal flour at weekends.*   Visitors *Easter to end Sep Sun
Bank Holidays.*

MERSHAM **Mrs. G. Christiansen Swanton Mill** Ashford Kent
TEL (0233) 72223   *A watermill in a 3 acre garden reinstated in 1975.*   Sales *organically
grown stoneground flour using wheat from Perrycourt Farm, near Canterbury.*
Visitors *Apr to Oct Sat Sun 3 to 6.*

MILNTHORPE **Heron Corn Mill—Beetham Trust** Heron Corn Mill Cumbria

TEL (0524) 734858   *A water-powered mill possibly dating from 1220.*   Sales *small quantities of stoneground wholemeal flour to visitors.*   Visitors *Apr to Sep daily except Mon 11 to 12.15, 2 to 5.*

NAFFERTON **Peter Thirsk Station Flour Mills** Near Great Driffield North Humberside
TEL (0377) 44267   *Recently installed stone mill wheels removed from a Warrington mill.*   Sales *stoneground flour.*   Visitors *groups by arrangement.*

NEWBRIDGE **Millers Damsel Enterprises Lower Mill** Yarmouth Isle of Wight
TEL (0983 78) 228   *A traditional mill now operated by a water turbine.*   Sales *stoneground flour · biscuits with lower than normal fat and sugar content.*   Visitors *by prior arrangement only.*

NEWCASTLE EMLYN **Felin Geri Mill** Cwm-cou Dyfed
TEL (0239) 710810   *A working watermill dating back to 1604.*   Sales *stoneground wholemeal flour · organically grown vegetables are used in the mill café · unpasteurised milk during summer months.*   Visitors *Easter to Oct daily 10 to 6.*

NEWNHAM BRIDGE **Dr. R. Lear Newnham Mill** Tenbury Worcestershire
TEL (058 479) 445   *Driven by an undershot 14' water-wheel and using French burr stones.*   Sales *stoneground wholemeal flour.*   Visitors *Easter to Sep Sat 2 to 5, Sun 10 to 5; flour sold year round by appointment.*

NEWTON FLOTMAN **William C. Duffield Saxlingham Thorpe Mill** Nr Norwich Norfolk
TEL (0508) 470661   *Dating in part from 1869 and on the river Tas, there is a large modern extension but two pairs of 4½' diameter French burr stones have been retained.*   Sales *stoneground wholemeal flour, trade only.*   Visitors *by appointment only.*

OVER **Mr. G. C. Wilson The Mill** Nr St. Ives Cambridgeshire
TEL (0954) 30742   *A restored windmill.*   Sales *stoneground locally grown non-organic, and 75% and 80% extract rates normally available too · customers own grain ground.*   Visitors *flour sales and tours by prior arrangement.*

PENTREFOELAS **Mrs. Margaret Horsfield Foelas Watermill** Clwyd
TEL (069 05) 603   *Water-powered mill.*   Sales *organically grown wholemeal flour · rye · barley flour.*   Visitors *Mon to Fri 10 to 5.*

PORTHYRHYD **Melin Maesdulais Watermill** Carmarthen Dyfed
TEL (026 786) 472   *Water-powered overshot water-wheel driving traditional French burr millstones.*   Sales *wholemeal, organically grown, stoneground flour · rye · 85% extraction rate wheat · seed flour · seed and herb flour · seed spice flour · bread and cakes baked on the premises.*   Visitors *Easter to end Sep daily 10 to 6, tearoom.*

PRISTON **Peter Hopwood Priston Mill** Nr Bath Avon
TEL (0225) 23894   *Driven by a 21' diameter pitchback water-wheel possibly dating from the 1850's. The mill is at the centre of a picturesque 300 acre farm growing semi-organic wheat; original millstones.*   Sales *wholemeal stoneground semi-organic flour year round.*   Visitors *daily 2.15 to 5 except Wed Thur; groups other times by arrangement.*

RAVENGLASS **Muncaster Mill** Cumbria
TEL (065 77) 232   *An old manorial mill serving the Muncaster Estate. Present building dates from 1700. Driven by overshot water-wheel.*   Sales *stoneground organic wheat products to which oatmeal will be added shortly; year round.*   Visitors *daily except Sat Apr May Sep 11 to 5, June July Aug 10 to 6.*

RETFORD **North Leverton Windmill Company** North Leverton Windmill Nottinghamshire
TEL (0427) 880662   *An early 19th century windmill.*   Sales *stoneground wholemeal flour · cracket wheat · bran.*   Visitors *the mill is worked irregularly and it is best to enquire first.*

ROWSLEY **M. J. Tilley Caudwell's Mill** Matlock Derbyshire
TEL (0629) 734374   *A water-powered roller-mill, the machinery installed early this century.*   Sales *wholemeal and strong white flour year round, wholesale and retail.*   Visitors *weekdays 10 to 5.30, usually weekends too.*

SHAFTESBURY **N. R. Stoate and Sons Cann Mills** Dorset
TEL (0747) 2475   *Dating from 1832 the mill consists of 5 pairs of French burr stones.*

Sales *wholemeal stoneground organically grown wheat flours · also ordinary wholemeal and 81%
extraction · rye flour · coarse and fine bran · self-raising shortly.* Visitors *by arrangement only.*

SKIPTON **George Leatt High Corn Mill** North Yorkshire

TEL (0756) 2883 *Two water-wheels driving two pairs of millstones.* Sales *stoneground
wholemeal flour.* Visitors *corn mill and folk museum open daily except for some winter
months.*

SOHAM **Nigel Moon Downfield Windmill** between Ely and Newmarket
Cambridgeshire

TEL (0533) 707625 *A wind-powered tower mill restored in 1980 with back-up engine for calm
spells.* Sales *stoneground organically grown English wheat in wholemeal, 85% and 80%
grades · also bran · extra wheat · gluten · stoneground oatmeal and animal feeds.*

THORNER **Edwin and Andrew England Thorner Mill** Elm Tree House Main Street
Leeds West Yorkshire

TEL (0532) 892629 Sales *conservation grade stoneground flour.* Visitors *by arrangement.*

UPAVON **C. B. Wookey** Rishall Wholemeal Flour The Manor Pewsey Wiltshire

TEL (098 0630) 264 *1,650 acre farm with flour produced from a Simon Barron Stone Mill.*
Sales *organically grown stoneground wholemeal flour, grown to Soil Association standard · some
barley as well · bakehouse producing bread and rolls, Tue and Fri.* Visitors *Mon to Fri
7.10 to 4.30, Sat 7.10 to 10.10; bread orders can be collected 9 onwards.*

UPPER DICKER **Sussex Archaeological Society Michelham Priory Mill** Hailsham
East Sussex

TEL (0323) 844224 *Newly restored watermill using French burr stones, the first recorded mill
on the site dated from 1434.* Sales *stoneground wholemeal flour.* Visitors *Apr to 3rd week
Oct daily 11 to 5.30; access through Priory grounds for which a charge is made.*

WALSHAM-LE-WILLOWS **Walsham Mills Limited** Wattisfield Road Nr Bury St. Edmunds
Suffolk

TEL (035 98) 679 *A modern stoneground electric-powered mill adjacent to an old windmill.*
Sales *stoneground wholemeal flour, some organic grade.* Visitors *tours by arrangement.*

WHITE MILL **The Mill** Carmarthen Dyfed

TEL (0267 88) 209 *Formerly a water-powered mill, now diesel engined following construction
of a nearby road bypass. First recorded in the Lickley family bible 1815.* Sales *stoneground
wholemeal flour.* Visitors *Mon to Fri 9 to 5.30, Sat 9 to 12.30.*

WORSBROUGH **South Yorkshire County Council Worsbrough Mill** Museum Barnsley
South Yorkshire

TEL (0226) 203961 *An early 17th century watermill.* Sales *stoneground wholemeal flour.*
Visitors *Wed to Sun 10 to 6 each week.*

GENERAL READING

Colour Book of Wholefood Cookery   Octopus   1985
Wholefood Baking *Sarah Bounds*   Hamlyn/NTP   1984
Not Just a Load of Old Lentils *Rose Elliot*   Fontana   1972
The Complete Wholefood Cuisine *Nikki and David Goldbeck*   Thorsons   1984
Good Housekeeping Book of Wholefood Cookery *Gail Duff*   Ebury Press   1980
A Book of Middle Eastern Food *Claudia Roden*   Penguin   1970
The Health Food Guide *Michael Balfour*   Pan   1981
Silent Spring *Rachel Carson*   Penguin   1982
Look Younger, Live Longer   *Gayelord Hauser*   Faber and Faber   1951
A—Z of Health Foods *Carol Bowen*   Hamlyn   1979
The Food Scandal *Geoffrey Cannon and Caroline Walker*   Century   1984
English Bread and Yeast Cookery *Elizabeth David*   Allen Lane   1977
The Natural Food Catalogue *Vicki Peterson*   Macdonald   1984
E for Additives *Maurice Hanssen*   Thorsons   1984
The Food Watch Alternative Cook-Book *Honor J. Campbell*   Foodwatch   1984
The Sunday Times Book of Real Bread *Michael Bateman and Heather Maisner*
    Rodale Press   1982
The International Vegetarian Handbook *Hania Gorzko (Editor)*   Vegetarian Society
    1985
Vegetarian Gourmet Cookery *Alan Hooker*   Pitman   1976
Vegetarian Kitchen *Sarah Brown*   BBC   1984
The Cranks Recipe Book *David Canter, Kay Canter and Daphne Swann*   Dent   1982
Vegan Cooking *Leah Leneman*   Thorsons   1982

Diets
Cooking for Special Diets *Bee Nilson*   Penguin
The Vegetarian on a Diet *Margaret Cousins and Jill Metcalfe*   Thorsons   1984
The Pritikin Programme for Diet and Exercise *Nathan Pritikin*
    Bantam/Grosset & Dunlap   1979
Bristol Diet *Dr. Alec Forbes*   Century   1985
Deliciously Low *Harriet Roth*   Century   1984
Good Food, Gluten Free *Hilda Cherry Hills*   Roberts Publications   1976
Healthy Eating Healthy Heart *Good Housekeeping Institute*   Ebury Press   1979
Diet for Life *Mary Laver and Margaret Smith*   Pan   1981
No-Salt Cookery *Sarah Bounds*   Thorsons   1984
Live Longer Now *Jon N. Leonard, J. L. Hofer and N. Pritikin*   Grosset & Dunlap   1974

Organic gardening and farming
Fertility without Fertilizers *Lawrence D. Hills*   Henry Doubleday Research Association
    1976
Animal Machines *Ruth Harrison*   1964
Food for Free *Richard Mabey*   Collins   1972
The Organic Food Guide *Alan Gear*   Henry Doubleday Research Association   1983
The Farmer, The Plough and The Devil *Arthur Hollins*   Ashgrove Press   1984
The Findhorn Garden *The Findhorn Community*   Turnstone Books and Wildwood
    House   1975

MAPS

Maps

The maps are only meant to give a rough guide to the location of a particular entry and should be used in conjunction with a large scale Ordnance Survey map, or an A–Z for London. If you are travelling in a new area the map will tell you what real food shops, restaurants, growers or mills are in the vicinity.

MAP 1

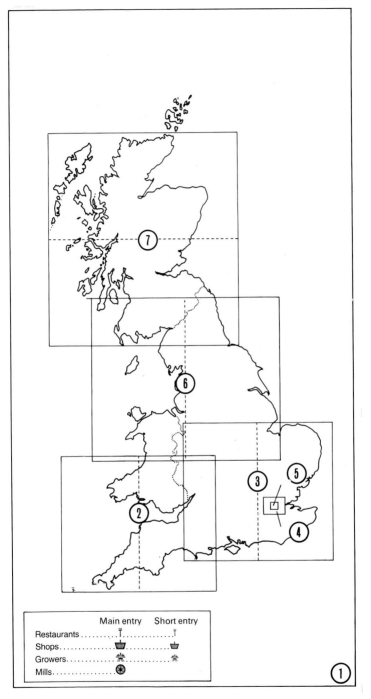

	Main entry	Short entry
Restaurants		
Shops		
Growers		
Mills		

MAP 2

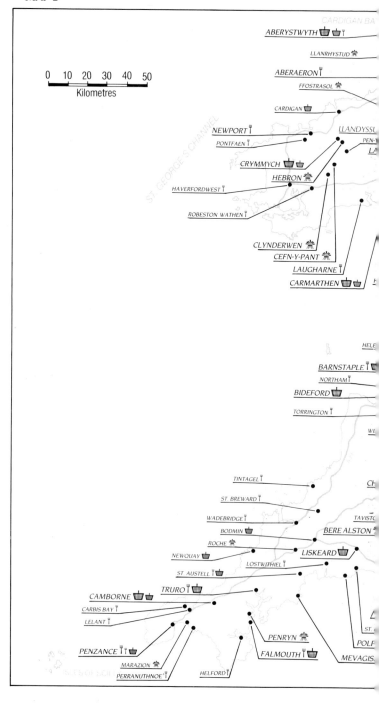

CARDIGAN BAY

ABERYSTWYTH

LLANRHYSTUD

ABERAERON

FFOSTRASOL

CARDIGAN

NEWPORT

PONTFAEN

LLANDYSSU

PEN-

LA

CRYMMYCH

HEBRON

HAVERFORDWEST

ROBESTON WATHEN

CLYNDERWEN

CEFN-Y-PANT

LAUGHARNE

CARMARTHEN

ST. GEORGE'S CHANNEL

0 10 20 30 40 50
Kilometres

HELE

BARNSTAPLE

NORTHAM

BIDEFORD

TORRINGTON

Wi

TINTAGEL

CH

ST. BREWARD

WADEBRIDGE

TAVISTO

BODMIN

BERE ALSTON

ROCHE

NEWQUAY

LISKEARD

LOSTWITHIEL

ST. AUSTELL

CAMBORNE

TRURO

CARBIS BAY

LELANT

ST.

POL

PENZANCE

PENRYN

MARAZION

FALMOUTH

MEVAGIS.

PERRANUTHNOE

HELFORD

MAP 2

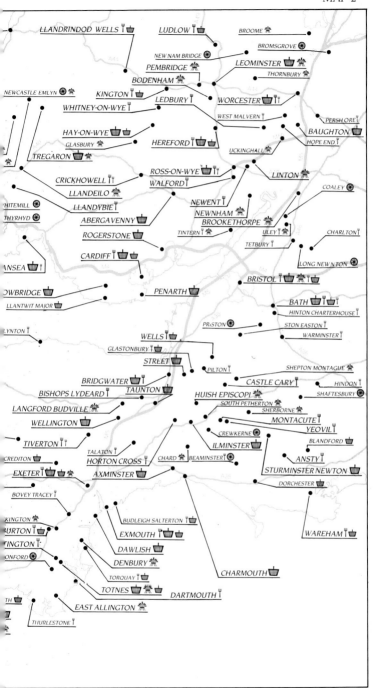

MAP 3

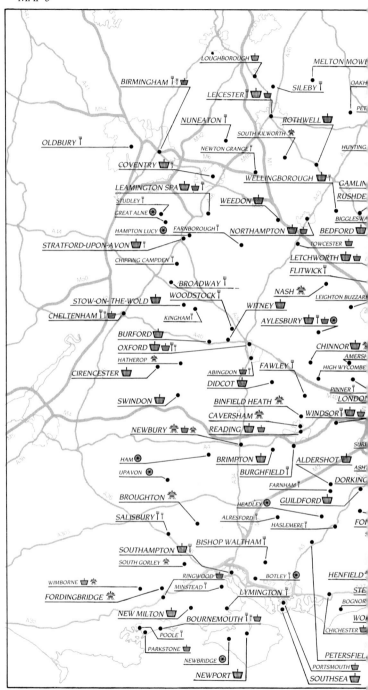

MAP 3

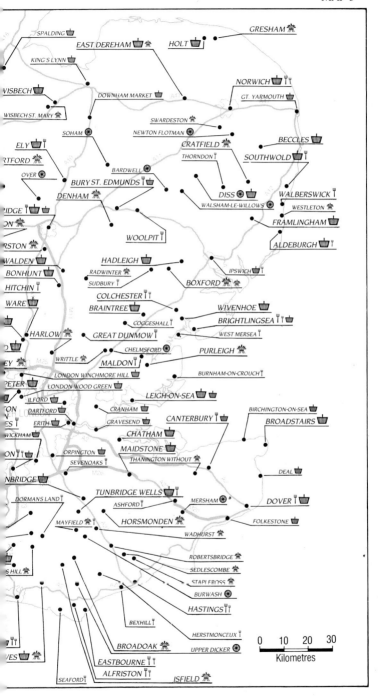

SPALDING

EAST DEREHAM

KING'S LYNN

HOLT

GRESHAM

WISBECH

DOWNHAM MARKET

NORWICH

GT. YARMOUTH

WISBECH ST. MARY

SWARDESTON

SOHAM

NEWTON FLOTMAN

BECCLES

ELY

CRATFIELD

SOUTHWOLD

RTFORD

THORNDON

OVER

BARDWELL

BURY ST. EDMUNDS

DISS

WALBERSWICK

RIDGE

DENHAM

WALSHAM-LE-WILLOWS

WESTLETON

ON

FRAMLINGHAM

RSTON

WOOLPIT

ALDEBURGH

WALDEN

HADLEIGH

BONHUNT

RADWINTER

IPSWICH

HITCHIN

SUDBURY

BOXFORD

WARE

COLCHESTER

BRAINTREE

WIVENHOE

HARLOW

COGGESHALL

BRIGHTLINGSEA

GREAT DUNMOW

WEST MERSEA

EY

CHELMSFORD

PURLEIGH

WRITTLE

MALDON

PETER

LONDON WINCHMORE HILL

BURNHAM-ON-CROUCH

LONDON WOOD GREEN

ON

LEIGH-ON-SEA

ILFORD

CRANHAM

BIRCHINGTON-ON-SEA

ES

DARTFORD

GRAVESEND

CANTERBURY

BROADSTAIRS

WICKHAM

ERITH

ON

CHATHAM

ORPINGTON

MAIDSTONE

SEVENOAKS

THANINGTON WITHOUT

DEAL

NBRIDGE

TUNBRIDGE WELLS

DORMANS LAND

ASHFORD

MERSHAM

DOVER

MAYFIELD

HORSMONDEN

FOLKESTONE

WADHURST

ROBERTSBRIDGE

S HILL

SEDLESCOMBE

STAPLECROSS

BURWASH

HASTINGS

BEXHILL

HERSTMONCEUX

BROADOAK

UPPER DICKER

EASTBOURNE

VES

ALFRISTON

SEAFORD

ISFIELD

0 10 20 30
Kilometres

MAP 4

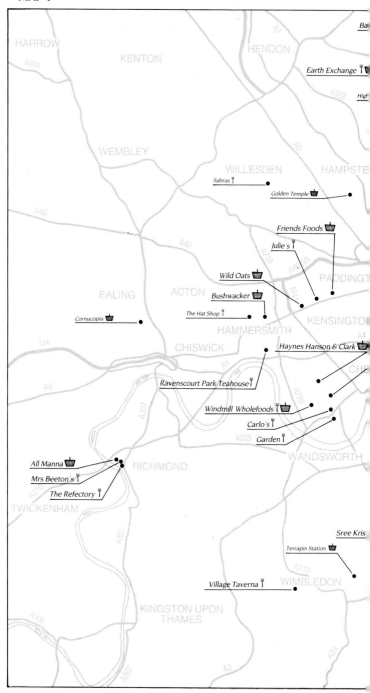

Ba

Earth Exchange

High

Sabras

Golden Temple

Friends Foods

Julie's

Wild Oats

Bushwacker

The Hat Shop

Cornucopia

Haynes Hanson & Clark

Ravenscourt Park Teahouse

Windmill Wholefoods

Carlo's

Garden

All Manna

Mrs Beeton's

The Refectory

Sree Kris

Terrapin Station

Village Taverna

HARROW

KENTON

HENDON

WEMBLEY

WILLESDEN

HAMPSTE

HAMPST

PADDINGT

EALING

ACTON

KENSINGTO

HAMMERSMITH

CHISWICK

CHE

WANDSWORTH

RICHMOND

TWICKENHAM

WIMBLEDON

KINGSTON UPON
THAMES

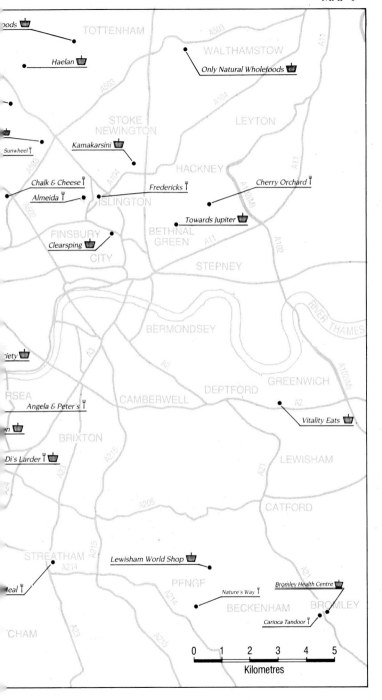

MAP 4

...oods

TOTTENHAM

WALTHAMSTOW

Haelan

Only Natural Wholefoods

A503

A104

STOKE
NEWINGTON

LEYTON

Sunwheel

Kamakarsini

HACKNEY

A11

Chalk & Cheese

Fredericks

Cherry Orchard

Almeida

ISLINGTON

A104

Towards Jupiter

A501

BETHNAL
GREEN

A11

FINSBURY

Clearspring

CITY

STEPNEY

BERMONDSEY

...iety

A3

A2

GREENWICH

...RSEA

Angela & Peter's

DEPTFORD

CAMBERWELL

Vitality Eats

...n

BRIXTON

A215

LEWISHAM

Di's Larder

A23

A205

CATFORD

STREATHAM

A214

Lewisham World Shop

...eal

PENGE

Bromley Health Centre

Nature's Way

BROMLEY

BECKENHAM

Carioca Tandoor

...CHAM

A215

Carioca Tandoor

0   1   2   3   4   5

Kilometres

MAP 5

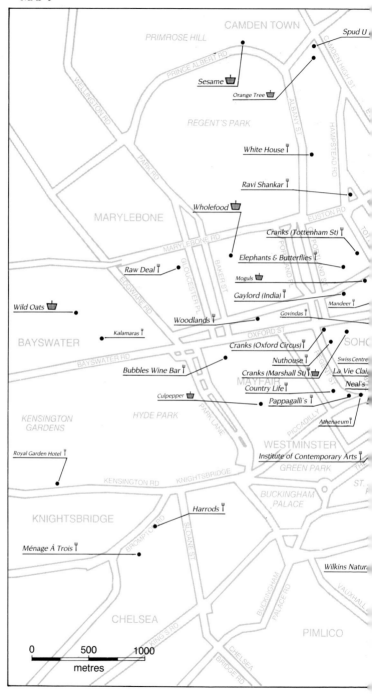

PRIMROSE HILL

CAMDEN TOWN

Spud U

PRINCE ALBERT RD

WELLINGTON RD

Sesame

Orange Tree

REGENT'S PARK

ALBANY ST

CAMDEN HIGH ST

HAMPSTEAD RD

PARK RD

White House

Ravi Shankar

EUSTON RD

MARYLEBONE

Wholefood

MARYLEBONE RD

Cranks (Tottenham St)

Elephants & Butterflies

GLOUCESTER PL

BAKER ST

EDGWARE RD

Raw Deal

Moguls

Gaylord (India)

Mandeer

Wild Oats

Woodlands

Govindas

BAYSWATER

Kalamaras

OXFORD ST

SOHO

BAYSWATER RD

Cranks (Oxford Circus)

Nuthouse

Swiss Centre

Bubbles Wine Bar

Cranks (Marshall St)

La Vie Clair

MAYFAIR

Country Life

Neal's

Culpepper

Pappagalli's

PARK LANE

HYDE PARK

PICCADILLY

Athenaeum

KENSINGTON
GARDENS

WESTMINSTER

Royal Garden Hotel

Institute of Contemporary Arts

GREEN PARK

KENSINGTON RD

KNIGHTSBRIDGE

ST.

BUCKINGHAM
PALACE

KNIGHTSBRIDGE

Harrods

BROMPTON RD

SLOANE ST

Ménage À Trois

BUCKINGHAM PALACE RD

Wilkins Natur

VAUXHALL

CHELSEA

KING'S RD

PIMLICO

CHELSEA

0   500   1000

metres

BRIDGE RD

MAP 5

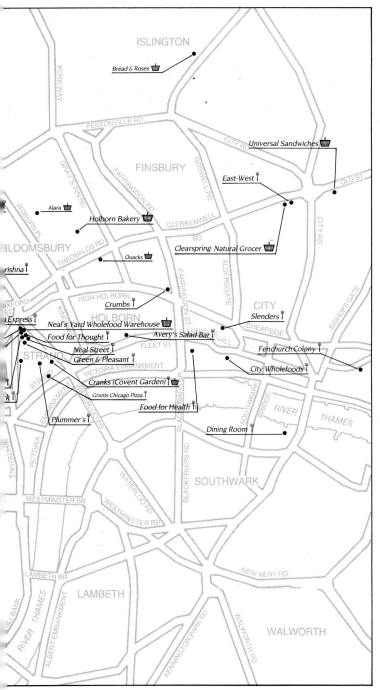

ISLINGTON

Bread & Roses

YORK WAY

PENTONVILLE RD

FINSBURY

CITY RD

Universal Sandwiches

GRAY'S INN RD

FARRINGDON RD

GOSWELL RD

OLD ST

East-West

WOBURN PL

Alara

CITY RD

CLERKENWELL RD

Holborn Bakery

BISHOPSGATE

BLOOMSBURY

THEOBALDS RD

Clearspring Natural Grocer

rishna

Quacks

ALDERSGATE

HIGH HOLBORN

FARRINGDON ST

CITY

XFORD

Crumbs

Slenders

HOLBORN

KINGSWAY

CHEAPSIDE

Express

Neal's Yard Wholefood Warehouse

LUDGATE HILL

Food for Thought

Avery's Salad Bar

Fenchurch Colony

STRAND

Neal Street

FLEET ST

Green & Pleasant

City Wholefoods

STRAND

Cranks (Covent Garden)

VICTORIA EMBANKMENT

Grunts Chicago Pizza

BLACKFRIARS BRIDGE

RIVER

THAMES

Food for Health

Plummer's

SOUTHWARK BRIDGE

Dining Room

WHITEHALL

VICTORIA

SOUTHWARK

BLACKFRIARS RD

WESTMINSTER BR

WATERLOO RD

WESTMINSTER RD

NEW KENT RD

LAMBETH BR

LAMBETH

RIVER THAMES

ALBERT EMBANKMENT

KENNINGTON PARK RD

WALWORTH RD

WALWORTH

MAP 6

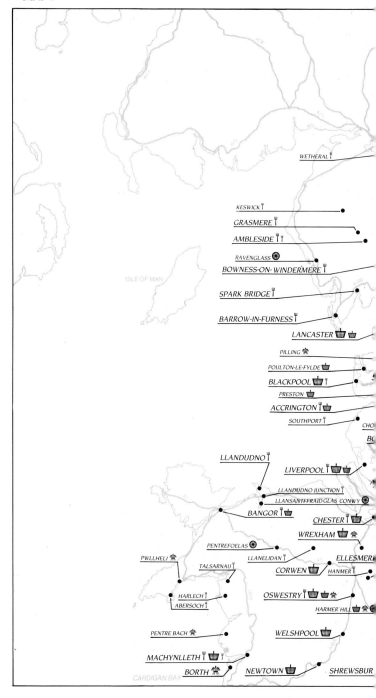

ISLE OF MAN

WETHERAL

KESWICK

GRASMERE

AMBLESIDE

RAVENGLASS

BOWNESS-ON-WINDERMERE

SPARK BRIDGE

BARROW-IN-FURNESS

LANCASTER

PILLING

POULTON-LE-FYLDE

BLACKPOOL

PRESTON

ACCRINGTON

SOUTHPORT

CHO

BC

LLANDUDNO

LIVERPOOL

LLANDUDNO JUNCTION

LLANSANTFFRAIDGLAS CONWY

BANGOR

CHESTER

WREXHAM

PENTREFOELAS

PWLLHELI

LLANELIDAN

ELLESMER

TALSARNAU

CORWEN

HANMER

HARLECH

OSWESTRY

ABERSOCH

HARMER HILL

PENTRE BACH

WELSHPOOL

MACHYNLLETH

BORTH

NEWTOWN

SHREWSBUR

CARDIGAN BAY

MAP 6

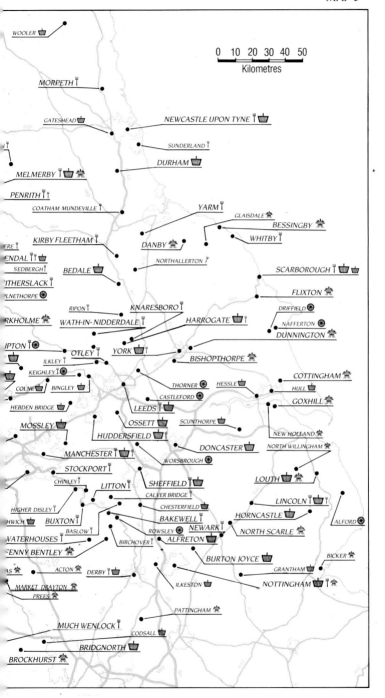

MAP 7

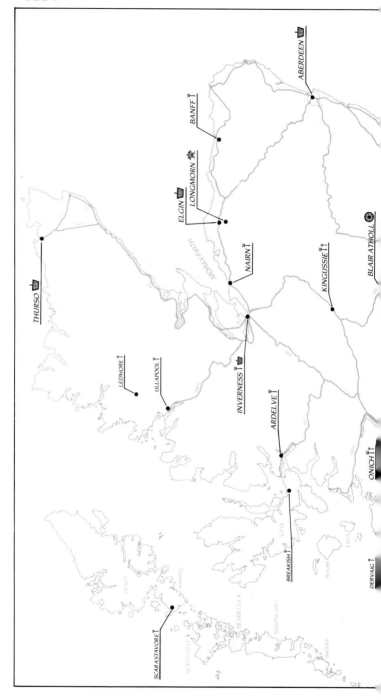

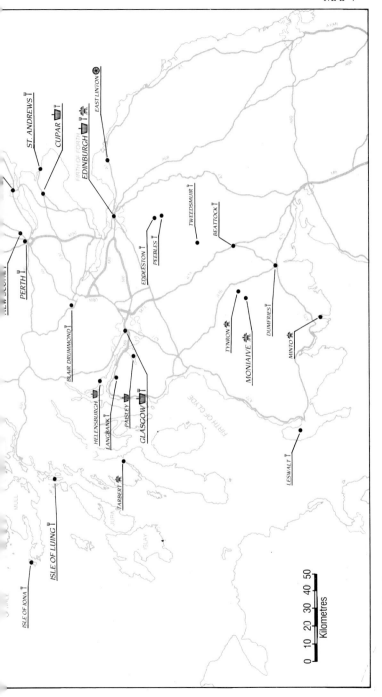

MAP 7

ST. ANDREWS

CUPAR

EDINBURGH

EAST LINTON

FIRTH OF FORTH

PERTH

TWEEDSMUIR

BEATTOCK

EDDLESTON

PEEBLES

BLAIR DRUMMOND

TYNRON

MONIAIVE

DUMFRIES

MINTO

HELENSBURGH

LANGBANK

PAISLEY

GLASGOW

FIRTH OF CLYDE

LESWALT

TARBERT

MULL

JURA

ISLAY

ISLE OF LUING

ISLE OF IONA

0 10 20 30 40 50

Kilometres

GLOSSARY

Additives   Colourings, preservatives or flavourings, sometimes all three, introduced into fresh and manufactured foods for the purposes of extending their shelf life, modifying their appearance and, supposedly, enhancing their flavour.

Bio-dynamic   This produce, marketed under the Demeter symbol, rejects any practices based on the use of artificially prepared products either for promoting plant growth, or for controlling adverse factors such as weeds, insect pests or fungal inspections.

Cold-pressed   or cold-pressing is a preferred method of extracting oil from olives, nuts and grapes for culinary purposes.

Conservation grade   A standard for produce grown by members of the Organic Farmers and Growers Association, a farmers' co-operative whose main produce is flaked grains.

The Farm and Food Society   Founded in 1966, Fritz Schumacher was one of the Society's early patrons. The secretary's address is: 4 Willifield Way, London N11.

Free range eggs   A liberally used term but only those shops and farms displaying a sign with a hen and her egg within a golden triangle are approved by the Free Range Egg Association.

Gluten-free   A term given to a dietary regime prescribed for those suffering from coelic disease, though the same gluten-free diet is sometimes felt to be beneficial in the treatment of certain other conditions.

Granary   Grain made from flour which is not 100 % extraction but which has had some malt flakes, bran and cracked wheat added, which makes a loaf of an interesting texture.

Macrobiotic   George Ohsawa who studied the ancient philosophies of Japan, China and India first used this term for a modern comprehensive philosophy.

The McCarrison Society   A society formed in 1966 by a group of doctors and dentists disillusioned by the never-ending prospect of patching up sick people. The secretary's address is: 23 Stanley Court, Worcester Road, Sutton, Surrey.

NACNE   Abbreviation for National Advisory Committee on Nutritional Education, a Government sponsored body set up in 1979 whose findings were eventually published in *The Food Scandal* by Geoffrey Cannon and Caroline Walker.

Organically produced foods   Foods from soils manured without the use of chemical fertilisers, or treatment with chemicals during the various stages of growth or storage.

Polyunsaturated fats   Unlike saturated fats, these are believed to be of beneficial value when present in foods though it should be borne in mind that it is also the expert view that the total quantity of fats consumed should, on average, be considerably reduced.

Stoneground   A traditional milling process using millstones which grind corn at lower temperatures than steel rollers.

Sugar-free   Meaning sugar has not been added in the course of food processing though sugar may well occur naturally in a food.

Tofu   This is a high protein food with a modest fat content (the fat element being high in polyunsaturated fats) and is a product of the soya bean.

Vegan   Veganism is a pattern of eating which eschews all food which is of animal origin including honey.

Vegetarian   Vegetarians do not eat any meat, poultry or fish or their by-products.

Wholefood   Nothing added, nothing removed, and if grown to organic standards, so much the better, might well sum up the wholefood philosophy.

Wholemeal   Wholemeal (still described confusingly, if not inaccurately, as wholewheat) means only one thing and that is flour of 100 % extraction.

INDEX TO MAIN ENTRIES

RESTAURANTS

Abbey Green Restaurant   *Chester*
Acorn Natural Food Centre   *Maldon*
Almeida Wine Bar   *London*
Angel Food   *Tiverton*
Angela and Peter   *London*
Annie's   *Wareham*
Applejack   *Ledbury*
Armless Dragon   *Cardiff*
Avery's Salad Bar   *London*

Balcraig House   *New Scone*
Ballymaloe House   *Shanagarry*
Beeton's Restaurant (Mrs.)   *Richmond*
Ben Bowers   *Nottingham*
Bistro (Mr.)   *Mevagissey*
Blue Frog Café   *Kington*
Bluebell Bookshop   *Penrith*
Bountiful Goodness   *Southampton*
Bradfield House   *Bury St. Edmunds*
Brambles   *St. Andrews*
Brants Health Food Restaurant   *Hastings*
Bread and Roses   *Leicester*
Bridge Restaurant   *Bridgwater*
Bridgefield House   *Spark Bridge*
Britons Arms   *Norwich*
Brothertons   *Woodstock*
Brown's Restaurant   *Oxford*
Bubbles Wine Bar   *London*
But'n'Ben   *Arbroath*

Café at Premises   *Norwich*
Carragreen   *Liverpool*
Carlo's Place   *London*
Carrington's   *Llandudno*
Carved Angel   *Dartmouth*
Casey's   *Bishop's Waltham*
Ceilidh Place   *Ullapool*
Chaise Lounge Too   *Manchester*
Chalice   *Bury St. Edmunds*
Chalk and Cheese Restaurant   *London*
Cheese Press   *Crickhowell*

Cherry Orchard   *London*
Chives   *Cheltenham*
Cindy's Kitchen   *Waterhouses*
City Wholefoods   *London*
Clifton Hotel   *Nairn*
Clouds   *Brighton*
Clouds   *Kingston Upon Thames*
Cnapan Restaurant and Country House
    Newport
Coconut Willy's   *Stockport*
Coffee Shop   *Yarm*
Coffee Tavern   *Rushden*
Coolings Wine Bar   *Exeter*
Counterpoint   *Aylesbury*
Country Kitchen   *Edinburgh*
Country Kitchen Restaurant   *Windsor*
Country Life   *London*
County Hotel   *Banff*
Cranks   *Dartington*
Cranks   *London—Covent Garden*
Cranks   *London—Marshall Street*
Cranks   *London—Oxford Circus*
Cranks   *London—Tottenham Street*
Creagdhu—The Lodge on the Loch
    Onich
Crown   *Southwold*
Crucible Theatre Coffee Shop   *Sheffield*
Crumbs   *London*
Crumbs Salad Restaurant   *Cardiff*
Curry Garden Tandoori   *Dover*

Delany's   *Shrewsbury*
Dining Room   *London*
Di's Larder   *London*
Drachenfels Vegetarian Restaurant
    Nuneaton
Dunain Park   *Inverness*

Earth Exchange Collective   *London*
East-West   *London*
Effy's   *Hereford*

245

Elephants and Butterflies   London
Evelyn & Owen's   Bath
Everyman Bistro   Liverpool

Farmhouse Fare   Liverpool
Farmhouse Kitchen   Manchester
Feathers   Ludlow
Fenchurch Colony   London
Flappers Restaurant   Hitchin
Flitwick Manor   Flitwick
Fodder   Hereford
Food for Friends   Brighton
Food for Health   London
Food for Thought   London
Fox   Ansty
Frederick's   London

Gannets Restaurant   Newark
Garden   London
Gaylord India   Manchester
Gaylord (India)   London
Good Companion   Oswestry
Good Earth   Wells
Good Food Café   Llandrindod Wells
Gourmet   Morpeth
Grape Expectations   Bangor
Green Apple   Bakewell
Green and Pleasant Salad Restaurant   London
Greenhouse Vegetarian Restaurant   London
Guild Café Restaurant   Bristol

Harboro Hotel   Melton Mowbray
Hare Krishna Curry House   London
Harrods Juice Bar   London
Harvest Vegetarian Restaurant   Ambleside
Health Food Restaurant   Accrington
Heavens Above!   Barnstaple
Hedgerow Vegetarian Restaurant   Bowness
Helios Fountain   Edinburgh
Hendersons   Edinburgh
Henry's Wholefood Restaurant   Bournemouth
Herbs   Skipton
Hive on the Quay   Aberaeron
Hobbs Pavilion   Cambridge
Hockney's   Croydon
Hole in the Wall   Bath
Holland and Barrett   Oxford
Honeypot   Colchester

Horizon Café   Ely
Huckleberry's   Bath

Inpulse   Bolton
Institute of Contemporary Arts   London

Jacobe's Hall   Brightlingsea
Jonathan's Restaurant   Oldbury
Julie's   London

Kalpna Restaurant   Edinburgh
Kate's   Falmouth
Kirby Fleetham Hall   Kirby Fleetham
Kitchen at Polperro   Polperro
Knights Farm   Burghfield

Lamb Inn   Ilminster
Little Barwick House   Yeovil
Loch Duich Hotel   Ardelve
Longhouse Buttery and Gallery   Isle of Luing
Lovin' Spoonful   Blackburn
Lygon Arms   Broadway

Magpie Café   Whitby
Maldon Coffee Shop   Maldon
Manna   London
Marches   Hereford
Market Restaurant   Manchester
McCreadies   Bristol
Meader's   Ross-on-Wye
Ménage à Trois   London
Michael Snell   Salisbury
Milk House   Montacute
Millwheel   Worcester
Moon Restaurant   Kendal
Moonrakers   Alfriston

Nathaniels Restaurant   Buxton
Nature's Way   Brighton
Nature's Way   Eastbourne
Nature's Way   Hove
Nature's Way   Worthing
Neal Street   London
Nettles   Cambridge

Nut and Meg   *Manchester*
Nutcracker   *Altrincham*
Nuthouse   *London*

Old Bakehouse Restaurant   *Castle Cary*
Old Bakery   *Woolpit*
Old Bank House   *Lymington*
Old Fire Engine House   *Ely*
Old Saddlery   *Ashburton*
Old School   *Sileby*
Old Vicarage   *Witherslack*
Olive Branch   *Penzance*
On the Eighth Day   *Manchester*

Pappagalli's Pizza Inc.   *London*
Pastures New   *Barrow-in-Furness*
Peppermint Park   *London*
Pilgrims   *Tunbridge Wells*
Pizza Express   *London*
Plummers   *London*
Poachers Restaurant   *Glasgow*
Pool Court   *Otley*
Potter's Wheel   *Walberswick*
Pottles   *Truro*

Quarry Shop   *Machynlleth*

Rainbow Vegetarian Restaurant
     Leamington Spa
Ravenscourt Park Teahouse   *London*
Ravi Shankar   *London*
Raw Deal   *London*
Red Lion Inn   *Litton*
Refectory   *Richmond*
Restaurant at Leeds Playhouse   *Leeds*
Rhyspence Inn   *Whitney-on-Wye*
Rose Cottage Inn   *Bishops Lydeard*
Round the Bend   *Exmouth*
Rowan Tree   *Grasmere*

St. Aldate's Coffee House   *Oxford*
Salad Centre   *Bournemouth*
Salvo's   *Leeds*
Sarah Brown's   *Scarborough*
Sasses Restaurant   *Norwich*

Schwallers   *Knaresborough*
Scott's   *Much Wenlock*
Seasons Kitchen   *Forest Row*
Shrimps Wine Bar   *Dublin*
Slenders   *London*
Slims Health Food Restaurant   *Brighton*
Soutters Restaurant   *Newent*
Sportsman's Arms   *Wath-in-Nidderdale*
Spud U Like Ltd   *London*
Square Peg Café   *Dundee*
Sree Krishna   *London*
Stable Door Wine Bar   *Laugharne*
Starr   *Great Dunmow*
Strawberry Fields   *Leeds*
Super Natural   *Newcastle-upon-Tyne*
Sweeney Todds Pizza Parlour   *Canterbury*

Teignworthy Country House   *Chagford*
Timothy's   *Perth*

Ubiquitous Chip   *Glasgow*

Verandah Tandoori   *Edinburgh*
Village Bakery   *Melmerby*
Village Taverna   *London*
Vintage   *Kinsale*

Waffle House   *Norwich*
Walford House Hotel   *Walford*
Walnut Tree   *Fawley*
White House   *London*
Whole Meal   *London*
Wig and Mitre   *Lincoln*
Wild Oats   *Birmingham*
Wild Oats II   *Bristol*
Wild Thyme   *Birmingham*
Wilkins Natural Food   *London*
Windmill Restaurant   *London*
Wood'n Spoon Restaurant and Creel Bar
     Kingussie
Woodlands   *London*

Xanadu   *Cambridge*
Xavia's   *Brighton*

SHOPS

Aardvark   *Carmarthen*
Acorn Natural Foods   *Bridgnorth*
Aetherius Society Health Foods   *London*
Aldeburgh Health Food and Delicatessen
    Aldeburgh
All Manna   *Richmond*
Allen's Wharf Stores   *Bath*
Alligator   *York*
Alternatives   *Chester*
Ambrosia Wholefoods   *Aberdeen*
Arcadian Wholefoods   *Bideford*
Arjuna   *Cambridge*

Barbara's Health Food Centre   *London*
Barber and Manuel   *Leominster*
Bean Machine   *Crymmych*
Beanbag Wholefoods   *Witney*
Beanfreaks Health Food Centre   *Penarth*
Beanos Natural Foods   *Bristol*
Beano Wholefoods Co-operative   *Leeds*
Bedale Bakery   *Bedale*
Booth & Co   *Clitheroe*
Bran Tub   *Petersfield*
Breadwinner   *Edinburgh*
Brewhouse Traditional and Wholefood Co
    Wicken Bonhunt
Brian Hardy Ltd   *Wisbech*
Bridge to Health   *Wembley*
Broad Street Bakery   *Bath*
Bushwhacker   *London*

Cardiff Wholefoods   *Cardiff*
Carley and Webb Grocery and Provisions
    Framlingham
Celestial Foods   *Chinnor*
Charles Riggs   *Totnes*
Cheeseboard   *Harrogate*
Clearspring Natural Grocer   *London*
Compleat Foods Wholefood Victuallers
    Cupar
Cornucopia Health Foods   *Abergavenny*

Counterpoint   *Aylesbury*
Country Bumpkin Bakery   *Exmouth*
Country Harvest   *Taunton*
Country Harvest Natural Foods   *Street*
Country Harvest Natural Foods
    Bridgwater
Country Health   *Stratford-upon-Avon*
Country Kitchen   *Horncastle*
Covered Market   *Carmarthen*
Crabapple   *Shrewsbury*
Crystal Harvest   *Watford*
Curds and Whey   *Swansea*

Daily Bread Co-operative   *Northampton*
Danaan Wholefoods   *Southampton*
Dancing Cat Trading Co-operative
    Liverpool
Dandelion Natural Foods   *London*
Di's Larder   *London*
Dover Health Food Centre   *Dover*
Down to Earth Wholefoods   *Ware*
Drop in the Ocean Wholefoods   *Coventry*
Drug and Wholefood Store   *Burton Joyce*

Ear to the Ground   *Swansea*
Earthbound Wholefoods   *Guildford*
Earth Exchange Collective   *London*

Fairhaven Wholefoods   *Letchworth*
Flour Bin   *Sheffield*
Fodder   *Ross-on-Wye*
Food for Thought   *Guildford*
Foodsmith   *Burford*
Foodwatch   *Sturminster Newton*
Forrest and Niven   *Glasgow*
Friends Food   *London*
Frost's Fruit and Flower Stalls
    Aberystwyth

Full of Beans   Lewes
Funny Foods   Ossett

Ganesha Wholefoods   Axminster
Gillygate Wholefood Bakery   `York
Good Health   Broadstairs
Good Food Shop   Hereford
Good Food Shop   Hertford
Goodness Foods   Weedon
Graham, W. J.   Co. Westmeath
Granary   Truro
Granary   Wrexham
Grassroots (Wholefoods and Herbs)
        Glasgow
Great Western Wholefoods   Cirencester
Green Door Bakery and Wholefood Shop
        Manchester
Greens Health Food Store   Lincoln
Guy's Health Store   East Dereham

Haelan Organic Food/Herbal Med. Centre
        London
Haggers Natural Foods   Dorking
Hampers of Aylesbury   Aylesbury
Harvest   Falmouth
Harvest Wholefoods   Bath
Hay Wholefoods and Delicatessen
        Hay-on-Wye
Haynes, Hansom & Clark   London
Health and Dietary Food Stores   Aberdeen
Health Food Centre   Thurso
Health Food Store   Blackpool
Health Foods   Camborne
Healthy Living   Tonbridge
Herbs, Spices and Wholefoods   Alfreton
Holborn Bakery   London
Honesty Wholefoods   Maidstone
Honeysuckle Wholefood Co-operative
        Oswestry
Horizon Health   Ely
House of Goodness   Leamington Spa
Hungate Health Store   Beccles

Ilminster Health Foods   Ilminster
Infinity Foods Co-op   Brighton

James Bowtell   Braintree
Jane's Bakery   Brimpton

Kamakarsini Health and Beauty Centre
        London
Kinbro Health Foods   Elgin

Ladywell Wholefood Bakery   Rothwell
Lansdown House Health Foods   Lewes
Larner Brothers   Holt
La Vie Claire   London
L'Epicure   Cowbridge
Lewisham World Shop   London
Linacre's Wholefoods   Barnstaple
Lovin' Spoonful   Blackburn

Maeth y Meysydd Wholefood Shop
        Aberystwyth
Maggie's Farm   Durham
Mandala Wholefoods   Newcastle-upon-Tyne
Melfoods   Aldershot
Milburn Health Foods   Newcastle-upon-Tyne
Millwheel   Worcester
Moores Health Foods   Bristol
Mossley Wholefoods   Mossley
Mother Earth Wholefoods   Leigh-on-Sea
Mulberry Bush Wholefoods   Lampeter
Mumbles Health Fayre   Swansea

National Centre for Alternative Technology
        Machynlleth
Natural Food Centre   Bridgwater
Natural Foods   Taunton
Natural Food Store   Diss
Natural Food Store   Norwich
Natural Life   Tunbridge Wells
Naturally   Doncaster
Nature's Best   Didcot
Nature's Corner   Hassocks
Neal's Yard Farm Shop   London
Neal's Yard Wholefood Warehouse   London
Newport Health Food Centre   Newport
Nitty Gritty Wholefoods   Leominster
Norwich Health Foods   Norwich
Nova Wholefoods Co-op   Bristol
Nuts in May   Saffron Walden
Nutters   Southwold

Oasis Wholefoods   Windsor

On the Eighth Day Co-operative *Manchester*
One Earth *Lancaster*
Only Natural Wholefoods
  Chalfont St. Peter
Only Natural Wholefoods *London*
Ough & Sons *Liskeard*
Ouroboros Wholefood Collective
  Nottingham

Peaceworks Co-op *Huddersfield*
Peck and Strong *Exeter*
Pilgrims Health Food Shop *Tunbridge Wells*
Poppadums *Dawlish*
Pulse (Pure Foods) *Lincoln*
Pulse Wholefoods *Cardiff*

Quarry Shop *Machynlleth*

Rainbow Wholefoods *Norwich*
Rawel's Super Foods *London*
Rawel's Super V.G. Foods *London*
Reading Wholefoods *Reading*
Real Foods *Edinburgh*
Redland Wholesome Foods *Bristol*
Renaissance *Norwich*
Robinsons of Charmouth *Charmouth*
Roots Wholefoods *Edinburgh*
Round the Bend *Exmouth*
Rowan Tree *Bristol*

Sacks *Totnes*
Sarah Brown's *Scarborough*
Seasons *Exeter*
Sesame *London*
Scoff's *Bath*
Scottocks Health Food *New Milton*
Simon's *Corwen*
Simple Supplies *Brighton*
Single Step Co-operative *Lancaster*
Solarstor Health Foods *Chatham*
Sparrow Wholefoods *Newtown*
Sparrow Wholefoods *Welshpool*

Specialité Foods *Hay-on-Wye*
Starbake *Newport*
Steyning Health Foods *Steyning*
Stoneground Bakery *Bristol*
Sunflower *Hadleigh*
Sunflower Wholefoods *Bedford*
Sunfood *Barnstaple*
Sunseed *Wellington*
Swindon Pulse Wholefood Co-operative
  Swindon

Taylor's Wholefoods and Herbs *Norwich*
Tayside Health Food Stores *Dundee*
Time for Change *Southsea*
Towards Jupiter *London*
Tregaron Foods *Tregaron*

Uhuru Wholefoods *Oxford*
Universal Sandwiches *London*

Village Bakery *Melmerby*
Vine Cottage *Baughton*
Vitality Eats *London*

Wellingborough Health Foods
  Wellingborough
Welshpool Herbs and Spices *Welshpool*
Wholefood *London*
Wholefood Co-op *Louth*
Wholefood Shop *Stow-on-the-Wold*
Wholefood Shop *Wivenhoe*
Wholemeal *Leicester*
Wicker Herbal Stores *Sheffield*
Widdicombe, J. P. *Millbrook*
Wild Oats *London*
Wild Oats Wholefoods *Bristol*
Wilkins Natural Foods *London*
Windmill Wholefoods *London*

York Wholefoods *York*

INDEX TO MAIN ENTRIES

GROWERS

Arkley Manor Farm   *Arkley*

Barrow Hill Farms   *Henfield*
Bindon Home Farm   *Langford Budville*
Boathouse Farm   *Isfield*
Bottom Village   *Danby*
Brentlands Farm   *Brookethorpe*
Broadfield Court Vineyard   *Bodenham*
Brunswick Nursery   *Bishopthorpe*
Bryn Saron Farm Produce   *Llandyssul*

Camphill Village Trust   *Newnham*
Carney's Organic Farm   *Dunmore East*
Charles Riggs   *Totnes*
Church Farm Gardens   *Bessingby*
Cracknell's Free Range Poultry Farm   *Huish Episcopi*
Craigdarroch Gardens   *Moniaive*

Denham End Farm   *Denham*
Dunkerton's Cider Company   *Pembridge*
Dunnington Lodge   *Dunnington*

Elgin Springs   *Longmorn*

Ferrocrete Farm   *Arkholme*
Furzehill Organic Produce   *Fordingbridge*

Gauntlet   *Bicker*
Gilbert's   *Brookethorpe*
Glanrhydwilym   *Clynderwen*
Gorgie City Farm   *Edinburgh*
Green Circle Growers   *Broughton*

Higher Birch Farm   *Bere Alston*

Hill Farm   *Boxford*
Holywell Farm   *Nash*

Icknield Nurseries   *Chinnor*

Lipton Farm   *East Allington*
Little Bottom Farm   *Caversham*

Michael Paske Farms   *Hartford*
Mill Farm   *Purleigh*
Moorfoot Organic Garden   *Denbury*
Mr. Brookman   *Potton*

New House Farm   *Melmerby*
North Sydmonton Nursery   *Newbury*

Old Railway House   *Louth*
Onaway   *Flixton*
Orchards Nursery   *Ellesmere*
Organic Produce   *Harston*

Pengelli   *Hebron*
Penrhiw Farm Dairy   *Cefn-y-Pant*
Pond House   *Binfield Heath*
Poplar Farm   *Cratfield*
Priory   *Fenny Bentley*

Qasid Stud   *Lee Brockhurst*

Rachel's Dairy   *Borth*
Red House Farm   *North Scarle*
Revells Fruit Farm   *Linton*
Roosters Rest   *Goxhill*
Rosehaven   *Gamlingay*

St. Werburgh's City Farm   *Bristol*
Sky Farm   *Broadoak*
Small's Farm   *Horsmonden*
Southerham Cottage Kitchen   *Lewes*
Stables   *Gresham*

Thrushes Bush Poultry Farm   *Harlow*
Trenance Fruit Growers   *Penryn*
Tyn Grug Farmhouse Cheeses   *Llandeilo*

Willows Nurseries   *Leominster*

York Grounds   *Cottingham*

REPORT FORM

We are always delighted to receive readers' views on *Guide* entries and a form is provided for this purpose. In this way we are able to build up a more complete picture of the establishments we list and future editions of the *Guide* can be improved accordingly. If you prefer to make your report on a separate piece of paper, please do so.

We should also be glad to hear of places—perhaps newly established—that have not already come to the *Guide*'s attention. Please tell us about them whether they are shops, hotels, restaurants, millers, fish curers or fishmongers, market gardens and farms. Please do not hesitate to write at length as we should like to know exactly what you felt was particularly worthwhile about these places. We should also like to hear of any reasons for dissatisfaction. We are not seeking routine information as this can easily be obtained later.

To give some idea of the details that would be particularly useful we list some points to consider.

- How did the food rate in terms of wholefood importance, variety and value?

- In what ways did the food distinguish the place from other establishments in the district.

- The standard of service.

- The style of the surroundings.

- The idiosyncracies—of management or place.

RECOMMENDATION FOR AN ENTRY

To the Editor, The Real Food Shop and Restaurant Guide
Freepost Burford Oxford OX8 4TE

Name of place recommended..

Address ....

....

Telephone number, if known ....

continue overleaf or report on a separate piece of paper if preferred

Name and Address (CAPITALS PLEASE)

....

....

REPORT FORM

We are always delighted to receive readers' views on *Guide* entries and a form is provided for this purpose. In this way we are able to build up a more complete picture of the establishments we list and future editions of the *Guide* can be improved accordingly. If you prefer to make your report on a separate piece of paper, please do so.

We should also be glad to hear of places—perhaps newly established—that have not already come to the *Guide*'s attention. Please tell us about them whether they are shops, hotels, restaurants, millers, fish curers or fishmongers, market gardens and farms. Please do not hesitate to write at length as we should like to know exactly what you felt was particularly worthwhile about these places. We should also like to hear of any reasons for dissatisfaction. We are not seeking routine information as this can easily be obtained later.

To give some idea of the details that would be particularly useful we list some points to consider.

- How did the food rate in terms of wholefood importance, variety and value?

- In what ways did the food distinguish the place from other establishments in the district.

- The standard of service.

- The style of the surroundings.

- The idiosyncrasies—of management or place.

RECOMMENDATION FOR AN ENTRY

To the Editor, The Real Food Shop and Restaurant Guide
Freepost Burford Oxford OX8 4TE

Name of place recommended..

Address ....

....

Telephone number, if known ....

continue overleaf or report on a separate piece of paper if preferred

Name and Address (CAPITALS PLEASE)

....

....

REPORT FORM

We are always delighted to receive readers' views on *Guide* entries and a form is provided for this purpose. In this way we are able to build up a more complete picture of the establishments we list and future editions of the *Guide* can be improved accordingly. If you prefer to make your report on a separate piece of paper, please do so.

We should also be glad to hear of places—perhaps newly established—that have not already come to the *Guide*'s attention. Please tell us about them whether they are shops, hotels, restaurants, millers, fish curers or fishmongers, market gardens and farms. Please do not hesitate to write at length as we should like to know exactly what you felt was particularly worthwhile about these places. We should also like to hear of any reasons for dissatisfaction. We are not seeking routine information as this can easily be obtained later.

To give some idea of the details that would be particularly useful we list some points to consider.

- How did the food rate in terms of wholefood importance, variety and value?

- In what ways did the food distinguish the place from other establishments in the district.

- The standard of service.

- The style of the surroundings.

- The idiosyncracies—of management or place.

RECOMMENDATION FOR AN ENTRY

To the Editor, The Real Food Shop and Restaurant Guide
Freepost Burford Oxford OX8 4TE

Name of place recommended...

Address ....

....

Telephone number, if known ....

continue overleaf or report on a separate piece of paper if preferred

Name and Address (CAPITALS PLEASE)

....

....